A History of Franco-German Relations in Europe

A History of Franco-German Relations in Europe

From "Hereditary Enemies" to Partners

by Carine Germond and Henning Türk

A HISTORY OF FRANCO-GERMAN RELATIONS IN EUROPE
Copyright © Carine Germond and Henning Türk, 2008.

First published in 2008 by PALGRAVE MACMILLAN® in the United States—a division of St. Martin's Press LLC, 175 Fifth Avenue, New York, NY 10010.

Where this book is distributed in the UK, Europe and the rest of the world, this is by Palgrave Macmillan, a division of Macmillan Publishers Limited, registered in England, company number 785998, of Houndmills, Basingstoke, Hampshire RG21 6XS.

Palgrave Macmillan is the global academic imprint of the above companies and has companies and representatives throughout the world.

Palgrave® and Macmillan® are registered trademarks in the United States, the United Kingdom, Europe and other countries.

ISBN-13: 978-0-230-60452-0
ISBN-10: 0-230-60452-8

Library of Congress Cataloging-in-Publication Data

A history of Franco-German relations in Europe : from "hereditary enemies" to partners / edited by Carine Germond and Henning Türk.
     p. cm.
  Includes bibliographical references and index.
  ISBN 0-230-60452-8
  1. France—Foreign relations—Germany. 2. Germany—Foreign relations—France.
I. Germond, Carine. II. Türk, Henning.

DC59.8.G3H57 2008
327.44043—dc22   2008017280

A catalogue record of the book is available from the British Library.

Design by Scribe Inc.

First edition: December 2008

10 9 8 7 6 5 4 3 2 1

Printed in the United States of America.

For centuries, the history of France and Germany has been a continual effort of the two nations to get closer, to understand, to unite, to merge: Indifference was never possible for them; they had to hate or love one another, fraternize or go to war. France's and Germany's destiny will never be established nor assured individually.

—Ludwig Börne, Menzel: Der Franzosenfresser

Contents

Preface

The idea for this book came from the somewhat unexpected difficulty in finding relevant and up-to-date scholarly literature on Franco-German relations in English. It is certainly the case that many studies in French and German have already been devoted to the subject, whereas the academic literature available in English is much sparser and, except for more recent studies examining the contemporary development of Franco-German cooperation in the European Union, often outdated as well. In fact, a comprehensive historical retrospective presenting the current state of international research on Franco-German relations is still not available in English, even as the contribution of France and Germany in and to Europe remains largely misunderstood outside the European Union and especially in the United States. It thus seems important to us to highlight the historical roots of the contemporary Franco-German partnership to an English-speaking readership and contribute to a better understanding of its role in Europe.

The fact that the editors are themselves descendants of "Marianne" and "Germania" gives an additional flavor to this book, which has truly been nurtured under the auspices of Franco-German collaboration and friendship. It is also a European and transatlantic venture of the cyber age; not only did the two editors live on opposite sides of the Atlantic during its conception but the contributors were spread out across Europe and the United States as well.

This book would never have been put to press without the financial support of the FAZIT foundation in Germany, which allowed the translation and proofreading of the articles written by nonnative speakers of English. We are particularly grateful for the excellent work done by Robert Hogg (University of Chicago), who translated the articles by Reiner Marcowitz, Ulrich Lappenküper, and Ulrich Pfeil from German into English and proofread almost all other contributions. We would also like to thank Eric Dere (Yale University) for his translation of Sylvain Schirmann's article and the individuals who translated the chapters by Martial Libera, Michèle Weinachter, and Georges Saunier from French into English. Furthermore, our thanks go out to Christopher Chappell, our editorial contact at Palgrave, and to the anonymous reviewers who provided insightful comments on earlier drafts. We are also deeply indebted to Professor Wilfried Loth (University of Duisburg-Essen) for his active support of our book project and to Clifford P. Hackett, who gave us many helpful stylistic advices. We owe a final word of thanks to our contributors for their patience throughout the whole process and for their contributions that are the substance of this book.

Old Foes and New Friends

Historical Perspectives on Franco-German Relations since Napoleon

Carine Germond and Henning Türk

I t is now a commonplace to regard France and Germany as playing a decisive role in Europe. Over the past few decades, numerous labels have been used to characterize their "special relationship": couple, pair, axis, tandem, privileged partnership, engine, motor, locomotive, linchpin, alliance within the alliance, detonator, and so forth.[1] These manifold characterizations refer in one way or another to the volume of communication and exchanges existing today between the two governments and the degree to which they have been institutionalized. What they all have in common is the dynamic and usually positive qualities they impart to Franco-German relations in Europe. That the two countries would play such a constructive role was by no means evident given the violent legacy of their history. Indeed, the history of Franco-German relations before 1945 is characterized by a long-lasting antagonism feeding on rivalry for territory and hegemony on the European continent, as well as humiliated national sentiments and revenge discourses.

The intertwined history of France and Germany has underpinned Europe's past unlike that of any other European country: both modern states can trace their origin to Charlemagne's empire; the founding dynasts of the French kingdom were of Germanic origin and, in subsequent centuries, strove to assert their independence vis-à-vis the Holy Roman Emperors. As the French veteran of reconciliation Joseph Rovan writes, "it took twenty-three Franco-German wars since the era of Charles V and François I to finally create Europe."[2] There was thus a long way to go before the former alleged "hereditary enemies" became the close partners they are now in the European Union (EU) and the world.

Following the path opened up by the historians Raymond Poidevin and Jacques Bariety,[3] the purpose of this book is to shed light on the major transformations and developments that relations between France and Germany have undergone since the early nineteenth century and to assess their significance in and for Europe. In contrast to the many contemporary studies available in English that first and foremost focus on post–1945 Franco-German relations, this broad chronological scope sheds light on the historical foundations on which the contemporary Franco-German relationship is based and highlights historical continuities and ruptures.

The contributions were penned by young emerging scholars from Europe and the United States working on recently opened archives or revisiting long-accessible collections. To head each section, more experienced hands were charged with the writing of broad-brush, preliminary surveys in which they contextualize the themes developed in the more detailed, research-based subsections. The international origins of the contributors are concrete proof of the ever-renewed interest in the subject—and not only in the two countries primarily concerned.

Although traditional diplomatic history predominates, other disciplines such as political science and cultural, social, and economic history are represented, too. This interdisciplinary approach brings to light the different aspects and dimensions of bilateral relations and integrates research on both European and Franco-German history. The methodological tools used by the contributors also mirror the many ways to approach Franco-German relations. Although most authors have privileged a comparative approach reflecting the contemporary trend to "bilateralize" Franco-German relations, in some cases they also reflect the vivid and ongoing scholarly debate about national versus comparative versus transnational versus transfers study versus "entangled" history versus *histoire croisée* that has involved historians of the Franco-German relationship in particular over the past decade.[4]

The book is divided into three chronological sections that mark epochal caesurae and show an internal unity, recognizable patterns of bilateral interactions, and thematic recurrences. Focusing on Franco-German relations from Napoleon to the First World War, the first section illustrates how those relations and the formation of both national identities were shaped by territorial conflicts, power rivalry, exacerbated nationalism, and revenge discourses. The second section deals with the interwar period from the end of the First World War to the immediate aftermath of the Second World War. It exemplifies instances of rapprochement in various realms—among them civil society, economics, and politics—as well as the persistence of distrust and conflicts. It analyzes the motives behind these reconciliation attempts and the national, bilateral, European, and international reasons for their failure. Finally, the third section explores post–1945 bilateral relations. It illustrates the dynamic interactions between Franco-German cooperation and European integration and highlights the radical transformation of the Franco-German relationship from confrontation into ever-closer cooperation. A selected bibliography of the English-language scholarly literature available on the subject ends the volume.

As Reiner Marcowitz points out, the "long nineteenth century" was "the century of Franco-German antagonism." This antagonism eventually gave birth to the concept of the "hereditary enemy," which became a constitutive element of Franco-German relations in that era and, as such, is extensively analyzed in several contributions. Marcowitz and Bernhard Struck both underscore that the origin of the idea of a "hereditary enmity" between France and Germany is, in fact, anterior to the Franco-Prussian conflict and can be traced back to the emergence of national consciousness and of modern nationalism on both sides of the Rhine. Jörg Ulbert further argues that Austria remained the actual "hereditary enemy" of France, at least until the rise of Prussia threatened French interests in Europe. Stefan Jordan and Hugo Frey scrutinize the intellectual construction of the concept by two leading French and German historians, Heinrich von Treitschke and Jacques Bainville. Although they belonged to two different generations, they made use of similar rhetoric to construct the image of the archenemy, one that was mixed with anti-Republicanism, anti-Semitism and, occasionally, social Darwinism. With their depictions of France and Germany, both historians fostered mutual resentment and hostility that was later instrumentalized in both countries for purposes of domestic and foreign policy.

Nineteenth-century Franco-German relations were also decisively influenced by nationalism that, in France, took on a missionary and expansive character after the French Revolution of 1789 and, in Germany, was successfully instrumentalized to throw off the yoke of Napoleonic occupation during the German Wars of Liberation (1813–15). The formation of both nation-states throughout the nineteenth century thus occurred largely as a conflictive and interactive process in which images and perceptions of the other served to buttress national sentiments. Nationalist episodes also occurred regularly during the Restoration era, for instance during the "July crisis" of 1830, the "Rhine crisis" of 1840, and the Revolution of 1848. France's national humiliation by the coronation of Emperor Wilhelm I at Versailles in January of 1871, the founding act of the Prussian-led *Kaiserreich* or German Empire, laid the groundwork for revenge and persistent resentment, as Nathan Orgill illustrates. He shows that Otto von Bismarck's complex system of alliances successfully managed both to isolate France in the concert of Europe and thwart a French war of revenge but rapidly broke down after the chancellor's fall from power, thus opening a way for France to reassert itself against its rival.

Struck and Ulbert also explore the implications of the existence of multiple "Germanies" for Franco-German relations, an aspect that has been neglected by the scholarly literature to a great extent. Indeed, a pluralistic Germany implies an additional interlocutor in the otherwise bilateral diplomatic game. Struck identifies a "Third Germany," belonging neither to Prussia nor to Austria and forming a kind of buffer zone, a borderland between France and Prussia. It is in this area, he argues, that entanglements of a cultural, political, or legal nature were the most intensive. Ulbert demonstrates that the primary aims of French diplomacy were to avoid the rise of a hegemonic power in Germany by playing either the Prussian or Austrian card so that France could control German affairs and keep both German powers in check. This policy, which had shown some positive results until the 1850s, was shattered by Austria's defeat in 1866. The victory of Prussia over its German rival paved the way for a Prussian-led *Kaiserreich*, striving to assert its dominance over France.

The long nineteenth century thus appears as a multifaceted period, during which a complex Franco-German relationship cannot be reduced to a one-dimensional "hereditary enmity."

In a pattern similar to that of the previous era, the dramatic interwar period witnessed constantly alternating surges of hostility and attempts at rapprochement that closely matched variations in the balance of power between France and Germany, as Sylvain Schirmann reveals. Characteristic of the interwar period, he argues, was the failure of both countries to develop new modes and patterns of interaction other than conflict and competition.

This is particularly well-exemplified by Laura Fasanaro, Elana Passman, and Verena Schöberl, each of whom examines very different realms of bilateral interactions. Fasanaro takes the sensitive problem of coal, then the prime energy resource, and the related issue of the Ruhr basin and illustrates how an unresolved divisive bilateral factor of the interwar era was successfully turned after 1945 into a force for unity between France and Germany on the one hand and Western Europe on the other. Leaving the governmental sphere, Passman and Schöberl explore para-public and public examples of Franco-German rapprochement during the second half of the 1920s. Passman looks at instances of civic activism in favor of Franco-German rapprochement and turns her attention to three private organizations that, buoyed by the "spirit of Locarno," had an original approach to bilateral relations and created a (narrow and ephemeral) space of communication and cooperation for civil society. By establishing new forms of mediation between France and Germany, she makes the case that, despite their failure to redefine bilateral relations during the interwar period, these early attempts at cooperation laid the groundwork for the post–1945 reconciliation process. Schöberl then shows that, beyond the political divide and positions of the French and German intellectual elite for or against Franco-German rapprochement, a deep-seated distrust persisted in both countries and underlay reconciliation discourses. Even the European enthusiasm stirred up by the signing of the Treaty of Locarno proved too superficial to profoundly alter older dynamics at work between France and Germany.

The political relevance of Franco-German economic relations comes to light in Frédéric Clavert's and Martial Libera's chapters. The former demonstrates that Franco-German efforts to improve economic and trade policy relations during the second half of the 1930s had a primarily political motive. Clavert explains that France sought to tie the economic settlement of bilateral disputes to a wider political agreement in Central and Eastern Europe that would also include the United Kingdom and the United States. Indeed, Franco-German initiatives toward economic rapprochement were part of a larger effort to alleviate growing tensions between weakened, pacifist democracies and ambitious, revisionist dictatorships. Revisiting traditional explanations for France's economic policy toward

Germany in the immediate aftermath of the Second World War, Libera argues that France, in fact, pursued an imperialist and expansionist policy in Germany based on a mixture of political, economic, and security considerations. He also investigates the motivations and roles of the different political and industrial players and sheds light on the decision-making processes regarding Germany in postwar France.

Another theme that stands out is the importance of leaders, networks, and mediators during the interwar period. Indeed, bilateral rapprochement was purposefully advanced by a handful of influential personalities, such as Aristide Briand, Gustav Stresemann, Robert Schuman, and Emile Mayrisch. Voluntarism thus appears as a defining characteristic of interwar rapprochement and highlights the decisive role of a small Franco-German vanguard. The various instances and realms of interwar rapprochement also bring out the complexity of plans developed in these crucial years. Although interwar proponents of Franco-German reconciliation failed to perpetuate what they had achieved, post–1945 reconciliation between France and Germany would continue to be primarily embodied by those who actively promoted it and would be achieved by a relatively small pioneering group.

In this context, it is also interesting to draw a parallel between the interwar and postwar notions of rapprochement. As in the post–1945 era, interwar rapprochement refers to and defines processes by which France and Germany sought to gradually remove obstacles to cooperation. These processes lay within both a bilateral and multilateral—partly European—framework with the signing of a series of treaties seeking to regulate divisive issues. In both cases, Franco-German rapprochement was underpinned by a system of alliances and pacts. As several authors show, alliances between France and its Western and Eastern allies were central to its attitude toward Germany. But the interwar alliance system was undermined by growing interallied disagreements on reparations, war debt, and protectionist reactions to the economic crisis, as well as divergent strategic interests. In contrast, Soviet containment gave the postwar Western alliance system its political, economic, and ideological cement. Moreover, interwar rapprochement lacked the two fundamental elements of convergence and harmonization, which would greatly contribute to the success of postwar rapprochement, as a recent study on Franco-German rapprochement in the 1950s has convincingly demonstrated.[5]

By the end of the 1940s, a redefinition of the whole Franco-German relationship in the wider European context had become necessary. A new order in Franco-German relations would emerge and inaugurate one of the longest and most stable periods in bilateral interactions. The "hereditary enmity" of the nineteenth century evolved after 1945 into a hereditary friendship, a long and sinuous path reconstructed by Ulrich Lappenküper.

A key development of the postwar era was the emergence of the Franco-German "couple" that came to stand for the partnership ruling the countries' relations from 1950 onward. Although the metaphor was used in previous centuries to describe relations between "Marianne" and "Germania" (or the somewhat naïve young man Michel),[6] it was popularized after 1945 to epitomize reconciliation, portray a pacified relationship between France and Germany, and underscore the personal dimension of the bilateral partnership[7]—something that a few pairs of statesmen knew how to stage effectively with symbolic gestures intended to mark the collective memory of both peoples.

Historians of Franco-German relations have highlighted the significance of Franco-German couples, and Lappenküper sketches the way in which each one of them stands for a distinct period in bilateral interactions. The image of a unique Franco-German couple appears too simplistic, however. There has indeed been a variety of couples reflecting the degree of personal understanding and proximity existing between the French and German leaders who embody it. Mathieu Segers sheds light on the surprising (and largely overlooked) couple of Guy Mollet and Konrad Adenauer whose entente, he argues, was decisive for the creation of the European Economic Community (EEC). Ronald Granieri stresses the close and friendly relationship that existed between Charles de Gaulle and Adenauer, which had a personal dimension but was also based on realpolitik calculus and came to symbolize Franco-German reconciliation. Lappenküper, Granieri, and Garret Martin illustrate the difficulties encountered by Adenauer's successors, Ludwig Erhard and Kurt Georg Kiesinger, in attempting to establish similar relations with de Gaulle; in the case of Erhard, there even developed a kind of "noncouple" or "anticouple." Katrin Rücker revisits the complex relationship between Georges Pompidou and Willy Brandt that, above all, rested on the will to collaborate. Michèle Weinachter analyzes the pragmatic and amicable couple formed by Valéry Giscard d'Estaing and Helmut Schmidt, who both played a crucial role in the advancement of European integration. Georges Saunier considers the "special relationship" between François Mitterrand and Helmut Kohl, who in spite of dissimilar personal backgrounds and occasional disagreements, showed real solidarity. Focusing on the personal dimension of Franco-German relations demonstrates that the performance and the efficiency of the Franco-German couple in the European and international arena have largely depended on the political will of the two partners.

The idea of the Franco-German couple is also closely related to the counterpart image of the engine or motor. Indeed, the analogy of the engine implies that France and Germany provide the impetus driving the European construction, but it also expresses the idea that there is an indivisible connection between Franco-German relations and Europe. In fact, since the creation of the first European institutions, both countries have used their reconciliation and their reliance on joint leadership to sustain the momentum of European integration so as to bolster their claim for leadership in Europe.

The authors extensively illustrate how the preliminary entente between France and Germany became a prerequisite for the integration of Europe and how the two countries were able to provide an impulse for European projects and then implement them. Victor Gavin explains that, very early on, France purposefully pushed European integration by means of the European Coal and Steel Community (ECSC) and the European Defense Community (EDC) in order to serve its national interest in a stable and long-lasting solution to Franco-German problems through a new European framework—rather than doing so out of any European idealism. Mathieu Segers contends that the Adenauer-Mollet agreement to save the endangered negotiations on the EEC and the European Atomic Energy Community (EAEC-Euratom) marks the actual birth of the Franco-German axis, and he brings to light the nuclear dimension of the Franco-German rapprochement in the second half of the 1950s. Granieri analyzes the particular combination of practical, geostrategic interests and aspiration to reconciliation that provided and reinforced the momentum eventually leading to the institutionalization of Franco-German relations with the signature of the Elysée Treaty in 1963. This agreement served to underpin France's and Germany's claims for leadership in Europe, legally and formally. However, Lappenküper, Martin, and Granieri demonstrate that the objectives laid down in the treaty were not fulfilled by Adenauer's successors. Yet, it is precisely in difficult periods that the agreement proved its value as an instrument of dialogue whose mechanisms guaranteed the continuity of the Franco-German couple beyond governmental changes or occasional disagreements, as Georges Saunier rightly reminds us. In fact, the 1963 treaty survived its authors and successive actors to remain the institutional basis of bilateral cooperation up to the present. The stalled Franco-German engine was reactivated by Georges Pompidou and Willy Brandt, who, as Rücker points out, were able to assert their authority both in Europe and the world whenever they acted together, although their ability to deal with global challenges, such as the energy crisis and monetary disorders, did have certain limits. Weinachter analyzes how Valéry Giscard d'Estaing and Helmut Schmidt successfully instrumentalized their entente to advance European integration with the creation of two new institutional tools: the European Council and the European monetary system. Also, Saunier credits François Mitterrand and Helmut Kohl with giving European integration decisive impulses. Although German unification profoundly altered the internal structure of the Franco-German relationship, it served as a catalyst to further the political and economic integration of Europe and pave the way for the creation of the EU in 1992.

The authors show that the failure of France and Germany to achieve consensus on essential issues and to harmonize their visions often resulted in bilateral crises and European stagnation as the couple lost its force of attraction for the other European member states. By contrast, when they found common ground, progress toward integration could be achieved.

Despite its apparent continuity, the character of the Franco-German couple has changed over time, too. Curtailed by the legacy of the Second World War, West Germany contented itself with the role of junior partner. Franco-German reconciliation fostered the Federal Republic's reintegration into the community of nations and gave Bonn greater possibilities to articulate its own interests in the European and world arenas. Consequently, the relationship was one of unequal partners very early on, as many authors rightly note. The Elysée Treaty, which allowed France to cooperate with and control Germany at the same time, mirrored this particular balance of power within the couple. A rebalancing of the relationship started in the 1970s when, in the wake of the economic recession following the two oil shocks, the scales of power clearly tipped in favor of West Germany. The Federal Republic was then able to translate economic strength into political power more actively. *Ostpolitik* also gave it a new legitimacy apart from French support and widened its leeway in Europe. The withering of historical constraints on Germany was thus decisive in shifting power within the Franco-German duo. German reunification accelerated this preexisting trend, since it emphasized the country's key geo-strategic role in Europe as a bridge between the center and the new periphery of the EU. Twenty-first-century Franco-German relations are those of equal partners, but the reshaping of the two countries' relations is still an ongoing process, as the recent celebration of the fortieth anniversary of the Elysée Treaty has shown.

Furthermore, an original and often ignored aspect of postwar Franco-German relations comes to light in the chapters written by Garret Martin, Ulrich Pfeil, and Wolfram Vogel, who analyze the influence of third parties on the couple, as either a potential source of conflict or a source of increased strength for the bilateral relationship. Although triangular relations have a long tradition in Franco-German history, the specific post–1945 international context of the cold war provided new leeway for a third party, such as the United States—whose role is indirectly discussed in other chapters—the Soviet Union, or the German Democratic Republic (GDR) to influence the development and test the cohesion of the Franco-German partnership. Analyzing the dynamic triangle formed by Paris-Bonn-Moscow during de Gaulle's presidency, Martin illustrates the ways in which the Soviet factor acted alternately as a centrifugal and a centripetal force on the Franco-German couple, bringing together or, conversely, pushing the partners away from one another. Pfeil looks at the triangular relations among France, West Germany, and the "other" (East) Germany, a direct consequence of the postwar division of Europe into two spheres of influence. He depicts the overall unsuccessful attempts by the East Germans to bring the GDR factor into the relationship between its West German counterpart and France on a political and cultural level, both before and after the official recognition of the GDR by France in 1973. However, with its complex mixture of intra-German rivalry and seemingly contradictory Franco-West German and Franco-East German interests, Pfeil argues that the GDR was nonetheless a "stimulating element" in the Paris-Bonn relationship.

Although its role has been largely downplayed, if not neglected, Poland's rise to the status of a third party in post–cold war relations between Paris and Bonn by way of the Franco-German-Polish "Weimar Triangle" is by no means irrelevant, especially in the context of Europe's latest enlargement. Vogel emphasizes that its creation in 1990 fulfilled different objectives—in the case of France, to keep a dreaded German *Drang nach Osten* under control; in the case of Germany and Poland, to accelerate enlargement and integration into the European Community. The Weimar Triangle's creation also coincides with questions by member states, both old and new, as to the Franco-German couple's ability to exert its leadership in an enlarged Europe. Vogel concludes that the Weimar platform, despite is flaws, evidenced the will of France and Germany to continue shaping European integration processes in the future and is primarily used as a strategic instrument to underpin their political leadership in the enlarged EU.

Despite their differences, certain similarities can be identified in the three triangular relationships portrayed. History seems crucial to all of them. Indeed, there is an ancient tradition of bilateral alliances that bound France, Germany, and Russia (the Soviet Union), on the one hand, and Poland, on the other. Also, France had a long tradition of dealing with multiple "Germanies," which for centuries has been a constitutive element of its policy toward its neighbors beyond the Rhine. Another commonality among these triangles appears to be the asymmetry of power relations existing among the three partners.

The Franco-German partnership stands out in Europe by virtue of its history, intensity, and institutional framework. It is a highly codified cooperation that is firmly anchored, both in the political and societal realm of the two countries. However, the generational replacement that took place in France and Germany has altered the contents and practices of bilateral cooperation. Most of the ideals and objectives, which were formulated during the reconciliation phase, have been achieved. The relationship between both countries is no longer the only aim of cooperation but is first and foremost shaped by common interest in the world and in Europe. If France and Germany want to be able to affront the manifold challenges of the twenty-first century, from globalization to demographic changes and Europe's future enlargements, they will have to redefine their privileged partnership.

Notes

1. Douglas Webber, ed., *The Franco-German Relationship in the European Union* (London: Routledge, 1999); Robert Picht and Wolfgang Wessels, eds., *Motor für Europa? Deutsch-französischer Bilateralismus und europäische Integration* (Bonn: Europa-Union Verlag, 1990); Robert Picht, *Das Bündnis im Bündnis. Deutsch-französische Beziehungen internationalen Spannungsfeld* (Berlin: Severin und Siedler, 1982); Haig Simonian, *The Privileged Partnership: Franco-German Relations in the EC, 1969–1984* (Oxford: Oxford University Press, 1985); Julius Friend, *The Linchpin. Franco-German Relations 1950–1990* (New York: Praeger, 1991); Valéry Guerin-Sendelbach, *Ein Tandem für Europa? Die deutsch-französische Zusammenarbeit der 80er Jahre* (Bonn: Europa Union Verlag, 1993); David P. Calleo and Eric R. Staal, eds., *Europe's Franco-German Engine* (Washington, DC: Brookings Institution, 1998); Gisela Hendriks and Annette Morgan, eds., *The Franco-German Axis in European Integration* (Cheltenham: Elgar, 2001); Laurent Leblond, *Le couple franco-allemand depuis 1945—chronique d'une relation exemplaire* (Paris: Le Monde-Editions, 1997); Henri Ménudier, ed., *Le couple franco-allemand en Europe* (Asnières: Publications de l'Institut d'Allemand d'Asnières, 1993); Daniel Colard, *Le partenariat franco-allemand du traité de l'Elysée à la République de Berlin 1963–1999* (Paris: Gualino Ed., 1999).

2. Quoted in Ulrich Krotz, "Social content of the International Sphere: Symbols and Meaning in Franco-German Relations," Harvard University, Minda de Gunzburg Center for European Studies, 11.

3. Jacques Bariety and Raymond Poidevin, *Les relations franco-allemandes 1815–1975* (Paris: Armand Colin, 1977); *Frankreich und Deutschland: Die Geschichte ihrer Beziehungen 1815–1975* (München: Beck, 1982).

4. For a compact summary of the theoretical debate in English, see Michael Werner and Bénédicte Zimmermann, "Beyond Comparison: *Histoire croisée* and the Challenge of Reflexivity," *History and Theory* 45 (2006): 30–50; Jürgen Kocka, "Comparison and Beyond," *History and Theory* 42 (2003): 39–44; Philippe Ther, "Beyond the Nation: The National Basis of Comparative History of Germany and Europe," *Central European History* 36, no. 1 (March 2003): 45–73. For the specific debate among historians of Franco-German relations, see Michel Espagne, *Les transferts culturels franco-allemandes* (Paris: PUF, 1999); Jacques Leenhardt and Robert Picht, eds., *Au jardin des malentendus: Le commerce franco-allemands des idées* (Arles: Actes sud, 1997); Hans-Jürgen Lüsebrink and Rolf Reichardt, eds., *Kulturtransfer im Epochenumbruch. Frankreich—Deutschland 1770 bis 1815* (Leipzig: Leipziger Universitätsverlag, 1997), 9–26; Horst Möller and Jacques Morizet, eds., *Franzosen und Deutsche. Orte der gemeinsamen Geschichte* (München: Beck, 1996)—*Allemagne-France. Lieux de mémoire d'une histoire commune* (Paris: Albin Michel, 1995); Michael Werner, "Le prisme franco-allemand: à propos d'une histoire croisée des disciplines littéraires," in *Entre Locarno et Vichy. Les relations culturelles franco-allemandes dans les années 1930*, ed. Hans Manfred Bock, Reinhart Meyer-Kalkus, and Michel Trebitsch (Paris: CNRS-Editions, 1993), 303–16.

5. Helène Miard-Delacroix and Rainer Hudemann, eds., *Wandel und Integration. Deutsch-französische Annäherungen der fünfziger Jahre—Mutations et intégration. Les rapprochements franco-allemands dans les années cinquante* (München: Oldenbourg, 2005), 27–30.

6. Joseph Hurt, "Le couple franco-allemand. Naissance et histoire d'une métaphore," in *France-Allemagne, passions croisées*, ed. Karl-Heinz Götze (Aix-en-Provence: Université de Provence, 2001), 51–60.

7. Cyril Buffet and Béatrice Heuser, "Marianne-Michel: The Franco-German Couple," in *Haunted by History: Myths in International Relations*, ed. Cyril Buffet and Béatrice Heuser (Providence: Berghahn Book, 1998), 174–205.

PART I

Franco-German Relations from Napoleon to World War I

CHAPTER 1

Attraction and Repulsion

Franco-German Relations in the "Long Nineteenth Century"

Reiner Marcowitz

Franco-German relations are a central theme in both nations' historical writing. The period from 1789 to 1919 is of special significance.[1] Mutual attraction and repulsion alternated in especially quick succession during that era. Both peoples admired one another. Yet, they both feared and even hated one another. To that extent, the "long nineteenth century"[2] between the French Revolution and the First World War was also the century of Franco-German antagonism. That view may seem exaggerated and excessively focused on developments in the years after 1867. However, it was not the prehistory of the Franco-Prussian War of 1870–71 that first signaled new developments in the bilateral relationship but rather the much earlier Wars of Liberation of 1813–15. For the first time, traditional power-political rivalry and the age-old territorial conflicts of earlier centuries were combined with national passion. The *Grande Révolution* of 1789 had instilled in the French a "sense of mission"[3] that seemed to justify and even mandate a duty to bring their neighbors the blessing of *liberté égalité, et fraternité*; that many Germans initially welcomed. The victorious march of the French through Europe at the beginning of the nineteenth century thus made enduring changes in the political geography of Germany. The emperor was compelled to abdicate and the "Holy Roman Empire of the German Nation" splintered into different groups of collaborating, neutral, and dispossessed princes. The French calculus of playing the various "Germanies" against one another seemed to be effective at first, with France having "become the actual arbiter of German affairs."[4] At the same time, important administrative and sociopolitical reforms introduced in the French-ruled Rhineland and Westphalia gave those occupied regions a decisive push toward modernization. Yet, under Napoleon I, the French mission became a fig leaf for a barely disguised expansionism against which a significant German resistance soon coalesced. What began at the grassroots was soon taken up by the elites. The territorial rulers, above all Prussian King Friedrich Wilhelm III, put themselves at the head of the popular outrage against France in 1813, raising their armies by resorting to national fervor.

The struggle against revolutionary France began in 1792 as a traditional cabinet war but ended in 1814 as a war between the nations. Out of the transnational Holy Roman Empire of the German Nation there arose a national alliance of interests during the Wars of Liberation. Opposition to the one-man rule of Napoleon I and general hostility toward France led to the intensification of German national consciousness.[5] Germany, which up to that time had been little more than a geographic expression, took on a political dimension for many of its people for the first time. However, its adherents constituted a minority that, after the defeat of Napoleon I by the restored German princes and their European colleagues, was easily outmaneuvered at the Congress of Vienna. The German Confederation did not meet either the political or the national hopes of those Germans who had risen up against the French occupation. The price for peace and stability in Europe in the subsequent decades was both a moderate restoration of the old lordships (*Standesherrn*) in Germany and the sharp repression of the new liberal, if not actually democratic, movements within the German Confederation. Nationalism no longer burdened Franco-German relations, and indeed, the first half of the nineteenth century was essentially characterized by the well-known network of connections between the French and their German neighbors. Yet, at least for the representatives of the nationalist movement, France remained a potential enemy of Germany. When their demands for German unity succeeded in the second half of the nineteenth century, the nationalist antipathy between both peoples once more took center stage.

At first, the successful suppression of the national movement in Germany convinced the French that things had remained unchanged beyond the Rhine. It was Madame de Staël's depiction of Germany before the Wars of Liberation that determined the perception of the country for generations after 1815: the image of a people somewhat uncouth but decent, philosophically and artistically talented but incapable of great political action.[6] Moreover, her book made Germany "into the central object of foreign interest among the leading intellectual classes in Paris."[7] In Germany, fears of renewed French aggression predominated along with a grudging acceptance of France as a legitimate child of the European family of nations. The France of the Bourbon restoration held itself aloof from its eastern neighbors, careful not to stir up any fears given the experience of Napoleonic expansionism.[8] From the beginning, there were attempts to link up with traditional French policy on Germany by working against the hegemony of any one German state, whereby the old rival, Austria, was joined by the new opponent, Prussia, or by supporting the desire for independence of the small and medium-sized German states constituting the "Third Germany," among which

Bavaria especially seemed a "natural ally." After France had succeeded in shaking off the supervision of the victorious powers at the congress in Aachen in November of 1818 and thus had once again joined the European pentarchy, these policies seemed more than ever to offer new possibilities. Altogether, however, France was far from pursuing an active German policy between 1815 and 1830 and instead kept a low profile, especially since it remained a domestically unstable and internationally isolated "great power on probation."[9]

The July Revolution of 1830 conjured up memories of 1789 both in France and in neighboring countries.[10] Once again, the French had driven a hated ruler from his throne, this time Charles X, who had attempted to hollow out the Constitutional Charter conceded by his brother in 1814. The peaceful unfolding of this second attempt to realize the ideals of 1789 gained France the sympathies of at least the liberally oriented segments of the German public, even though worries about possible expansionist developments in French foreign policy persisted. Meanwhile, Paris had once again become the "Mecca of Progressives of all countries,"[11] including many German democrats and liberals escaping persecution at home or simply eager to follow the exciting developments firsthand. In terms of German policy, the July revolution constituted a caesura to the extent that France now seemed to be more of an example of political self-determination and revolutionary transformation worthy of imitation in the eyes of the German national movement that, after years of suppression, was now striving to make its voice heard. This positive image of France contained negative traits as well; the very same supporters of German unification perceived France as a potential aggressor seeking to annex the left bank of the Rhine, against which some of them advanced the goal of regaining Alsace-Lorraine, notably at the 1832 Hambach Festival. This demonstrates again how durable the experience of Napoleonic rule and the Wars of Liberation were in the German view of the neighbor to the west.

In 1839 and 1840, the "European front of suspicion" formed once again.[12] France was isolating itself within the European pentarchy by supporting Mehmet Ali, the Egyptian vassal of the Turkish sultan, in his efforts to become independent. In the frustrated French public, reaction against the other powers' opposition suddenly transformed itself into demands for pushing the national boundary to the Rhine, which the Thiers government initially embraced. The subsequent "Rhine crisis" was to have far more lasting effects than the Oriental crisis that had precipitated it: In Germany, old fears of an aggressive France fixated on its "natural border" along the Rhine manifested themselves in a catchy battle lyric. Although there were some voices raised against this anti-French national pathos, they did not alter the fact that "1840" served a similarly catalytic function for the development of German national consciousness as the Wars of Liberation had: once again, the image of France as an enemy was used to sharpen the German national image, and this view of the neighbor to the west would once again become a given for a younger generation.[13]

In the revolutionary year 1848, it was not only the sociopolitical order in France and the states of the German Confederation that were changed but also the whole system of mutual relations. Early on, the first revolutionary government in France sought to eliminate concerns of possible French aggression and work with its eastern neighbor.[14] When governments in Germany were toppled a month later, it seemed that during a brief "revolutionary spring," cooperation under the banner of national self-determination would even be possible. After the rapid conservative swing in France, however, such revolutionary dreams withered completely, and the traditional power-political calculus again took center stage. On the French side, this meant not supporting the emergence of a unified German state, which had become the main focus of revolutionary energies beyond the Rhine. The delegates at the Paulskirche in Frankfurt furthered this classic French reflex in German policy by making excessive territorial demands. Without reservations, the new German ethnocentricity subordinated to its own right of self-determination the corresponding claims of other nationalities—in Schleswig-Holstein, in Posen, and even in Alsace-Lorraine—and sought to incorporate these regions into the new Reich. It also failed to define its own competencies vis-à-vis those of the remaining individual German states. By the late summer of 1848, the German national movement had already lost all French sympathy.

Louis Napoleon was elected president of the Second French Republic in December of 1848, then secured for himself dictatorial powers for a period of ten years, in December of 1851, and proclaimed himself emperor a year after that. He strove to replace the Vienna order of 1815 with a new system based on the national self-determination of peoples, in which France would play a dominant role.[15] He needed international recognition for this purpose. In the first half of the 1850s, he dealt mainly with Austria rather than its junior partner Prussia, especially since Austria eventually joined the Western powers in the Crimean War (1853–56) against Russia, whereas Prussia and the German Confederation remained neutral, thereby isolating themselves in the short term. Only in the years after the Crimean War, in the run-up to the Italian War of 1859 and thereafter, did the French emperor incorporate Prussia more fully into his German policy calculus: First of all, he was concerned to secure the neutrality of Prussia and the Confederation, in which he was successful despite significant opposition. Subsequently, his thoughts were dominated by the idea that the sought-after transformation of the map of Europe would allow and even necessitate a change in the status quo within the Confederation. For this, it seemed appropriate to back Prussia as a means of revising the traditional order.

The Prussians remained suspicious of Napoleon III and his political unpredictability and respected the traditional solidarity of the German great powers. These factors hindered comprehensive cooperation with France. Only the appointment of Otto von Bismarck as Prussian prime minister in September of 1862 and, one month later, also as foreign minister marked a real course change in Prussia's policy toward France.[16] The new head of government had developed his own political philosophy and finally came out against any policy based on principles. Wholly the "Realpolitiker," Bismarck demanded that Prussia enter only those alliances that served its political interests. As early as the end of the 1850s, this meant, in his view, cooperation with France, which was interested in elevating Prussia's status in Germany, rather than with Austria, which denied its north German neighbor equal status in the Confederation. Napoleon III encouraged Bismarck during the latter's brief stint as Prussian ambassador in Paris in 1862 to have Prussia pursue a national policy in order to expand its power in Germany.

In the run up to the German-Danish War, the French government adopted a conciliatory policy and intensified its solicitation of an alliance with Prussia. The time of the great successes represented by the Paris Peace Conference of 1856 was over; there was no longer any hope of using restrained support for nationalist movements in order to gain a leading position for France within a new European order or personal popularity for its emperor by revising the hated Vienna system. Thus, the French leadership was now supporting the greatest possible territorial expansion of Prussia without directly linking this with its own territorial demands. The recovery of the Rhine border was by no means the leitmotiv of Napoleon III's foreign policy, since that would have provoked a new anti-French coalition.[17] Rather, the emperor was seeking an alliance with Prussia to increase his influence in Western Europe, exactly as the map of the Continent was being altered by Prussian successes. Above all, he wanted to foil any agreement between the two major German powers that would exclude France from a possible reordering of the German Confederation. By the summer of 1866, during the period preceding the "German War," there developed "a kind of three-way political game"[18] among France, Austria, and Prussia. At the outbreak of this "German War" in June of 1866, the French government anticipated a long struggle that would wear down the two leading German powers, finally leading to a peace settlement with the decisive involvement of France and a transformation of the German Confederation and, indeed, of Europe itself. The French were therefore all the more disappointed when Prussia sought a military decision as early as July 3 at the Battle of Königgrätz and achieved a decisive victory there. This battle—in France named after the nearby Bohemian town of Sadowa—proved to be a decisive caesura in Franco-Prussian relations: The quick and thorough victory over Austria meant a profound change in power relations within the German Confederation—one offering Prussia the possibility of a small-German unification but not one compatible with an increase of French power.

Yet, exactly that was wanted by a disappointed French public opinion, upon whose support Napoleon III had been increasingly dependent since he had begun liberalizing the governmental system in 1860. The emperor, who had repeatedly sought domestic support in the past by means of invoking the foreign policy greatness of France, became "the prisoner of his prestige policy."[19] The fact that the new situation, above all the exclusion of Austria from Germany, also offered France objective advantages remained unnoticed by such forces or was regarded as less significant than Prussia's increase in power. The initial sympathies of great segments of the French populace for the German unification movement and for self-determination vanished after 1866; henceforth, most Frenchmen regarded a small German unification under Prussian leadership "as an almost fatal danger."[20] After Königgrätz, France made territorial demands for Belgium and Luxemburg that would determine if the fundamentally peace-oriented emperor or his pro-war entourage, supported by a strong anti-Prussian mood in the country, would prevail.

After Bismarck finally made a public disavowal of the French during the Luxemburg crisis of 1867,[21] the Second Empire could expect no further compensation from Prussia. A new war did not thereby become unavoidable, but due to the tense French domestic political situation, it at least became more likely. Everything now depended on whether new points of conflict would arise. This happened in 1870 with the candidacy of a prince of the House of Hohenzollern-Sigmaringen for the Spanish throne.[22] From early on, French public opinion held Prussia responsible for this unwelcome initiative. That view was unjustified, as was the assumption that Bismarck had been pushing for the Hohenzollern candidacy from the beginning. In fact, he learned of it only in February of 1870 but had forcefully pushed it thereafter against the opposition of his king, since he saw the possibility of further weakening France in Europe and thus keeping its ruler eager for peace. As the candidacy became known in Paris in early July, the populace, frustrated over their nation's foreign policy failures during the past five years, reacted with indignation. Foreign Minister Antoine de Gramont demanded in an ultimatum as early as July 6, 1870, before the French Chamber of Deputies that Prussia reject the candidacy. He seemed to have succeeded since the Hohenzollern prince subsequently withdrew his name. Instead of savoring this victory, however, the French government attempted to expand upon it: On July 12, French ambassador Vincent Benedetti sought from the Prussian king, who was taking the cure in Bad Ems, a declaration guaranteeing that the Hohenzollern would not seek the Spanish throne in the future. Wilhelm I refused this politely and informed Bismarck of the matter via telegram. This excessive demand by the French government offered Bismarck the possibility of transforming a Prussian defeat into an opportunity to dupe France: he edited the "Ems Dispatch," making Wilhelm's refusal appear to be a brusque rejection of Benedetti, thereby putting the French government in the position of accepting a new foreign policy defeat or resorting to war. In France, outrage broke out at France's public humiliation by Prussia. On July 19, 1870, Napoleon III declared war.

Neither the French nor the Prussian government had initially been seeking war, but when the threat of war arose in the context of the July crisis of 1870, neither was prepared to avoid one. They both viewed military conflict as a legitimate continuation of a political disagreement. Additionally, the French leadership's poor management of the issue of Spanish succession and its emphasis on national honor and greatness led to a situation in which a simple rejection of the throne by the House of Hohenzollern-Sigmaringen no longer sufficed. Gramont's declaration of July 6 supported the idea that war was not necessary but acceptable. Likewise, it was clear to Bismarck that the "Ems Dispatch" had to be "a calculable spark for military conflict."[23] Thus, the "Franco-Prussian War" ultimately originated "from the collision of two political offensives."[24] It was admittedly the case that Bismarck for his part had pursued a "tactic of provocative defense,"[25] so that the French declaration of war would be the casus belli for the South German states, which had signed defensive treaties in 1866 and thereby also become the cornerstone of a "small" German unification. All this resulted not from the Prussian prime minister's policy goals but rather from unexpected developments and ultimately from poor French decision making based on falsely understood considerations of prestige.

The official statements of both sides bore witness to the widespread pathos of national testing and the conviction of the justice of one's own cause. This feeling increased to a seemingly indisputable certainty on the French side when the emperor was toppled after his capture at the Battle of Sedan on September 2, 1870, and the new "Government of National Defense" declared itself ready to concede to the Germans their national self-determination as long as France's own territorial integrity were preserved. That was not acceptable on the German side, however; already in the early phase of the war, demands were being voiced for the annexation of Alsace-Lorraine. For both nationalist and military reasons, Bismarck did not believe those demands could be rejected. Thus, the "Franco-Prussian War" had escalated into a "national war"[26] no later than September of 1870. Whereas the Germans had initially believed themselves the victims of French aggression, the French now felt called upon to defend their newly founded republic against Prussian-German expansion. After the surprising initial successes of the republican armies, the Prussian leadership reacted with the decision to march on Paris. At the beginning of January 1870, the French capital was subjected to bombardment, a measure that Bismarck had succeeded in pushing through over the objections of the Prussian chief of the general staff, Helmuth von Moltke, who would have preferred to starve out the besieged city. Bismarck feared that any further delay in a peace settlement could provoke the intervention of the other great powers. His calculation was successful: On January 28, 1871, the two sides signed an armistice. Ten days earlier, Wilhelm I had been proclaimed "German Kaiser" in the Palace of Versailles. More than a mere coincidence, it made "the enmity of France against Germany into a defining component of the foundation on which the Reich had to stand."[27] The military act on the soil of the defeated opponent placed the foundation of the German Empire within the continuity of the Franco-German conflict over foreign domination and national self-determination that had shaped the relations between the two countries since the beginning of the century. During the Wars of Liberation, the German national consciousness developed in opposition to France; the unified "small" German Reich that decades later made a reality of these national hopes had emerged in a new war with France and had solidified the Franco-German opposition for the long term, indeed transforming it into the notion that the two countries were "hereditary enemies," a conviction that was then passed down from one generation to the next.

Of course, this concept of "hereditary enemies" was primarily an ideological construct, developed in previous decades in the states of the German Confederation by societal groups seeking to strengthen German identity using the image of an enemy and simultaneously seeking to popularize their demand for a German nation-state by means of this "negative integration."[28] A dominant historiography of national apologetics in both countries contributed to this by working well into the first half of the twentieth century to project this view anachronistically onto the past and also perpetuate it for the future.[29] On the French side, this manifested itself in the desire for revanche and in the final dissolution of Madame de Staël's positive image of Germany in favor of the idea of a "dual Germany."[30] The stereotype of the land of poets and thinkers, though not totally abandoned, was immediately overlain with the image of a barbaric and domineering Germany. Conversely, there reigned in Germany a permanent anxiety over possible French aggression. At the same time, the image of a politically progressive France that, in any event, had only fascinated democratic and liberal circles while terrifying conservatives was replaced by that of an unpredictable and dangerous enemy. To sum up, it was in 1871 that the process of the "nationalizing" of enmity begun during the Wars of Liberation sixty years earlier was completed. Thenceforth, the enemy image on both sides became "a constitutive element of the national consciousness . . . [that] in crisis situations [created] a union of the nationalist minimal consensus."[31] Despite continuing bilateral transfers and linkages of a cultural, scientific, and economic nature as well as temporary political approaches that naturally occurred repeatedly even after 1870–71, this minimal consensus could be rapidly reactivated at any time.

The terms of the Treaty of Frankfurt of May 1871 contributed to the long-term burden on Franco-German relations. The demand for reparations totaling five billion francs within three years as a precondition for the permanent withdrawal of occupation forces from France was actually within the realm of traditional demands placed on defeated states and therefore acceptable. The annexation of Alsace-Lorraine, however, seemed anachronistic and even barbaric in the age of nation-states and the self-determination of peoples, even if a French victory would certainly have entailed comparable German territorial concessions.[32] The German government regarded possession of those border areas as indispensable: It did not believe that France would ever really accept the founding of the Reich and thus regarded another war as likely. The loss of a strategically important area would make French aggression more difficult. Moreover, this new artificial construct, the German Empire, needed a strong emotional foundation that was to be provided by the experience of the common struggle against France and the winning of a new "Imperial Territory." Ultimately, the annexation of Alsace and a part of Lorraine proved to be a heavy foreign policy burden because it became the "centerpiece of the idea of *revanche*"[33] in France and all the more so because the Reich could never win over the residents of the occupied regions, who remained second-class citizens.

The French government managed to finish paying the reparations in 1873, one year earlier than planned, and the last German soldiers withdrew from their posts in eastern France in October of 1873. With surprising rapidity, then, the French regained their ability to act on the foreign stage. For its part, the German government continued to regard France only as a negative element:[34] Long-lasting cooperation between the two countries seemed impossible due to the poisoned climate, whereas new conflicts appeared likely and thus necessitated appropriate precautions. Within this context, Bismarck believed it possible to frighten France once again with a massive threat of war in 1875. The effort failed this time, however, due to the solidarity shown by the other great powers with a France under threat. Ultimately, this "War-in-Sight" crisis demonstrated "the change in rank between France and Germany in the role of preponderant power on the Continent"[35] that had occurred in 1871. This increase in power, a "half-hegemonial position,"[36] although a positive development in and of itself, for the Reich, raised the danger of Germany's using its potential against the other great powers, as Napoleon I had once attempted, or of seeking a special role within the European pentarchy for a policy of prestige as Napoleon III had sought. Bismarck was immune to both dangers, especially after the experience of 1875 and because of his fundamental rejection of plans for preventive war. His efforts to thwart and control French cravings for revanche were henceforth transferred to the purely diplomatic realm. The goal of his complex alliance policy in subsequent decades was to achieve a "universal political situation in which all the powers except France need us and, by dint of our mutual relations, are kept as much as possible from forming coalitions against us," as he summarized it in his famous "Kissinger Diktat" of 1877.[37] Given the Russians' dissatisfaction with Germany resulting from the 1878 "Congress of Berlin," such an optimal constellation proved illusory, but France was still to be excluded wherever possible. At the very least, a lasting wedge was to be driven between the neighbor to the west and the neighbor to the east so that Germany would be spared a two-front war, thus pulling the rug out from under any French attack.

Between 1880 and 1885, it was nevertheless the case that a settlement between Germany and France seemed possible on the basis of close colonial cooperation. Since Bismarck regarded the Reich as a "satisfied" power, he was willing to promote French overseas territorial aspirations—in the hope that new possessions would allow the French to forget "the blue ridges of the Vosges" and free the Reich from the "birth defect of alienation from its French neighbor."[38] Beyond that, a forceful French colonial policy would, of necessity, divide France and Great Britain and thereby improve Germany's foreign policy position still further. On the French side, Prime Minister Jules Ferry (1880–81 and 1883–85) placed a high priority on the acquisition of new regions overseas and therefore made a congenial partner for Bismarck's policy. The highpoint of this honeymoon was the Berlin Congo Conference of November 1884 to February 1885, at which the Germans and the French worked closely together and largely against British interests. However, this cooperation remained a brief episode: Ferry's government fell in late March of 1885, his pro-German foreign policy having been extremely unpopular. Bismarck realized that colonial solidarity indeed produced temporary successes but could not eliminate long-term Continental animosity. From this point onward, he once again regarded France primarily as an irreconcilable opponent. This overlapped with a general tendency in the latter decades of the nineteenth century toward stronger societal, economic, and civilizational linkages in Europe—at the level of Franco-German bilateralism, too—that can certainly be characterized as an integration of the Continent avant la lettre.[39]

Bismarck's resignation and the "New Course" did not fundamentally alter relations between the two states. The usual expressions of antipathy alternated with transitory demonstrations of sympathy. The intensification of German colonial policy engendered new points of conflict that did not, however, rule out occasional agreements. The issue of Morocco twice led to genuine crises, in 1905–6 and again in 1911, both of which demonstrated the growing isolation of the German Reich. On the eve of the First World War, the position of France in the international system had improved to the extent that Germany's had worsened: First, the "World Policy" pursued by the Reich since 1890 had transferred its activities from the Continent to the far reaches of the globe and thereby had inevitably lessened the pressure that was kept on France up to that time. Secondly, German aspirations for the status of "world power" had given rise to new conflicts, above all with Britain but also with Russia, such that France was fully able to escape its European isolation, the very isolation that Bismarck at Bad Kissingen had warned ought to be the central goal of German foreign policy. France's new position was to be seen in the Franco-Russian conventions of 1892 and 1912, the Anglo-French Entente Cordiale of 1904, and the Triple Entente linking France, Britain, and Russia in 1907. These developments destroyed Bismarck's system of alliances and exposed Germany to the danger of a two-front war, a prospect the first German chancellor's policies had always sought to avoid. What was perceived among the German diplomatic establishment as foreign "encirclement" was in actuality self-created "exclusion"; not only had Bismarck's successors wasted the alliances he had bequeathed them, they had also ignored the lesson he had been taught by the "War-in-Sight" Crisis of 1875: The newest member of the Concert of Europe was forbidden to pursue any policy of prestige, a course that could easily have subjected it to the fate of France under both Napoleons. Instead, the foreign policy of "Wilhelmine Germany" was characterized by demonstrative swagger and pathological sensitivity resulting from a dangerous mixture of self-overestimation and an inferiority complex, hallmarks of both the Kaiser and his empire. It was no longer France but Germany that seemed to be arrogating to itself the status of "something very special"[40] in the concert of the great powers, seeking to claim special rights. If need be, this could justify war or make war seem unavoidable if a presumably hostile environment failed to concede those rights.

The murder of the heir to the Austrian throne, Franz Ferdinand, and his wife on June 28, 1914, was initially condemned by all the European great powers as a despicable act deserving of harsh punishment. Despite the risks that such a crisis presented in an age of arms races and nationalist agitation, there initially seemed to be no threat of a "great war." As things escalated after the Austrian ultimatum to Serbia on July 23, followed five days later by a declaration of war, coordinated efforts at crisis diplomacy by the Germans and French should have been obvious given that the latter had significant influence in Russia and the former was the very close ally of Austria. However, this was not undertaken or, at best, was not pursued energetically enough, since the German government was subordinating all its decisions to the primacy of military matters from late July onward—and that meant the exigencies of the Schlieffen Plan, which called for mobilization both in the west and in the east. Therefore, Berlin issued an ultimatum to Paris on July 31 demanding its neutrality in the event of war between Germany and Russia. The evasive French response of August 1 was followed two days later by Germany's declaration of war against France. Thus, the German government had brought upon itself the odium of being the aggressor, just as Napoleon III had done forty-four years earlier.

The subsequent conflict was a "great" or "world" war in which all the major powers participated, but it was at the same time one more link in a chain of Franco-German confrontations since the dawn of the nineteenth century. In both countries, euphoria over the war vanished rapidly because the conflict in the West had by year's end hardened into a war of position whose horrors were experienced by French and German soldiers alike. In the following years, attempts to break through the enemy front cost millions of lives on both sides. The oft-evoked "bath of steel" that was to cleanse the nations and from which they were to emerge free of the dross of a long period of peace revealed itself to be a blood bath for which, above all, Germans and Frenchmen were to pay a high price. Politicians in both countries quickly realized that the extent of the victory had to correspond to the greatness of the sacrifice if they wanted to remain in power. Merely reinstating the peace would have been seen as an insult to the dead; hence, each side developed far-reaching war goals that had this much in common: rather than seeking to weaken the opponent for a time, they aimed to eliminate the threat permanently. In France, Jacques Bainville's "History of Two Peoples" popularized the new image of Germany that in 1870–71 had already superseded Madame de Staël's one-sided, favorable portrait of the neighbor beyond the Rhine: Henceforth there dominated the image of a belligerent, violent, and power-hungry Prussiandom that had subjected the traditional "Germanies" to an artificial centralism and in response to which France must make recourse to the policy of the time of the Peace of Westphalia—a policy of divide et impera.

Views such as this—rather than appeals to what the two peoples had in common, that is, appeals made by well-intentioned people on both sides even during the war—were to shape France's policy on Germany after the armistice of November 11, 1918. From "an abyssal feeling of anxiety"[41] there arose maximal demands[42] that could be only partially realized at the Paris Peace Conference of 1919. This was due to France's need to avoid a break with the more conciliatory United States and Britain, two allies it could not dispense with in the postwar period. Hence, France was unable to bring about the founding of separate states on the left bank of the Rhine under a French protectorate. Nor would the Saar region be permanently turned over to France but instead was to be administered for fifteen years by the League of Nations, albeit with significant economic privileges for France. Nor did the French prevail in requiring that the future German army be a small conscript force; instead, the Allies permitted a professional force of 100,000. The terms of the Treaty of Versailles, signed on June 28, 1919, were not sufficient to weaken Germany over the long term but were indeed sufficient to cause decisive harm to Franco-German relations in the first half of the twentieth century. Given that France, more than any other victorious power, oversaw a "coalition peace,"[43] its image in Germany was most closely associated with the seeming despotism of the victors. Who in Germany was prepared as early as 1919 to admit the possibility that a "German" Versailles would have been hardly less harmful to France as the actual historical treaty was to Germany? After twenty years of "false peace"[44] Hitler unleashed a new and much greater war by exploiting old hatreds. Only after that war could reconciliation between the two peoples for the first time gain a real chance and the long century of Franco-German antagonism—beginning with the French Revolution in 1789 and the Wars of Liberation in 1813—come to an end.

Notes

1. See Raymond Poidevin and Jacques Bariéty, *Frankreich und Deutschland. Die Geschichte ihrer Beziehungen 1815–1975* (München: Beck, 1982), 17–316; Reiner Pommerin and Reiner Marcowitz, eds., *Quellen zu den deutsch-französi -schen 1815–1919* (Darmstadt: Wissenschaftliche Buchgesellschaft, 1997); Etienne François, Marie-Claire Hoock-Demarle, and Reinhard Meyer-Kalkus, eds., *Marianne—Germania. Deutsch-französischer Kulturtransfer im europäischen Kontext 1789–1914*, 2 vols. (Leipzig: Leipziger Universitätsverlag, 1998).

2. Jürgen Kocka, *Das lange 19. Jahrhundert* (Stuttgart: Klett-Cotta, 2004).

3. Karl Epting, *Das französische Sendungsbewusstsein im 19. und 20. Jahrhundert* (Heidelberg: Vowinkel, 1952).

4. Thomas Nipperdey, *Deutsche Geschichte 1800–1866. Bürgerwelt und starker Staat* (München: Beck, 1984), 12. Cf. Karl Otmar Freiherr von Aretin, *Heiliges Römisches Reich 1776–1806. Reichsverfassung und Staatssouveränität*, vol. 1 (Wiesbaden: Steiner, 1967), 251–506; T. C. W. Blanning, *The French Revolution in Germany. Occupation and Resistance in the Rhineland, 1792–1802* (Oxford: Clarendon, 1983); Ute Planert, *Der Mythos vom Befreiungskrieg. Frankreichs Kriege und der deutsche Süden. Alltag—Wahrnehmung—Deutung 1792–1841* (Paderborn: Schönigh, 2007).

5. Michael Jeismann, *Das Vaterland der Feinde. Studien zum nationalen Feindbegriff und Selbstverständnis in Deutschland und Frankreich 1792–1918* (Stuttgart: Klett-Cotta, 1991), 27–102.

6. Anne Germaine de Staël, *Über Deutschland*, ed. Monika Bosser (Frankfurt am Main: Insel Verlag, 1985).

7. Klaus Heitmann, "Das französische Deutschlandbild in seiner Entwicklung, Teil 1," *Sociologia Internationalis* 4 (1966): 79.

8. Klaus Hammer, *Die französische Diplomatie der Restauration und Deutschland 1814–1830* (Stuttgart: Hiesermann, 1963).

9. Reiner Marcowitz, *Großmacht auf Bewährung. Die Interdependenz französischer Innen- und Außenpolitik und ihre Auswirkungen auf Frankreichs Stellung im Europäischen Konzert 1814/15–1851/52* (Stuttgart: Thorbecke, 2001).

10. Winfried Baumgart, *Europäisches Konzert und nationale Bewegung. Internationale Beziehungen 1830–1878* (Paderborn: Schönigh, 1999), 271–80; Marcowitz, *Großmacht*, 99–126.

11. Franz Herre, *Deutsche und Franzosen. Der lange Weg zur Freundschaft* (Bergisch Gladbach: G. Lubbe, 1983), 136ff.

12. Anselm Doering-Manteuffel, *Die Deutsche Frage und das Europäische Staatensystem 1815–1871* (München: Oldenburg, 1993), 18. Cf. Baumgart, *Europäisches Konzert*, 287–301; and Marcowitz, *Großmacht*, 152–70.

13. Jeismann, *Vaterland*, 162ff.

14. Marcowitz, *Großmacht*, 185–211, 225–47.

15. William E. Echard, *Napoleon III and the Concert of Europe* (Baton Rouge: Louisiana State University Press, 1983); Marcowitz, *Großmacht*, 212–24.

16. See Andreas Hillgruber, *Bismarcks Außenpolitik* (Freiburg: Rombach, 1995), passim.

17. This against the interpretation of Hermann Oncken, *Die Rheinpolitik Kaiser Napoleons III. von 1863 bis 1870 und der Ursprung des Krieges von 1870/71. Nach den Staatsakten von Österreich, Preußen und den süddeutschen Mittelstaaten*, 2 vols. (Osnabrück: Biblio-Verlag, 1967). Cf. Elisabeth Fehrenbach, "Preußen-Deutschland als Faktor der französischen Außenpolitik in der Reichsgründungszeit," in *Europa und die Reichsgründung*, ed. Eberhard Kolb (München: Oldenburg, 1980), 109–37.

18. Hillgruber, *Außenpolitik*, 65.

19. Ibid., 79ff.

20. Josef Becker, "Der Krieg 1870/71 als Problem der deutsch-französischen Beziehungen," in *Eine ungewöhnliche Geschichte. Deutschland—Frankreich seit 1870*, ed. Franz Knipping and Ernst Weisenfeld (Bonn: Europa-Union-Verlag, 1988), 21.

21. Baumgart, *Europäisches Konzert*, 388–94.

22. Ibid., 394–405.

23. Becker, *Krieg 1870/71*, 23.

24. Lothar Gall, *Europa auf dem Weg in die Moderne 1850–1890* (München: Oldenburg, 2003), 61; David Wetzel, *Duell der Giganten. Bismarck, Napoleon III. und die Ursachen des Deutsch-Französischen Krieges 1870–1871* (Paderborn: Schöningh, 2005).

25. Becker, *Krieg 1870/71*, 24. Cf. idem., ed., *Bismarcks spanische "Diversion" 1870 und der preußisch-deutsche Reichsgründungskrieg. Quelle zur Vor- und Nachkriegsgeschichte der Hohenzollern-Kandidatur für den Thron in Madrid 1866–1932* (Paderborn: Schöningh, 2003–7).

26. Sebastian Haffner, *Von Bismarck zu Hitler. Ein Rückblick* (München: Kindler, 1987), 45. Cf. Frank Becker, *Bilder von Krieg und Nation. Die Einigungskriege in der bürgerlichen Öffentlichkeit Deutschlands 1864–1913* (München: Oldenburg, 2001); Alexander Seyferth, *Die Heimatfront 1870/71. Wirtschaft und Gesellschaft im deutsch-französischen Krieg* (Paderborn: Schöningh, 2005).

27. Doering-Manteuffel, *Deutsche Frage*, 51.

28. Jeismann, *Vaterland*; Gilbert Ziebura, *Die deutsch-französischen Beziehungen seit 1945. Mythen und Realitäten* (Stuttgart: Neske, 1997), 15–24.

29. Beate Gödde-Baumann, *Deutsche Geschichte in französischer Sicht. Die französische Historiographie von 1871–1918 über die Geschichte Deutschlands und die deutsch-französischen Beziehungen in der Neuzeit* (Wiesbaden: Steiner, 1971); Wolfgang Hardtwig, "Von Preußens Aufgabe in Deutschland zu Deutschlands Aufgabe in der Welt. Liberalismus und Borussisches Geschichtsbild zwischen Revolution und Imperialismus," *Historische Zeitschrift* 231 (1980): 265–324.

30. Wolfgang Leiner, *Das Deutschlandbild in der französischen Literatur* (Darmstadt: Wissenschaftliche Buchgesellschaft, 1989).
31. Jeismann, *Vaterland*, 374ff.
32. Eberhard Kolb, *Der Weg aus dem Krieg. Bismarcks Politik im Krieg und die Friedensanbahnung 1870/71* (München: Oldenburg, 1989).
33. Poidevin and Bariéty, *Frankreich*, 148.
34. See Klaus Hildebrand, *Das vergangene Reich. Deutsche Außenpolitik von Bismarck bis Hitler 1871–1945* (Stuttgart: DVA, 1995), 13–411; François, Hoock-Demarle, Meyer-Kalkus, eds., *Marianne—Germania*.
35. Becker, *Krieg 1870/71*, 23.
36. Ludwig Dehio, *Deutschland und die Weltpolitik im 20. Jahrhundert* (München: Oldenburg, 1955), 15.
37. *Die Große Politik der Europäischen Kabinette 1871–1914. Sammlung der Diplomatischen Akten des Auswärtigen Amtes. Im Auftrage des Auswärtigen Amtes*, ed. Johannes Lepsius, Albrecht Mendelssohn-Bartholdy, Friedrich Thimme, 40 vols. (Berlin: Deutsche Verlagsgesellschaft, 1922–27), vol. 2: *Der Berliner Kongress und seine Vorgeschichte* (Berlin: Deutsche Verlagsgesellschaft, 1922), 153.
38. Hildebrand, *Reich*, 91.
39. Peter Krüger, *Das unberechenbare Europa. Epochen des Integrationsprozesses vom späten 18. Jahrhundert bis zur Europäischen Union* (Stuttgart: Kohlhammer, 2006), 13, 67–135; Hartmut Kaelble, *Nachbarn am Rhein. Entfremdung und Annäherung der französischen und deutschen Gesellschaft seit 1880* (München: Beck, 1991).
40. Haffner, *Bismarck*, 89.
41. Hildebrand, *Reich*, 388.
42. Georges-Henri Soutou, "Die Kriegsziele Frankreichs im Ersten Weltkrieg," in *Über Frankreich nach Europa. Frankreich in Geschichte und Gegenwart*, ed. Wolf D. Gruner and Klaus-Jürgen Müller (Hamburg: Krämer, 1996), 327–39.
43. Poidevin and Bariéty, *Frankreich*, 301.
44. Jean-Baptiste Duroselle, *Histoire diplomatique de 1919 à nos jours* (Paris: Dalloz, 1993), 9.

CHAPTER 2

War, Occupation, and Entanglements

German Perspectives on the Napoleonic Era

Bernhard Struck

Introduction

When did the nineteenth century begin? Did it begin with Napoleon? This chapter considers Franco-German history around 1800. While briefly referring to aspects of that history before the French Revolution and also after the Napoleonic era, the main focus is on the Napoleonic Wars, on perceptions and experiences of them. The Franco-German relationship between 1800 and 1815 was largely asymmetrical due to Napoleon's military victories, the annexation of German territories to France, and the transfer of French administrative, legal, and constitutional systems to parts of Germany. Thus, the focus here is on "Germanies and Napoleonic France" rather than "France and Germany" so as to stress French domination over the German territories.

The concept of a pluralistic Germany is relevant because the historiography of Franco-German relations during the Revolutionary and Napoleonic eras has largely focused on Prussia. This has resulted in a master narrative of German history centered on the Hohenzollern kingdom and—in a teleological way—on the Prussian-led German Empire of 1871. Key elements of this Prussocentric master narrative are nation- and state-building, modernization, and nationalism. This concentration on Prussia has entailed simplification of a far more complex Franco-German relationship. The decision to focus primarily on the Third Germany, that is, those areas belonging neither to Prussia nor to Austria, is justified because parts of this Dritte Deutschland were annexed to France or integrated into the Confederation of the Rhine. This was therefore the region of the most intensive French-German entanglement around 1800.

From the perspective of rather ordinary contemporaries such as German travelers along with the insights of recent research on the experience of war, it will be argued that the categories in most late nineteenth- and even twentieth-century master narratives of German history, such as the (Prussian-led) nation-state and nationalism, hardly played a role in the perceptions of contemporaries. It was instead the case that the nation, the idea of national borders, and, above all, the image of a national enemy were mainly the result of the politics of memory and literary discourse in the aftermath of the Napoleonic era.

Within Franco-German history between 1800 and 1815, we will give preference to the notion of "entanglement." In addition to containing the notion of transfer, entanglement has a twofold meaning. First, transfer often concentrates on agents of transfer processes, on media, or on single objects, while entanglement stresses an intensified period of mutual perceptions and exchange processes on various levels, such as the legal system, administration, constitutions, or objets d'art. Second, this exchange between France and the German states around 1800 was largely driven by war and occupation, as well as by resistance to some extent. This is yet another difference from the concept of transfer, which is mainly based on the assumption of voluntary and peaceful relations between regions and their willingness to receive foreign goods.[1] There is yet another reason to prefer the notion of entanglement: both the comparative approach and the analysis of cultural transfer most often refer to a national framework—even though this is exactly what is questioned by the notion of transfer. In this case, the national framework would be a clear-cut Franco-German history in which both entities are distinctly separated by national borders.

From Borderland to National Frontier

Since the mid-seventeenth century, France had been one of the main travel destinations for Germans. Especially from the 1770s onward, the Bourbon monarchy and, above all, its centers, Paris and Versailles, attracted many German visitors.[2] Conversely, Germany was much less attractive for the French. Even during the French Wars between 1792 and 1814, there was a constant stream of German visitors toward France and intense production of German travel writing on the country.[3] One of the most common routes for entering France was through Baden via Kehl on the east bank of the Rhine. Before the revolution, the river itself was the border that had to be crossed before entering France. The route in Baden, the first stop in France at Strasbourg, and the continuing journey through Alsace and Lorraine toward either Paris or the southern parts of the country were described by many travelers.[4]

One such traveler was Johann Friedrich Carl Grimm, a physician from Saxony, who visited France in 1773. In his travelogue, he described the regions and different German states he traversed in great detail, focusing on the gradual change in manners, costumes, language, architecture, and agriculture. When he finally reached the Rhine, he mentioned "the bridge" with the "French guards and the tollhouse" in only a few words.[5] Grimm then continued by describing the entrance to Strasbourg as the border between the countryside and the city, providing far more detail than when describing the border between France and Germany.[6] Even though a clearly visible border between France and the Holy Roman Empire did exist, Grimm did not perceive it as a national border. In fact, his description of regional differences between French Alsace and Baden on the German side of the Rhine did not differ from other regions and territories with their local and regional character within the Holy Roman Empire. Instead of an unambiguous national border, Grimm perceived a zone of overlapping national cultures in which signifiers such as language, architecture, and certain customs changed only gradually. Johann Grimm is representative of perceptions of the Franco-German borderland not only before the French Revolution but also into the early years of the nineteenth century.[7] Sophie La Roche, a well-known writer by the 1780s, took the same route on the eve of the French Revolution. One must read her travelogue carefully in order not to miss the moment when the border was crossed because she did not devote a single word to it. She did not, in fact, perceive the border as playing any role. Having already ventured halfway through Alsace, the first characteristic that proved she had entered France was the change of language from German to French.[8] Moreover, she observed successive changes in agriculture, the social conditions of the rural population, and the appearance of the villages. Entering France did not mean crossing the state border at the Rhine. Instead, entering the "actual France" meant that all traces of the "former German national character" had vanished, which for La Roche was only the case once she was in Lorraine.[9] These examples demonstrate how little importance people of the late eighteenth century paid to the role and perception of the linear national border between France and Germany.[10] To them, the two countries were not clearly divided entities but rather were connected by an expanded, entangled Franco-German borderland.

In April of 1819, the merchant Johann Daniel Mutzenbecher departed from Hamburg for southern France. He took the same route via Kehl to Strasbourg as many of his compatriots had previously. In the aftermath of the Napoleonic Wars, he painted a completely different picture of the border than had La Roche. Before entering France, he stopped at the "border of his fatherland" to reflect on the Rhine, which he "had been longing to see for the first time in my life as every German does."[11] Before even entering France, he judged the neighboring country and its "inhabitants as completely different from us in terms of customs and behavior" and, above all, as being "morally corrupted." Altogether, Mutzenbecher dedicated several pages to the depiction of a linear national border that—in his view—clearly divided two nations. He repeatedly referred to the Napoleonic Wars in his description of the border and was convinced that the "French people was already longing to take revenge."[12] Mutzenbecher's depiction of the border could hardly offer a more dramatic contrast to those of his compatriots some twenty years earlier. Indeed, Mutzenbecher, who had been born in 1780, belonged to a generation that had experienced a period of almost constant warfare. Moreover, as an ordinary merchant from Hamburg, he might well have come to know hardship during that period.

Like other Hanseatic cities such as Lübeck and Bremen, Hamburg had been occupied by the French in 1806 and integrated into the French Empire in 1810. The cities suffered severe economic problems under French rule. After Napoleon had established the Continental Blockade in 1806 in order to weaken Great Britain by means of economic warfare, the Hanseatic cities had lost their traditional overseas economic connections and markets, which led to unemployment, poverty, and emigration.[13] Thus, the border description given by Mutzenbecher a few years after the French wars, when the memory of the events was still fresh, differed completely from those of his predecessors.

With his detailed and emotional depiction of an alienating, linear, national border, Mutzenbecher seems to be an excellent representative of a key element in the master narrative of nineteenth- and twentieth-century history—that the Napoleonic Wars brought about the transformation from traditional patriotism to modern nationalism and the birth of two hereditary nations.

Napoleon and Master Narratives of Nineteenth-century German History

In 1983, Thomas Nipperdey began his now canonical work on German history in the nineteenth century with a short but powerful sentence: "In the beginning was Napoleon."[14] As simple as this statement might appear, it embodies both the master narrative of the book and, to a large extent, the main features of the master narrative of nineteenth-century German history in general: modernization and the nation-state. For the first of his three volumes covering the long nineteenth century in German history, Nipperdey chose the time span 1800 to 1866. With his opening statement, he chronologically began with Napoleon's ascent from military general to leading political figure in France, hence acknowledging his impact on Germany as well.

Napoleon Bonaparte's career had started with his command of the French army in Italy in 1796 and 1797. He had gained political power by his coup d'état of 18–19 Brumaire Year VIII (November 9–10, 1799), which had brought down the Directory and established the Consulate. Five years later, in December of 1804, Napoleon ended the Consulate by crowning himself and establishing the French Empire—in reference to the medieval empire of Charlemagne, which only two years later itself came to an end at his hands.[15] When Napoleon became one of the three Consuls in 1799, the new government inherited the revolutionary foreign policy. After initial victories in 1792, the revolutionary army under the Directory had conquered the German speaking left bank of the Rhine in the autumn of 1794. This part of the Holy Roman Empire was de facto annexed by France in the following years. De jure it was incorporated into France only by the Treaty of Lunéville in 1801. Already in 1798–99, however, the region had been subdivided into four French-style departments—Roer-Département (Aachen), Rhin-et-Moselle (Koblenz), Sarre (Trier), and Mont-Tonnerre (Mainz)—which were legally and politically fully integrated into France in September of 1802. Thus, about 1.6 million German-speaking inhabitants were French citizens until the end of Napoleonic rule in 1814.[16] During that period, the population offered only meager resistance and its inhabitants in general proved themselves loyal citizens. Desertion after conscription, taken as an indicator for loyalty or resistance, was not higher than in other parts of the French Empire.[17]

The loss of territories in the west that had belonged mainly to Prussia or the Habsburgs along with the loss of the states of Baden, Württemberg, and Hesse-Kassel had far-reaching consequences within the Old Reich. Following the peace treaty of 1801, a *Reichsdeputation* (Imperial deputation) was established in order to investigate the issue of compensation for the lost territories. The means by which this territorial compensation was achieved were secularization, that is, confiscation of church property, and mediatization, that is, the end of the direct lordship of the Emperor over the Imperial cities (*Reichsstädte*) and the Imperial knights (*Reichsritterschaft*). Approval of these measures was given in the Final Recess of the Imperial Deputation in 1803. In fact, the aftermath of the treaty of Lunéville brought about a territorial revolution in the Holy Roman Empire. Roughly 1,500 miniature lordships with sovereignty vanished from the map. About three million people experienced a change of regime. Moreover, the *Reichs deputationshauptschluss* had far-reaching social consequences. Because the church lost large portions of its property in the west, it could no longer offer attractive positions to the nobility. In some territories such as Bavaria, the process of mediatization meant the abolition of serfdom. Elsewhere, as in the Rhineland, the confiscation and reselling of church property led to industrialization and intensified the modernization of agriculture.[18]

This territorial revolution within the Holy Roman Empire largely served Napoleon's interests. By ending the immediacy of the *Reichsstädte* and the *Reichsritterschaft* to the Emperor, Napoleon severed long-standing loyalties to the Habsburgs. In fact, his main aim was to weaken Austria and, above all, to push it away from the Rhine. In order to achieve this, the greatest benefits of territorial reorganization between 1801 and 1803 accrued to Prussia, Baden, and Württemberg. The latter was elevated to the status of a kingdom, as was Bavaria in 1805.[19] Thus, Napoleon had established middle-sized, independent counterparts to Austria within the Reich, a policy that paid off for France. Baden and Württemberg became core elements of the Confederation of the Rhine (*Rheinbund*) created in July of 1806. Even before that, they had proved themselves loyal to Napoleon by sending troops to support France in 1805. The war in that year ended successfully for the Napoleonic armies with the victory over allied Austro-Russian forces at Austerlitz in December.

Together with Russia and Saxony, Prussia decided to go to war against France in 1806. The military defeat at Jena and Auerstedt on October 14, 1806, was disastrous for Prussia, as was the Treaty of Tilsit, which brought Napoleon to the apex of his influence over Germany. The Hohenzollern kingdom lost about half of its territory. Its holdings west of the Elbe were integrated into the Confederation of the Rhine, as was the newly created Kingdom of Westphalia. Furthermore,

Prussia lost large parts of its Polish lands, which were transformed into the Grand Duchy of Warsaw. The Prussian army was severely reduced; French troops were stationed in the country; it was forced to join the Continental Blockade and pay a large indemnity to France, creating a financial crisis.

The Confederation of the Rhine was initially composed of seventeen German states. After annexing northern Germany, it consisted of thirty-five members in its final form in 1810. By then, all territories of the former Reich had become part of the Confederation except Prussia, Austria, Danish Holstein and the Swedish possessions in Pomerania.[20] Some states of the Confederation such as Westphalia, Berg, and Frankfurt were governed by the Bonaparte family and served as model states in which the French legal system (including the Napoleonic or Civil Code), administration, and social policy were implemented along with partial introduction of the French education system and language. Other states within the Confederation of the Rhine including Bavaria, Württemberg, and Baden had a much wider scope of independence. They partly followed the French example by combining French-style legal and administrative reforms with their own traditions.[21] Even though they were loyal to the French Empire until the wars of 1813–14, they were by no means simple vassals, as the disdainful interpretation of nationalist-orientated German historiography in the late-nineteenth and early-twentieth century would have it.

Comparing the Old Reich before 1800 with the map of Germany in 1806–7 or 1815, Nipperdey was correct to state that "in the beginning was Napoleon." Of more than three hundred territories before 1800, only thirty-nine remained after 1815.[22] However, to start German history in the nineteenth century with Napoleon and his impact on Germany only seems to be a chronological narrative. Analytically—and in keeping with the main themes of his master narrative, modernization and nation-building—Nipperdey started diachronically from 1871, the year in which the German Empire or Kaiserreich was founded. He looked back from the end of the century arguing that modernization, which to him and many other historians meant the emergence of the nation-state, was mainly brought to Germany from the outside, from Revolutionary and Napoleonic France. "In the beginning was Napoleon" meant that France in 1800, after ten years of revolution, after creating a "modern" army based on citizenship and conscription, was on its way to creating a "modern" nation-state and was thus *more* modern than the Holy Roman Empire of the German Nation.[23]

One could indeed argue that France was more modern than the Holy Roman Empire in 1800. Contemporaries were not sparing in their criticism of the "anachronistic" fragmentation of the Reich,[24] while historiography has also regarded the Holy Roman Empire for a long time as backward, military weak, economically underdeveloped in large areas, and simply old fashioned. Research has, however, largely changed that interpretation by revealing a far more positive situation, proving the empire's effectiveness even though its institutions were complex and had to be balanced against one another.[25] On the other hand, recent studies have stressed that France was by no means a modern, centralized nation-state by 1800 or 1815. Certainly, the French army, for instance, brought men from all over the country together and thus ensured that almost 75 percent spoke standard French in 1799, whereas only a quarter had done so a decade earlier.[26] Still, it took until the second half of the nineteenth century to bind the peripheries to the center and to create a widespread notion of nation and citizenship.[27] Finally, research in recent years has questioned to a great extent the ruptures of 1789 for French history and 1806 for German history. Referring largely to Alexis de Tocqueville's *L'Ancien Régime et la Révolution* (1856), the continuities between the ancient régime, French Revolution, and Napoleonic Empire are now being highlighted. The same is true of the reforms of Enlightened Absolutism in Prussia and Austria as well as the Prussian reform movement after 1806. Thus, in a longer chronological perspective from about 1770 to 1815, France and Germany are now seen as having been far more similar to one other than Nipperdey suggested with his first sentence.[28]

Perceiving French Germany: Experiences of War and Occupation

As with many historical concepts and narratives, modernization and its analytical tools (state- and nation-building) are mainly categories created *ex post facto* from the perspective of the historian who frames his or her object, often by a classical top-down approach. But to what extent did these categories play a role for contemporaries?

Even though travel became more difficult during the Napoleonic era, people still visited France and the annexed territories.[29] One such visitor was the physician Friedrich Albrecht Klebe. In the autumn of 1800, he journeyed along the Rhine and through the now French departments of Donnersberg, Mosel, and Roer. His travelogue, published the following year, stands in the tradition of late-eighteenth-century Enlightened travel writing. He described French Germany in an objective way by listing statistical data on demography and providing extensive information on agriculture and the conditions of the peasantry, for instance. However, Klebe was not only interested in giving his readers pure information.[30] He was also critical of French rule in the Rhineland. Most of all, however, he opined that the population was certainly suffering from the strong French military presence. He also stressed the devastation that the war had brought to the region.[31] What Klebe did not do was claiming these territories as "German" or as belonging to the "German nation" and thus reclaiming them from France. As long as the French governed well, he did not see any point, it seems, in objecting to foreign rule. Around 1800 it was regarded as natural that warfare led to territories changing hands, the main difference from earlier periods being that it now did not matter so much who governed but rather how a territory was governed. The nation as a central category, applied by Johann Daniel Mutzenbecher some fifteen years later when he described the Rhine, did not yet play a role.

How can we explain the shift in the travelogues of the French Rhineland in 1800 from Klebe to that of Mutzenbecher, who depicted the Rhine as a national frontier in the aftermath of the wars? The birth of modern German nationalism has often been described as occurring in the period between 1806 and the so-called Wars of Liberation in 1813–14.[32] This seems to be true, if one mainly takes into account the writings of early national-oriented writers such as Ernst Moritz Arndt, Johann Gottlieb Fichte, or Friedrich Ludwig Jahn. For a long time, research on German nationalism has stressed the impact of these exclusively Prussian writers. There is no question that publications such as Arndt's pamphlet *Der Rhein, Teutschlands Strom, nicht Teutschlands Grenze* from 1813 had an impact on reinforcing national sentiments. But research over the last few years has considerably modified our picture of the Wars of Liberation. Instead of masses of young volunteers rushing into an army under a national banner in order to fight in the name of the nation, it has been demonstrated that large numbers deserted the Prussian forces. Authors such as Michael Broers have gone so far as to declare the *Befreiungskriege* a "myth" invented mainly by nationalist historiography or literature following 1815.[33] Furthermore, studies of the impact of the wars on identities have stressed that in large parts of occupied Germany, the war against Napoleonic France did not necessarily strengthen national identity but rather local and regional identities.[34] In fact, authors such as Arndt and Fichte were the exception and must be situated at the radical end of the spectrum of opinion on French occupation. Even among well-educated elites, the attitude toward French occupation varied. French rule on the Rhine was seen by many in a rather pragmatic light. This might be illustrated by the various reactions to the confiscation of art objects and cultural goods by the French.

Following the French victories, a vast number of cultural goods—mostly valuable books, paintings, and objects from cabinets of curiosities—were taken from the Rhineland, Bavaria, Prussia, and Vienna between 1794 and 1809. What was a simple confiscation in the beginning soon developed into tthe ideology of *patrimoine libéré*: it was not only the people who lived in the "freed territories" who should have the right to join France, but cultural artifacts also had to be freed, collected and, finally, displayed in the capital of "freedom."[35] The confiscated objects were brought to Paris and integrated into the Musée Napoléon. In 1807, they were made accessible in a large exhibition at the Louvre, along with artistic objects from other occupied countries. During these campaigns, the French government sent a number of specialized *commissaires* to Germany who worked closely with local specialists in order to choose objects and list them carefully. Until the end of French rule in Germany in 1814–15, the discourse in newspapers and correspondence among experts had an Enlightened, cosmopolitan air. Almost all experts dealing with the topic greeted the transfer of the goods to Paris warmly, since the reputation of the French specialists was excellent.[36] National sentiments on stolen art objects did not play a role until the end of Napoleonic rule in Germany. Only later during the nineteenth century were the confiscations declared to be "Raubzüge" and "Kunstraub" of what was now regarded as national art.[37] Only after 1815, once the cultural goods transferred to France had been brought back, did a larger public in Germany began relating these objects to a German identity and see them as part of a national heritage.

If national sentiments had a limited impact among well-educated elites, how did the rest of the population experience war and occupation? For the south-western regions of Germany, Ute Planert has stressed that the population directly confronted with the burdens of war had a far more differentiated view of the French army and the French in general than authors such as Arndt or Fichte suggested. The image of the other was largely dependent upon the behavior of the foreign armies. "In contrast to late nineteenth-century interpretations," Katherine Aaslestad has argued regarding northern Germany, "antagonism toward the French stemmed from the destruction of individual livelihoods, not nationalist aspirations."[38] Thus, the enemy was not only the French but could also be Prussian or Russian troops.[39] Even resistance and popular uprisings during the wars were not necessarily directed against the French enemy. For most segments of the population, "[n]otions of modern nationalism were alien."[40]

After the War: Writing Memories and History—Creating Enemies

When Johann Daniel Mutzenbecher arrived at the Rhine in 1819, which in his view constituted a national border dividing Germany from France, he seemingly described the moment of entering the enemy's territory. The author may have expressed his actual feelings or may have simply aimed at writing a bestselling travelogue. At the very least, Mutzenbecher's text embodies developments after the war rather than the period before 1815—even though that is what he was referring to.

The Napoleonic Wars had brought a shift toward reinforced national thinking. But this was limited. The writings of a minor group of mainly Prussian authors hardly had a widespread effect on the population as a whole. Most of the population in the annexed territories and in the Confederation saw neither the French nor Napoleon as an enemy. To ordinary people, who suffered the most from war when troops were stationed in their region or town, it did not matter who had brought the war or whence the troops had come. The war itself and its consequences were the enemy. In this respect, it is obvious that Napoleon profited from the image of the one who had ended the chaotic revolution and brought peace, at least in the beginning (1801 and 1802).[41] When war returned, the Napoleonic troops at least were far more disciplined than the revolutionary troops had been. Thus, many German writers had hoped for someone like Napoleon who was capable of taming the revolution and warfare. Even members of the Prussian army, such as Karl Friedrich von Klöden, saw a "contented future" with Napoleon leading France forward.[42] This positive image outlasted Napoleon's rule in France and over large parts of Europe. In the formerly French parts of Germany such as the Rhineland or the model states, the image of the "liberal Emperor" was cultivated after 1815 in order to confront the new rule by Prussia. Napoleon was depicted as the emperor who had brought the Civil Code, equality in taxation, emancipation of the Jews, and an end to aristocratic privilege.

Veterans' associations founded in the Rhineland played an important role in perpetuating this positive picture.[43]

In the early 1840s, however, the image of Napoleon and France in general started shifting. The French government publicly claimed the Rhine as the Franco-German border in 1840 and thus the territories on the west bank as French. This rhetoric immediately recalled the era of Napoleonic rule. It provoked an increase in national sentiment and a surge in patriotism that until then had hardly gained ground in the Rhineland. Here, as elsewhere in the formerly French-dominated parts of Germany, local and regional identities, strongly linked to dynastic loyalties, remained powerful during the nineteenth century.[44]

In December of 1852, Louis Napoleon became French emperor as Napoleon III. His reign promptly led to a reassessment of the memories of Napoleon I and French rule at the beginning of the century. The era of French occupation before 1815 had soon been transformed into a time of national dishonor. The historical image of Napoleon I shifted from that of the liberal emperor to that of a national enemy, especially in the writings of Heinrich von Treitschke and Heinrich von Sybel, two of the most prominent national historians of the Prussian-dominated German Empire after 1871.[45] Alongside more formal historical writing, there was a large number of memoirs, more than 470 autobiographies and, most importantly, more than 560 historical novels shaping the collective memory of the wars and the image of the French.[46] Widely read novels such as Ludwig Rellstab's *1812*, published in 1834, or Theodor Fontane's *Vor dem Sturm*, published in 1878, took up the issue of the Napoleonic Wars, linking the time of war to the search for national identity in which the "French" served as a counteridentity. Especially in times of crisis and war, as in 1840, 1870, and once again in 1914, the narrative of a hereditary enemy grew stronger in literary and historical works.[47]

Notes

1. Johannes Paulmann, "Internationaler Vergleich und interkultureller Transfer. Zwei Forschungsansätze zur europäischen Geschichte des 18. bis 20. Jahrhunderts," *Historische Zeitschrift* 267 (1998): 649–85.

2. Thomas Grosser, *Reiseziel Frankreich: Deutsche Reiseliteratur vom Barock bis zur Französischen Revolution* (Opladen: Westdeutscher Verlag, 1989).

3. At least seventy travelogues on France in book form were published in Germany between 1800 and 1820. See Bernhard Struck, *Nicht West—nicht Ost. Frankreich und Polen in der Wahrnehmung deutscher Reisender zwischen 1750 und 1850* (Göttingen: Wallstein, 2006), 80.

4. See Peter Sahlins, "Frontiers Revisited: France's Boundaries since the Seventeenth Century," *American Historical Review* 95 (1990): 1423–51.

5. Johann Friedrich Carl Grimm, *Bemerkungen eines Reisenden durch Deutschland, Frankreich, England und Holland in Briefen an seine Freunde* (Altenburg: Richter, 1775), 1:141.

6. Ibid., vol. 1, 142.

7. Struck, *Nicht West—nicht Ost*, 193–229.

8. Marie Sophie von La Roche, *Journal einer Reise durch Frankreich, von der Verfasserin von Rosaliens Briefen* (Altenburg: Richter, 1787), 17–18.

9. La Roche, *Journal*, 23. See also Heinrich Sander, *Beschreibung seiner Reisen durch Frankreich, die Niederlande, Holland, Deutschland und Italien, in Beziehung auf Menschenkenntnis, Industrie, Litteratur und Naturkunde insonderheit*, 2 vols. (Leipzig: Jakobäer, 1783/84), 1:3–4, 16–23.

10. Struck, *Nicht West—nicht Ost*, 209–12.

11. Johann Daniel Mutzenbecher, *Bemerkungen auf einer Reise aus Norddeutschland über Frankfurt nach dem südlichen Frankreich im Jahr 1819* (Leipzig: Rein'sche Buchhandlung, 1822), 88.

12. Ibid., 88–91.

13. Katherine B. Aaslestad, *Place and Politics: Local Identity, Civic Culture, and German Nationalism in North Germany during the Revolutionary Era* (Leiden: Brill, 2005), 245–320; Idem, "Paying for War: Experiences of Napoleonic Rule in the Hanseatic Cities," *Central European History* 39 (2006): 649.

14. Thomas Nipperdey, *Deutsche Geschichte 1800–1866. Bürgerwelt und starker Staat* (München: Beck, 1994), 1.

15. Jean Tulard, *Napoléon ou le mythe du sauveur* (Paris: Fayard, 1999), 79–83, 115–26.

16. Michael Rowe, "Between Empire and Home Town: Napoleonic Rule on the Rhine, 1799–1814," *The Historical Journal* 42, no. 3 (1999): 643–74; Idem, *From Reich to State. The Rhineland in the Revolutionary Age, 1780–1830* (Cambridge: Cambridge University Press, 2003), 87–115. See also Stuart Woolf, *Napoleon's integration of Europe* (London: Routledge, 1991).

17. Michael Rowe, "Resistance, Collaboration or Third Way? Responses to Napoleonic Rule in Germany," in *Popular Resistance in the French Wars: Patriots, Partisans and Land Pirates*, ed. Charles J. Esdaile (London: Palgrave, 2005), 67–90.

18. Tulard, *Napoleon*, 222–23.

19. John G. Gagliardo, *Reich and Nation. The Holy German Empire as Idea and Reality, 1763–1806* (Bloomington: Indiana University Press, 1980), 206–41.

20. Hans A. Schmitt, "Germany without Prussia: A Closer Look at the Confederation of the Rhine," *German Studies Review* 6, no. 1 (1983): 11–12.

21. Paul-L. Weinacht, "Les Etats de la Confédération du Rhin face au Code Napoleon" in *Napoléon et l'Europe*, ed. Jean-Clément Martin (Rennes: Presse Universitaire de Rennes, 2002), 91–102.

22. John Breuilly, "Napoleonic Germany and State-formation," in *Collaboration and Resistance in Napoleonic Europe. State-formation in an Age of Upheaval, c. 1800–1815*, ed. Michael Rowe (London: Palgrave, 2003), 121–52.

23. Hans-Ulrich Wehler, *Vom Feudalismus des Alten Reiches bis zur defensiven Modernisierung der Reformära 1700–1815, vol. 1 of Deutsche Gesellschaftsgeschichte* (München: Beck, 1996).

24. Gagliardo, *Reich and Nation*, 117–40.

25. Karl Otmar von Aretin, *Das Alte Reich 1648–1806*, 4 vols. (Stuttgart: Klett-Cotta, 1993–2000).

26. Michel Vovelle, *La Révolution Française* (Paris: Armand Colin, 1992), 177.

27. Eugen Weber, *Peasants into Frenchmen. The Modernization of Rural France, 1870–1914* (Stanford: Stanford University Press, 1992).

28. Helmut Berding, Etienne François, and Hans-Peter Ullmann, eds., *Deutschland und Frankreich im Zeitalter der Französischen Revolution* (Frankfurt/Main: Suhrkamp, 1989), 8–9.

29. Astrid Küntzel, *Die Nationalisierung des Fremden. Integration und Ausgrenzung des Fremden in Köln 1750–1814* (Köln: Böhlau, 2008), forthcoming.

30. Friedrich Anton Klebe, *Reise auf dem Rhein durch die deutschen Staaten von Frankfurt bis zur Grenze der Batavischen Republik und durch die Départements des Donnersbergs, des Rheins und der Mosel und der Roer im Sommer und Herbst 1800* (Frankfurt: Friedrich Esslinger, 1801), 1:165–67. See also Johann Friedrich Droysen, *Bemerkungen gesammelt auf einer Reise durch Holland und einen Theil Frankreichs im Sommer 1801 (Göttingen* (Göttingen: Heinrich Dieterich, 1802), 23–33.

31. Klebe, *Reise auf dem Rhein*, vol. 1, 165, 202, 241. See also Rowe, "Between Empire," 617.

32. Otto Dann, *Nationalismus* (Frankfurt/Main: Suhrkamp, 1985), 25; Michael Jeismann, *Das Vaterland der Feinde. Studien zum nationalen Feindbegriff und Selbstverständnis in Deutschland und Frankreich 1792–1918* (Stuttgart: Klett-Cotta, 1992).

33. Michael Broers, *Europe under Napoleon 1799–1815* (London: Arnold, 1996), 234–39.

34. Aaslestad, *Place and Politics*.

35. Bénédicte Savoy, "L'exposition des œuvres saisies par Dominique-Vivant Denon en Allemagne: 1807–1808, catalogue critique," in *Patrimoine Annexé. Les biens culturels saisis par la France en Allemagne autour de 1800*, vol. 1 (Paris: Edition de la Maison des Sciences de l'Homme, 2003), 15.

36. Ibid., 217–20.

37. Ibid., 203, 239–66.

38. Aaslestad, "Paying for war," 660.

39. Ute Planert, "From Collaboration to Resistance: Politics, Experience, and Memory of the Revolutionary and Napoleonic Wars in Southern Germany," *Central European History* 39 (2006), 676–705; Aaslestad, "Paying for war," 668–69.

40. Planert, "From Collaboration to Resistance," 686.

41. Ibid., 681–684.

42. Hagen Schulze, "Napoleon," vol. 2 of *Deutsche Erinnerungsorte*, ed. Etienne François and Hagen Schulze (München: Beck, 2001), 29.

43. Ibid., 33–36; Planert, "From Collaboration to Resistance," 694.

44. Abigail Green, *Fatherlands. State-building and Nationhood in Nineteenth-Century Germany* (Cambridge: Cambridge University Press, 2001).

45. Schulze, "Napoleon," 39–41.

46. I would like to thank Maria Schultz, Berlin, for these figures.

47. See Planert, "From Collaboration to Resistance," 695–97.

CHAPTER 3

France and German Dualism, 1756–1871

Jörg Ulbert

The Holy Roman Empire of the German Nation was a conglomerate of several hundred more or less independent states. From the late Middle Ages to the early eighteenth century, it was dominated by a single family: the Habsburgs. From 1452 to the dissolution of the Empire in 1806, the elected emperor was a member of the Habsburg family, apart from the interlude between 1742 and 1745 that saw an emperor belonging to the Wittelsbach family. From their base in Austria, the Habsburgs gradually extended their power outside the borders of the Empire: first toward Bohemia, Hungary, and Croatia, then toward Spain (and its colonies), the Netherlands, Franche-Comté, Northern Italy, and Sardinia. In the eighteenth century, a rival emerged from within the Holy Roman Empire itself: Prussia. Raised to the rank of kingdom in 1701, the modest electorate of Brandenburg became a major power in just a few decades and quickly began to challenge Austria. A few weeks after he succeeded to the throne in 1740, the King of Prussia, Friedrich II, invaded Silesia, the richest of the Austrian provinces. This particular conquest not only reinforced Prussian power but also created a long-lasting enmity between the two countries. The stakes in this conflict quickly rose from just the control over Silesia to supremacy in Germany. After the Napoleonic wars and the political reorganization of the German lands by the Congress of Vienna, the struggle between Prussia and Austria for hegemony, henceforth called "German dualism," quickly became part of the "German question." Like the "Greek question" or the "Italian question," it concerned a state whose borders would not be set by the changing fortunes of conquest or marriages but by national, cultural, and linguistic considerations. Due to the geographical situation of the Holy Roman Empire, within the very heart of Europe, its size, and its considerable population, the German question took on an

The author wishes to thank Joanna Ropers for her translation of this article.

international dimension. France was the nation most directly concerned and sought to act as the arbitrator in this power struggle.

From the late fifteenth century to the mid-eighteenth century, the relations between France and the Empire were shaped by the dynastic rivalry opposing the Valois family and, as its successors, the Bourbons to the House of Habsburg. Through various legacies, the Habsburgs, in only a few decades, succeeded in accumulating vast possessions which, at the time of the election of Charles V as emperor (1520), ended up completely surrounding France. From that time on and for over a century and a half, the struggle against this "Habsburgian noose"[1] and against the threat of a Habsburgian universal monarchy[2] became the main concern of French foreign policy.[3]

The Peace of Westphalia (1648) and the Treaty of the Pyrenees (1659) eventually loosened the noose. Even though the danger of a Habsburgian universal monarchy had disappeared, the fundamentals of French foreign policy hardly changed. Only the scope of the French fears changed: while before Paris had feared a Habsburgian universal monarchy in Europe, it now dreaded Habsburgian supremacy within the Empire, with an emperor who was thought to be on the verge of instituting a monarchy by suppressing the "German liberties" of its members.[4] Traditionally, France used allies recruited from within the Empire or from its borders to counterbalance Austrian power. After the decline of its long-standing ally, Sweden, during the second half of the seventeenth century and the first third of the eighteenth century, French diplomats turned to Prussia who henceforth filled the role, not as a natural ally as Sweden had done but as a "necessary ally" to "keep a counterweight to maintain perfect balance."[5]

French support of Prussia supposed that the latter established and upheld the balance of power within the Empire. Prussia, however, continued to extend its influence. From 1755, Prussia's power was deemed too large and even threatening for French interests.[6] As a consequence, at the behest of King Louis XV and the proimperial party in his court, France entered a diplomatic alliance with Austria (Treaty of Versailles of May 1, 1756), thus putting an end to more than two centuries of open hostilities between the two dynasties.[7] At that point, France was not hoping for the total annihilation of Prussia but rather hoped to be able to bring it back to its level of power before 1740 when Friedrich II took over Austrian Silesia.[8] At the same time, during the Seven Years' War (1756–63), France refused to consent to even the slightest Habsburgian territorial gain, as this could have once again tipped the scales in favor of Austria.[9]

While this reversal of alliances, often referred to as a "Diplomatic Revolution," marked a breach from the traditional principles of French foreign policy, it also fell within the continuity of France's desire to avoid the rise of a hegemonic power in Germany. This goal was never explicitly formulated as a doctrine; nevertheless, French diplomacy observed it in the following centuries no matter who was in power in Paris. France adapted and adjusted this guiding line to the political evolutions in Europe and to the political and philosophical mutations within France but continued to believe that a unified Germany would have nothing but disastrous consequences for France's own vital interests. However, the reversal of alliances was also meant to further another goal that was not directly linked to the Empire: by entrusting the German war scene to Austria, France was free to concentrate on its naval war against England.

The alliance with Austria was upheld after the Seven Years' War. If the alliance had already been generally disapproved of in 1756, it now became even more controversial. French public opinion demanded the reinstatement of the Prussian alliance. From 1740, there was a real Friedrich-mania, which portrayed Friedrich II of Prussia, on the one hand, as a king who applied Enlightenment principles and, on the other, as a warrior-king whose victories, even when against the French army, were widely applauded.[10] A large part of the political and diplomatic circles also hoped for a return to the pre-1756 arrangements; in their opinion, Austria had regained ground and was preparing once again to strive for hegemony in Germany, the alliance with the Habsburgs seemed unnatural.[11]

The accession of Louis XVI to the French throne did not change this general tendency. The Austrian alliance, which became a means of "mutual containment,"[12] was indeed more and more contested, as much in public opinion[13] as in the ministerial circles,[14] but was nevertheless upheld. During the 1780s, French diplomats hoped to use the alliance not only to keep the Habsburgian aspirations under closer scrutiny containing them peacefully but also to keep Austria from entering an alliance with England.[15] Moreover, Prussia continued to play its role as a counterweight within the Empire without the necessity of making an alliance through a treaty; some observers even went as far as maintaining that only through the Seven Years' War debacle had any real balance within the Empire been maintained.[16] Even the relative decline of Prussian power after the death of Friedrich II (1786) and the instatement of his nephew, Friedrich Wilhelm II, did not alter France's position. The Austrian alliance, gradually emptied of its original engagements, continued until the Revolution and the declaration of war in 1792,[17] even though Prussia became the representative of French interests in the Empire, and throughout Eastern Europe,[18] going as far as creating a league of princes (*Fürstenbund*) directed against the Habsburgs, of which France had been a secret member until at least 1787.[19]

Even if, at first, the Revolution changed nothing in the diplomatic orientation of France's German policy, things began to change from 1792. The radicalization of the revolutionary movement, along with a change of staff in the Ministry of Foreign Affairs rapidly brought about a reversal of the situation. Two new principles emerged: (1) war against tyrants and (2) natural borders. The concern with the balance between Austria and Prussia within the Empire, eventually counterbalanced by a third party made up of minor German princes, which had occupied French foreign affairs since the early eighteenth century, now became of secondary importance even though it did not disappear completely.[20] It gave way to an ideological vision, the main goal of which became the spreading of the French Revolution. Consequently, the Empire, which was considered a stronghold of despotism, had to disappear to be reconstructed according republican principles: "The Holy Empire, that monstrous assembly of small and large despots who damn one another in society with their excessive politeness, very well! The

Holy Empire must also disappear by the effects of our incredible revolution. The kingdom of France supported it, the French Republic shall work for its destruction."[21] The first plans to reorganize the Holy Empire were made as early as the spring of 1791. A diplomat suggested the abolition of the imperial title and the redistribution of imperial territory to set up larger entities, the members of which would unite in a confederation to be used as a buffer state against the main neighboring powers.[22]

The project of reorganizing the German States was accompanied by the claim that the Rhine was a natural border of France. This idea did not emerge during the French Revolution. In fact, the issue of natural borders had already arisen with the French intervention in the Thirty Years' War and the occupation of Alsace and was taken up again during the War of the Reunions under Louis XIV,[23] to eventually disappear from French diplomatic vocabulary for almost a century. The success of the revolutionary wars finally made it possible for the Republic to act upon this claim by occupying and then annexing the left bank of the Rhine, without obtaining the rest of the Holy Roman Empire, however. This changed under Napoleon. After the victory of Austerlitz (December 2, 1805), the French emperor found himself in the entirely novel situation of being able to redraw the map of a substantial part of Germany. Indeed Napoleon ultimately reduced the number of states in the Holy Roman Empire to around forty, sixteen of which were forced to join the Rhine Confederation. In the three following years, twenty-three other German states entered the Rhine Confederation; only Prussia, Austria, and the two Danish and Swedish possessions remained outside. The creation of the Confederation brought about the end of the Holy Roman Empire of the German Nation (August 6, 1806) and Franz II had to relinquish his Imperial crown following an ultimatum from Napoleon.

Although the Rhine Confederation's principal role was military, it also allowed France to fulfill its longstanding ambition of creating a third party in Germany that would counterbalance the two dominant powers, Austria and Prussia. Unfortunately for the French the Confederation had only a brief existence and began to fall apart after the battle of Leipzig (1813).

During the first restoration, French policy toward Germany remained very similar to that of Napoleon. Both Louis XVIII and Talleyrand sought to prevent Austria, still the hereditary enemy, and Prussia from becoming the dominant powers in Germany. They considered that the best way to achieve this aim was to support the constitution of a third party made up of Francophiles. Talleyrand went to the Congress of Vienna with this aim in mind and began to increase his influence during the negotiations until the Hundred Days, Napoleon's short-lived return to office, put an end to these attempts.

The Hundred Days left France with no real power to exert any influence on the form that the new Germany would take. On the fringe of the Congress of Vienna, the German Confederation (*Deutscher Bund*) was created. It comprised the states of the former Rhine Confederation but it also included Austria and Prussia. This put an end to the French dream of perpetuating a third party of the small and medium-sized German states and revived the risk of seeing one of the two dominant powers take control of the whole German region.

Furthermore, a vast national and liberal movement had developed in Germany since the occupation by Napoleon's troops, and even more so since the Hundred Days. It was with extreme concern that the French diplomats described the rise of a profoundly anti-French feeling that brought together claims for a unified Germany and signs of an imminent revolution. One of them went as far as to compare the situation to that of "the French crisis of 1788."[24]

To prevent the Liberals and the supporters of a unified Germany from gaining ground, during the Conference of Carlsbad (August 1819), the States of the German Confederation ratified restrictive measures introduced by the chief Austrian minister, Prince Metternich. Initially approved in France, it quickly became clear that the agreements were used not only to counter the revolutionary risks in Germany but also to secure Austria's role as the dominant power within the Confederation. For the French foreign ministry, the emperor of Austria had become, if not by right at least in practice, "emperor of Germany" and Metternich its "dictator."[25] Prussia, which at the end of the Napoleonic campaigns seemed to be the greatest danger for French interests,[26] also stepped into the Austrian sphere. In France, Prussia was then considered as crushed by the "Austrian yoke," as an "Austrian prefecture" governed by ministers reduced to the rank of Metternich's "lieutenants."[27]

The Second Restoration, which was more concerned by the Italian scene where Austria had also succeeded in extending its influence considerably, pursued a low-key German policy.[28] First excluded by the Congress of Vienna, then preoccupied with maintaining the established balance and peace of the continent, it had no support in Germany that would have allowed it to have any influence on the events. Nevertheless, it remained true to the principles of the ancient régime, seeking to use its influence, however limited, to counter the projects of whichever of the two dominant powers in Germany was likely to get the upper hand.

As a result, French diplomacy became more interested in a stronger Prussia hoping to find "its natural ally against Austrian supremacy,"[29] although later this position changed when French diplomats eventually sized up Prussia's strength. The main concern of the French was thus the Prussian attempts at achieving a customs union in Germany. As soon as the first page of the project was signed creating the union between Prussia and Hesse (1828), the diplomats started alerting their minister. Some went as far as seeing it as the most serious event in Germany since the Reformation and the Peace of Westphalia.[30] In fact, the French representatives understood from the beginning that an economic union under the leadership of Prussia was likely to bring about a political union of Germany. Although, on several occasions, France tried to slow down the process,[31] it could not however stop it: March 22, 1833, thirteen German states joined Prussia and Hesse, to form a larger customs union (the *Zollverein*), which was soon to be joined by almost all of the remaining states, except for Austria.

The July Monarchy (1830–48), certainly brought about changes within France itself but changed nothing in its German policy, at least not during the first decade of its existence.[32] Austria remained the main opponent, and Prussia, even though it was unsuccessfully approached twice by French diplomats to enter into an alliance, remained a concern, while the small and medium-sized states were actively supported in their desire of independence.[33]

Relations did not change until the Franco-German crisis of 1840.[34] The humiliation felt in France when the Oriental crisis was settled by the four major powers without its participation stirred up strong resentment.[35] National sentiment in France soon demanded a settlement of the Congress of Vienna, and a long forgotten claim reappeared: that of natural borders and in particular that of the Rhine. The more the French government raised the tone, even going as far as threatening the German Confederation with war (without however actually ever having the intention to act upon it),[36] the more German public opinion was angered, and in the process the Rhine became the very symbol of confrontation in the propaganda opposing the French and German camps.[37] From a political point of view, the 1840 crisis disappeared as quickly as it had flared up and did not trigger the war that a section of French public opinion demanded. In Germany, however, its effects were long-lasting. The year 1840 stood for "the breakthrough of mass nationalism,"[38] which rapidly found an ideological base and a clear objective: national unification. It is in these terms that the crisis of 1840 paved the way for the 1848 revolution.

In France, the German Revolution of 1848 created much enthusiasm at first. A "fraternal pact" was drawn up between "two nations of free citizens who quite naturally will find common interests."[39] During the spring of 1848, on the French side the natural borders issue disappeared, and on the German side, there was a willingness to give up rights to Alsace, as it was admitted that the population—although of German descent—wanted to stay French. But as soon as the young German Nation appeared ready to take up arms to give the inhabitants of Danish Schleswig the possibility to join them, French foreign policy went immediately back to its old habits. Oddly enough, from the summer of 1848, the Second French Republic feared a unified republican Germany more than a federal monarchic state, assuming that once "restructured according to democratic principles, it would become arrogant and predatory due to the violence of the circumstances."[40] The minister of foreign affairs at the time, Jules Bastide, a major advocate of a German policy "of division and balance of power," considered a Germany of forty-five million inhabitants that all obeyed "a single impetus" a great danger for his own country, and therefore strongly encouraged antiunitarian tendencies in Austria, Prussia, and Bavaria,[41] aiming to foil the aspirations of German nationalists.

However, at least until 1866, neither in France nor anywhere else in Europe could a unified Germany really be imagined.[42] It had been thought that the sense of identity of the members of the German Confederation and the legitimist, reactionary, and antinational attitude of the two dominating dynasties would always take the upper hand.

Just as the Second Republic, but for different reasons, the Second Empire defended the principle of nationalities. Napoleon III, the "champion of nationalities," supported it personally[43] and then saw in it the possibility to use its dynamics and its explosive potential in favor of France's interest.[44] This specifically held true in Italy: on the one hand, he supported an Italian nation, and, on the other, he wanted to reduce Austrian influence. Concerning Germany, however, Napoleon III's policy was more hesitant. While acknowledging the well-founded claims of the nationalists, he also feared a unified Germany. For a long time he considered Austria as the main danger for France. Prussia, as had been usual since the death of Friedrich II, was considered a second-rate power and, consequently, was militarily underestimated. It was not until the Austrian defeat against Prussian troops in Sadowa (July 3, 1866) that France realized its error: "It is in the Emperor's interest not to allow Prussia to destroy for its own profit the European balance by reinstituting under another form the German Empire that France took so many centuries to pull down."[45] Faithful to its traditional strategy, France then sought an alliance with Austria, the weaker of the two dominant powers in Germany. However, the unifying process had already started, France was isolated, and when the Franco-Prussian war began, Napoleon III was alone, facing Prussia.

The background of the war was the dynastic struggle between the Bourbons and the Hohenzollerns for the vacant Spanish throne. When in the early summer of 1870 the prospects of the Hohenzollern candidate improved and thus a personal union between Spain and Prussia could at least hypothetically come to pass, the primal fear of being surrounded arose in France once again. The pressure brought to bear by French foreign policy was indeed able to force the withdrawal of the Hohenzollern candidacy but proved unable to defuse the crisis over the long term. This was because King Wilhelm of Prussia refused to renounce the claims of his house permanently. Bismarck wrote a press release—dubbed the "Ems Dispatch" after the town of Bad Ems where the king was staying—related to this issue but presenting it in a severely truncated and ambiguous form. A mediocre translation into French made things worse by increasing the text's severity. Spurred on by an outraged public and a reckless overestimation of its own military capabilities, the French government jumped at the opportunity to declare war against Prussia on July 19, 1870. [46]

Numerical inferiority, poor preparation, and command errors brought France to the brink of defeat within a few weeks. Although an armistice was not signed until January 28, 1871, the outcome of the war had actually been decided at the Battle of Sedan on September 1, 1870—a day after that defeat, a quarter of the French army had become Prussia's prisoners of war, as had Emperor Napoleon III himself. [47]

After the French defeat, the declaration of the King of Prussia as Emperor of Germany, January 18, 1871, in the Hall of Mirrors in the Château de Versailles put an end to a long standing central principle of French foreign policy. Since François I and throughout the different political regimes, France had wanted to prevent any single power from taking control of Germany. Now this precise situation had arisen, since the German Empire was in fact a Greater Prussia. But far from accepting this state of affairs, France, each time it found itself in a position of strength, after the First and the Second World War, would try to overturn the results of 1871 to break up Germany. The fall of the Berlin Wall made these rather old reflexes resurface for the last time.

Notes

1. François Bluche, *Louis XIV* (Paris: Fayard, 1986), 346, 920; our translation.
2. Franz Bosbach, *Monarchia Universalis. Ein politischer Leitbegriff der frühen Neuzeit* (Göttingen: Vandenhoeck und Ruprecht, 1988), 35.
3. For an excellent summary of the struggle, see Rainer Babel, *Deutschland und Frankreich im Zeichen der habsburgischen Universalmonarchie 1500–1648* (Darmstadt: Wissenschaftliche Buchgesellschaft, 2005), 15–101.
4. On this subject, see: Jörg Ulbert, "Die Angst vor einer habsburgischen Hegemonie im Reich (1715–1723)," in *Deutschlandbilder—Frankreichbilder 1700–1850*, ed. Thomas Höpel (Leipzig: Leipziger Universitäts-Verlag, 2001), 57–74.
5. "Aperçu de la situation politique de la France," s.l., 1781, Archives des Affaires étrangères, Paris (AAE), Mémoires et Documents (MD) France 587, fol. 9v; our translation.
6. See among others: "Tableau Politique . . . ," anonymous, ca. 1756, AAE, MD France 581, fol. 17v–18v.
7. See recent publications on this subject: Sven Externbrink, *Friedrich der Große, Maria Theresia und das Alte Reich* (Berlin: Akademie-Verlag, 2006). See also Lothar Schilling, *Kaunitz und das Renversement des alliances* (Berlin: Duncker und Humblot, 1994).
8. Eckehart Buddruss, *Die französische Deutschlandpolitik, 1756–1789* (Mainz: von Zabern, 1995), 81.
9. Ibid., 129.
10. See Stephan Skalweit, *Frankreich und Friedrich der Große* (Bonn: Röhrscheid, 1952).
11. See for example: "Mémoire présenté au Roi Louis XV par le Duc de Choiseul vers la fin de février 1765," AAE, MD France 581, fol. 40r; "Mémoire secret sur les affaires générales de l'Europe," 1767, AAE, MD France 446, fol. 346r–346v.
12. Buddruss, *Deutschlandpolitik*, 140.
13. Ibid., 151.
14. "Mémoire présenté à Son Excellence Monseigneur le Comte de Vergennes," 1 XI 1781, AAE, MD France 587, fol. 31v-33r; "Sur les mesures à prendre soit avec l'Empire . . . Par Mr Favier," 1781, AAE, MD France 587, fol. 81v; "Mémoire de Politique extérieure générale présenté par Vergennes au Roi," 29 III 1784, AAE, MD France 587, fol. 218r–220r; "Système politique de la France au dehors," anonymous, 1789, AAE, MD France 587, fol. 230r–232r.
15. Buddruss, *Deutschlandpolitik*, 144, 175.
16. Ibid., 163.
17. "Résumé. De l'Etat actuel des cours et des Pays qui sont dans mon département. Par M. de Rayenval," February 1787, AAE, MD France 586, fol. 244r–271v.
18. Buddruss, *Deutschlandpolitik*, 171, 233, 294, 296.
19. Ibid., 284.
20. "Quelques idées sur les raports [*sic*] actuels de la France avec les principales puissances de l'Europe, soumises . . . par Ant. Bern. Caillard," 1795, AAE, MD France 655, fol. 9v–10v; "La République française doit-elle désirer de conclurre [*sic*]

une paix générale avec les puissances coalisées?" anonymous, 1795, MD France 655, fol. 75r.

21. "Précis du sistême politique . . . " signed de Maillot, 1795, AAE, MD France 655, fol. 199v; our translation.

22. "Mémoire sur le changement à apporter à la constitution de la Confédération germanique," anonymous, April 1791, AAE, MD France 587, fol. 285r–285v, 288v; our translation.

23. See Daniel Nordman, *Frontières de France* (Paris: Gallimard, 1998), 88–105.

24. Cited from Karl Hammer, *Die französische Diplomatie der Restauration und Deutschland 1814–1830* (Stuttgart: Hiersemann, 1963), 69. Also see Michael Jeismann, *La patrie de l'ennemi. La notion d'ennemi national et la représentation de la nation en Allemagne et en France de 1792 à 1918* (Paris: CNRS Ed., 1997), 23–147.

25. Hammer, *Diplomatie*, 82.

26. Ibid., 15–16, 18, 42, 93.

27. Cited from Ibid., 93–94.

28. Ibid., 12, 79–80, 105.

29. Dieter Roghé, *Die französische Deutschland-Politik während der ersten zehn Jahre der Julimonarchie (1830–1840)* (PhD diss., University of Würzburg, 1971), 220.

30. Hammer, *Diplomatie*, 229; Roghé, *Deutschland-Politik*, 150.

31. For this subject, see Roghé, *Deutschland-Politik*, 149–67.

32. Anna Owsinska, *La politique de la France envers l'Allemagne, 1830–1848* (Varsovie Ossolineum, 1974), 11–38.

33. Roghé, *Deutschland-Politik*, 223–24, 231.

34. For this subject, see: Irmline Veit-Brause, *Die deutsch-französische Krise von 1840* (PhD diss., University of Cologne, 1967).

35. See Wolf D. Gruner, "Der Deutsche Bund, die deutschen Verfassungsstaaten und die Rheinkrise von 1840," *Zeitschrift für bayerische Landesgeschichte* 53 (1990): 51–78.

36. Roghé, *Deutschland-Politik*, 239.

37. See these verbal jousts: Jean-Marie Carre, *Les écrivains français et le mirage allemand 1800–1940* (Paris: Boivin, 1947); André Monchoux, *L'Allemagne devant les lettres françaises. De 1814 à 1835* (Paris: Colin, 1953); and Heinz-Otto Sieburg, *Deutschland und Frankreich in der Geschichtsschreibung des 19. Jahrhunderts*, 2 vols. (Wiesbaden: Steiner, 1954–58).

38. Heinz-Otto Sieburg, "Nationales Selbstverständnis und Gegensatzbewusstsein in der Ära der Julimonarchie und des Vormärz," in *Aspects des relations franco-allemandes 1830–1848*, ed. Raymond Poidevin and Heinz-Otto Sieburg (Metz: Centre de Recherches Relations Internationales, 1978), 9; also see Rudolf Buchner, "Der Durchbruch des modernen Nationalismus in Deutschland," in *Festgabe dargebracht Harold Steinacker* (Munich: Oldenbourg, 1955), 309–33.

39. Rudolf Buchner, *Die deutsch-französische Tragödie, 1848–1864* (Würzburg: Holzner, 1965), 178.

40. Alexander Scharff, "König Friedrich Wilhelm IV., Deutschland und Europa im Frühjahr 1849," in *Geschichtliche Kräfte und Entscheidungen*, ed. Martin Göhring and Alexander Scharff (Wiesbaden: Steiner, 1954), 166.

41. Ibid.

42. Anselm Doering-Manteuffel, *Die deutsche Frage und das europäische Staatensystem 1815–1871* (Munich: Oldenbourg, 2001), 30.

43. Pierre Milza, *Napoléon III* (Paris: Perrin, 2006), 368–70.

44. Wolf D. Gruner, "Frankreich und der Deutsche Bund 1851–1866," in *Aspects des relations franco-allemandes*, 39–61.

45. Reculot to minister, July 6, 1866, AAE, CP Allemagne 842, cited from: Gruner, "Frankreich und der Deutsche Bund," 61.

46. For further details see: Eberhalb Kolb, *Der Kriegsausbruch 1870: Politische Entscheidungsprozesse und Verantwortlichkeiten in der Julikrise 1870* (Göttingen: Vandenhoeck & Ruprecht, 1970).

47. For more details on the course of war refer, amongst others, to François Roth, *La guerre de 1870* (Paris: Fayard, 1990); Geoffrey Wawro, *The Franco-Prussian War. The German Conquest of France in 1870–1871* (Cambridge: Cambridge University Press, 2003); David Wetzel, *Duell der Giganten. Bismarck, Napoleon III. und die Ursachen des Deutsch-Französischen Krieges 1870/71* (Paderborn: Schöningh, 2005).

CHAPTER 4

Between Coercion and Conciliation

Franco-German Relations in the Bismarck Era, 1871–90

Nathan N. Orgill

"The great powers of our age are like passengers, unknown to one another, who have accidentally come together in a railroad car," Otto von Bismarck told Prince Orlov in 1879. "They all watch each other, and when one of them sticks his hand in his pocket, the passenger next to him prepares his own revolver in order to be ready to shoot first."[1] Bismarck's description of the Great Powers was an accurate depiction of European politics after 1871, when mutual suspicion grew at an alarming rate. Its most symptomatic expression could be found in the relations of France and the newly united Germany. In the years that followed the Peace of Frankfurt, Franco-German relations can be divided into three periods: from 1871 to 1877 relations were relatively poor, as Bismarck feared a war of revenge and the restoration of a monarchy that might conduct it; from 1877 to 1885 relations between the two countries steadily improved, as republican sentiment became firmly entrenched in France and both countries made efforts in the direction of conciliation; but with the fall of the Ferry government in 1885 relations once again became icy, a trend that ultimately culminated in the Franco-Russian alliance in the early 1890s.

Nevertheless, in each of these phases there were certain trends in Franco-German relations that remained static. In the first place, Germany played the senior role in the relationship from 1871 to 1890. As the main force behind German diplomacy, Bismarck consistently tried to prevent France from gaining allies and fighting a war of revenge. In addition, the tactics he employed to isolate France were dictated by the parameters of her domestic politics; when anti-German or monarchist governments came to power, Bismarck time and again checked French ambitions by diplomatic isolation and intimidation; when the French government was more conciliatory, he was more likely to encourage a policy of friendship himself. Nevertheless, both sides assumed there would always be disagreement over Alsace-Lorraine.

The Imposed Peace, Revanche, and the Recovery of France, 1871–77

The peace inaugurated in 1871 made clear that the constellation of power in Europe had dramatically altered. The most obvious manifestation of this development was the displacement of France by Germany as the preeminent military and diplomatic power in Europe. Berlin became the center of the international system and Bismarck its effective manager. In France there was a backlash against the transformation that found expression in the idea of revenge (revanche). Bismarck suspected that any peace settlement would merely be a "truce" for France to violate as soon as possible. As the arbiter of the states system after 1871, he sought the maintenance of peace in order to ensure that his creation would not be torn apart. Since he believed that France was most likely to violate the peace, an all-important objective in his foreign policy was the isolation of France and the suppression of her military power.

In the Frankfurt peace settlement, Bismarck utilized every means available to him to keep France weak. First, Germany imposed a large war indemnity of five billion francs. Second, the German army would occupy a "neutral zone" in northeastern France until the war debt was paid.[2] Finally, France had to cede Alsace and parts of Lorraine to Germany, a great humiliation to French patriots. Historians have viewed this move variously as an instance of the old man's "unwisdom,"[3] or his Machiavellian machinations.[4] Nonetheless, it is doubtful that Bismarck ever believed a defeated France could be reconciled to the new situation, even without the seizure of territory; instead, he believed—like the generals—that Alsace-Lorraine was a necessary buffer against any future French aggression in southern Germany.[5]

In any event, the settlement seemed to guarantee future popular animosity in France. In Paris the German army conducted in March 1871 a triumphal parade through the heart of the city to the *Arc de Triomphe*. The inhabitants of Alsace-Lorraine, moreover, were incensed by the cession of the two provinces, and they began to emigrate immediately after 1871; as much as one-third of the original population may have fled to the west altogether.[6] But perhaps the most forgotten fact of the settlement was the feeling of dishonor it engendered in northeastern France, where forty-three departments had to live under German military rule for up to three years in some cases.[7] All told, the situation must have seemed little more than an imposed peace to the average French citizen.

For many in France it offered obvious rationale for revanche, as Germany came to be viewed increasingly after 1871 as the "hereditary enemy" of France. Early on, the revanche movement had an obvious leader in Léon Gambetta. A leader of the resistance after Sedan and a nationalist voice in the Assembly,

Gambetta founded the newspaper *La République Française* to protect France and her vanquished provinces from the German menace. He was also the man who made revanche an unspoken assumption of politics in the early Third Republic, something supported by a populist literature of nationalist thinkers.[8] The ideology of revenge thus made significant inroads into the heart of the nation after 1871.[9]

In the face of such hostility, it became a watchword in Bismarck's thinking that France would never be reconciled to the results of the Battle of Sedan. Aside from the stipulations of the Treaty of Frankfurt, he sought to deflect the ominous confrontation by encouraging republicanism in France. A republican government, he believed, could not wage a war of revenge; bitter infighting would characterize the party system, there would be a rapid turnover in governments, and a republic would be unacceptable to potential allies in the east—namely, to Russia.[10] Hence, Bismarck adamantly promoted the government of President Adolphe Thiers from 1871 to 1873. He also remarked somewhat insincerely in the peacemaking process that Germany would only negotiate with representatives of the people, "the ultimate sovereign" in France.[11]

But Bismarck's policy took a worrisome turn in 1873. In May, Thiers lost the support of the Assembly and had to resign. "Without doubt," Bismarck grumbled at the time, "our political situation has been made worse by the change."[12] The new foreign minister, Duc Louis de Decazes, hoped to score cheap victories in foreign policy as a way of clearing ground for the restoration of the monarchy.[13] Worse still, the French completely paid off the war indemnity—six months ahead of schedule, by borrowing money abroad from the U.S. banking institution J. P. Morgan & Co.—and the German army finally had to give up its occupation of France in September 1873. As a final blow, the Assembly began to reform the French army along Prussian lines making every Frenchman liable for five years of military service.[14] Altogether the reforms seemed to increase the size of the French army, according to German figures, by nearly 144,000 men.

Domestically, Bismarck responded with the *Kulturkampf*, seeing the large Catholic minority in Germany as a kind of fifth column that would disrupt the unity of the Kaiserreich. Bismarck's activities in this sense spilled into the domestic politics of France and her neighbors. In late 1873, for example, he called upon the French government to prosecute bishops who had publicly criticized the Kulturkampf and encouraged resistance in the dioceses of Lorraine.[15] Further, between 1873 and 1877—Marshal MacMahon's term as president of France—Bismarck conducted a deliberate campaign to support similar liberal and anticlerical governments in Belgium, Spain, and Italy, in order to "contain" monarchist France.[16] Bismarck also met the renewed French threat with diplomatic isolation. He formed, along with the responsible ministers of Austria-Hungary and Russia, the Three Emperors' League in October 1873. The bloc lacked the hard-and-fast pledges of Bismarck's later alliances and instead seemed a throwback to the Holy Alliance of the early nineteenth century, based as it was on the principle of blocking domestic revolution through the maintenance of peace abroad.[17] But in practice, Bismarck found it useless in committing the eastern monarchies to Germany against France: as the foreign minister of Austria-Hungary, Count Andrássy, remarked in 1874, a "powerful France was needed more than ever for the balance of power in Europe."[18]

The general ineffectiveness of Bismarck's attempts to isolate France became obvious during the "war scare" of 1875.[19] The crisis developed directly out of the chilliness of Franco-German relations after 1873. Most of the burden for the renewed hostility between the two states lies squarely on Bismarck's shoulders, as increasingly he resorted to intimidation and coercion to check France's recovery. The alarm bell first rang with the famous Radowitz mission of February 1875, when a rumor arose that Bismarck had tried to get Russian approval for an attack on France. News of the army cadre law of 1875 broke shortly afterward, giving rise to open talk of preventive war in Germany. In an attempt to curb the growth of French power, Bismarck inserted an article in the *Kölnische Zeitung* on April 5, 1875, which argued that the cadre law was really a French attempt to exact revenge upon Germany. Subsequently, the Berlin *Post* on April 8 wrote that France was going to begin a war of revenge—that war was "in sight." The event reached a climax when a German diplomat supposedly told the French ambassador at a dinner party that a preventive war would be justified by the bellicose attitude of the French.[20] The result was a resounding diplomatic defeat for Germany. The British told Bismarck they would not tolerate the destruction of France; what was even worse, the Russians agreed. Needless to say, the whole episode allowed the French to play the role of victim and ensured the other powers would not sit idly by as in 1870. French isolation was no longer such an assured thing.

Bismarck's Diplomatic Realignment and the Franco-German Détente, 1877–85

In the wake of the war-in-sight crisis, the attention of Europe shifted away from the west to the question of the death of Europe's "sick man," the Ottoman Empire. The revolt of Bosnia and Herzegovina in July 1875 sparked a crisis in the Near East, which escalated the next year when Bulgaria revolted in May and Serbia and Montenegro declared war in the summer. Sympathy for the revolts ran high in Russia, and the pan-Slavs there pushed for intervention. Britain had long stood in the way of Russian expansion into the Mediterranean and found a friend in Austria-Hungary, which feared the loss of influence in the Balkans. After a lengthy waiting game, the tsar finally declared war in April 1877, fighting until the fortress of Plevna in Bulgaria surrendered to the last Russian armies in December. The Treaty of San Stefano that followed enlarged Bulgaria so that it would become the largest state in the Balkans. This new larger Bulgaria was henceforth to be the heart of the Russian sphere in the Balkans, while the territory the Ottoman Empire retained in Europe was now dramatically restricted to the region in the immediate vicinity of Constantinople, Thrace. Not surprisingly, Austrian diplomats called for a congress of the great powers to discuss the matter, public opinion in Britain supported the idea, and representatives of the powers met at Berlin in June 1878 to revise the peace settlement. At the Congress of Berlin, the Russian sphere that had been created by San Stefano was greatly truncated; and Britain, France, and Austria-Hungary all received compensation for the little bit of territory that Russia retained. Many Russians viewed the settlement as a diplomatic defeat engineered by Bismarck, and, in this sense, the congress helped pave the way for the Franco-Russian Alliance of 1894 by encouraging the growth of Pan-Slavism.

At about this time, Bismarck seriously began to fear a revival of a "nightmare of coalition": an alliance in which Germany was surrounded by hostile powers on three sides (i.e., France, Russia, and Austria). His response to this problem was that Russia and Austria should in the future center their activities in the Near East, where Russia would take a defensive stand and need a German alliance. Neither Russia nor Austria would dream of joining an anti-German bloc; and Britain specifically would compete with France over control of the Mediterranean and Egypt. The common denominator behind each of these goals was that France was assumed to be as "hostile" as ever to Germany; a common result of their accomplishment would be the isolation of France. It was, in other words, "a complete political situation in which all the powers excepting France will need us and be held back as far as possible from a coalition against us by their relations to one other."[21] It signaled a shift to a more subtle tactic: the indirect isolation of France.

The first move in the fulfillment of this goal was the creation of the Dual Alliance in October 1879, which called for military assistance if Russia should attack either of the two states and for neutrality if either were attacked by another state. By directly linking Austria-Hungary to Germany, the alliance implied that the Habsburgs would not join with France to attack the Kaiserreich. The agreement became the linchpin of Bismarck's diplomatic reconfiguration. The second move in Bismarck's foreign-policy reorientation was the renewal of the Three Emperors' League, which developed from a vague monarchical agreement into a hard-and-fast defensive alliance. The treaty, signed in June 1881, called for neutrality if one of the countries found itself at war with a fourth power. The main advantage of the maneuver for Bismarck was that it completely eliminated the possibility of a Franco-Russian alliance. The last move in Bismarck's diplomatic reorientation came with the adhesion of Italy to the Dual Alliance in the spring of 1882. Like the earlier treaties, the agreement itself was aimed directly at isolating France: it provided for military aid if any of the three powers were attacked by France or a combination of two other powers.

A major aspect behind these developments was related to an improvement in Franco-German relations after 1877. In December 1875 elections were held for the Assembly in France, and republican candidates won a majority in the Chamber of Deputies and a near majority in the Senate. The election signified the growing strength of the republican ideal in France. It did not take long for Marshal MacMahon to challenge the republicans by turning out his cabinet and dissolving the Assembly in the so-called seize mai crisis of 1877. The move seemed ominous for Franco-German relations, for President MacMahon appointed a monarchist cabinet under the Duc de Broglie. Bismarck made it known that any turn in a reactionary direction would inevitably mean war with Germany.[22] Despite a determined campaign by the monarchists to win the elections of October 1877, a majority of republican candidates were returned to the Chamber of Deputies, a victory that was supplemented the following year when the republicans won a majority in the Senate as well. Republicanism had won the day, and President MacMahon had to resign office in January 1879, allowing for reconciliation between France and Germany.

In the immediate aftermath of the French elections of 1877, William Henry Waddington took charge of the portfolio for foreign affairs: he informed the ambassador in Berlin, Viscount Elie de Gontaut-Biron, it was crucial to communicate "the great value" he attached "to maintaining with [the government in Berlin] relations based upon mutual confidence."[23] Going further in the direction of détente, the new government replaced Gontaut-Biron himself with Count Charles de Saint-Vallier in January 1878, who was supposed to cultivate peaceful relations with Germany.[24] The relationship got even better with the accession of the new president, Jules Grévy, an open advocate of rapprochement. The fruition of these developments was a period of relatively friendly relations that lasted from the solidification of the Third Republic in late 1877 to the fall of Jules Ferry in 1885. The new relationship found expression first of all in Bismarck's attitude toward France at the Congress of Berlin. Bismarck went so far as to suggest that the meeting be held in Paris under the chairmanship of the French delegation, and, when that failed, tried his hardest to portray Waddington as the most important mediator of the thorny questions hashed out by the Congress.[25] Bismarck, moreover, downplayed the object of his alliance system to the French; it was mainly intended, he averred, to prevent a war between Austria-Hungary and Russia; indeed, the basis of his foreign policy was the Austrian alliance and the maintenance of good relations with France.[26]

But even more important was the encouragement Bismarck gave to the French in the world outside Europe, which he hoped would direct their energies away from revanche. In 1879, for example, after expressing his peaceful intentions to the French ambassador in Berlin, Bismarck remarked frankly, "I am prepared to give assistance to you in your endeavors where they do not contradict with our own interests. But, I say again, what is necessary for the French people . . . is some gratification of its self-esteem, and I desire sincerely to see it achieve this gratification . . . in the Mediterranean Sea, its natural sphere of expansion."[27] In his exhortation to Saint-Vallier, Bismarck had in mind the seizure of Tunis, which had been set aside for France at the Congress of Berlin. These measures were directly in accordance with the blueprint Bismarck had devised in 1877 and served the purpose of finding outlets for French expansion outside Europe, especially in North Africa and Asia, where France might come into conflict with other powers besides Germany. Bismarck, for example, repeatedly offered support on the issue of French occupation of Tunis after 1879. He ordered the German representative at the Madrid Conference in 1880 to support the French representative and received the grateful thanks of Saint-Vallier in return.[28] Finally, in 1881 the French—under the leadership of Jules Ferry—occupied Tunis, and, as he had promised, Bismarck backed the French move.

The trend by 1881 was such, then, that relations between Germany and France seemed at a highpoint. Bismarck went so far as to ask the ambassador to Paris, Prince Chlodwig von Hohenlohe, to express the desire that "a friendly German empire with forty-five million inhabitants may be more useful and a stronger situation for the French than [having] a million Alsace-Lorrainers."[29] The rapprochement even extended to the darkest corners of the revanche movement; Gambetta silently approved of the improvement in Franco-German relations, hoping it might lead to the peaceful restitution of the lost provinces.[30]

The culmination of this trend came in the second Ferry ministry, when Bismarck made his brief bid to acquire overseas colonies. The primary motivation for the move has been interpreted variously, but one major aspect of the demarche was an attempt by Bismarck to construct a Franco-German entente directed against Britain.[31] The main goal behind the maneuver, Bismarck frankly told the French ambassador in Berlin, was to get the French to forget Sedan, as they had once before forgotten Waterloo; he would help the French fulfill their ambitions everywhere except on the Rhine.[32] Between 1884 and 1886, Bismarck acquired the lion's share of Germany's colonial empire, obtaining New Guinea, the Cameroons, Togoland, German East Africa, and German South-West Africa. At the same time, the French experienced a similar kind of success in the colonial field that led to the eventual acquisition of Madagascar and territories in Indochina. But the entente quickly deflated in 1885, when Ferry's government collapsed as a result of military reverses faced by French forces at Tonkin in March. The climate of French political opinion turned against new colonial adventures, and after 1885 French diplomacy shifted dramatically away from the colonial sphere back to Europe. The main focus was once again centered on strengthening the army and ending France's isolation in Europe.

Boulangism and Bismarck's Response, 1885–90

The most important manifestation of the shift in Franco-German relations was the phoenix of Boulangism that arose from the ashes of Ferry's political demise. General Georges Boulanger, who was minister of war from early 1886 to May 1887, was primed to play the role of dashing conqueror on a horse in a France that needed a strong man to sweep away political disunity and to conduct a more successful foreign policy.[33] He introduced minor reforms into the army, won the admiration of the common people in Paris, and generally gained a reputation as the general who personified *la revanche*.[34] What was perhaps most striking, though, was Boulanger's meteoric rise. Hohenlohe indicated this when he wrote that Boulanger had seemed to play the fool in the spring of 1886, but enjoyed by November the support of a majority of the Chamber. "If he remains two years later in office," Hohenlohe elaborated, "the conviction will have become general that he is the man who can conquer Germany and recover Alsace-Lorraine, and as Boulanger is a man without any scruples, whose ambition soars very high, he will drag the masses into war."[35]

The détente of the Ferry years had never enjoyed a total political consensus, anyway. It was in the early 1880s that Paul Déroulède had formed the Ligue des Patriotes (League of Patriots) as a nationalist pressure group and oversaw its growth to include 300,000 members. Furthermore, he completely dismissed the value of the recent French colonial acquisitions, remarking at one point to Ferry, "I have lost two children, and you offer me twenty domestics."[36] He offered the support of the Ligue to Boulanger in 1883, and the general received an obvious boost from the endorsement. After 1885, then, the biggest threat from Bismarck's standpoint was that the populist Boulanger would form a government of his own or overthrow the government of another—and either option seemed the obvious prelude to a new war between France and Germany.

In response, Bismarck himself turned away from the détente and focused domestic attention by early 1887 on the threat posed by a Boulangist France. He introduced a new army bill into the Reichstag that provided increased armaments and the funds to pay for them for seven years. Because the oppositional parties would only agree to a three-year provision, Bismarck dissolved the Reichstag and called for new elections, calculating that government-supporting parties would thereby win a majority in the body. Bismarck called up 71,000 reservists in the midst of the campaign, ramped up the press in support of the army bill, and generally created a new war scare. The situation must have seemed eerily familiar to 1875 when the Berlin *Post* proclaimed on January 31, in an article entitled "On the Razor's Edge," that Boulanger had won the heart of the French masses and responsible statesmen in France had to do something to prevent a war.[37] Bismarck echoed these thoughts privately to the French, asserting that if Boulanger formed his own government or were elected president himself, a war would result.[38] Bismarck's campaign led to the most dazzling conservative electoral success before 1890: he was able to form the Kartell as a government-supporting bloc in the Reichstag that would ensure the passage of the army bill.

In spite of this, if Bismarck had whipped up public opinion against France to create support for the Septennat Bill, the real threat he saw behind the scenes was Russia. Once again, relations with France were a part of a larger crisis Bismarck faced that led to the refinement of his alliance system in the latter half of the 1880s. Tsar Alexander III had never been happy with the situation in Bulgaria after the Congress of Berlin, and, after a drawn-out crisis, he intervened in August 1886 to depose Prince Alexander of Battenberg, who had been elected to the throne of Bulgaria in 1879. This action alarmed the Austrians, who felt that Russia was making another move to dominate the Balkans; they therefore began to prepare for a war, and the situation remained very tense for a number of months. In response the tsar refused to renew the Second Three Emperors' League when it expired in 1886. To solve the problems posed by renewed Austro-Russian conflict and the Boulangist threat in France, Bismarck had to reconstruct his system of alignments.

This reorientation was accomplished through a series of complicated maneuvers in 1887. All of the European great powers—excluding, of course, France—were involved in these negotiations in one form or another. The first step in this reconfiguration was the signature of the two Mediterranean Agreements in 1887 between Italy, Austria-Hungary, and Great Britain, which called for the maintenance of the status quo in the Mediterranean and the Balkans. As such, the agreements were a check on both French aspirations in Africa and Russian ambitions in the Near East. The second new arrangement was the Reinsurance Treaty between Russia and Germany of June, which called for both Russia and Germany to remain neutral in a war with a third power.

By the end of 1887, then, Germany's position vis-à-vis France was secure as ever. The Reinsurance Treaty and continued adherence of Austria-Hungary and Italy to the Triple Alliance kept France isolated and facing potential enemies to the south and the west; the Mediterranean agreements checked French colonial expansion and affiliated Britain with the German bloc; and every major power in Europe except France was now tied in one form or another to Germany.[39] At the same time, however, the system Bismarck devised to isolate France and check the Austro-Russian friction contained the seeds of its own demise. It lacked durability because it depended to a high degree on the intervention of Bismarck personally, while increasingly the political and military leadership of Germany had come to fear Russia over the 1880s.

By the time Bismarck passed from the scene in 1890, Franco-German relations had waxed and waned between the two extremes of outright hostility and working détente. The flux back and forth between coercion and conciliation was primarily related to the domestic situation in France and Bismarck's estimate of which political groups there were most likely to try to exact revenge. In the periods when monarchist governments were in power or revanchist leaders were in the ascendancy—from 1871 to 1877, and again from 1885 to 1890—Bismarck consistently dealt with the French threat by military intimidation and diplomatic isolation. From 1877 to 1885, on the other hand, when republican sentiment was firmly entrenched in France, Franco-German relations went through a thaw that culminated in the diplomatic cooperation Bismarck offered the Ferry government to help fulfill its colonial aspirations. Two factors remained constant in these years, however: Bismarck always maintained the diplomatic initiative as the central figure in European diplomacy up to 1890; and the lost provinces of Alsace and Lorraine continued to be a constant reminder that Germany and France were essentially "hereditary enemies" who would inevitably find themselves embroiled in a conflict at some time in the future. In a sense, then, the reentrenchment of the Franco-German antagonism after 1885 heralded major changes for the future. Germany lost the diplomatic initiative in Europe with Bismarck's dismissal in 1890, while she simultaneously dropped the secret alliance with Russia embodied in the Reinsurance Treaty. As a result, French statesmen were gradually able to win over Tsar Alexander III to a Franco-Russian alliance in the early 1890s, making Bismarck's "nightmare of coalitions" a distinct reality by 1894.

Notes

1. Orlov to Alexander II, October 1, 1879, *Krasnyi Arkhiv* 1 (1922): 86; my translation. Henceforth all translations are my own unless otherwise noted.
2. Frankfurt Peace Treaty, May 10, 1871, no. 17, J. Lepsius, A. Mendelssohn-Bartholdy and F. Thimme, eds., "Der Frankfurter Friede und seine Nachwirkungen 1871–1877," *Die Grosse Politik der Europäischen Kabinette. Sammlung der diplomatischen Akten des Auswärtigen Amtes*, vol. 1 (Berlin: Deutsche Verlagsgesellschaft für Politik und Geschichte, 1922), 38–43. Henceforth this source will be abbreviated as *GP*.
3. George P. Gooch, "Franco-German Relations 1871–1914," in *Studies in Diplomacy and Statecraft*, ed. George P. Gooch (New York: Longmans, Green and Co., 1942), 1.
4. Harvey Clark Greisman, "The Enemy Concept in Franco-German Relations, 1870–1914," *History of European Ideas* 19 (1994): 42.
5. Gabriac to Rémusat, August 14, 1871, no. 42, *Documents diplomatiques français, 1871–1914*, series 1, vol. 1 (Paris: Imprimerie Nationale, 1929), 62. Henceforth this source will be abbreviated as *DDF*.
6. Raymond Poidevin and Jacques Bariéty, *Les relations franco-allemandes 1815–1975* (Paris: Armand Colin, 1977), 103; and Gooch, *Franco-German Relations*, 2.
7. Allan Mitchell, *A Stranger in Paris: Germany's Role in Republican France, 1870–1940* (New York: Berghahn Books, 2006), 10.
8. E. Malcom Carroll, *French Public Opinion and Foreign Affairs, 1870–1914* (Hamden, CT: Archon Books, 1964), 73.
9. Greisman, "The Enemy Concept," 43.
10. Allan Mitchell, *Bismarck and the French Nation* (New York: Pegasus, 1971), 78.
11. A.J.P. Taylor, *The Struggle for Mastery in Europe, 1848–1918* (Oxford: Oxford University Press, 1954), 217.
12. Bismarck to Manteuffel, June 2, 1873, no. 114, *GP*, vol. 1, 189.
13. William L. Langer, *European Alliances and Alignments 1871–1890*, 2nd ed. (New York: Knopf, 1950), 38–39.
14. Poidevin, Bariéty, *Les relations franco-allemandes*, 117.
15. Otto Pflanze, *Bismarck and the Development of Germany*, vol. 2, *The Period of Consolidation, 1871–1880* (Princeton, NJ: Princeton University Press, 1990), 263.
16. James Stone, "Bismarck and the Containment of France, 1873–1877," *Canadian Journal of History* 29 (August 1994): 281–304.
17. Lothar Gall, *Bismarck: Der weiße Revolutionär*, 2nd ed. (Munich: Ullstein, 2002), 586–87.
18. Le Flô to Decazes, February 17, 1874, no. 284, *DDF*, ser. 1, vol. 1, 313.
19. On the "War-in-Sight" Crisis of 1875, see Joseph V. Fuller, "The War Scare of 1875," *The American Historical Review* 24, no. 2 (1919): 196–226; and James Stone, "The War Scare of 1875 Revisited," *Militärgeschichtliche Mitteilungen* 53 (1994): 309–26.
20. Gontaut-Biron to Decazes, April 21, 1875, no. 395, *DDF*, ser. 1, vol. 1, 415–21. It is still not entirely certain if Radowitz ever made these comments exactly. *See* Radowitz to Bismarck, May 12, 1875, *GP*, vol. 1, 275–77; and Joseph Maria von Radowitz, "1839–1877," in *Aufzeichnungen und Erinnerungen aus dem Leben des Botschafters Joseph Maria von Radowitz*, ed. Hajo Holborn, vol. 1 (Osnabrück: Biblio-Verlag, 1967), 318–32, both of which make the comments seem less noxious.

21. Memorandum by Bismarck, June 15, 1877, no. 294, *GP*, vol. 2, 153–54.
22. Mitchell, *Bismarck*, 87.
23. Waddington to Gontaut-Biron, December 14, 1877, no. 219, *DDF*, ser. 1, vol. 2, 223.
24. Robert H. Wienefeld, *Franco-German Relations 1878–1885* (Baltimore: Johns Hopkins, 1929), 47–48.
25. Taylor, *The Struggle for Mastery*, 253.
26. Saint-Vallier to Courcel, November 12, 1880, no. 294, *DDF*, ser. 1, vol. 3, 259.
27. Saint-Vallier to Waddington, January 5, 1879, no. 369, *DDF*, ser. 1, vol. 2, 412. Saint-Vallier's emphasis.
28. Hohenlohe to Solms-Sonnenwalde, May 27, 1880, no. 665, *GP*, vol. 3, 398–99.
29. Busch to Hohenlohe, July 16, 1881, no. 668, *GP*, vol. 3, 401.
30. Gooch, *Franco-German Relations*, 16.
31. The argument is posed in A. J. P. Taylor, *Germany's First Bid for Colonies 1884–1885: A Move in Bismarck's European Policy* (New York: Norton, 1970).
32. Courcel to Ferry, November 29, 1884, no. 471, *DDF*, ser. 1, vol. 5, 495.
33. On Boulanger, see William D. Irvine, *The Boulanger Affair Reconsidered: Royalism, Boulangism, and the Origins of the Radical Right in France* (New York: Oxford University Press, 1989).
34. W. R. Fryer, "The Republic and the Iron Chancellor: The Pattern of Franco-German Relations, 1871–1890," *Transactions of the Royal Historical Society* 29, no. 5 (1979): 181–82.
35. Chlodwig von Hohenlohe, *Memoirs of Prince Chlodwig of Hohenlohe-Schillingsfuerst*, vol. 2, trans. George W. Chrystal (New York: Macmillan, 1906), 367.
36. Quoted and translated in Gooch, *Franco-German Relations*, 18.
37. E. Malcom Carroll, *Germany and the Great Powers 1866–1914* (New York: Prentice Hall, 1938), 243.
38. Herbette to Flourens, January 29, 1887, no. 415, *DDF*, ser. 1, vol. 6, 426.
39. Mitchell, *Bismarck*, 100.

CHAPTER 5

Traditions of Hate among the Intellectual Elite

The Case of Treitschke and Bainville

Hugo Frey and Stefan Jordan

The historical profession has made the international rivalry between France and Germany in the modern period into a *locus classicus* of scholarship. Recently it is cultural historians who have contributed the most to new thinking on Franco-German enmity. Their best work illustrates how crossnational hatreds were a prominent part of everyday life in both of the states.[1] Demography, industry, cuisine, and children's literature were all vectors for the public expression of Francophobia and Germanophobia. Among the elite, geographers, anthropologists, and historians provided detailed studies that "proved" the ownership of the disputed territory of Alsace-Lorraine for their nation-state.[2] Some historians, like Jules Michelet and Ernest Renan, were themselves popular national heroes. To illustrate and to analyze the apogee of Franco-German enmity via the means of a short case study we will compare and contrast the writings of the historians: Heinrich von Treitschke (1834–86) and Jacques Bainville (1879–1936).

Both writers discussed in this chapter are notorious. The German, Treitschke, was professor of history at the University of Berlin, and his thinking is often cited as a significant precursor to Nazism.[3] This profile as a reactionary was not lost on Treitschke's contemporaries. During the First World War, Allied intellectuals, including Emile Durkheim, identified him as a significant cause of bellicosity.[4] After 1945 it was political philosophers who returned to Treitschke to establish the roots of Nazism.[5] Jacques Bainville is no less central a figure from the European extreme right-wing. He was an enthusiastic member of the royalist movement *Action française*, and he wrote extensively for this movement's newspaper of the same title. Bainville researched and lectured on the German threat to French security. This subject became his obsession and he published volumes on it from the eve of the First World War to his death (1936).[6]

We will analyze two publications in particular: Treitschke's *Was fordern wir von Frankreich?* (1870) and Bainville's *Histoire de Deux Peuples* (1915).[7] These are classics that have been overlooked in recent years by historians despite the fact that they were once influential and bestselling publications. An analysis of these texts illustrates the heart of Francophobia and Germanophobia. Treitschke's and Bainville's visions of the other's nation function as a mirror image. The positions the historians expressed in their writings blur into a common xenophobia. Similarly, Treitschke's and Bainville's attitudes toward social revolution (1789) closely resemble one another. We will also pinpoint a common anti-Semitism that colors the writers' thinking. In addition, there are links to be made in the historians' attitude to the idea of power. For here, too, the historians shared attitudes. However, we underline that *not* everything was mirrored. Notably, Treitschke's and Bainville's thinking on religion and race is dissimilar. Certainly, the comparative approach we adopt is not without its risks. For instance, some readers might object that Treitschke and Bainville were of different generations or were writing for different readerships. However, as we will explain, the older man, Treitschke, directly influenced the younger one. Similarly, while not holding a chair in history at a French university, Bainville was appointed to the Academie Française in 1935. As Eugen Weber noted in his famous work on the Action française, the royalist historian proved influential beyond the limited circles of extreme right-wing clubs and so he was in that respect held in comparable, albeit necessarily different, public esteem to Professor Treitschke in Germany.[8] In any case, our selection to compare these two opinion formers is based neither on the rigorous methods of comparative biography nor on the narrative prescriptions, which are perhaps associated with the writing of a history of History as scientific discipline. Our modest aim is to analyze the contribution of these men when they were important actors in the nationalist feud that intermittently raged between France and Germany.

Treitschke's imaginary France presented in *Was fordern wir von Frankreich?* (1870) is a pitiful place. He suggests that the country is inhabited by savages. For Treitschke the French are "half educated barbarians"; they are "wild beasts." He teaches that the French are a "reckless" and "frivolous people" who have become too arrogant to be ignored by their peaceful German neighbors. Treitschke contends that the Revolution of 1789 created a centralizing state that encouraged a "domineering national spirit" in France that was disproportionate to the true strength of these weak people. Notably, Treitschke uses the common pejorative term *Welsch* to describe all non-Germans who are living to the west of the Vosges Mountains.[9] Treitschke's only praise for France is offered toward its German speaking citizens of Alsace. He explains that these soldiers, albeit now serving in the French army, are the strongest and most honorable people. He promises that in the Vosges Mountains the German visitor glimpses healthy men with German "blood," even if they can only speak the French language.[10]

Treitschke denies all "moral" qualities to the French. He establishes opposition between a robust, natural, healthy, and "good" German culture-race, which he contrasts with the failings of French civilization and its "Welsch immorality." He asserts that, after 1870, France must take a lesser role in European affairs and that the German victory means that this will be the case. The most important distinction made by Treitschke is between "German Culture" and "Western Civilization." This distinction became very popular by the end of the century and is repeated by both right-wing nationalist and liberal German thinkers, including Ernst Troeltsch and Max Weber.

Jacques Bainville's assault on Germany, published in the opening phase of the 1914–18 war, is as ferocious as Treitschke's polemic. Bainville's explanation of European history is founded on the idea that the continent is repeatedly shaken into war by the barbaric race of the Germans. To simplify the central *Bainvillean* argument, he thinks that France and Europe's eternal problem is Germany. Thus, Bainville stigmatizes the Germans as an aggressive race that must be controlled to defend peace. He notes that they live in an "état monstrueux," which is authoritarian, militarist, and lacks culture. Bainville labels Germany as a "brigand-state," which is the "plague of the European world." He explains that any German achievements in politics, trade, or art are founded on military superiority. Furthermore, the Germanic obsession with war has its origins in a significant historical truth. Bainville teaches that the united Germany is an "abnormal" state, and because it is a fake community, without any genuine national identity, it relies on militarism.[11]

Treitschke and Bainville employ common rhetorical devices. The insults they level at each other's state and people can be viewed as a mirror image of each other. For example, both the historians reduce their object of hate to a few, repeated, simplistic, insults. In Treitschke's work the French are viewed as the *Welsch* or the "savages." Bainville reifies Germany into being a militarist warrior state. Neither author elaborates on the characteristics of their enemy in any detail or with reference to empirical research. In this style they imply that the enemy's homeland is unimportant and insignificant. Both men represent the enemy's land as an empty space which is open to attack. They impute irrationality on the part of their enemy's actions. They ascribe policies or behavior patterns of extreme violence to the other community. For example, Treitschke accuses Republican France of "annihilating" German-Alsatian particularism. Comparably, Bainville fears a future time that will be dominated by German inspired wars of "extermination."

The historians share a preference for the use of metaphors of health and illness. Treitschke calls France sick and Bainville labels Germany as being the plague of Europe. Much of the content of the two publications is exemplary of hard, integral or closed, nationalism. The nation's rival, in each case the neighboring foreign power, is stigmatized as inferior but is then, equally, perceived as a deadly threat. The national historians' homelands are associated with positive values of natural order while the opponent's country is identified as being uncivilized, barbarous and "diseased." The very idea that Franco-German confrontation was a natural historical state of affairs, a hereditary experience, is shared by the writers. On either side of the Rhine, or for Treitschke the Vosges mountain range, the men concur that much in European affairs is shaped by Franco-German conflict. However, the term "hereditary" is predominantly used by Treitschke and Bainville as a metaphor. They borrow the term from the scientific, and the dynastic, usage to imply that there is a continual struggle between their communities that is repeated over generations. The concept of hereditary conflict is not elaborated on in a pseudoscientific mode. There is, therefore, no reason to believe that the authors considered Franco-German conflict to be an immutable and irresolvable, permanent, "scientific" necessity. Both of the historians consider the past to be more complex, richer, than the literal use of the term "hereditary" implies. Furthermore, they each desire that their own nation might eventually assert a definitive victory against the other, which would conclude the struggle. A hereditary condition, taken literally and not metaphorically, would mean that such a definitive victory is impossible.

Treitschke's and Bainville's visions can be plausibly discussed as functioning as a "mimetic double." When they expressed their contempt for each other's community they increasingly imitated the other's language and meaning. This means that the historians begin to share a nationalist ideology that transcends German and French cultural differences and almost becomes a single discourse. As the philosopher René Girard posits, "mimetic violence makes the antagonists more and more interchangeable as they try to succeed in destroying each other."[12] Francophobe Treitschke and Germanophobe Bainville drift toward this accommodation. That these publications were written at times of war, 1870 and 1914, explains the rhetorical ferocity. Treitschke was writing his essay on France precisely when the German army won at Sedan (1870) and, similarly, Bainville reviews Franco-German relations when the next war was in its infancy. Certainly, until 1865 Treitschke had little interest in claiming Alsace for Germany.[13] Likewise, Bainville was not always so hostile to Germany. When studying in Munich in 1898 and in Berlin in 1899 he wrote letters home to the effect that he was enjoying life very much in Germany. Describing Berlin, he reported: "a very pretty town, very lively and very gay. One always finds something to do or see."[14] Certainly Bainville's first publication, *Louis II de Bavière* worked with a common popular notion of the French literary elite that Germany was a divided land that was split between positive and negative identities. For many French writers at this time it was a country with a "dual nature." Nonetheless, these ambiguous sympathies for the country across the Rhine were youthful indiscretions. By 1909 Bainville's work was attacking Germany and the positive side of the duality model was dropped. His *Bismarck et la France* (1909) and the subsequent *Le Coup d'Agadir* (1913) display Germanophobia that is near to the content of *Histoire de Deux Peuples*.[15]

Not every aspect of the content of the two publications can be interpreted with reference to René Girard's perceptive notion of the mimetic double. The sharpest difference between the two men's historiography is their treatment of religion. The tensions here are obvious and do not blur into a common discourse.

Treitschke asserts the importance of Lutheran Protestantism in German nation-building. The period of the reformation is a "crowning summit" of history to which the people of Alsace contributed. Protestantism is, to quote the historian, "the mightiest of all the forces at the root of German ways."[16] In complete contradiction, Bainville asserts that French grandeur is best guaranteed when the nation is working in harmony with Catholic Rome. He claims that the natural French alliance is with Rome and Italy.

There were, however, further shared perspectives, notwithstanding the Protestant–Catholic division. Common right-wing conservatism links the two versions of history that the men popularize. This is best illustrated in their overlapping interpretations of the French revolution. Treitschke, anticipating Bainville's later argumentation by some forty years, and also much of *Action française* ideology, instructs his German readership by explaining that 1789 led France to abandon any love of history and that France is terribly weakened by this error. Treitschke diagnoses the French "disease" as being a failure to any longer understand the importance of tradition and history.[17] Jacques Bainville would have agreed on this analysis. In addition, Treitschke notes that it is the same revolution that, paradoxically, has encouraged France to be bold on the international stage and to create a dangerously centralized power base in Paris.

Bainville's *Histoire de Deux Peuples* contains another negative interpretation of 1789. For Bainville the Enlightenment and the Revolution are the cause of all French suffering. It is these terrible events that empower Germany and provoke war in 1870 and 1914.[18] In brief, Bainville argues that the Republic's greatest crime is to forget the key French strategy of limiting German strength. Treitschke's and Bainville's negative interpretations of 1789 therefore sound superficially alike.

The lines of argument adopted by the authors are inversions of each other. Both men despised the Revolution. On the one hand, Treitschke read it as a threat toward Germany, because it unified France and threatened Alsatian specificity. On the other hand, Bainville considered 1789 had divided France and established a liberal foreign policy that was too pro-German. For him the Revolution had created a bizarre exchange of fortunes between France and Germany. Under the ancien régime it had been the French that had controlled German affairs through a successful policy of divide and rule. As a consequence of the Revolution this healthy state of affairs had ended.

The proximity of the arguments that Treitschke and Bainville developed is further illustrated in their representation of Napoleon. Treitschke suggests that Napoleon had developed a policy to destroy Germany. He teaches that Napoleon's project was to create a divided sovereignty by encouraging an Austro-Bavarian (Catholic) kingdom in the South of Germany. It was a French scheme to "bar the way against a real and powerful Germany," lead by the Prussian King.[19] Bainville is in agreement with much of this discussion when he considers that France must always adopt a policy of divide and rule toward Germany. Thus, Bainville's thinking corresponds to Treitschke's claim that France aims to prohibit a united Germany. The fundamental difference in perspectives is that Treitschke considers French policy to be a disgrace whereas Bainville praises it as a necessity.

While neither *Was fordern wir von Frankreich?* nor *Histoire de Deux Peuples* contains any overt anti-Semitic argument, this perspective unites the ardent Prussian nationalist and Parisian royalist. The historians' attitudes toward "the Jews" run in parallel. Treitschke supported popular German anti-Semitic movements and demanded that the German Jewish people assimilate completely into the national community. Furthermore, Treitschke deliberately links the perceived Jewish threat with France in his *Deutsche Geschichte im 19. Jahrhundert* (5 vols., 1879–94). Therein, and in popular newspaper articles as well, Treitschke despairs that German Jews are influencing public life without abandoning their "Jewish separatism." He claims that German Jews are responsible for the promotion of a dangerously positive image of France in the country. Treitschke suggests that the German Jews are especially sympathetic to Republican France. He identifies links between "the Jews" and France. According to his reasoning, he considers that the French, like the Jews, have broken with the idea of history. This means that neither people could be concerned with a true German love of the past because as "moderns" they reject history. For example, he asserts: "To the Jews German veneration of the past appeared ludicrous; but modern France had broken with her history, here they felt more at home in this raw new state."[20] Thereby, Treitschke associates his vision of the internal threat, the nonassimilating Jews, with the external rival the "French." In some publications, albeit not in *Histoire de Deux Peuples*, Bainville displays comparable anti-Jewish prejudice. For example, when confronted with empirical data that disproved the anti-Semitic slander the "Protocols of the Elders of Zion," he replied, "What does this prove about Bolsheviks and Jews? Absolutely nothing."[21] Writing in his published *Journal* he reflects further on "the problem of Jewry" in France. There he rehearses classic anti-Semitic claims that Jewish peoples are unable to become fully part of the French national community. Like Treitschke he identifies the Jews as outsiders from the national community. Bainville explains: "The Jew doesn't plant because he himself doesn't put down roots. He doesn't plant because his cast of mind perpetually tends towards abstraction."[22] Some years later, in 1912, he was to comment again that Paris must be defended from "all barbarities, the democratic barbarity, the Jewish barbarity."[23] Writing in his *Troisième République* (1935) he dismisses the established facts of the Dreyfus case (1898) and continues to throw suspicion on Dreyfus. Such comments serve to align Bainville very closely to Treitschkean nationalist anti-Semitic rhetoric.[24] Put boldly, Treitschke's Jewish-French alignment is replaced with Bainville's loosely implied Jewish-German conspiracy.

Bainville is inconsistent in his anti-Semitism. Research has indicated that in private he took up a position as a Dreyfusard, an interpretation that was completely out of sync with *Action française* and his treatment of the topic in his study, *Troisième République*. In letters to the husband of his cousin, he admitted that he considered Dreyfus was probably innocent.[25] There are other ambiguities in the record. Some years later, in 1935, his study of contemporary history, *Les Dictateurs*, includes a criticism of the Protocols of the Elders of Zion's slander. In the same book Bainville criticizes the absurd excesses of Hitler's Wagnerian neopaganism. Bainville concludes his analysis by stating that Hitler is France's most redoubtable enemy.[26] We conclude that Bainville's anti-Semitism is ambiguous. Close analysis of *Histoire de Deux Peuples* leads to the conclusion Bainville's mortal enemy is Germany and that France's primary historical error is the Revolution and the Republic. This is a reading of history that did not stop groups of *Action française* supporters from crying anti-Semitic abuse during Bainville's funeral on February 13, 1936. Pierre Birnbaum recalls the horrendous scene when royalist mourners spied that the politician Léon Blum was trapped in his car behind the funeral cortege. They cried out against Blum: "Kill him! Death to the Jew!"[27]

It is next important to draw attention to how the concept of race is used differently by the writers. Not every aspect of Treitschke's and Bainville's thinking neatly works as a mimetic replication of the other as we have already seen with regards to their treatment of religion and use of anti-Semitism. The comparison of the use of the concept of race by these authors shows that their mindsets were quite different on this important doctrine. Treitschke's work is far more colored by racist assumptions than is the case with the work of his French counterpart. The term *Volk* is consistently used by Treitschke, and it is on the basis of this concept that Treitschke claims that the Alsacians and Lothringians were Germans. Already in 1870, Treitschke confirms that German life is conserved in Alsace because the "Alemanic farmers" have stayed close to the earth and to nature. It is because of this ethnic-racial survival that the Alsatians will rediscover their home in the German state. It is a matter of nature and blood. Treitschke adds deep romantic myth as a further ingredient to the discourse when affirming that this type of mythological heritage further pulls Alsace to Germany.[28]

If one wants to generalize on Treitschke's idea of history and the relationship toward France contained in it, it is obvious to regard it as a first step in the development of the National Socialist idea of society and history. Treitschke uses *Völkisch* categories like blood, tribe, and soil. He characterizes *Volk* as a faith community that is influenced neither by particular interest nor by rational reasons. To see Treitschke as a forerunner of National Socialism (NS) is appropriate. A linkage not ignored by National Socialists themselves. He was an idol for NS historians like Walter Frank precisely because of these aspects.[29]

Bainville is unsystematic in his use of race thinking. He does not develop a full race theory in the manner of Treitschke's comments on the blood ties between Alsace and Germany. Nevertheless, he does assert that the German problem is because the "German race" has a propensity to wish to turn westward, to migrate, and to "live in other people's nests." Later, too, he profiles the French people in terms that evoke racist notions. Proudly, he underlines that despite the Revolution the ordinary Frenchman, through blood, is still able to fight and win the war of 1914. Thus, Bainville claims that French blood, biology, has triumphed over liberal politics and the error of 1789. However, almost contradicting this position, he expresses fears of the domination of race thinking in international relations. The precise short passage is to be found in the latter pages of *Histoire de Deux Peuples*. Here Bainville warns that if the idea of race becomes too popular it will be catastrophic for France and Europe because it will engender new and terrible wars. He implies that use of violent race thinking is a warrant for anarchy.[30] It is an anachronistic statement by a historian who is often best discussed in terms of the internal contradictions of his work.

Writing in 1902 Bainville declared some affection for the thinking of Friedrich Nietzsche. He explained that this German had delivered a helpful blow against moralists, democrats, and humanitarians. Reino Virtanen argues that besides Nietzsche there was also a debt to Treitschke, as well as the British conservatives Edmund Burke and Thomas Carlyle.[31] While these links are not discussed in any elaborate detail Bainville did once explain that Treitschke was a direct influence on his thinking. In 1903 he wrote that the German historians, from Mommsen to Treitschke, had taught some in France a lesson about love of national grandeur, and they instructed on the necessary conditions for order and authority. As this short acknowledgement to German historiography indicates, there are further direct similarities in the two historians' belief in the legitimacy of power politics.

Treitschke's discussion of the future status of Alsace-Lorraine reveals an overwhelming belief in "the right of the sword." Treitschke's idea of justice is not based on the idea of an obligatory set of European rights or a more universal set of human rights. Nor is it founded on a divine order, as in the work of his predecessor in Berlin, Leopold Ranke. Instead, for Treitschke all international decisions are to be founded on the idea of the right of the strongest power. Despite all the race theorizations, Treitschke admits that this is not perfect science and should not be used to shape all international affairs.[32] Instead, he acknowledges that the only determining factor in European border disputes should be power. He explains that language is not sufficient to organize state boundaries. This would be an impossible principal to implement. Hence, Germany must take those territories beyond the Rhine that are simply needed for its defense. The driving factor in European state relations is therefore pragmatic, military, authority. Towns like Metz and Belfort might be French-speaking areas, but their strategic importance means that they must be held by the victor, Germany.[33] This belief in pragmatism and power politics is distinctive from other German historians, who primarily used linguistic arguments in favor of the Germanization of Alsace. For example it was precisely on this basis that Theodor Mommsen in several newspaper articles had claimed Alsace to be German. It is also different from French historian Fustel de Coulanges' response to Mommsen's claims. De Coulanges suggests in his *Questions historiques* that the peoples of the border territory were French because they chose to be. For him, "will," not race or language, dictated nationality.[34] However, there are closer similarities to Treitschke's thinking in Bainville's considerations on international relations. The underlying philosophy that informs all of *Histoire de Deux Peuples* is the moral rights of the dominant nation. For Bainville, just like Treitschke before him, it is completely ethical that a dominant force, for him France, does all in its power to control and to limit the development of its rival. The rationale for engaging in this policy is self-defense, but this is just a small step from a policy of continued preemptive control, and dominance, of Germany. Like Treitschke, Bainville claims that an aggressive, proactive, foreign policy is justified by reasons of state. It contrasts from the earlier liberal French writers like Michelet, who wished for a "concert of nations" to protect European peace.

The possible influence of Treitschke's thinking on Bainville's authoritarianism is unusual. Far more commonly, nationalist historians provoke counterattacks from their enemies. This is the story of much of the reception of Treitschke in France. In 1899 the Swiss based historian Antoine Guilland wrote extensively about the dangers of new German nationalism that was exemplified by Treitschke. His work, published in French in Paris, is an authoritative and logical critique of the underlying politics of Treitschke's oeuvre.[35] During the First World War Emile Durkheim's analysis of Treitschke's historiography highlights how the historian rejected all common human values in favor of a brutal authoritarian nationalism. Durkheim's work was published in an important series of texts provided by intellectuals to assist in the war effort against Germany. It is an important, if now long forgotten, act of intellectual critique in the service of France.[36]

What of Bainville's reputation in Germany? It, too, would become a source of German war propaganda that well illustrated the pernicious nature of the French. Just as Treitschke appeared to confirm all of the worse French suspicions of the Germans in 1914, Bainville was to evoke comparable fears in Weimar and National Socialist Germany. By the interwar period, Bainville had become a notorious figure in Germany where his work was increasingly used to legitimate National Socialist expansionism against France. Thus, *Histoire des Deux Peuples* was translated by the legal scholar Friedrich Grimm and it was soon a popular and influential work. Specifically, it was read to justify the National Socialist policy of revision of the Treaty of Versailles. Bainville's anti-German book was used to justify a policy of German National Socialist retaliation against the "malicious" French. The NS argument ran that, if France had indeed pursued a policy of divide and rule against the Germans then, now was the time to stop this "injustice" and to "turn the tables." Remarkably, in 1940 the German edition of Bainville's book, *Frankreichs Kampf gegen die deutsche Einheit*, sold over 150,000 copies.[37] By 1941 Grimm was making a career out of criticizing the French foreign policies revealed in Bainville's writings. A young Belgian journalist, Paul de Man, noted Grimm's arguments in his column in the newspaper *Le Soir* on August 19, 1941. There de Man reflects that the tragedy of the contemporary period was that the French had not looked for collaboration with Germany long before the debacle of 1940. De Man names Bainville as being a significant cause of the French blindness toward Germany.[38]

In conclusion, this case study provides a snapshot of anti-French and anti-German nationalism in the period that preceded the First World War. It reveals that, despite the obvious antipathy, there are fundamental similarities at play. Regarding historiographic rhetoric, we find common tropes in the two publications: the association of the enemy with disease and violence; the nondiscussion of the enemy's homeland, a nonplace to be attacked. We have also suggested that there are deeper levels of shared thinking, not least in a crossnational hostility toward Republicanism and the Jewish community. We note the presence of race as a category of analysis in both of these writers' arguments. However, in the selected texts Bainville did not develop his use of this concept as fully as Treitschke. There is also the shared belief in the right of power to determine international relations. There is a more obvious confrontation regarding religious beliefs: a very direct contrast between Treitschke's Prussian Protestantism and Bainville's French Catholicism. Finally, these writings added to a vicious circle of Franco-German conflict. Rightly, Treitschke was cited in Paris as a particularly unpleasant force in German nationalism. Rightly, Bainville was read in Berlin as a hostile critic of Germany. Only after National Socialists, Vichy collaborators, and French fascists combined forces to plunge Europe in to human despair, did historians of this type fall into some disrepute.

Notes

1. See Michael Jeismann, *Das Vaterland der Feinde. Studien zum nationalen Feindbegriff und Selbstverständnis in Deutschland und Frankreich* (Stuttgart: Klett-Cotta, 1992); Christian Simon, *Staat und Geschichtswissenschaft in Deutschland und Frankreich 1871—1914: Situation und Werk von Geschichtsprofessoren an den Universitäten Berlin, München, Paris*, 2 vols. (Bern: Peter Lang, 1998); Christian Geulen, ed., *Vom Sinn der Feindschaft* (Berlin: Akademie, 2002); Michael E. Nolan, *The Inverted Mirror. Mythologizing the Enemy in France and Germany, 1898–1914* (Oxford: Berghahn, 2005).

2. Peter Schöttler, "The Rhine as an Object of Historical Controversy in the Inter-War Years," *History Workshop Journal* 39 (1995): 1–22.

3. For biographies of von Treitschke, see Walter Bußmann, *Treitschke. Sein Welt- und Geschichtsbild* (Göttingen: Muster-Schmidt, 1981); Ulrich Langer, *Heinrich von Treitschke. Politische Biographie eines deutschen Nationalisten* (Düsseldorf: Droste, 1998). See also Irmgard Ludwig, *Treitschke und Frankreich* (München: Oldenbourg, 1934).

4. See Emile Durkheim, *L'Allemagne au dessus de tout* (Paris: Armand Colin, 1914); Ernest Baker, "Nietzsche and Treitschke: The Worship of Power in Modern Germany," *Oxford Pamphlets* 20 (1914): 3–28; Cannon E. McClure, *Germany's War Inspirers* (Brighton: Society for Promoting Christian Knowledge, 1914); J. A. Cramb, *Germany and England* (London: John Murray, 1914). One year earlier, G. P. Gooch was more positive in *History and Historians in the Nineteenth Century* (London: Longman, 1913), 147–55.

5. See Hans Kohn "Treitschke: National Prophet," *The Review of Politics* 7, no. 4 (October 1945): 418–40; Stefan Breuer, *Nationalismus und Faschismus: Frankreich, Italien und Deutschland im Vergleich* (Darmstadt: Wissenschaftliche Buchgesellschaft, 2005).

6. See Jacques Bainville, *Louis II de Bavière* (Paris: Fayard, 1900); Bainville, *Le Coup d'Agadir et la guerre d'orient* (Paris: Nouvelle librairie nationale, 1913); Bainville, *Bismarck (Paris: Editions du Siècle, 1932)*; and Bainville, *L'Allemagne* (Paris: Librairie Plon, 1939).

7. Heinrich von Treitschke, *Was fordern wir von Frankreich?(1870)* in vol. 3 of *Aufsätze, Reden und Briefe*, ed. Heinrich von Treitschke (Meersburg: Hendel Verlag, 1929), 450–89. Herein see, *What We Demand from France* (London:

Macmillan, 1870). Jacques Bainville, *Histoire de Deux Peuples: la France et l'Empire Allemand* (Paris: Fayard, 1915).

8. Eugen Weber, *Action Française* (Stanford: Stanford University Press, 1962), 518.

9. The term *Welsch* was commonly used to describe all people who do not speak German. The expression is not tightly linked to race thinking but is usually defined as a cultural–linguistic term of derision.

10. Treitschke, *What We Demand From France*, 37.

11. Bainville, *Histoire de Deux Peuples*, 293–94.

12. René Girard, *To Double Business Bound* (Baltimore: Johns Hopkins University Press, 1988), 223.

13. See Heinrich von Treitschke, *Briefe*, vol. II, ed. Max Cornelius (Leipzig: Hirzel, 1914), 403.

14. Cited in Henri Rollet "Jacques Bainville, Dreyfusard. Lettres de 1898–1899," *Revue d'histoire diplomatique* 1 (1981): 78–80.

15. William R. Keylor, *Jacques Bainville and the Renaissance of Royalist Historiography in Twentieth Century France* (Baton Rouge: Louisiana State University Press, 1979), 14–15, 51–78. For discussion of the French vision of Germany as a "dual nation," see Allan Mitchell, "German History in France after 1870," *Journal of Contemporary History* 2, no. 3 (1967): 81–100; and Claude Digeon, *La Crise allemande de la pensée française* (Paris: Presses Universitaires de France, 1959).

16. Treitschke, *What We Demand from France*, 48, 73.

17. Ibid., 57–58.

18. See Bainville, *Histoire de Deux Peuples*, 285.

19. Treitschke, *What We Demand from France*, 101.

20. Heinrich von Treitschke, *Deutsche Geschichte im 19. Jahrhundert*, 5 vols. (Leipzig: Hirzel, 1879–94). For an English translation, see *History of Germany in the Nineteenth Century*, ed. Gordon Craig (Chicago: University of Chicago Press, 1975). For "Radicalism and the Jews" see p. 254 therein.

21. Cited by among others, Eugen Weber, *Action française* (Stanford: Stanford University Press, 1962), 201.

22. Cited in Stephen Wilson, "A View of the Past," 146. The remarks date from August 1905 and were reprinted in Bainville, *Journal* (Paris: Plon, 1945).

23. Cited in Rollet, "Jacques Bainville," 69.

24. Jacques Bainville, *Troisième République* (Paris: Fayard, 1935), 201–32.

25. Rollet, "Jacques Bainville," 71–72.

26. Jacques Bainville, *Les Dictateurs* (Paris: Denoël et Steele, 1935), 271–93. See also the final pages of the reprinted and expanded edition of *Histoire de Deux Peuples, continuée jusqu'à Hitler* (Paris: Fayard, 1936), 244–45; 251–2.

27. Pierre Birnbaum, *Un mythe politique: la République juivée* (Paris: Gallimard, 1995), 316.

28. Treitschke, *What We Demand from France*, 44.

29. See for example Walter Frank, "Eine Studie über Hermann Oncken," *Völkischer Beobachter*, February 3–4, 1935, 5–6.

30. Bainville, *Histoire de Deux Peuples*, 306–7.

31. See Bainville in *Enquête sur l'influence allemande*, ed. Jacques Morland (Paris: Société de Mercure de France, 1903), 22–23. See also Reino Virtanen, "Nietzsche and the Action Française: Nietzsche's significance for French Rightist Thought," *Journal of the History of Ideas* 11, no. 2 (1950), 194.

32. Treitschke, *What We Demand From France*, 39.

33. Ibid., 40.

34. Fustel de Coulanges, *Questions historiques* (Paris: Hachette, 1893).

35. Antoine Guilland, *L'Allemagne nouvelle et ses historiens* (Paris: Alcan, 1899).

36. Durkheim, *L'Allemagne au dessus de tout.*

37. Dominique Decherf, *Bainville: l'intelligence de l'histoire* (Paris: Bartillat, 2000), 387–88; see also Fritz Taubert "Friedrich Grimm—patriote et allemand, européen convaincu," in *Entre Locarno et Vichy. Les relations culturelles franco-allemandes dans les années 1930*, ed. Reinhart Meyer-Kalkus et al., 2 vols. (Paris: CNRS, 1993), 108–19.

38. Paul de Man, "Le Testament politique de Richelieu," *Le Soir*, August 19, 1941. Reprinted in Paul de Man, *Wartime Journalism* (Lincoln: University Nebraska Press, 1988), 135–36.

PART II

Franco-German Relations in Interwar Europe

CHAPTER 6

Franco-German Relations, 1918–45[1]

Sylvain Schirmann

Hardly a period in Franco-German relations was as dramatic as that which ran from the end of World War I to the surrender of Nazi Germany on May 8, 1945. France and Germany were each partly responsible for World War I, and their relationship formed the heart of the European problem in the interwar period. Nothing, however, was inevitable. The Treaty of Versailles did not actually preclude Franco-German reconciliation. Versailles need not have become a mechanism that perpetuated mutual grudges. In actuality, the brief episode from 1924 to 1929 witnessed significant progress toward rapprochement.

One can divide the period in Franco-German relations from 1918 to 1945 into several time stages. Immediately after World War I, Paris and Berlin began a time of "cold war" over the unresolved status of the Ruhr region. When Aristide Briand and Gustav Stresemann came into prominence, their policies ushered in a new stage of encouraging rapprochement. Stresemann's untimely death in October 1929 reversed this process, and the next few years were a time of crisis and regression for bilateral relations. Adolf Hitler's ascent in Germany brought yet another stage characterized by outright antagonism. The Reich held a strong advantage: not only had France's influence eroded, but the country would soon lose its independence. Finally, Nazi Germany's defeat in 1945 inaugurated a new order in Franco-German relations.

The Time of Cold War between France and Germany (1918–24)[2]

In the aftermath of World War I, the balance of power seemed to favor France. It emerged from the conflict as both military and moral victor, standing as one of the key pillars of the European order. French troops held the left bank of the

Rhine. Among Paris's allies were various nations of Central and Eastern Europe, which were arrayed along Germany's vulnerable backside. The Germans had lost territory in both the east and the west; their country had been disarmed and demilitarized. German economic power was under leash, and its government had ceded control of the Saar economy to a commission of the League of Nations. The Silesian Basin was returned to Poland; Danzig, with its strategic port, became a "free city" under protection of the League of Nations. Furthermore the economic dispositions of Versailles obliged Germany to unilaterally accord most-favored-nation trade status to France and to allow Alsatian and Lorrainian products to enter Germany tariff-free. These five-year measures undeniably favored France. When one also considers the burden of reparations, as stipulated by the Treaty of Versailles and the following reparations conferences, the strained position of the Reich becomes clear. Moreover, Germany was explicitly named in the treaty as having instigated hostilities. France basked in this moral victory.

Still, the German position was not without advantages. Territorial concessions had freed the Reich of certain nonindigenous and diasporic national groups (Danes, Alsace-Lorrainians, and Slavs), centered the German nation exclusively on its own people and reinforced Germany's cohesion. The new configuration of Central and Eastern Europe also meant there were now German minorities living in nearby states. Berlin could use the German diaspora as leverage to influence other parts of the Continent, thereby weakening the alliances that supported France. In addition, the German homeland had been neither razed nor destroyed. The economic might of the Reich was largely intact. There was, of course, the obligation for Germany to aid in rebuilding the European continent. Paris expected substantial reparations to help fund French reconstruction. The Treaty of Versailles affirmed this, but only in principle. It failed to specify either the precise amount of reparations due from the Reich or the means of payment. This lack of clarity presented a great opportunity for Germany, since France and Britain were not in complete agreement over the exact amounts and modalities of payments. The two victors ultimately agreed on the sum of 132 billion gold marks, which Germany was bound to respect. After some initial equivocation, France and Germany seemed to be making headway toward rapprochement. Louis Loucheur, the French Minister of Reconstruction, and Walter Rathenau, the German Minister of Foreign Affairs, met in Wiesbaden to sign a series of accords that would govern Germany's participation in French reconstruction. However, the Wiesbaden Agreement could not be implemented largely because of British opposition. As an alternative, the British proposed, toward the end of 1921, the creation of a European economic reconstruction fund in which Soviet Russia would be allowed to participate. The initiative was debated at the Cannes conference (December 1921 to January 1922) and then at the Genoa conference (April 1922) but was ultimately rejected by Raymond Poincaré, the new president of the French Council. Admittedly, the Gold Exchange Standard was adopted, but no resolution of the European question was reached. This drove Germany into the arms of Russia; the two countries signed the Rapallo treaty on

April 16, 1922, sealing their rapprochement. This move isolated Paris and disquieted the young states of Central and Eastern Europe.

It was Poincaré's decision to capitalize on the first shortfall by Germany in reparations payments and better France's fragile position. Poincaré's strategy was to make it one step toward a French Europe. Such an opportunity came at the end of 1922 when Germany missed a deadline for payment of in-kind reparations. On January 10, 1923, French, Belgian, and Italian troops seized control of factories and coal mines in the Ruhr area. France's occupation of the Ruhr region had begun. It met with staunch German resistance, orchestrated by the government of Chancellor Wilhelm Cuno. The general strike unleashed by the Germans clashed with the resolve of the French, who did not hesitate to shatter the movement through force. The situation brought Germany to the edge of financial bankruptcy and political implosion. France's aim was to detach the Rhine and Ruhr regions from German control. A customs barrier was erected to isolate western Germany from the Reich. Paris pressed for Rhineland autonomy and the creation of a separate currency. Nevertheless, France lacked the wherewithal to realize these ambitions: its meager fiscal resources and the instability of the franc were too large an obstacle. When, in September 1923, Gustav Stresemann, Germany's new Chancellor, entreated his countrymen to cease resisting, the two countries opened negotiations, and Paris readily agreed to participate since the chief issue at stake, reparations, would be treated in the presence of the Americans. Jacques Bariéty's scholarship has largely verified that Poincaré's true intent in seeking Ruhr coal was to bring the Americans into the European game. Because Paris could not obtain the American guarantee it had hoped for, it aimed to tie the United States into overseeing reparations and thereby gain a measure of security against German non-compliance.

The Dawes Plan, adopted in April 1924, responded in large part to the expectations of the two antagonists, France and Germany. A loan, more than half of whose amount was guaranteed by the United States, was awarded to Germany. Germany, in turn, would issue up to 10 billion marks in additional reparations payments in the succeeding five-year period. The installments were progressively scheduled so as not to adversely impact the German economy. Moreover, a general agent in charge of reparations, Parker Gilbert of the United States, was empowered to exempt Germany from transfers of reparations in case of economic or financial crisis. However, the German government was obligated to provide guarantees in the form of mortgages on the Reichsbahn and a number of the country's leading industrial enterprises. The Dawes Plan also further encouraged European economic prosperity, because it was linked to hefty U.S. investment in Germany and Central and Eastern Europe. The plan facilitated Franco-German rapprochement by temporarily removing the motives for bilateral conflict and charting a path for the departure of French forces from the Ruhr area.

The Time of Franco-German Rapprochement (1924–29)[3]

The Ruhr issue and the Dawes Plan negotiations led to the downfall of Poincaré in the 1924 elections. The leftist coalition, the *Cartel des gauches*, and the new Council President, radical Edouard Herriot, modified the course of French foreign policy. Herriot hearkened to the cause of collective security and aimed to make the League of Nations the cornerstone of peace in Europe. Encouraged by the British, the German government, and notably Stresemann, the French authorities dispatched a memorandum in early 1925 regarding the issue of French security. Herriot was caught up in dealing with a financial crisis and could not respond personally to the Berlin leadership. The issue fell instead to Aristide Briand. Since 1921, Briand had perceived France's weakness and concluded the politics of force were no longer the best strategy. As France's new foreign policy chief, Briand felt it essential that Germany be integrated into the European concert so it might be inclined to recognize French borders. In Berlin, Gustav Stresemann was similarly committed to dialogue with Paris, having identified this as the only way to loosen the restraints weighing upon the Reich. His aim was to negotiate so Germany could regain equality of rights with the other powers. Thus in the summer of 1925, a Franco-German dialogue was begun that would prove too superficial to survive the death of Stresemann in October 1929.

The Locarno conference in October 1925, and the Rhine Pact signed during the conference, coaxed Germany into acknowledging its western borders and gave France an implicit guarantee that it would not dispute its territory. In turn, these treaties were also a reassurance to Germany, since they functioned as a deterrent against future clashes similar to what had happened in the Ruhr. Nevertheless, Berlin did not actually pledge restraint in Central and Eastern Europe, which suggested that German revisionist aims in Europe had not been quenched by Locarno. The pact had the primary consequence of awarding Germany entry into the League of Nations in September 1926, and as a member of the permanent council. By accepting this invitation, Berlin had tacitly acknowledged the borders of the other member states, but Germany now had a means to leverage its diaspora, using it as an excuse to influence national minority policy in Eastern Europe, since the League of Nations acted as defender of these groups' rights.

In 1926, the Nobel Peace Prize was awarded dually to Briand and Stresemann for having been the two principal architects of Franco-German rapprochement. A year later, France and Germany signed their only bilateral treaty of the interwar period, the Franco-German Commercial Treaty of August 1927. This commercial accord extended general and unconditional most-favored-nation status to both signatories.[4] Earlier in May 1927, following the international economic conference, Paris and Berlin had also accorded each other most-favored-nation trading status. This signaled the intent of both countries to enter a privileged partnership and gradually abandon protectionism. The volume of bilateral trade swiftly increased, and the balance, until then favorable to France, clearly tipped in favor of Germany. Paris calculated this concession might solidify the peace.

Furthermore, in 1928 Briand approached the Americans with a multilateral pact designed to consolidate peaceful relations. The resulting Briand-Kellog Pact was signed in Paris in August of that year, but it did not fulfill all of the French foreign minister's hopes. The signatories, which included Germany, renounced war as a means for settling disputes, though the treaty included no automatic guarantees to that effect. France soon saw its position weakened when Germany called for French withdrawal from the left bank of the Rhine, since there was no apparent justification for a continued French armed presence after the signature of the Paris treaty. The bulk of 1929 was then dedicated to negotiations over the anticipated Young Plan—a successor to the Dawes Plan—that proposed a hopefully lasting solution to the issue of reparations. Payment would occur in (1) unconditional installments that Germany must deliver regardless of circumstance and (2) conditional installments that would be linked to fulfillment of interallied debt owed to the United States. International loans were issued to benefit Germany and a new international body, the Bank for International Settlements, was established to oversee payments between sovereign nations. These mechanisms were scheduled to serve a fifty-nine-year duration; they were also supposed to underpin economic stability in Europe, though this proved elusive. The Young Plan was supposed to eliminate a long-standing Franco-German bone of contention. A further gesture of conciliation came with Briand's proposal of September 5, 1929, that a *"lien federal"* (federal link) be created in Europe, with Paris and Berlin standing as joint guarantors of the peace.

The five years that elapsed under the Dawes Plan and Briand's leadership are evidence that Versailles did not preclude Franco-German rapprochement. The political calculations of Briand and Stresemann had fostered Franco-German linkages, and this endeavor was aided by economic prosperity and the existing Europeist movement. National aspirations also lurked below the surface, with Briand considering rapprochement an expedient to restrain Germany and prevent a shift to revisionist politics. The bilateral dialogue reinforced the security of France and preserved a configuration of European politics favorable to the interests of Paris. On the German side, Stresemann used rapprochement to help emphasize the legitimate basis for his country's demands and to open the possibility for adjustment of the Versailles terms. As long as the dialogue yielded mutual concessions, the relationship progressed. However, this quid-pro-quo also exemplified the fragility of the arrangement. The economic prosperity that followed the U.S. investments in Europe yielded bilateral rapprochement, which Washington, London, and the Europeist movement supported. The Europeists, and particularly militants such as Coudenhove with his Pan-Europe movement, favored a united Europe where France and Germany would play the roles of model and motor to help pacify the continent. Certain Catholic circles (Marc Sangnier, Maurice Vaussard) hoped for such reconciliation and counted on the youth to help accomplish this. Economic and intellectual elites rallied around the idea. For example, there was the Franco-German Committee for Information and Documentation and the Colpach circle, organized by Luxembourg industrialist Emile Mayrisch. It was Mayrisch who, in 1926, was the driving force behind the first international steel entente, which regrouped the producers of Belgium, Luxembourg, France, and Germany. Industrialists on both sides of the Rhine flocked together more and more frequently in the cartels that were formed in Europe during this period of economic prosperity. These groups approved of Locarno, the trade treaty from 1927, and Briand's initiative from 1929. Regrettably, this would mark the apogee of the Franco-German dialogue. Could the Reich truly endorse the idea of a federal link in Europe that would compel it to relinquish any claim to revision of the Treaty of Versailles? France had proposed a treaty that, if accepted, would have forced Germany to abandon its ambitions in Central and Eastern Europe. Suppose Germany had then fielded a counterproposal, demanding as a concession redress for the injustices imposed at Versailles? The resulting compromise might have enabled the countries to move in the direction envisioned by Briand. However, could the French leadership ever agree to such a concession? The death of Stresemann in 1929 rendered all of these questions irrelevant and deprived Briand of his negotiating partner. In this troubled context, marked by the revival of national propaganda in Germany and economic disarray following the New York Stock Exchange's "Black Tuesday," progress would be difficult to achieve.

The Time of Crisis (1929–33)[5]

Stresemann's successor, Julius Curtius, and the new Secretary of State, Bernhard Wilhelm von Bülow, gauged the time was ripe for a reignition of German revisionist sentiment. The departure of French troops from the left bank of the Rhine and the prevailing climate of hostility toward France allowed the Reich to strive against the restrictions that impinged on its sovereignty. Facing economic crisis, heavily indebted Germany began to question its reparations burden, and harbor concerns over its foreign commercial and financial relations. The conditions presented Reich authorities with an opportunity to regain equality of rights with the other powers. The compliance of the French government was by no means certain. Paris's strength lay in its control over finance and it could become a weapon.

The authorities at the *Auswärtiges Amt* greeted Briand's memorandum with a lukewarm response. They were hardly enamored of the proposed community institutions. Following the creation of the Study Commission for a European Union Berlin had made no secret of its aims to secure membership for the Soviet Union and Turkey, both of whose opposition to the prevailing European order had aligned them with the Reich's interests. Germany enjoyed other advantages as well. The economic crisis revived the idea of rapprochement between Germany and Austria. March 1931 gave way to the Curtius-Schoeber project, which proposed a customs union between the two countries. French leaders could not tolerate this prospect, a sentiment echoed by the United Kingdom. Paris and London exerted pressure on Berlin to abandon the effort, which it did in autumn 1931. Nevertheless, Germany's economic plight and Austria's financial difficulties, which began in May 1931, could not simply be ignored by France. The French authorities were willing to increase aid to Austria (through the League of Nations or initiatives such as the Tardieu Plan, named after French Council President André Tardieu) but were more reluctant to assist Germany. When the weakness of Germany's banking system became apparent, U.S. president Herbert Hoover suggested a one-year moratorium on intergovernmental debts. The proposal applied to reparations but did not cover most interallied debts, which were of a private nature. The Laval government gave half-hearted approval to Hoover's plan. On July 18, 1931, Chancellor Brüning traveled to Paris to meet Pierre Laval, Council President, and Briand, Minister of Foreign Affairs. Brüning hoped to secure assistance that would enable him to overcome the financial difficulties plaguing the Reich. If Laval offered him a substantial lump-sum payment, he would match it with political guarantees. Paris demanded a cease to German rearmament, recognition of all standing European borders, and the silencing of revisionist intentions for the next decade. However, Brüning, pressured by the nationalist and extremist right, could not accede to France's demands. Even in September 1931 when a mixed, Franco-German economic commission was inaugurated in Berlin, feelings of suspicion and mistrust were thick between the two Rhineland neighbors. These tensions were subsequently mirrored in all aspects of the two countries' relations.

In the commercial sphere, Germany and France relaunched their trade war. French business circles clamored for quotas that would restrict German imports. The Franco-German cartels that flourished in the late 1920s collapsed and new examples of bilateral cooperation became rare (only three instances in 1932). Germany's response was to practice export dumping and impose strict regulations on French agricultural products. However, the Reich's strongest response was in regard to the control of the exchange rate. After a yearlong negotiation, Paris and Berlin agreed in December 1932 to modify the treaty signed in 1927. The new texts fixed the compensation in commercial payments and abolished the most-favored-nation clause. A Franco-German office of commercial payments seconded by the Paris Chamber of Commerce would administer the new arrangement.

In the diplomatic sphere, the Franco-German debate was dominated by three issues: the reorganization of Europe, the problem of reparations, and the conference on disarmament. The reorganization of Europe placed France and Germany in direct opposition. Paris advocated a regionalist economic policy in Central and Eastern Europe that would benefit its allies. In 1932, France called for the creation of a common market of Danube countries, consisting of Hungary, Austria, and the three nations of the Little Entente. To ensure currency stability, the new market arrangement would be endowed with French capital. In September 1932 at the Stresa conference, French diplomats proposed the revaluation of cereal prices to favor Eastern European nations. The idea met with little success. In failing to field a viable commercial policy, Paris gave the Reich an opening in which to advance its own set of bilateral accords with Eastern Europe. The accords of 1931 and 1932 between Germany and the Danube countries embraced both trade in industrial goods, and trade in agricultural products and raw materials. This aggressive use of bilateralism enabled Berlin to make progress in a diplomatic realm that Paris had formerly dominated. The system of alliances erected by France was beginning to crumble. Paris's inability to resolve the Eastern European crisis at a time of heavy German trade penetration in these countries left France isolated in two important areas: reparations and disarmament.

The states undertook to run dry the deep quagmire of reparations at Lausanne in early summer 1932. From the opening of the conference on June 16, 1932, there was a clear struggle between France and Germany, supported by Great Britain, over the annulment of reparations. For Herriot, security was the prime issue. He would not waive reparations without an agreement on disarmament. Paris envisioned concessions on the order of payment reductions or a final lump-sum transfer but opposed outright forgiveness of reparations. Berlin on the contrary wanted reparations to be annulled but in exchange was prepared to sanction a customs union between the two countries and reinforce commercial cooperation in Europe and equality of rights with respect to armaments. The German government also argued for a military entente underpinned by summits with the principal powers. Herriot refused the German terms on July 7, 1932. The following day, an imprudent Gentlemen's Agreement was concluded between the United Kingdom, Germany, France, Italy, and Belgium. Germany was obligated to pay a final reparations balance of three billion gold marks. Any further reparations claims against Germany would be waived, contingent however, on America's voidance of corresponding interallied debts.

Lausanne was a grievous setback for France. It had conceded reparations cuts, but by failing to link the gesture to German concessions on disarmament, France's position was dramatically weakened in the following Geneva conference, where disarmament issues were discussed in detail. The Reich refused to participate unless it was granted full military autonomy. Britain lent its support, and the German maneuver succeeded, winning the Reich military equal status on December 11, 1932. France was isolated in Europe, and the balance of power was shifting inexorably to Berlin. Thus, before the ascendance of Hitler to power (January 30, 1933), Germany had utilized the economic crisis to shake off the fetters of the Versailles Treaty. Its reparations obligation had been annulled. With regards to disarmament should the Reich rearm, its partners would disarm. Berlin had leapfrogged Paris to assume the leading role in Central and Eastern Europe, due in large part to its tactics of economic complementarity. The result was a power imbalance in favor of the Reich that Hitler would gladly inherit.

The Time of Antagonism (1933–40)[6]

The writings and speeches of Hitler left no doubt of his opinion: France was the enemy to destroy as it would always obstruct Germany in its quest to occupy the "vital area" to the east. In the eyes of Nazi leaders, a war was not only inevitable but also manifestly desirable. Only then could the Reich realize its goal of controlling and subjugating other European nations. It was a natural response to the racial vision of the *Volk*. It was therefore necessary to prepare for the coming conflict and recreate a German army worthy of the name. Beginning in 1933, the early rudiments of the future German war economy—ruled by autarchy, aggressive commerce abroad—and control over foreign exchange and clearings were set in place. Domestically, commercial policy steered German industry into activities useful to the production of arms. The measures led to tight control of an economy now fully oriented toward military production. Living standards were affected, but the relative frugality of domestic consumption was overshadowed by Germany's foreign policy successes. The Nazi regime was also recognized for its markedly effective employment policy. These events understandably disquieted Paris, which stood in relative isolation. The French government struggled with ministerial crisis after ministerial crisis, which sparked political activism in the form of leagues. At international summits, Paris was unable to gather support for its views. For instance, a French-envisioned "Gold Block" composed of Belgium, the Netherlands, Switzerland, Italy and Poland proved unviable because it priced the goods of bloc members out of international markets. The breaking point came in 1933 when the Reich opted to quit the League of Nations and not participate in disarmament talks. Paris did not object, leading its allies to question France's ability to shield them from the growing German menace. Poland first manifested this doubt officially when it signed a nonaggression pact with the Reich in January 1934.

Hitler's rise in Germany would have presumably elicited menacing attitudes from France. The French political elite, however, was divided into two camps: leaders such as Edouard Daladier and André François-Poncet, who favored broaching a tentative entente with Berlin, and others such as Joseph Paul-Boncour, who urged that no action be taken unless the United Kingdom could be secured as a partner. If Berlin still sought an integral revision of the Versailles treaty, caution would be needed to avoid a preemptive war initiated by Paris. As a measure calculated to deescalate the conflict, Hitler pledged before the Reichstag on May 17, 1933 not to seek revision of the Versailles Treaty except through peaceful means. He additionally called for nonaggression pacts to be signed with all of Germany's neighbor states. Impressed with these declarations, the United Kingdom counseled France to adopt a moderate policy and pressed it to sign the Pact of Four, an initiative of Benito Mussolini that stipulated the powers (Germany, France, Italy, and the United Kingdom) could modify the European status quo via unanimous agreement. On July 7, 1933, Hitler was officially offered his seat at the table of European leaders. Shortly after on July 20, the Concordat with the Vatican enabled the government to divide the "moral opposition" that it had engendered throughout the world. Hitler was poised to enjoy a strong advantage for the remainder of 1933, considering that he had accumulated recognition through his numerous diplomatic successes and elevated his party to the dominant position in Germany by July 14, 1933.

The Reich then strove to make France appear as the intransigent partner. First, it was the French government that objected to German rearmament and effectively compelled Berlin to abandon rearmament talks and even quit the League of Nations on October 14, 1933. The decision to withdraw from the League had met with overwhelming support from the German people (92 percent in a

November 12, 1933, plebiscite). Second, it was Paris that resumed the trade war in January 1934 by denouncing the commercial treaty of 1927. However, Paris had little option since the currency exchange controls imposed by Germany had handicapped French exports. France was at a disadvantage and chose to mimic the United Kingdom's policy of avoiding any action that would demonize Hitler. The situation changed with the arrival of Louis Barthou to the Ministry of Foreign Affairs. In 1934 he resolved to free his country from alignment with London and aimed to contain the German threat. This spurred the Ministry to approach the Soviet Union and Italy and to tighten links with allies in Central and Eastern Europe. In July 1934, during the attempted coup of the national-socialists in Austria, Paris lauded Mussolini for positioning his troops on the Brenner. Barthou's leadership was short-lived, though: three months afterward he was assassinated along with King Alexander of Yugoslavia. On the surface, Laval, Barthou's replacement, appeared to espouse almost identical policies. However, the new leading voice at the Quai d'Orsay would not confine himself strictly to the compositions penned by Barthou. Laval thought a network of tentative alliances and rapprochement with the Reich would guarantee French security. This prompted him to declare on the occasion of the Saar plebiscite in 1935 that the Saar "was German" and that France should accept the remilitarization of the Reich, which Hitler announced in the spring of that year. The Stresa front imagined by Paris, Rome, and London to contain the German threat was irreparably shattered once the diverging interests of the three powers became clear. On the anniversary of the victory at Waterloo (July 1935), the United Kingdom signed a naval treaty with Nazi Germany. Mussolini launched his Ethiopian campaign and concluded that it was preferable to make overtures to Berlin rather than count on his allies from Stresa. On March 7, 1936, one month before key elections in Paris, Hitler dispatched forces to occupy the left bank of the Rhine and—in direct contravention of existing treaties—remilitarized the region. French Council President Albert Sarraut was indignant, but French military leaders could not afford to indulge in outrage. Instead, they recommended a course of prudence, one in keeping with the conciliatory stance adopted by Britain. Hitler perched his troops directly on France's borders. The Reich had recovered full sovereignty on the territory granted to it by the Treaty of Versailles. To pursue the program of the Nazis, the Reich needed only to intensify rearmament. In April 1936, Hitler set his nation to this task and appointed Göring to supervise the effort.

What was the Front Populaire to do in the face of national-socialist Germany? Léon Blum distrusted Hitler but chose nonetheless to pursue the conservative path of collective security and reliance on the League of Nations. Paris stood passive during hostilities in Spain, denying meaningful assistance to the Spanish Republicans and allowing Hitler to exploit the country's civil war as a training ground for his own forces. By autumn 1936, the Axis had been created. Paris continued to align itself with the British position, joining the United Kingdom in its efforts to appease the Reich. The logic was that economic concessions might be able to "buy peace". In late 1936, a Western trust was created in Paris by Britain, Italy, France, and the Reich to control raw materials. Why not offer colonial concessions in order to gain German concessions in Europe? In 1937, Paris signed an accord governing coke and iron production; this would supply the Reich with the iron ore needed for rearmament. The exchange was further enshrined in a trade agreement that followed. France maintained its policy of appeasement even as Austria was annexed in March 1938 and Czechoslovakia portioned. For French authorities, Munich, in particular, was critical, since it inaugurated the politics of "zones of influence." Their decision to abandon Central and Eastern Europe to the Reich's control was calculated to prolong the peace. France had prepared still further concessions: mixed Franco-German corporations in the colonies and joint commercial structures controlled by the two countries. March 1939 witnessed the total disappearance of Czechoslovakia as a nation, and Germany emerged with a fresh set of demands—this time concerning Poland. France confronted the bitter truth: its policy of appeasement had failed, and Hitler would not be sated. At that point, war was inevitable.

The Time of War (1940–45)[7]

By June 25, 1940, France was overrun and an armistice was signed. Franco-German relations devolved into a relationship of forced collaboration with France. Under the armistice, France was divided into multiple zones. Three-fifths of the territory was designated a German-controlled zone. Italy was accorded a small zone in the Alps. The remaining territory to the south was declared a "free zone" and left to the administration of the French government. All costs of occupation were to be borne by France. The French army was reduced and ordered to surrender its arms and equipment; France's navy was demobilized. Nevertheless, France's colonial Empire remained intact. Why did Hitler spare a country whose government had collapsed? The reality was Hitler desired to preserve a French government sufficient to oversee day-to-day management of the occupation; it would lift the burden from his own personnel. He also calculated that French citizens might be more tolerant of occupation if it was imposed under the façade of self-government. In any event, defeat in World War II spelled death for France's Third Republic. The succeeding "French state" and National Revolution were artifacts of a France reshaped to serve German needs.

On the foreign policy stage, Marshal Philippe Pétain and other French elites chose open collaboration with the Reich. By November 11, 1942 the entirety of France had fallen under occupation. The new French state imposed policies that were authoritarian, anti-Communist, and anti-Semitic, and its longevity was predicated on further victories by Germany. Vichy France perceived its interests lay in enthusiastic collaboration with the occupiers but with enough restraint to maintain support from at least a majority of French citizens. This policy suited Germany brilliantly. It was the best assurance the Reich could obtain that France would fulfill its financial, economic, and social obligations. Germany was correct in assuming that the Vichy government would ensure stability; the puppet state successfully maintained calm and social order in France throughout the major part of the war. Through such acts of collaboration, the French state hoped to win less stringent treatment for native Frenchmen and support for the National Revolution that would contribute to anchoring the reactionary regime. Vichy France could also be called upon by the Reich to participate in joint actions against left-wingers and the Resistance. Pétain and Laval, the council vice-president, had effectively bet on Germany's victory. Collaboration was a means to reserve some status for France in a German-dominated Europe and to safeguard the Empire.

Such designs were condemned by the Resistance and the Free French. The French National Liberation Committee and its successor, the Provisional Government of the French Republic (PGFR), had focused its sights on Germany since 1943. Its primary motive was one of vengeance. According to its dogma, the preponderance of guilt lay with the Reich. As a long-term goal, the PGFR aspired to restore security to France and all of Europe, something that German aggression had long prevented. Consequently, the Free French first sought to weaken and dismember the Reich. This shed light on General de Gaulle's ambition to obtain a seat for the PGFR at the Allied negotiating table and to demand that France be allocated an occupation zone. Since 1943, some at Algiers, the stronghold of the Free French, had dreamed of ensconcing Germany in a grand new Europe that would be organized along the lines of a federation. De Gaulle also envisioned a united Western Europe with France at its helm; however, he was pragmatic enough to put this objective off and to focus on dismantling Nazi Germany. Did France have in 1945 the resources necessary to carry out such a project? Before it could truly turn its attention to postwar Germany, France would have to address its own need for reconstruction.

Conclusion

Undeniably in a strong position at the end of World War I, in 1945 France was again among the victors, but, unlike the previous experience at Versailles, it enjoyed much less freedom to dictate terms regarding Germany. Postwar dispositions would be settled by the Allies as a group, and the specifics hinged on the demands of two new players: the United States of America and the Soviet Union. Franco-German relations, first dominated by Paris and then by Berlin in the 1930s and during the occupation, could no longer be shaped by conflict and the competition for supremacy. Attempts at hegemony, both French-led and German-led, had failed repeatedly. The interwar period of rapprochement was marred by thinly concealed nationalist ambitions. It was followed by a devastating and climactic struggle that underscored how Paris and Berlin had failed to learn from the experience of World War I and develop new modes of interaction. Only after a second and more terrible conflict did the seeds for genuine cooperation emerge, beginning a new order in Franco-German relations that would deliver these two neighbors of the Rhine into peaceful coexistence.

Notes

1. Raymond Poidevin, Jacques Bariety, *Les relations franco-allemandes 1815–1975* (Paris: A. Colin, 1977), 377; Raymond Poidevin, *L'Allemagne et le monde au XXe siècle* (Paris: Masson, 1983), 292; Sylvain Schirmann, *Quel ordre européen? De Versailles à la chute du IIIe Reich* (Paris: A. Colin, 2006), 335.

2. Jacques Bariety, *Les relations franco-allemandes après la première guerre mondiale* (Paris: Pedone, 1977), 797; Paul Letourneau, *Walter Rathenau 1867–1922* (Strasbourg: Presses Universitaires de Strasbourg, 1995), 271; Stanislas Jeannesson, *Poincaré, la France et la Ruhr (1922–1924). Histoire d'une occupation* (Strasbourg: Presses Universitaires de Strasbourg, 1998), 432; Ragna Boden, *Die Weimarer Nationalversammlung und die deutsche Außenpolitik* (Frankfurt am Main: Peter Lang, 2000), 191; Karl J. Mayer, *Die Weimarer Republik und das Problem der Sicherheit in den deutsch-französischen Beziehungen, 1918–1925* (Frankfurt am Main: Peter Lang, 1990), 216; Klaus Schwabe, ed., *Die Ruhrkrise 1923* (Paderborn: F. Schöning, 1984), 111.

3. Jacques Bariety, ed., *Aristide Briand, la Société des Nations et l'Europe, 1919–1932* (Strasbourg: Presses Universitaires de Strasbourg, 2007), 542; Christian Baechler, *Gustav Stresemann (1878-1929) De l'impérialisme à la sécurité collective* (Strasbourg: Presses Universitaires de Strasbourg, 1996), 956; Matthias Schulz, *Deutschland, der Völkerbund und die Frage der europäischen Wirtschaftsordnung 1925–1933* (Hamburg: Krämer, 1997), 478; Franz Knipping, *Deutschland, Frankreich und das Ende der Locarno-Ära 1928–1931* (München: Oldenburg, 1978), 261; Jean Marie Valentin, Jacques Bariety, and Alfred Guth, *La France et l'Allemagne entre les deux guerres mondiales* (Nancy: Presses Universitaires de Nancy, 1987), 244.

4. Zara Steiner, *The Lights that Failed: European International History 1919–1933* (Oxford: Oxford University Press, 2005), 400.

5. Hans Manfred Bock, Reinhardt Meyer-Kalkus, Michel Trebitsch, eds., *Entre Locarno et Vichy. Les relations culturelles franco-allemandes dans les années 1930*, 2 vols. (Paris: CNRS Editions, 1993), 891; Willy A. Boelcke, *Deutschland als Welthandelsmacht 1930–1945* (Stuttgart: Kohlhammer, 1994), 234; Sylvain Schirmann, *Crise, coopération économique et financière entre Etats européens 1929–1933* (Paris: CHEFF, 2000), 401; Hermann Graml, *Zwischen Stresemann und Hitler. Die Außenpolitik der Präsidialkabinette Brüning, Papen und Schleicher* (München: Oldenburg, 2001), 259.

6. CNRS, *Les relations franco-allemandes 1933–1939, Actes du colloque de Strasbourg 7–10 Octobre 1975* (Paris: Editions du CNRS, 1976), 424; CNRS, *La France et l'Allemagne 1932–1936, Actes du colloque de Paris, 10–12 mars 1977* (Paris: Editions du CNRS, 1980), 417; Wilhelm Deist, Manfred Messerschmidt, Hans-Erich Volkmann, Wolfram Wette, *Ursachen und Voraussetzungen des Zweiten Weltkrieges* (Frankfurt am Main: Fischer, 1989), 951; Wolfgang Geiger, *L'image de la France dans l'Allemagne nazie 1933–1945* (Rennes: Presses Universitaires de Rennes, 1999), 412; Robert W. Mühle, *Frankreich und Hitler 1933–1935* (Paderborn: Schöningh, 1995), 406; Stephan A. Schuker, ed., *Deutschland und Frankreich. Vom Konflikt zur Aussöhnung. Die Gestaltung der westeuropäischen Sicherheit 1914–1963* (München: Oldenburg, 2000), 280; Sylvain Schirmann, *Les relations économiques et financières franco-allemandes 1932–1939* (Paris: CHEFF, 1995), 304; Karl Rohe, ed., *Die Westmächte und das Dritte Reich 1933–1939* (Paderborn:

Schöningh, 1982), 231; Franz Knipping, Klaus-Jürgen Müller, eds., *Machtbewusstein in Deutschland am Vorabend des Zweiten Weltkrieges* (Paderborn: Schöningh, 1984), 390. Hans-Jürgen Döscher, *Das Auswärtige Amt im Dritten Reich. Diplomatie im Schatten der "Endlösung"* (Berlin: Siedler, 1987), 333; Charles Bloch, *Le IIIe Reich et le Monde* (Paris: Imprimerie Nationale, 1986), 545.

7. Philippe Burrin, *La France à l'heure allemande 1940–1944* (Paris: Seuil, 1995), 560; Pascal Ory, *La France allemande (1933–1945)* (Paris: Gallimard Folio-Histoire, 1995), 371; Annie Lacroix-Riz, *Industriels et banquiers sous l'occupation. La collaboration économique avec le Reich et Vichy* (Paris: A. Colin, 1999), 661; Eberhard Jäckel, *La France dans l'Europe de Hitler* (Paris: Fayard, 1968), 554.

CHAPTER 7

Franco-German Relations and the Coal Problem in the Aftermath of the First and Second World Wars

From Bilateral Conflict to European Energy Cooperation

Laura Fasanaro

Coal and coke were of major importance in the Franco-German puzzle during the first half of the twentieth century, coal being the main energy resource in Europe and coke being a rarer coal by-product necessary for the steel industry. Both of these commodities were concentrated near the Franco-German border. France in particular suffered from a structural dependence on imports of coal and coke from the Ruhr basin in order to fuel its national steel industry, which Paris planned to relaunch after each world war. For its part, Germany was a major European coal exporter with a strong metallurgical industry. Despite the growing prominence of oil during the interwar period, the primary and diversified use of coal by European populations and by industry made that resource into a political conundrum for European and transatlantic diplomatic relations from the end of the First World War onward.[1]

This chapter will explain why Franco-German competition for coal turned into French-led military action in the aftermath of the Great War, namely the occupation of the Ruhr basin, whereas after the Second World War, it paved the way for European integration. An interpretation of Franco-German interdependence and rivalry in the coal and steel sector is given here by means of a comparative approach examining both the early 1920s and the late 1940s. The chapter first points out some analogous aspects of the German problem in the two postwar periods and the similar position initially defended by France against its wartime allies in each instance, seeking alternative solutions, such as the creation of a frontier between Germany and the Ruhr and the establishment of an international administration of the region. Second, the chapter stresses the different kinds of solutions developed by the French leadership in subsequent years of political and economic recovery. Eventually, this culminated in the use of force against Germany in 1923, whereas French leaders opted for a novel agreement in 1950–51 by which France finally managed to gain control over German coal producing areas and particularly the Ruhr basin through the first successful example of supranational cooperation in Europe, the European Coal and Steel Community (ECSC).

Among the numerous factors influencing Franco-German relations and the settlement of the energy issue, three will be examined here. The first is the French leadership—the political beliefs of Raymond Poincaré in 1922–23 and Robert Schuman in 1948–50 and the influence of pressure groups on the French Foreign Ministry in particular. The second factor is the network of economic ties between the industries of the two countries, reflecting Franco-German interdependence more than rivalry. The third is France's position toward its major allies, namely the diplomacy of coal and steel among France, Britain, and the United States.

The issue of coal and steel after the Great War is part of the historical debate on French and German war aims and peace objectives,[2] the problem of reparations and interallied debts,[3] and the political and military preparation for the Ruhr invasion by France.[4] On the other hand, more specialized works on coal as a European problem in postwar reconstruction mostly focus on the aftermath of 1945.[5] Franco-German political and economic relations after Potsdam, moreover, have been thoroughly explored.[6] This chapter further investigates the numerous connections between Germany's interallied occupation, the rise of the cold war, and the beginnings of European integration.

France's German Policy after the Two World Wars: Security, Coal, and the Recovery of the Steel Industry

In 1919 and 1945, France's German policy focused on preventing unrestrained economic recovery and avoiding the reemergence of German expansionism. Security against Germany was at the core of French public debate and interallied talks. Control over the Ruhr resources in particular was both a domestic and a foreign policy issue for the French government.

After the Great War, France advocated the end of Germany's territorial unity—specifically, the French sought an independent Rhineland or, alternatively, a permanent occupation of that region—as a solution to both its economic and strategic problems.[7] Contrary to the initial expectations of France, however, the Treaty of Versailles confirmed Germany's western borders, with the exception of Alsace-Lorraine. The economic organization of the Ruhr and access to its resources thus remained crucial issues in France: The basin represented the pivot of Germany's economic power and of its war industry. Additionally, whether as reparations or as simple exports, the Ruhr would provide coal and coke, the essential resources to fuel the French steel industry,[8] which was highly dependent on German coke. While the gap between France's coal production and domestic demand could be filled by imports from allied countries, such as Britain and Belgium, coke for French steel mills could either be purchased or received as reparations only from the Ruhr. Furthermore, regaining sovereignty over Alsace-Lorraine as stipulated in the Versailles Treaty and in renewed economic ties with Luxembourg served to increase its steel investments, thereby raising French demand for German coke.[9] The Versailles reparations settlement, however, was not adequate to meet these needs, as it provided only a ten-year arrangement for reparations in coal products. Immediate needs for German raw materials were therefore less important in 1922 than long-term objectives,[10] such as the ownership of Ruhr mines, a guarantee of coke deliveries to France after the deadline set by the treaty, and increased independence in the energy sector.

In the aftermath of the Potsdam Conference in 1945, French policy on Germany included a revision of German borders, creation of an independent state in the Rhineland, and international administration of the Ruhr basin—all these points are strikingly similar to French policy after the First World War. Between 1944 and early 1946, Charles de Gaulle supported the division of Germany and the creation of a federation of independent states.[11] This stance was officially maintained by Georges Bidault as French foreign minister until at least 1947.[12] Bidault had personal doubts about the success of this strategy, and yet he knew that French public opinion would not support capitulation on the German problem[13] and that changing France's position could reduce the political credibility of his own party, the *Mouvement républicain populaire*.[14] Both territorial changes along the Franco-German border and reparations were to contribute to Germany's "economic disarmament."[15] This idea also included the reduction of and control over certain key industries, such as steel. Economic disarmament was not, however, an idea new with de Gaulle's government. A similar strategy had already been envisaged by French Minister of Commerce Etienne Clémentel after the Great War.[16] At the end of the Second World War, Germany's economic disarmament was, once again, complementary to the French government's commitment to speed up the recovery of the domestic steel industry, driven by both economic and political considerations.[17]

The very idea of "security" in both periods thus included not only military defense but also the economic disarmament of Germany, international political control over the heart of its coal and steel production—the Ruhr basin, possibly together with an autonomous government in the Rhineland—and a boost to France's heavy industry. Finally, there is continuity between the two periods regarding the interdependence between the French steel industry and German resources. Between 1945 and 1947–48, the French government seemed inclined to take the same tough approach toward Germany it had taken during the Versailles conference and through the period of the Ruhr invasion. Instead of persisting in a hard-line policy, however, an innovative and long-term solution to the problem of coal was put forward by France itself in May of 1950.

From the Ruhr Crisis to European Energy Cooperation

This section will analyze, how leaders, industry, and alliances determined or influenced the French decision to launch a military invasion of the Ruhr in 1923 and the plan for a European coal and steel pool in 1950.

The Leaders

The first factor is the role of leadership and ideas, namely the political beliefs of Raymond Poincaré, on the one hand, and Robert Schuman, on the other, as well as the ideological environment surrounding them. It has long been held that Poincaré, prime minister and foreign minister of France from 1922 to 1924, had been focusing primarily on an occupation of the Ruhr since January of the crucial year 1922, largely motivated by his own political views. Conversely, Robert Schuman is frequently recalled as the leader who was able to give up nationalist competition and lead Europe to its first successful supranational project in 1950–51. Poincaré has, for a long time, been associated in European public opinion with nationalism, *revanchisme*, and the strict implementation of the Versailles Treaty at the expense of diplomacy, whereas Schuman has been considered the advocate of peace and one of Europe's "fathers." Views of Poincaré's nationalism and some of the more extreme accusations of Germanophobia against him were, however, revised and softened by scholars as early as the 1970s, given that French archival sources have revealed all the complexity of the Ruhr crisis. John F.V. Keiger, the author of a recent biography, stresses the role of Poincaré's contemporary political adversaries and of the press in exaggerating his anti-German feelings. A well orchestrated campaign against Poincaré, led by a segment of the German press and industrialists, was the main reason he became so unpopular in Europe.[18] Historians such as Jacques Bariéty have argued against the traditional description of the French leader as lacking diplomatic skill and as a champion of force and a hard-line position against Germany.[19] While rejecting simplistic explanations, some scholars do stress, however, the crucial role of Poincaré and a few other political personalities, such as the lobby of French officers and civil servants in the Rhineland, and figures in the French Parliament[20] who supported French intervention and penetration into the Rhine region. The military occupation of the Ruhr was not a new idea in 1922: It had been discussed during the Versailles negotiations[21] and was considered by the French government as a possible solution, although an extreme one, in the event Germany was unable to afford reparations.[22] Nevertheless, Poincaré did not immediately or exclusively focus on the military option.[23] The Ruhr occupation was decided only between August and November of 1922 in the context of domestic pressures and international uncertainties. Contrary to received opinion, Poincaré's own political thoughts thus played only a minor role in the Ruhr crisis, while his distrust of Germany's willingness to implement the peace treaty has been frequently mistaken for Germanophobia. The transition from negotiation with Germany to military intervention was instead due in part to the ideas put forward by a lobby of military and civil servants who advocated the theory of making the Ruhr a "productive guarantee." These ideas also had some appeal in the French political environment of the time, which eventually contributed to Poincaré's resolution and granted him the necessary parliamentary support to implement it.[24]

A coal and steel pool featuring equal rights and restrictions for France and Germany under a supranational High Authority was an idea drafted by Jean Monnet in the spring of 1950 and endorsed by French Foreign Minister Robert Schuman.[25] This initiative was rooted in the ideological debate on European integration, renewed between 1948 and 1950, and furthered by those ideas. Interdependence and solidarity among European countries were essential components of Schuman's political thought; "supranational" integration would be another step forward. Since he became foreign minister in 1948, moreover, Schuman openly advocated a new foreign policy, aimed at bringing Germany back into the community of European nations with equal rights and responsibilities.[26] Lastly, on the coal and steel issue, Schuman emphasized that imposing restrictions on the German economy was insufficient to solve the old structural problems of this sector, such as long-term coal and coke supplies for France and the lack of competitiveness of French steel against German. Both a bilateral understanding in this sector and European cooperation were considered necessary.[27]

Beyond any idealistic portrait painted by his contemporaries or by later apologists for European integration, Schuman thus had a straightforward idea of the European postwar order that included a new model of Franco-German relations based on equality and close interstate cooperation.[28] The foreign minister's ideological approach did indeed give momentum to Monnet's document, not only because it was part of a broader wave of European movements and ideas spreading throughout the continent in many different forms but also because these ideas were fostered by the United States.

The Industry

The role of French steel industrialists in the Ruhr military occupation was a minor one and was overestimated by contemporaries. Recent historical interpretations of the events of 1922 and 1923 minimize the pressure coming from French industrial groups, such as the Comité des Forges.[29] Punitive measures against Germany were unpopular in large sectors of French heavy industry and business: The French government's economic and political ambitions threatened the network of close links with German counterparts that French industrialists wanted to revive.[30] Aware of the constraints on French steel production due to its dependence on Ruhr coke, they aimed at improving Franco-German relations and advocated long-term agreements to gain the necessary coke supplies at the domestic German price and assure products from Alsace-Lorraine easy access to the German market. The policy of the French steel industry was far from a military initiative: It focused first on direct agreements with the Ruhr producers in order to restart the coke-*minette* trade and second on buying German mines.[31] Rebuilding the commercial relations of the prewar period would stabilize the interdependent regions of Lorraine, Luxembourg, the Saar, and the Ruhr, which was in the interest of both sides.[32]

The French steel industry had a similar attitude after the Second World War. In 1945, France could count on a new advantage in the unrelenting competition between the two countries. By the end of hostilities, the German steel industry was largely under Allied control.[33] France's intention to become the main continental steel power was reflected in the national Modernization Plan, largely focused on the reconstruction and takeoff of the steel sector.[34] Already in 1945 and 1946, however, French industrialists were inclined to restructure the partnership with their German counterparts if not on an equal basis, at least under conditions that would enable the reconstruction of both countries. The French government's advocacy of international control over the Ruhr basin was in this sense not helpful to French industrialists: It delayed a solution to the German problem and left the other Allies a free hand to anticipate France with other commercial agreements on German soil. Not only were French steel industrialists unopposed to German industrial reconstruction, they also favored the beginnings of "European construction" as early as 1946–48.[35] Bilateral contacts between the steel industrialists of both countries resumed officially within the Organization for European Economic Cooperation (OEEC). Historians of industrial relations generally agree on a postwar trend in the European industrial environment aiming at the resumption of prewar commercial partnerships.[36] Proposals for international steel agreements of different kinds came from the German producers as well: Some of them included the revival of prewar international steel cartels and the old exchange system between Ruhr coke and *minette* from Lorraine; others aimed at offering major participation in the Ruhr trusts to French investors; some included Ruhr coal supply arrangements in a broader Franco-German economic partnership (similar to the 1921 Wiesbaden Agreements); still others went so far as to envision some loss of sovereign authority. John Gillingham takes this wave of "new internationalism" in Germany mainly as a product of military defeat and postwar disarray.[37]

This cooperative attitude was now probably more influential than after the Great War. At that time, it had not prevented France's use of force in the Ruhr even though they had not really provided support either, whereas between 1945 and 1950, it helped restore Franco-German relations and paved the way for the development of European projects.[38] And yet, the "liberal Europe" defended by French heavy industry after the Second World War, in which both French and German industrialists would be free to "renew and consolidate special agreements that existed before the war,"[39] was certainly not the same model of Europe later inaugurated by the Schuman Plan. The pattern of the ECSC would open debate on a liberal but also an integrated Europe in which liberalism would be combined with (and limited by) supranational institutions. French steel industrialists would not support a settlement of the coal and steel problem involving equal restrictions (and extensive ones) for all, as the High Authority would be entitled to set according to the ECSC founding treaty. The supranational formula was launched only with a true political initiative that would be challenged—with surprising cohesion—during the months of the ECSC negotiations by the same industrial confederations of both countries that had supported bilateral free trade agreements, as if mistrust of a supranational and anticartel authority had replaced the French and German industrialists' longstanding mutual distrust of one another.[40]

The Alliances

In the years 1919 to 1922, relations among France, Britain, and the United States had been embittered by the inability of the signatory countries to enforce Germany's implementation of the Treaty of Versailles. In the period from 1945 to 1950, relations were affected by the split in the wartime alliance between the Anglo-Americans and the Soviets and by the rise of the cold war. In both periods, France suffered from fear of isolation.

Different French governments in the aftermath of the Great War, including Poincaré's, shared a common feeling that amicable and cooperative relations with London and Washington were necessary, to the point that some scholars have defined them as "the key to France's foreign policy in the early 1920s;"[41] most of all, they were the key to France's policy toward Germany. Yet, neither Britain nor the United States agreed with France's views on postwar Europe, which focused on France's own recovery of great-power status in Europe and on its security against Germany. After the difficult negotiations in Versailles, other tensions grew among the three allies, due in part to the end of the Anglo-American guarantee on France's eastern borders: As an alternative to Paris's advocacy of the permanent occupation of the Rhineland and the creation of an independent state between France and Germany, the French government considered the Anglo-American guarantee fundamental to its own security. Besides, tensions arose because of the link between war debts and German reparations. Paris would pay its debts only on condition: that Germany fulfilled its reparations duties.[42]

Contrary to what happened in the aftermath of the Second World War, however, the political involvement of the United States in European politics was limited after the Great War: In terms of its relations with the other powers, what really affected France's shift toward a resolute and almost unilateral initiative to seize control of the Ruhr was the failure of an understanding with London. The year of tensions was 1922, rife with disagreements and misunderstandings with Britain on all the crucial issues: reparations, interallied debts, the Rhineland, and the Ruhr. From the Genoa Conference in April—where France blamed Britain for its soft and ambiguous behavior toward the Russo-German Treaty of Rapallo—to the failure of the London Conference on reparations in early August, relations between Paris and London were marked by growing disagreement and distrust.[43] Differences in the political approach and style of the British and French leaders gave rise to negative mutual perceptions: Scholars have not been generous in describing either Lloyd George's negative opinion of Poincaré's formalism and rigidity or the Frenchman's distrust of the Briton's ambiguity toward France.[44] Beyond personal differences and individual concerns, however, one additional factor complicated Franco-British relations: Competition for the control of the coal and steel markets. This rivalry had two interrelated facets. First, France and Britain were both steel producers and competitors, which prevented Britain from supporting France's proposal of August 1922 to seize control of the German state mines in the Ruhr.[45] Second, Britain was in competition with Germany, as they were both France's coal suppliers: Both London and Berlin were eager to fuel French reconstruction.[46] A Franco-British understanding on a stable and long-term settlement of the Ruhr issue was therefore almost impossible. The two were uneasy partners both in the implementation of the peace settlement and in its revision, mostly because they clearly disagreed over setting strategic controls on coal resources. Britain did not support France's ambitions to build a stronger and more competitive steel industry nor did it favor a Franco-German bilateral agreement on coal. These circumstances eventually isolated the Third Republic and facilitated the French leadership's shift toward military intervention in the Ruhr.

After the Second World War, in contrast, there were chances for a consolidation of Franco-British relations as early as 1945. Alleviating France's fears of Germany and preserving its friendship with Paris were now considered by the British government much more important than in the past due mainly to the Soviet threat and to the increasing need for cooperation in occupied Germany. In 1946, moreover, Charles de Gaulle's resignation and the political instability in France raised concerns in both Britain and the United States about the consolidation of a democratic government in the country.[47] Britain, however, opposed France's plans for the separation of the Rhineland and the Ruhr from Germany in 1945–47, as it had in 1919. Severing the Ruhr would definitely deprive the future German state of any chance to recover economically and politically, and this would ultimately increase the Soviet Union's political weight in Europe.[48] The British and the American Occupation Zones of Germany were merged in 1947, and British Foreign Secretary Ernest Bevin definitely recognized that a relaunch of Ruhr industry in particular was necessary to facilitate German economic reconstruction.[49] Steel was crucial to the postwar balance of power in Europe:[50] A revision of the restrictions imposed on the German steel industry was therefore advocated by Britain with the support of the United States as an additional political device to counterbalance the Soviet danger in Europe.

Complementary to this policy were British and American decisions on the allocation of German coal and on the future organization of the Ruhr mines. Since 1946–47, increasing quotas of coal produced in the British occupation zone, including both the northern Rhineland and the Ruhr, were assigned to domestic consumption in occupied Germany while export quotas were reduced.[51] This helped the British and American zones and thus accelerated Germany's recovery, even at the expense of coal importing countries such as France.[52] One further step in this direction was taken in November of 1948 when the United Kingdom and the United States decided that the administration of West German mines should be temporarily left to German trusteeships and that a final decision on the mines' ownership and organization should be transferred to the new German state.[53]

Coal was a keyword in most of the talks between the French and their Western Allies in the period from 1945 to 1950. The United States viewed it as the pivot of European economic reconstruction.[54] Coal shortages, due primarily to the broader energy crisis engulfing all of Western Europe in the aftermath of the war,[55] were particularly dramatic in France: The destiny of the Ruhr thus seemed even more crucial in the period from 1945 to 1950 than it had after the Great War. France's German policy eventually became more conciliatory between 1947 and 1948: France obtained from Britain and the United States a temporary, advantageous agreement on German coal supplies in 1947,[56] and a supervising body for the Ruhr was created the following year. This International Ruhr Authority soon proved ineffective, however. In the spring of 1950, when Monnet drafted the Franco-German coal and steel pool proposal, an effective and long-lasting international system of control over Ruhr resources had therefore not yet been implemented. In the economic, political, and ideological division of Europe, France was definitely part of the Western bloc, tied to the other Western European countries and the United States by the Marshall Plan, the Brussels Pact, and the Atlantic Pact. Nevertheless, Anglo-American commitment to the restoration of Germany caused deep anxiety in France, increasing its sense of impotence and fear of isolation. These feelings grew when the emergence of the cold war in Europe caused the British and the Americans to change their focus from Germany's economic recovery to its rearmament.[57] The international environment and the rise of the cold war ultimately drove the French leadership to transform its endless competition with Germany on coal and steel into a European deal that allowed France to regain the diplomatic initiative in Europe.

Conclusion

Nationalism and anti-German feelings influenced the Ruhr crisis only to a very limited extent. A group of politicians and officials who advocated an ambitious economic policy in the Rhineland supported by military intervention did, however, significantly influence the French government in 1922. Conversely, the Schuman Plan was simultaneously a political, economic, and ideological turning point. It included the "Europeanization" of the German problem on the one hand and an experiment with a supranational community on the other. The plan clearly took inspiration from the lively and diverse debate on European unity in those years.

Contrary to received opinion, the French steel industry played a minor role—or an ambiguous one—in both French solutions. A punitive and coercive policy toward Germany was regarded as obsolete and unfruitful. There were continuities in the desires of the French metallurgical industry in the aftermath of the First and the Second World Wars: long-term agreements with Germany, easy access to the German market, and peaceful political relations in the background.

Crucial to the creation of the Schuman Plan, however, were France's relations with its Western Allies and the risk of isolation vis-à-vis the Federal Republic in the new European order of the cold war. Although France and Britain were much closer in the late 1940s than in the early 1920s, their approaches to Germany were opposed and irreconcilable in both periods. This gave momentum to French initiatives aimed at redefining the country's position as a power in Europe. In times of complete disagreement and confrontation with Britain, the initiative was a military one, namely the Ruhr occupation. In 1950, within the context of the growing economic and political cooperation of Western Europe, the Schuman Plan instead represented an innovative diplomatic solution to old economic and political problems. Washington sided with Britain in supporting German reconstruction on the one hand, while overtly encouraged a revival of Franco-German relations within a European framework on the other.

Finally, the coal and steel issue can hardly be compared in the aftermath of the two wars without relating it to the transition from a "multipolar" Europe, in which political and economic competition was balanced between different nation-states, to a bipolar setting, in which competition between the European countries was dramatically affected by an increasing political, ideological, military, and economic dichotomy.

Notes

1. Georges-Henri Soutou, "Le coke dans les relations internationales en Europe de 1914 au plan Dawes (1924)," *Relations internationales*, no. 43 (1985): 249; John G. Clark, *The Political Economy of World Energy* (Chapel Hill: University of North Carolina Press, 1991), 15.

2. Manfred F. Boemeke, et al., eds., *The Treaty of Versailles. A reassessment after 75 years* (Cambridge: Cambridge University Press, 1998).

3. Marc Trachtenberg, *Reparation in World politics: France and European economic diplomacy, 1916–1923* (New York: Columbia University Press, 1980).

4. Jacques Bariéty, *Les relations franco-allemandes après la Première Guerre Mondiale* (Paris: Pédone, 1977); Stanislas Jeannesson, *Poincaré, la France et la Ruhr 1922–1924* (Strasbourg: Presses Universitaires de Strasbourg, 1998); Conan Fischer, *The Ruhr Crisis 1923–1924* (New York: Oxford University Press, 2003).

5. John Gillingham, *Coal, Steel and the Rebirth of Europe, 1945–1955. The Germans and French from Ruhr Conflict to Economic Community* (Cambridge: Cambridge University Press, 1991); Regine Perron, *Le marché du charbon, un enjeu entre l'Europe et les Etats-Unis de 1945 à 1958* (Paris: Publications de la Sorbonne, 1996); Alan S. Milward, *The Reconstruction of Western Europe, 1945–51* (London: Methuen & Co, 1984).

6. Andreas Wilkens, ed., *Die deutsch-französischen Wirtschaftsbeziehungen 1945–1960* (Sigmaringen: Jan Thorbecke Verlag, 1997); Sylvie Léfèvre, *Les relations économiques franco-allemandes de 1945 à 1955. De l'occupation à la coopération* (Paris: Comité pour l'histoire économique et financière, 1998); Gérard Bossuat, *La France, l'aide américaine et la construction européenne, 1944–1954* (Paris: CHEFF, 1992); Georges-Henri Soutou, "Georges Bidault et la construction européenne 1944–1954," *Revue d'histoire diplomatique* 26, no. 3–4 (1991): 267–306; Rainer Hudemann, "L'occupation française après 1945 et les relations franco-allemandes," *Vingtième siècle*, no. 55 (1997): 58–68; Henri Ménudier, *L'Allemagne occupée 1945–1949* (Paris: Editions Complexes, 1990).

7. Georges-Henri Soutou, "The French Peacemakers and Their Home Front," in *The Treaty of Versailles*, eds. Boemeke, et al., 168.

8. Bariéty, *Les relations*; Jeannesson, *Poincaré* 23–27; Georges-Henri Soutou, "La France et les Marches de l'Est, 1914–1919," *Revue Historique* 102 (1978): 341–88; Eric Bussière, *La France, la Belgique et l'organisation économique de l'Europe, 1918–1935* (Paris: CHEFF, 1992).

9. Soutou, *Le coke*, 249–67; Milward, *Reconstruction*, 130.

10. Soutou, *Le coke*; Jeannesson, *Poincaré*.

11. Raymond Poidevin, *Robert Schuman, homme d'Etat 1886–1963* (Paris: Imprimerie Nationale, 1986), 185; Léfèvre, *Les relations économiques*, 7–45.

12. For example: MAEF, *Documents Diplomatiques Français*, Annexes, 1946, Meeting of the Foreign Ministers, May 15, 1946.

13. Soutou, "Bidault," 268–69.

14. *FRUS*, vol. II, 1946, Caffrey to Secretary of State, November 13, 1946.

15. Léfèvre, *Les relations économiques*, 7; Marie-Thérèse Bitsch, "Un rêve français: le désarmement économique de l'Allemagne (1944–1947)," *Relations internationales*, no. 51 (Fall 1987): 314–16.

16. Elisabeth Glaser, "The Making of the Economic Peace," in *The Treaty of Versailles*, eds. Boemeke, et al.

17. Léfèvre, *Les relations économiques*; Wilkens, *Die deutsch-französischen Wirtschaftsbeziehungen*; Gillingham, *Coal*, 148–77; Milward, *Reconstruction*, 126–67; Philippe Mioche, "Aux origines du Plan Monnet: les discours et les contenus dans les premiers plans français (1941–1947)," *Revue Historique* 105 (1981): 405–38.

18. John F. V. Keiger, *Raymond Poincaré* (Cambridge: Cambridge University Press, 1997), 276–307.

19. Bariéty, *Les relations*, 91.

20. Ibid., 99–101 and Jeannesson, *Poincaré*, 78–83.

21. Arthur S. Link, ed., *The Deliberations of the Council of Four (March 24–June 28, 1919)* (Princeton: Princeton University Press, 1992).

22. Keiger, *Poincaré*, 294.

23. Jeannesson, *Poincaré*, 73–75; Bariéty, Les relations, 91–95; Keiger, *Poincaré*, 275–94.

24. Keiger, *Poincaré*, 294.

25. Milward, *Reconstruction*, and Gillingham, *Coal*, emphasize Monnet's paternity of the plan and take Schuman's contribution for modest.

26. Poidevin, *Schuman*, 208, 244–74; William I. Hitchcock, "Origins of the Schuman Plan, 1948–1950," *Diplomatic History*, no. 4 (1997): 603–30. See also Bossuat, *La France*, 735–46.

27. This was also Jean Monnet's opinion. See Jean Monnet, *Mémoires* (Paris: Fayard, 1976), 335–36.

28. Raymond Poidevin, "Der Faktor Europa in der Deutschlandpolitik Robert Schumans (Sommer 1948 bis Frühjahr 1949)," *Vierteljahrshefte für Zeitgeschichte* 33, no. 3 (1985): 406–19.

29. Jeannesson, *Poincaré*, 142–43.

30. Soutou, "The French Peacemakers," 169.

31. Soutou, *Le coke*, 250–55; Milward, *Reconstruction*, 130.

32. Jeannesson, *Poincaré*, 366–67.

33. Françoise Berger, "Les patrons de l'acier face à l'Europe (1930–1960)," in *Milieux économiques et intégration européenne en Europe occidentale au XXème siècle,* ed. Eric Bussière and Michel Dumoulin (Arras: Artois Presses Université, 1998), 189.

34. Milward, *Reconstruction,* 126–67.

35. Berger, "Les patrons," 190–91; Andreas Wilkens, "L'Europe des ententes ou l'Europe de l'integration?" in *Milieux économiques,* 267–83.

36. Wilkens, "L'Europe des ententes," 267–72; Léfèvre, *Les relations économiques.*

37. Gillingham, *Coal,* 217–27.

38. Adam Adamthwaite, *Grandeur and misery: France's bid for power in Europe, 1914–1940* (London: Arnold, 1995), 43–44.

39. Berger, "Les patrons," 191.

40. Wilkens, "L'Europe des ententes," 280–81; Philippe Mioche, *Le patronat de la sidérurgie française et le Plan Schuman en 1950–52: les apparences d'un combat et la réalité d'une mutation,* in *Die Anfänge des Schuman-Plans 1950/51,* ed. Klaus Schwabe (Baden-Baden: Nomos, 1988), 305–18; Léfèvre, *Les relations économiques,* 254–55.

41. Keiger, *Poincaré,* 278–83.

42. Trachtenberg, *Réparation.*

43. Jeannesson, *Poincaré,* 91–96; Bariéty, *Les relations,* 101–8.

44. Keiger, *Poincaré,* 288–89.

45. Jeannesson, *Poincaré,* 93.

46. Bariéty, *Les relations,* 80–81.

47. European Community Historical Archives (ECHA), (COL) JMDS/ 58, Caffrey to Secretary of State, no. 1595, April 4, 1946 (a political analysis of the domestic political situation in France in the eve of the 1946 elections). See also John W. Young, *Britain, France and the Unity of Europe, 1945–1951* (Leicester: Leicester University Press, 1984), 36–37.

48. Milward, *Reconstruction,* 128.

49. Anne Deighton, *The impossible peace: Britain, the Division of Germany and the origins of the Cold War* (Oxford: Clarendon, 1993), 121.

50. Gillingham, *Coal,* 178–79.

51. Perron, *Le marché du charbon,* 115–18.

52. Raymond Poidevin, "La France et le charbon allemand au lendemain de la deuxième guerre mondiale," *Relations Internationales,* no. 44 (1985): 366.

53. Alan Bullock, *Ernest Bevin: Foreign Secretary, 1945–1951* (London: Heinemann, 1983), 434–35.

54. ECHA, (COL) JMDS/58, Bernstein to Vinson. French Coal Requirements, April/May 1946; (COL) JMDS/59, Problems of European Reconstruction, 4 October 1947; Léfèvre, *Les relations économiques.*

55. Perron, *Le marché du charbon.*

56. Milward, *Reconstruction,* 140; Perron, *Le marché du charbon,* 129–30; Vincent Auriol, "1947," in *Journal du Septennat (1947–1954),* vol. 1 (Paris: Librairie Armand Colin, 1970), 167–68.

57. Hitchcock, "Origins," 603–30.

CHAPTER 8

Civic Activism and the Pursuit of Cooperation in the Locarno Era

Elana Passman

The 1925 signing of the Treaty of Locarno seemed to breathe new hope into Franco-German relations. Indeed the "spirit of Locarno" moved not just governments but also individuals to explore new roads to rapprochement. Once the French and German governments explicitly sanctioned a policy of détente, the efforts of concerned activists who had urged Franco-German cooperation found greater purchase and spread beyond the fringes of the political left. But even as civic debate came to reframe the Franco-German "problem" and welcome cooperation, it often remained mired in deep-rooted mistrust.

This chapter explores competing strategies to alleviate Franco-German tensions in the 1920s. Rather than looking to diplomatic instances of rapprochement—Locarno, Germany's entrance into the League of Nations, Thoiry, and the Franco-German Treaty of Commerce[1]—this chapter instead considers the ways in which an array of private organizations challenged the traditional Franco-German antagonism by constructing new models of cooperation. Focusing on civic activism, it examines the creation of an imaginary, negotiated space of cooperation between France and Germany, where engaged citizens conducted a new form of mediation, generally complementary—but at times in opposition—to the efforts of national governments.

After a brief survey of the strained postwar relationship between France and Germany, this chapter turns to specific attempts to bring about cooperation in the realm of civil society. Pacifists in the 1920s were at the forefront of efforts toward Franco-German entente and spearheaded civic and charitable activities long before the ink dried on the Locarno accords. In similar fashion, some element of Franco-German cooperation was often folded into the agendas of groups with a broad international base: international organizations affiliated with the League of Nations such as the Carnegie Foundation, political parties with international aspirations such as the Socialists, and religious associations such as the Catholic Church. A number of industrialists, too, favored cooperation in the form of transnational cartels or customs unions.

The chapter then examines three organizations exclusively devoted to improving Franco-German relations: the Mayrisch Komitee,[2] the Deutsch-Französische Gesellschaft, and the Sohlbergkreis. Born under the star of Locarno, these groups illustrate how Locarno energized the drive toward cooperation and channeled it in new directions. Activists frequently invoked the Treaty of Locarno, relevant for its recognition of the 1919 border between France and Germany, as the emblematic foundational moment of their quest, and the "spirit of Locarno" became their rallying cry. But Locarno was both a progenitor and beneficiary of the impulse toward cooperation. The accords granted cooperation legitimacy, bringing a variety of new champions to its cause. Groups born of the spirit of Locarno in turn broadened and deepened efforts at Franco-German rapprochement. Yet, government interference and internecine disputes limited such initiatives, as the final section of this chapter makes clear.

In the years after the Great War, Germany remained largely isolated from the international community politically, culturally, and economically. Its sole contact, outside the limited reach of the 1922 German-Soviet Treaty of Rapallo, was with Allied—especially French—troops seeking to compel compliance with the terms of Versailles. Consensus on German guilt for the war effectively barred the Germans from participation in the League of Nations until 1926. Similarly, the international scientific community's boycott of Germany persisted until 1926 and was only lifted due to diplomatic pressures. Even then, Germans only reengaged the international scientific community by fits and starts, in part due to their own official counter-boycott.[3] Economically, Germany only slowly reestablished normal trade relations.

Diplomats struggled to effect Franco-German rapprochement under the weight of fifty years of enmity, the war, and Versailles. Their convoluted efforts at conciliation would give rise to what Jean-Baptiste Duroselle has termed the "pactomania" of the late 1920s,[4] which seemed to attenuate tensions. In a similar fashion, disparate unofficial initiatives strove for Franco-German understanding. As Ilde Gorguet has noted, the 1920s witnessed a "constant preoccupation with reconciliation."[5]

Unlike several organizations in the late 1920s, which focused exclusively on Franco-German cooperation, most efforts of the early 1920s sought to curb the antagonism between France and Germany as part of a larger internationalist or transnational agenda. On the other hand, the programs of conservative-oriented European movements like Karl Anton Rohan's European *Kulturbund* (1922) and Richard Coudenhove-Kalergi's Paneuropa Union (1923), and, on the other hand, leftist international movements like socialism and pacifism all dovetailed with the pursuit of Franco-German cooperation. It was particularly in leftist spheres that early postwar efforts were concentrated. In addition, a number of religious, intellectual, and economic groups tried to bridge the Franco-German schism. Yet the Franco-German cause was not the raison d'être of any of these circles; thus, most actions in this arena remained circumscribed and sporadic at best.

The pacifist movement tended to frame the Franco-German "problem" as a humanitarian issue. German feminist pacifists raised funds for the reconstruction of war-torn French towns; the *Ligue des mères et éducatrices pour la paix* donated toys to the children of Germany's unemployed.[6] The 1923 Ruhr crisis, rather than undermining such efforts, further spurred pacifists to action. In France, pacifists joined an array of union leaders, socialists, and communists in protesting the occupation. The *Ligue des femmes pour la paix et la liberté* not only denounced Raymond Poincaré's incursion into the Ruhr but also established a program to sponsor starving children in the region.[7] In a gesture of proletarian solidarity, the International Workers Relief invited the hungry children of German workers to stay with the more prosperous families of French workers.[8]

Religious groups also viewed cooperation through a moral, humanitarian lens. For example, Marc Sangnier's Christian Democratic movement considered Franco-German cooperation an important aspect of its quest for world peace; it therefore attacked French Catholics' ardent nationalism and promoted reconciliation in its stead. Paralleling the charitable work undertaken by socialists and pacifists, German women at Sangnier's Freiburg Conference sacrificed their jewels to rebuild the cities of their victorious opponent. German youth in attendance vowed to enlist in the French reconstruction effort itself.[9] Although some Protestants, such as Germanist Henri Lichtenberger, wholeheartedly dedicated themselves to the pursuit of cooperation, Catholics were more involved on an organizational level; German Protestant youth groups, for one, more often worked in tandem with their counterparts in Britain or Scandinavia.[10]

Whether similarly grounded in religious affinities or from a solely political viewpoint, certain political parties also supported some form of rapprochement as a component of their broad transnational outlook. They, too, did not exclusively revolve around the Franco-German dynamic. The new Parti démocrate populaire and the Center Party in Germany—along with several other Catholic parties across Europe—pushed for a Christian Democratic coalition that transcended national boundaries. Socialists and Communists, of course, pursued internationalist agendas that at times placed the spotlight on France and Germany.

The message of cooperation likewise played a role in the arts. A few years after his own service in the Rhineland, Pierre Descaves penned a short story collection about a French administrator in the occupied Rhineland that served as a rather transparent allegory of Franco-German relations. Descaves emphasized the importance of communication and openness across borders and the "contagion of rancor and hatred."[11] More famously, Jean Giraudoux's 1922 novel *Siegfried et le Limousin* and his popular 1928 play *Siegfried* about an amnesiac soldier torn between France and Germany exposed the fluidity and even insignificance of national identity. The lesson of cooperation resonated more loudly after Locarno with Georg Wilhelm Pabst's film *Kameradschaft* (1931), a joint Franco-German production based on the 1906 Courrières mining disaster. *Kameradschaft* yoked a message of Franco-German cooperation to a socialist trope: French and German workers would unite to save each other from their oppressors.

French and German intellectuals also took more direct steps, both symbolic and practical, to bring about cooperation. In 1922, Paul Desjardins invited a number of celebrated intellectuals including Heinrich Mann and André Gide to Pontigny to renew the regular cycle of discussions that had lapsed during the war. The French *Union pour la Vérité* opened its doors to a handful of German journalists and professors to engage in vigorous debate to help lay the basis for a "rapprochement without illusions."[12] Salons held by, among others, Jean de Pange in Alsace, Aline and Emile Mayrisch in Luxembourg, Maurice Boucher in Paris, and Brigitte Bermann Fischer in Berlin likewise all sought meaningful dialogue. Whereas the frequency of such intellectual encounters helped forge strong networks and enhance expertise, intellectuals' timely political action served to publicize their agenda for cooperation. In July 1925, for example, a group of French intellectuals associated with pacifism—among them writers Henri Barbusse and Victor Margueritte—signed a manifesto advocating revision of Articles 227 through 231 of the Versailles Treaty, which most infamously had laid guilt for the war at the feet of the Germans.[13]

As Mona Siegel has pointed out, the quest for cooperation was not limited to elites. Notably, schoolteachers in France preached a message of harmony to their students. The teachers' syndicate called for rapprochement in 1925 and launched a "textbook war" the following year to boycott so-called bellicose textbooks; German teachers began to reciprocate such efforts in the early 1930s. Significantly, French teachers' less vindictive, more magnanimous view of Germany trickled down to the schoolchildren themselves, yielding a fundamental transformation of mentalities.[14]

Buoyed by the newly elected *Cartel des Gauches*, official efforts at rapprochement first gained ground with the 1924 London Accords, followed by a meeting between Prussian Minister of Culture Carl Heinrich Becker and French Education Minister Anatole de Monzie in Berlin as well as the Treaty of Locarno the next year. In different ways, the meetings at London, Berlin, and Locarno pulled the notion of rapprochement from the leftist, pacifist margins into more prominent, influential circles. The London Accords, which resulted in the Dawes Plan and the resumption of reparation payments, brought about a more secure landscape for trade. The September 1925 Becker-de Monzie meeting marked the first visit to Berlin by a French sitting minister in over fifty years. Although undertaken with extreme temerity, the Berlin meeting signaled at least a nominal interest in cultural and intellectual cooperation.[15] The Locarno Agreements further stabilized the Franco-German relationship by guaranteeing the 1919 border. By 1925, then, officials had left the door to negotiation open, and in swept a number of new proponents of change.

These diplomatic initiatives catalyzed and legitimated earlier efforts for economic cooperation. Desperate for new markets, French industrialists had tentatively explored the notion of rapprochement as early as 1920, but did not pursue it seriously until 1924.[16] Most prominent were those in steel and coal, but their desire for rapprochement was echoed by producers of potash, aluminum, and even wine. As Jacques Bariéty has argued, no real economic cooperation was possible without first securing political negotiation; thus the financial stability of the London Accords and the border security of Locarno enabled joint ventures.[17] If economic cooperation only began once some basic political conditions were secured, once initiated, economic cooperation proceeded apace with the International Steel Entente (1926) and a Commercial Treaty in 1927 along with an array of cartels from silk to dye.[18] Together, these diplomatic and economic initiatives provided much more fertile soil for the seeds of cultural cooperation.

The example of the Mayrisch Komitee perfectly illustrates the nexus of diplomatic, economic, and cultural efforts for cooperation. For Emile Mayrisch, head of the Luxembourger steel concern ARBED, Franco-German cooperation was necessary for a stable steel market. According to Mayrisch, international cartels "constitute an important factor for peace and reconciliation. But it is also quite certain that a minimum of preliminary political confidence is necessary as a foundation for such pacts."[19] Mayrisch's faith in economic entente materialized with the International Steel Entente, an accord among the top steel producers in France, Germany, Luxembourg, and Belgium ratified by, among others, Théodore Laurent, Ernst Poensgen, and Mayrisch. That same year these signatories joined with prominent representatives of society, the academy, and the press to form the Mayrisch Komitee to lobby for Franco-German understanding. In this way, these men melded their economic self-interest with a more cultural understanding of the Franco-German antagonism.

By bringing together big business interests and intellectuals around the Franco-German question, the Mayrisch Komitee forged ties among those who would not otherwise share much common ground. Unlike the humanitarian, religious, political, and intellectual circles previously discussed, the Mayrisch Komitee created and helped sustain new, exclusively Franco-German channels of communication. Members' prestige—as top industrialists, celebrated intellectuals, and former government ministers—lent a certain gravitas to the notion of cooperation. At the heart of the Mayrisch Komitee's credo lay the idea that Franco-German cooperation was in the national interest and transcended party differences. Members lauded its "realistic foundation in contrast to all the other similar works that pursue moral or philanthropic goals," namely the pacifist movement.[20]

Rather than approaching the Franco-German problem through the tangled avenues of diplomacy or through complicated trade negotiations as Mayrisch had long been advocating, Pierre Viénot, the Komitee's principal architect, wanted to tackle the problem head-on by addressing public opinion. Viénot proposed reorienting the "routine imagination" of the public and successfully steered the group in this direction.[21] As early as the spring of 1926, Mayrisch Komitee members agreed that without better communications between the two nations, the promise of the Locarno treaties "threaten[ed] to remain illusory."[22] The Komitee thus acted as a pressure group, urging the French and German press to avoid stale stereotypes and negative propaganda. By actively lobbying journalists, moreover, the Mayrisch Komitee incorporated some of these powerful voices into the Franco-German network.

Whereas the Mayrisch Komitee united business interests with a desire to reshape mentalities, its sometime rival the Deutsch-Französische Gesellschaft (DFG) worked to build a Franco-German community. The handiwork of art critic Otto Grautoff, the DFG arranged talks by French and German intellectuals and artists, screened films, sponsored educational trips, managed student exchanges, and matched up young pen pals. With a focus on sociability as well as on knowledge, the German association provided an active and ambitious forum for mutual understanding. Its associated journals, the *Deutsch-Französische Rundschau* (*DFR*) and the *Revue d'Allemagne* reinforced and expanded this community by reaching out to a diverse binational readership of teachers, lawyers, students, business people, and journalists, approximately one quarter of whom were women.[23] Although the DFG had no corollary corollary in France, it was loosely associated with the Ligues d'études germaniques, which reached out to German-language teachers.

Covering contemporary French literature, philosophy, music, art, politics, and the economy as well as Franco-German relations, the *Deutsch-Französische Rundschau* aimed to "avoid sentimental pacifism" in favor of pursuing "the spirit of mutual enlightenment and rational understanding."[24] An announcements section in each issue illuminated the many connections between France and Germany springing up from community to community, person to person. These announcements not only listed items of importance to the DFG, such as donations and new members, but also extended to a much broader range of French-German points of contact. These ranged from exhibitions and exchanges to more symbolic triumphs, such as Oleander, the first German horse to race at Longchamps since the war.

The *DFR*'s French counterpart, the *Revue d'Allemagne* aimed to spread and deepen French readers' knowledge about Germany. By not overtly aligning themselves with rapprochement politics or party politics more generally, the editors established their independence and credibility in three principal ways. First, the journal's neutrality implied that it was scientific and unbiased; however, at the same time, the *Revue d'Allemagne* provided an alternative to the academic, less accessible *Revue Germanique*. Second, it attracted writers and readers of all political and social backgrounds who might hold an interest in Germany whether from hatred or fascination or pacifist tendencies. Finally, it seemed to be about culture, a potentially less divisive subject than politics. In this way, the *Revue d'Allemagne* created a lieu de rapprochement—a space in which Franco-German relations could be negotiated and a certain idea of Germany (or even multiple visions of Germany) mapped out for French readers, just as the *DFR* did for its German audience with regard to France.

Rather than reaching out to bourgeois professionals, the Sohlbergkreis[25] sought to harness the energy of youth to the cause for cooperation. Conceived by Otto Abetz, the president of a coalition of youth groups in Karlsruhe, and organized by Abetz and journalist Jean Luchaire, the 1930 Sohlberg Congress brought together one hundred French and German youth of all professions, classes, political orientations, and religious affiliations. In one week of conferences and lectures, they learned about each other's culture and discussed their differences, similarities, and responsibilities. Luchaire explained that the encounter served as a "vast and honest examination of the conscience."[26]

Such meetings continued for the next few years, alternating locations from Germany to France, beginning with Sohlberg in the Black Forest. Around the campfire, in the woods, on ski slopes, and in hostels, the youth not only discussed cultural difference but also practiced rapprochement. Through Luchaire, the group maintained close ties to the Briandist newspaper *Notre Temps*, and after the first two conferences, Abetz launched a new journal *Sohlbergkreis*. In this way, the message of the Sohlbergkreis reverberated beyond the confines of the meetings.

Created in 1930 at the end of the age of Locarno[27] with its first meeting on the heels of the French evacuation of the Rhineland, the Sohlbergkreis exemplifies both Locarno's promise and its fragility. Yet equally important, it demonstrates the flexibility and durability of the message of Franco-German cooperation, which did not disappear with the end of the Locarno era in 1931. Although the succession of meetings became increasingly fraught with tensions as German nationalists became a more active and vocal element of the German contingent, Sohlbergkreis participants persisted in their efforts even after the Nazi takeover in Germany. The Sohlbergkreis, eventually absorbed by a new organization named the Deutsch-Französische Gesellschaft (DFG), continued to operate under Nazi leadership. Whereas some proponents of cooperation turned away from this cause during the 1930s, Abetz and other alumni of the Sohlbergkreis, the Weimar-era DFG, and the Mayrisch Komitee were active in the Nazi-era DFG or its French counterpart, the Comité France-Allemagne. Although their involvement in these groups in the 1930s and into the 1940s has rightly been criticized, it can and should be viewed in the context of their participation in Locarno-era efforts for cooperation.

Together, the Mayrisch Komitee, the DFG, and the Sohlbergkreis expanded and disseminated the notion of cooperation, just as they injected it with a new dynamism. But if movements for cooperation adopted a broader range of strategies and remained far more flexible than official government efforts, they, too, faced a variety of constraints. Most obviously, private efforts, like government initiatives, encountered vigorous nationalist opposition. In early 1926, *Action Française* members provoked a skirmish at a Paris talk by Elisabeth Rotten of the German branch of the League for Human Rights; subsequent talks by Alfred Kerr, Thomas Mann, and Hermann Keyserling were hardly publicized out of fear of further violence. Edouard Herriot himself admitted that the potential threat of the reactionary league the *Camelots du Roi* hindered efforts for intellectual rapprochement in Paris.[28] German officials echoed such pessimism. According to Ambassador Leopold von Hoesch, though "intellectual cooperation" provided a popular catchphrase since the war and many claimed to work in its name, it was in reality not widespread.[29] Clearly, the movement for cooperation faced an uphill battle.

Less obviously, a number of other factors limited private efforts. Advocates for cooperation had to reconcile their own visionary agendas with the need for government and public approbation. This balancing act began with the enormous challenge of where to position themselves on the spectrum of internationalism and nationalism. The fact that many early advocates of cooperation came from the political margins hampered their influence and led some to temper their positions. In this sense, post–Locarno activists recognized the need to demonstrate their patriotism to ensure credibility among the general public and thus give weight to their message. Even within the organizations themselves, members, despite their best intentions to remain open-minded, often fell back upon familiar patterns of mistrust and thereby undermined their own ambitions. Moreover, they had to navigate internecine rivalries and avoid working at cross-purposes. On another level, the German and French Foreign Offices wavered between support of and resistance to private initiatives. Officials' insistence on reciprocity—each measure toward entente taken in one country would be mirrored in form, content, and degree in the other—ensured a useful balance but also placed limits on the elasticity and the potential for expansion of such efforts.

Reciprocity had informally governed Franco-German cultural politics since Locarno; it implied a partnership of equals, relative openness, and shared political risk. The Mayrisch Komitee, supported by both Foreign Offices, resolved the issue of reciprocity relatively neatly. With one branch in Paris and one in Berlin and its annual meeting in Luxembourg, the Mayrisch Komitee considered structural balance as a sign of equality. Despite the Mayrisch Komitee's assurances of reciprocity, this could be threatened in practice by lack of attendance at meetings;[30] the 1928 death of Luxembourger Emile Mayrisch, who presided over the two national branches as a Solomon-figure, only exacerbated the fear of one side's dominance. A similar logic compelled Maurice Boucher, the chief editor of the *Revue d'Allemagne*, to serve on the editorial board of the *DFR*, just as his *DFR* counterpart Otto Grautoff sat on the editorial board of the *Revue d'Allemagne*.[31] Sohlbergkreis conferences likewise showed a careful sense of balance, with French and German speakers on each subject.

The French and German governments engaged in a politics of reciprocity after Locarno as well. The two Foreign Offices, for example, constantly questioned the legitimacy of the twinned journals the *Deutsch-Französische Rundschau* and the *Revue d'Allemagne* precisely because they were not in true balance. Complications regularly ensued when one country learned its subsidies outweighed those of the other. More importantly, the German review was affiliated with a friendship society, whereas the French review had no parallel association to advocate for Germany. Insisting on true reciprocity, the German Foreign Office threatened to cut funds to the *DFR* altogether unless its French counterpart immediately developed a Franco-German Society. Yet, even when the *Revue d'Allemagne* began to list its affiliation to the already extant Ligues d'études germaniques, the official German response was that reciprocity had not been achieved. The associations in each nation had to be founded at the same time, with the same structure and goals, and had to have a similar caliber of members to attain reciprocity and thus be entitled to support from the German government. After all, why should the German government assist an organization that promoted France, unless there was a corresponding group that championed Germany to the French?

Governments, moreover, expected these mediators to represent their nation as informal diplomats and often became frustrated when their infelicities—and especially their critiques of their own homeland—betrayed their amateurism or worse yet, their apparent disloyalty. High expectations in no small part stemmed from the fact that such groups received financial support from both governments. Otto Grautoff was particularly prone to gaffes, as the German Foreign Office regularly noted. But more serious infractions revolved around activists who publicly took a stand on hot-button political issues like reparations or the Saar. A *DFR* article on the evacuation of the Rhineland led to a firm dressing down of Grautoff by the German Foreign Office.[32] Although the journal's mission explicitly revolved around informing readers about contemporary France and Franco-German relations, the German Foreign Office had resolved from the outset that its support for the journal was conditional upon its avoidance of contemporary bones of contention, notably the issues of war guilt and the occupied Rhineland.[33] Such reticence also helps explain why French officials denied Otto Abetz permission to hold his youth group's first Franco-German congress—with its controversial central themes on borders and identities—in recently recovered Strasbourg, instead the gathering took place at Sohlberg in the Black Forest.[34]

Organizations devoted to cooperation in turn bristled when their own members undermined their agenda by criticizing the other nation. Jacques Seydoux, for example, was obliged to leave the Mayrisch Komitee after writing a number of allegedly anti-German articles on disarmament that "added grist to the mill" for opponents of rapprochement.[35] At Sohlbergkreis meetings beginning with Rethel (1931), some French participants decried the mounting nationalism they observed in their German peers. If nationalist suspicions infiltrated even their own circle, surely they represented an escalating threat.

The movement for cooperation was constrained by diplomats' guidelines, tensions within the individual groups, and jousting between the societies. The Mayrisch Komitee and Grautoff's DFG, for example, sustained a fierce competition. If anything, the two organizations were more similar than different; therein lay the root of their rivalry. Both groups clamored for the attention—and funds—of the French and German foreign ministries and of powerful private donors. The Mayrisch Komitee feared the DFG would splinter the effort for understanding and thereby strengthen the already dominant nationalist cause. If the DFG in many ways reflected the means and aims of the Komitee, it also threatened its uniqueness and vulgarized the task of cooperation by opening it to the broader educated reading public.

To be sure, a number of members of the two organizations overlapped. And members of both the Mayrisch Komitee and the DFG participated in the second major conference of the Sohlbergkreis in Rethel. Sociologist Arnold Bergstraesser of the University of Heidelberg taught both Pierre Viénot and Max Clauss, two of the main forces behind the Mayrisch Komitee, of which Bergstraesser himself would become a member. The sociology professor also spoke at Sohlbergkreis meetings and belonged to the DFG. Germanist Henri Lichtenberger similarly served on the editorial boards of the *Revue d'Allemagne* and the *DFR*, wrote regularly for both and was the honorary president of the Ligues d'études germaniques and an especially active member of the Mayrisch Komitee.

The interpenetration of these groups helped weave a dense network of activists devoted to the pursuit of cooperation. If they tussled over strategies, their varied tactics served to attract a broader scope of adherents to the cause. Moreover, their debates—at conferences and in print—suggested innovative approaches to reconciling national identity with transnational "understanding." Above all, they created both an intellectual and organizational framework exclusively dedicated to facilitating cooperation between France and Germany on which future champions of cooperation would rely. Inspired by Locarno, with a defining mission to address the Franco-German "problem," these private efforts bolstered diplomatic initiatives. Civic activists had adopted a diplomatic function (though not always with official approbation).

What, then, was the long-term legacy of the "spirit of Locarno" on Franco-German relations? Many scholars have claimed that Locarno-era efforts toward understanding yielded little fruit, did not stave off the rise of nationalism, or, at most, served as models for cooperation after the Second World War. Such arguments underestimate the resilience of joint French and German attempts at rapprochement in the face of the prevalent nationalist spirit in both nations. Civic debates about Franco-German cooperation in the Locarno years resonated throughout the 1930s and beyond. Locarno-era activists built a network of those pledged to Franco-German cooperation and helped define the rhetoric and methods of future associations devoted to this cause. In vastly different ways, these early efforts at cooperation shaped both the notorious collaboration of the Second World War as well as the post-1945 push for reconciliation. If we are to take seriously the ideas of this dedicated core, we must focus on the myriad (re)incarnations of their efforts beyond the ruptures of 1933 and 1945.

Notes

1. Hermann Hagspiel, *Verständigung zwischen Deutschland und Frankreich? Die deutsch-französische Außenpolitik der zwanziger Jahre im innenpolitischen Kräftefeld beider Länder* (Bonn: Ludwig Röhrscheid, 1987); Jon Jacobson, "Strategies of French Foreign Policy after World War I," *The Journal of Modern History* 55, no. 1 (1983): 78–95; Franz Knipping, *Deutschland, Frankreich und das Ende der Locarno-Ära 1928–1931. Studien zur internationalen Politik in der Anfangsphase der Weltwirtschaftskrise* (Munich: Oldenbourg, 1987).

2. Also known as the *Deutsch-Französisches Studienkomitee* and the *Comité franco-allemand d'information et de documentation*.

3. Archives Nationales (henceforth AN) AJ16 6958; Brigitte Schroeder-Gudehus, "La science ignore-t-elle vraiment les frontières? Les relations franco-allemandes dans le domaine des sciences," vol. 1 of *Entre Locarno et Vichy: Les relations culturelles franco-allemandes dans les années 1930*, ed. Hans Manfred Bock, Reinhart Meyer-Kalkus, and Michel Trebitsch (Paris: CNRS, 1993), 393–403.

4. J. B. Duroselle, "The Spirit of Locarno: Illusions of Pactomania," *Foreign Affairs* 50, no. 4 (1972): 752–64.

5. Ilde Gorguet, *Les mouvement pacifistes et la réconciliation franco-allemande dans les années vingt (1919–1931)* (Bern: Peter Lang, 1999), 4–5.

6. Siân Reynolds, *France between the Wars: Gender and Politics* (London: Routledge, 1996), 192.

7. Bibiliothèque de Documentation Internationale Contemporaine, Papier Duchêne, Dossier Allemagne 1923–1934. Gabrielle Duchêne, "Sacrifices de Réconciliation" (November 16, 1923).

8. Dieter Tiemann, *Deutsch-französische Jugendbeziehungen der Zwischenkriegszeit* (Bonn: Bouvier, 1989), 63.

9. Peter Farrugia, "French Religious Opposition to War, 1919–1939: The Contribution of Henri Roser and Marc Sangnier," *French History* 6, no. 3 (1992): 279–302; Gorguet, *Les mouvements pacifistes*, 67–69, 85–86.

10. Tiemann, *Jugendbeziehungen*, 86.

11. Pierre Descaves, *L'enfant de liaison* (Paris: Ernest Flammarion, 1929), 71.

12. *Problèmes franco-allemands d'après-guerre. Entretiens tenus au siège de l'Union pour la Vérité* (Paris: Valois, 1932).

13. Jean-Claude Delbreil, *Les catholiques français et les tentatives de rapprochement franco-allemand (1920–1933)* (Metz: SMEI, 1972), 29.

14. Mona L. Siegel, *The Moral Disarmament of France: Education, Pacifism, and Patriotism, 1914–1940* (Cambridge: Cambridge University Press, 2004), 103, 124–57.

15. Katja Marmetschke, "Un tournant dans le rapprochement franco-allemand? La rencontre entre C.H. Becker, ministre de l'Education de Prusse, et Anatole de Monzie, ministre français de l'Instruction publique, en septembre 1925 à Berlin," in *Echanges culturels et relations diplomatiques: Présences françaises à Berlin au temps de la République de Weimar*, ed. Hans Manfred Bock and Gilbert Krebs (Paris: PIA, 2004), 35–50.

16. Edward D. Keeton, "Economics and Politics in Briand's German Policy, 1925–1931," in *German Nationalism and the European Response, 1890–1945*, ed. Carole Fink, Isabel V. Hull, and MacGregor Knox (Norman: University of Oklahoma Press, 1985), 157–80.

17. Jacques Bariéty, "Industriels allemands et industriels français à l'époque de la République de Weimar," *Revue d'Allemagne* 4, no. 2 (1974): 1–16.

18. Guido Müller, *Europäische Gesellschaftsbeziehungen nach dem Ersten Weltkrieg. Das Deutsch-Französische Studienkomitee und der Europäische Kulturbund* (Munich: Oldenbourg, 2005), 41–42.

19. Emile Mayrisch, "Les ententes économiques internationales et la paix," in Centre de Recherches Européennes, Emile Mayrisch Précurseur de la construction de l'Europe (Lausanne: Centre de Recherches Européennes, 1967), 53.

20. Politisches Archiv des Auswärtigen Amts [henceforth PAAA] DBP 702a. Pierre Viénot, "Vorschläge zur Errichtung eines deutsch-französischen Informierungsausschusses," 7.

21. AN 411/AP/1, dossier 7. Pierre Viénot, "Le problème franco-allemand" (August 2, 1925).

22. PAAA DBP 702a. "Versammlung des Comité" (May 29, 1926).

23. I count 724 female members and 83 members whose gender cannot be determined definitively.

24. PAAA R70550 zu No. II Fr 441126 Prospectus. "Deutsch-Französische Rundschau" signed Grautoff (September 29, 1926).

25. It was not called "the Sohlbergkreis" until October 1930; its French counter part was called the "Comité d'entente de la jeunesse française" beginning in 1931. Following convention, I refer here to the entire circle as the Sohlbergkreis.
26. PAAA R98888. Jean Luchaire, "Une expérience franco-allemande: Au camp de Sohlberg," *La Volonté*, August 8, 1930.
27. Knipping, *Deutschland, Frankreich*, 220–24.
28. PAAA DBP 542b No. 913. Telegram, Hoesch to AA (August 20, 1927).
29. PAAA DBP 542b No. 353. "Geistige Zusammenarbeit" signed Hoesch (February 6, 1926); PAAA DBP 542b No. A555. "Geistige Zusammenarbeit" Hoesch to AA (February 15, 1927).
30. PAAA DBP 702a. Telegram 475, No. A 1571. Rieth to AA (May 19, 1926).
31. PAAA R70550 No. II Fr 5490. Grautoff to AA (December 17, 1926).
32. See internal reports and correspondence from Fall 1930 in PAAA R70553.
33. PAAA R70550 Aufzeichnung signed Köpke (January 13, 1927).
34. Barbara Lambauer, *Otto Abetz et les Français ou l'envers de la Collaboration* (Paris: Fayard, 2001), 25.
35. PAAA DBP 702a. "An die Herren Mitglieder der deutschen Gruppe," signed Krukenberg (November 29, 1927). See also Jacques Seydoux, *Pax*, November 25, 1927, and "Encore le désarmement," *Pax*, December 2, 1927.

CHAPTER 9

Two "Naughty Siblings"

France and Germany in the Public Discussion of the Interwar Period

Verena Schöberl

Introduction

In the interwar period, Franco-German relations were of great importance for European politics. They determined the stability and the development of Europe—for better or for worse. France and Germany still confronted one another after the First World War. As the victor, the former defended its achievements, and the latter, as the loser, fought for the revision of the outcome. This was a constant problem in the interwar period. Only in the years 1925 to 1930—between the Locarno Treaty and the Briand Plan—did the two neighbors honestly try to settle their differences. This gave a major impetus to the idea of a European reconciliation as well. After these hopeful years, however, relations deteriorated due to the Great Depression, the death of German Foreign Minister Gustav Stresemann, who had followed the path of reconciliation, and the subsequent rise of the National Socialist Party in Germany.

The importance of Franco-German relations in the interwar period is reflected in the public discourse of the time. Newspapers and journals in both France and Germany discussed the relationship intensively. Politicians, economists, and writers were engaged as well. Party affiliations came very clearly to the fore in this discourse. Thus, the first question this chapter poses is about which groups participated in the Franco-German discussion. The second question deals with the time frame of the discussion. During the era of reconciliation between 1925 and

1930, the discussion was most intense. Was it the most positive then too? What role did Locarno and the Briand Plan play in this discussion?

Often, both press and personalities judged a Franco-German reconciliation as the first step toward a unified Europe. The point of reference for most articles was the Pan-European plan of Richard Count Coudenhove-Kalergi, who proposed a United States of Europe (excluding Great Britain and Russia). His idea provoked an immense public response. The third issue of this essay is therefore the role of the Pan-European idea in Franco-German discourses.

France and Germany in the Public Discourse

Within the German press, leftwing publications strongly advocated a Franco-German reconciliation. Arnold Kalisch, a well-known pacifist and member of the German Social Democratic Party (SPD), argued in the pacifist magazine *Friedenswarte* for ending the "illness of Europe, the hate between Germany and France." He dubbed the two countries "naughty siblings" whose dangerous conflicts Europe should no longer take for granted.[1] The Social Democratic newspaper *Vorwärts* called for a Franco-German reconciliation as a prerequisite for the unification of Europe.[2] *Vorwärts* was assisted by *Gesellschaft*, the theoretical journal of socialism, which implored its readers to believe in Franco-German solidarity.[3] Additionally, a strong supporter of a Franco-German association was the *Sozialistische Monatshefte*, a journal that was very hostile to Great Britain, because it viewed the country as not contributing positively to Europe.[4]

However, it was not just Socialists and Social Democrats who stood up for France and Germany. Catholics did so as well. *Germania*, the newspaper of the German Catholic party the Center, called Franco-German unanimity the precondition for European unity.[5] It was one of the most committed participants in the Franco-German dialog. Since 1925, it had reported on "Germany and France" in a weekly section and exchanged articles with *L'Europe Nouvelle*, a journal equally oriented toward reconciliation.[6] The Catholic journal *Hochland* also fought for a Franco-German agreement.[7] The *Soziale Revue* concluded: "a Pan-European union is the only remedy for preventing the two neighbors France and Germany from grappling with locked jaws and bleeding to death from their wounds."[8]

Not every German newspaper supported a Franco-German reconciliation. Most of the critics were conservatives, however. They mistrusted France, largely due to its alleged efforts to achieve hegemony in Europe and the future of the Versailles Treaty. The conservative *Deutsche Allgemeine Zeitung* (*DAZ*) ran a headline in 1925 on "Gallic striving for glory," which would prevent any unification.[9] Four years later it still claimed that France's cry for security aimed at reinforcing its military, political, and financial hegemony on the European continent.[10] The journal *Deutschlands Erneuerung* even turned the idea of reconciliation into its opposite: It expected in Europe's future the "duel [between] Germany [and] France" and proceeded to utter an anti-Western tirade.[11]

One important aspect of this discussion, as Count Coudenhove suggested, was the fear of being left alone in a Europe that included France but not Britain. Johann Count Bernstorff, German Democratic Party (DDP), announced in 1926 in the Reichstag that France proclaiming a European Idea was like Greeks bearing gifts: "This would lead to the United States of Europe that Napoleon I had imagined while on St. Helena. . . . This is [a] United States of Europe we can never accept."[12] Wilhelm Heile (DDP) also affirmed that the "rise of a great power through ruthless application of power" was the wrong way to European unity.[13] Even without Napoleon, however, the fear of France was deeply rooted in German minds. The *DAZ* and the *Kölnische Zeitung* both were afraid that in a purely continental European bloc, "the Slavic-Romanic element" would prevail. Germany would thus be deprived of influence. Regarding Pan-Europe, they asserted that "to support such a political object is impossible for Germany."[14] Two conservative politicians uttered similar concerns. The "system of illusions" [that is] Pan-Europe was nothing other than a Europe of French hegemony."[15]

The French discussion about Franco-German reconciliation was characterized by strong similarities with the German one. The most fervent support for an understanding came from the political left. Many authors saw in Franco-German relations the "key to European Union," explained *La République*.[16] Pierre Renaudel of the French Socialist Party postulated in a 1928 New Year's message to *Vorwärts* that Germany needed to abolish its policy of revenge and France its policy of occupation.[17] One year later, Léon Blum, head of the French Socialists, hoped that the Young Plan, which foresaw the establishment of an international court in The Hague and the end of the French occupation of the Rhineland, had opened the path to the United States of Europe. The next steps depended on an honest and perhaps even cordial approach between France and Germany.[18] However, this cordiality failed to manifest itself. In 1930, Blum stated that the French press was leading a campaign against the secret re-armament of Germany. This was partly understandable, he admitted, but if one returned to the era of mistrust, any attempt at European federation would be doomed to failure.[19] The Radical-Socialist Jean Luchaire supported Blum. He believed that the Germans were true pacifists and Pan-Europeans who embraced Franco-German reconciliation, and so the French had to comport themselves equally well and become rational too.[20]

Rejections of Franco-German friendship were astonishingly rare. The authors did not lose sight of French interests but put them in a European perspective. Thus, *L'Oeuvre* claimed that France's security was a very good guarantee of European peace.[21] However, some intellectuals such as the French senator Jacques Bardoux and the sociologist Georges Blondel maintained their distrust of Germany.[22] This attitude was attributable in part to German Foreign Minister Gustav Stresemann, who before and during the First World War had been an annexionist. The French ambassador, Alexandre Conty, thus compared Stresemann to one of his predecessors who had been particularly unruly in French eyes: He saw a "pupil of Bismarck" lurking in the guise of a "good European."[23] *Le Figaro*, a conservative newspaper, reproached Stresemann for his wish to eliminate customs and political borders. It suspected that he wanted to secure a field of expansion for German overproduction and achieve German hegemony.[24] Thus, both countries continued to distrust one another.

A special characteristic of the French discussion was the constant emphasis on another policy option: France tried to maintain good contact with Great Britain and keep the country in Europe—whereas the Pan-European Idea foresaw a United Europe without the British Isles (or Russia). In French eyes Europe would hence become a group of powers "dominated by Germany."[25] Thus, Germany and France both had fears of being left alone in Europe with the other.

The Locarno Treaty:
A Silver Lining?

The Locarno Treaty of 1925 gave great impetus to the general discussion about France and Germany. In this agreement between the two neighbors and guaranteed by Great Britain and Italy, the German Reich acknowledged its western borders and agreed to the demilitarization of the Rhineland. This left the German Reich free hands to achieve its main and primary objective, that is, revision of its eastern borders. At the same time, the entry of Germany into the League of Nations was foreseen. This provoked an enormous response in the press and a wave of hope for European reconciliation. Even the national-conservative *DAZ* praised the Locarno Treaty as a good way out of the European crisis.[26] French Foreign Minister Aristide Briand is said to have announced after the signing of the treaty: "the United States of Europe is born."[27]

The greatest approval that Locarno received in Germany immediately after the negotiations was, again, from Social Democrats and Catholics. The head of the SPD, Otto Wels, declared passionately in parliament: "only now is there comprehension of the fact that we all . . . are connected through a common destiny . . . and that we need to be good Europeans if we want to be good Germans, good Frenchmen."[28] The position of the SPD was praised by the *Sozialistische Monatshefte*. They felt vindicated in their view on the European question: one of its authors called the treaty the "beginning of the gathering of the European peoples" within which Franco-German collaboration needed to be the first step.[29] The trade unionist journal *Gewerkschaftszeitung* also cheered Locarno as the "first step toward a European reconciliation." However, it hoped that the political act would be followed by an economic one.[30]

The head of *Germania* called Locarno a "public holiday for the whole of Europe." The "unity of the Occident" had now been reestablished.[31] Nevertheless, *Germania* stressed at the same time that revision of the Versailles Treaty was the ulterior motive of Locarno. This was symptomatic—supporting the Franco-German understanding but not losing sight of German interests. The Catholic journal *Abendland*, which above all fought for the reestablishment of the Occident, followed the same strategy. A revision of the Versailles Treaty had priority. If this was accomplished, however, one could easily handle the Pan-European problems of the present without the problems of the past.[32]

Liberals too welcomed Locarno. The *Vossische Zeitung* saw a general change in European status.[33] Wilhelm Heile (DDP) praised the development as well. For him, the Locarno Treaty was the best "that under the given circumstances could be achieved." Locarno would lead directly to Europe, "to the final goal of a European federation built on freedom and the equality of nations."[34] In the *Vossische Zeitung*, the president of the German Supreme Court, Walter Simons, called Locarno the "central piece of a political organization of Europe."[35] It is known, however, that Simons was an active advocate of the "Anschluss," the unification of Austria and the German Reich. He probably hoped that Locarno would bring him closer to his aim.

However, Locarno was not greeted only with praise. Most of the German conservatives rejected the treaty. The right-wing Reichstag Deputy Wilhelm Henning replied to a solemn speech of Otto Wels (SPD) by saying that his own party saw in the Locarno Treaty a "very cunning attempt to mock the German people."[36] That was a provocative statement. The Catholic *Germania* declared that the conservatives rejected the agreement because they regarded it as a new acknowledgement of the Versailles Treaty.[37] There was a fundamental difference between the documents: the Versailles Treaty was concluded about Germany, whereas the Locarno Treaty was concluded with Germany, as Wilhelm Heile explained. He interpreted the rejection by the conservatives as a last rearguard action and as a consequence of their demagogy.[38] The conservative *Deutsche Zeitung* countered sharply that Germany had to pay the piper of Locarno. It quoted former German Chancellor Bethmann-Hollweg, who had spoken about unlimited submarine warfare during the First World War: "Locarno—first step toward the United States of Europe! This is what was written recently by the triumphant organ of the Center Party, *Germania*. This first step has been paid with German land and people! If the next steps need to be paid in the same way, then *Finis Germaniae!*"[39] In France too, the conclusion of the Locarno Treaty dominated the press. Here, adherents of the European idea cheered very loudly. *L'Europe Nouvelle*, founded to promote the European idea, dealt with Locarno for weeks. Joseph Barthélemy, a Member of Parliament and vice president of the French Pan-European Union, hailed the "new spirit" of Locarno and regarded the treaty as a "primary contract of the United States of Europe." One only had to continue down this path.[40] *Le Monde Nouveau* likewise felt the "European spirit." Very polite toward its neighbor, it stressed what it regarded as decisive progress—for the first time after Versailles, the Germans had been allowed to negotiate a treaty. This would justify Briand's talking of the United States of Europe.[41] Even an author from the conservative newspaper *Le Figaro* emphasized in a very reconciliatory way the equality of the Germans in the "Rhine pact." At the same time, the newspaper remained cautious. Treaties could not always deliver what they promised. In the end, the only thing that counted was population.[42] And the Germans outnumbered the French. Deputy August Gauvain, who had grown up close to the German border, remained cautious as well, suggesting that in contrast to the peaceful French, the Germans were only keen on revenge. What happened if the treaty were to be broken?[43] A colleague summed up that Locarno was not enough to guarantee security and disarmament.[44] The agreement thus could not completely abolish the mistrust of the French people toward Germany.

Even some time after its conclusion, the echo of the Locarno Treaty could still be heard both in Germany and in France. The "policy of Locarno" was used as a catchphrase and was synonymous with Franco-German as well as European reconciliation despite German ulterior motives. Until 1927, Locarno was considered a very successful project; the policy of regional security pacts seemed to be a good strategy.[45] However, it was the case that disillusionment increasingly took over. No similar event, meeting, or treaty followed the agreement, making Locarno a one-time development. One ray of hope, though, was the meeting of the German and the French foreign ministers, Gustav Stresemann and Aristide Briand, in Thoiry on September 17, 1926. Both came to a basic understanding on the points of contention between their countries. For example, they agreed on the evacuation of the Rhineland and the return of the Saar region in exchange for German payments. However, the conversation was not turned into a treaty, because there were numerous public protests against the agreements, especially in France.[46] At first, the press reported intensively on the conversation; enthusiasm very quickly turned to disappointment, however, when it became obvious that the conversation would not have a positive outcome. Thus, an author complained in the *Sozialistische Monatshefte* that the "seed of Thoiry" had not sprouted.[47] While adherents of a united Europe despaired, Euro-skeptics felt encouraged. Hence, the conservative Adolf Grabowsky explained in 1928: "the fact that Locarno and Thoiry remained almost fruitless for true friendship between the two powers is seen in how unlikely any intimate combination of Germany and France is today."[48] Even the optimistic *Revue universelle* wrote in 1929 that the results of Locarno had not been very encouraging.[49] While the agreement might well have opened a door for constant reconciliation, no one actually walked through it.

The Briand Plan: European Intention or National Calculation?

In addition to Locarno, a second event stirred up emotions in this period. On September 5, 1929, Aristide Briand announced before the League of Nations in Geneva that he wished to create "a federal link" between the peoples of Europe. They should have the possibility of contacting each other at all times to discuss their interests and to make common decisions.[50] Eight months later, on May 17, 1930, he published a memorandum with the same message. Briand confirmed his wish for a European union and invited every European government to support his suggestion. They, however, answered reluctantly and were reserved.

The German government, for example, intended to give the Briand Plan a "first class burial" in the words of Julius Curtius, who had become foreign minister after Stresemann's death in the autumn of 1929.[51] Whereas Stresemann had supported European reconciliation, German politics after his death changed. The desire to revise the Versailles Treaty came more and more to the fore, and the Briand Plan was thought to hamper this aim.[52] In spite of all negative responses, the League of Nations founded a European study group to work on the plan. This was neither productive nor effective and the Briand Plan failed.

Nearly all over Europe, the Briand Plan created an enormous response in the press, wherein the debate over proposals for European unity peaked. From then on, the response continuously decreased. In Germany, it was overwhelmingly negative. Above all, the conservative press worked itself up expressing sharp criticism of the plan. Only the *Sozialistische Monatshefte*, again, fought for the plan and lamented that the German point of view was ignorant. Instead of honestly judging the proposal itself, the press would be content to cling to ancient anti-French prejudices.[53] The conservative author Reinhold Quaatz countered that the *Sozialistische Monatshefte* would act in a pro-French way and would be "politicians of fulfillment"—a reproach that was directed toward German politicians who had tried to fulfill the requirements of the Versailles Treaty at the beginning of the 1920s.[54] This shows the importance assigned to the Briand Plan. It aimed at a final reconciliation, whereas the adversaries felt it to be a threat to the very basis of the German Reich. A neutral stand was apparently not possible.

The critique of the German participants in the discussion covered two main points: First, it was said that Briand was not acting for the benefit of Europe but instead for "national egoist" reasons.[55] The French "security complex"[56] had made the foreign minister look for a new power politics,[57] one whose goal was still to preserve the Versailles "violation"[58] and the status quo.[59] The conservative *Preußische Kreuzzeitung* thus judged: Briand's "Pan-European Idea is for that reason—to make it simple—nothing other than a second dictation of Versailles . . . which hands over our native country completely to France."[60] *Das freie Deutschland* scoffed that while France may have changed its methods, "the aim of keeping Germany down has remained the same."[61] The editor-in-chief of *Deutsche Gedanke* regarded the plan as an attempt to daze those defeated in the war, "to make sure they will not feel the pain and the mutilation of the Versailles Treaty as much as they [currently] do."[62] The second argument was that Briand was looking to secure French hegemony,[63] albeit "benevolently disguised."[64] Germany was relegated to a very subordinate role in Briand's Europe[65] that was incompatible with the "interests and legitimate aspirations" of the German Reich.[66] The *Völkischer Beobachter* was particularly exercised about a Europe under the "protection of French bayonets."[67] Napoleonic fears were coming into play. The author Wilhelm Gürge warned against "the French idea of taking up the heritage of Napoleon."[68] Reinhold Quaatz also declared that Briand would follow a "Rheinbundpolitik" just like Napoleon.[69] The *Arbeitgeber* was equally afraid of "French hegemony" and the "fulfillment of the ambitious plans of Napoleon I."[70]

The French reception of Briand's proposal was significantly more favorable. The major newspapers welcomed it with one voice. The radical-socialist *Volonté* even declared effusively that the day of the memorandum's publication was one that no one would ever forget.[71] *Le Quotidien*, which was radical-conservative, was pleased that Europe was becoming conscious of its own existence. Now it was to express "its will to secure its civilization in peace."[72] The conservative *Le Temps* did not doubt either that the plan was "a great political idea"—not omitting to state, however, that under no circumstances should France's security be sacrificed.[73]

The Briand Plan did not remain undisputed in France. The most fervent critique was uttered from the very far left and the very far right wing, just as in Germany. The Communist *Humanité* complained: "Proletarians have nothing to expect from this federation."[74] The nationalist *Action française*, on the other hand, did not engage in that level of critique regarding its content; instead, the newspaper simply mocked the plan's author. Neither in his speech at the League of Nations nor in his memorandum could one single clear idea be found: "the whole world has the impression that Briand spoke to say nothing."[75]

Conclusion

The discussion about France and Germany clarifies basic elements of the political situation in the interwar period. On both sides of the border, Social Democrats, Catholics, and Liberals—to an extent—were relatively open-minded about reconciliation, especially between 1925 and 1930. They even hoped for general European reconciliation and unification. Nevertheless, mutual distrust could not be overcome. Both Germans and Frenchmen, especially conservatives, believed in the evil of the other—even during the period of reconciliation. Above all, national traumas—such as that caused by Napoleon—continued to linger in the collective memory of the societies. Thus, even protagonists of reconciliation were regarded with skepticism.

In this context, the Locarno Treaty was a ray of hope for both nations. Each welcomed it as a promise of lasting peace. Only conservatives were fearful for national aims and judged that Locarno was not the right way to start revising the Versailles treaty. Social Democrats, Catholics, and Liberals were the most active in advocating the Locarno Treaty. The most optimistic among them even regarded Locarno as the first step toward a United States of Europe. Yet, German adherents of the Occident and the "Anschluss" combined non-European ulterior motives with the treaty. This abuse of the European idea for nationalist aims is typical of European thinking in the interwar period. However, after it became clear that Locarno was not to be followed by other positive events apart from the Thoiry conversation, disappointment spread and the belief in Franco-German reconciliation faded away.

The Briand Plan could not link up with Locarno. The French foreign minister's proposal provoked a massive outcry in Germany. All anti-French prejudices of the previous years and even from centuries before took the stage once again. The plan was not regarded as an idea for European Union but as an attempt to secure French security and hegemony. This is also symptomatic of the interwar period: Everyone saw the ghost of nationalism lurking everywhere. True European thinking was unimaginable. Thus, a last chance for an enduring European understanding had lapsed. After 1930, any attempt to reconcile the neighboring states was obsolete.

Notes

1. Arnold Kalisch, "Paneuropa," *Friedenswarte* 25, no. 7 (July 1925): 207.
2. "Paneuropa," *Vorwärts*, October 3, 1926: 1.
3. Naphtali, "Die Einigung Europas," *Gesellschaft* (1926): 342.
4. Ludwig Quessel, "Ludwig: Frankreichs Europäische Aufgabe," *Sozialistische Monatshefte*, August 19, 1924: 482–85.
5. "Wien als Kongressstadt," *Germania*, October 7, 1926.
6. Guido Müller, *Europäische Gesellschaftsbeziehungen nach dem Ersten Weltkrieg. Das Deutsch-Französische Studienkomitee und der Europäische Kulturbund* (München: Oldenbourg, 2005), 64.
7. Speculator, "Paneuropa," *Hochland* 22 (October 1924): 116.
8. Ludwig Heilmaier, "Paneuropa," *Soziale Revue* 27 (September 1927): 399.
9. Hollweg, "Pan-Europa," *Deutsche Allgemeine Zeitung (DAZ)*, September 2, 1925: 1.
10. "Paneuropa oder deutsche Realpolitik?" *DAZ*, October 18, 1929.
11. Karl Toth, "Paneuropa. Eine grundsätzliche Untersuchung," *Deutschlands Erneuerung*, no. 10 (1926): 463ff.
12. *Verhandlungen des Reichstags*, vol. 389, 6483 A, March 22, 1926.
13. Wilhelm Heile, "Warum ich für Paneuropa bin," *Friedenswarte* 25 (September 1925): 236.
14. "Deutschland und Paneuropa. Graf Coudenhoves Irrtümer," *Kölnische Zeitung*, October 18, 1926.
15. Willy Hellpach, *Politische Prognose für Deutschland* (Berlin: S. Fischer, 1928), 477.
16. "Le rapprochement franco-allemand clef de voûte de l'Union européenne," *République*, September 4, 1929.
17. Pierre Renaudel, "Pour le rapprochement franco-allemand," *Vie socialiste*, 31 December 1927/7 January 1928, 3–4.
18. Léon Blum, "Les Etats-Unis d'Europe," *Le Populaire*, September 9, 1929.
19. Léon Blum, "Le Mémorandum de M. Briand. Contradiction et difficultés," *Populaire*, May 23, 1930.
20. Jean Luchaire, "Le détente franco-allemande est un fait incontestable," *Volonté*, November 14, 1929.
21. "Pan-Europa," *Oeuvre*, October 11, 1924.
22. Jacques Bardoux, "Mysticisme européen et réalisme politique," *Temps*, March 12, 1930; Georges Blondel, *Les Etats-Unis d'Europe: Ce qu'on pense à l étranger* (Paris, 1930), 9.
23. Conty, "Les Etats-Unis d'Europe," *Académie Diplomatique International: Séances et Travaux*, no. 1–3 (1930): 61.
24. Saint-Réal, "La production française et les Etats-Unis d'Europe," *Figaro*, September 5, 1929.
25. Archives du Ministère des Affaires Etrangères, Série Société des Nations, V-Union Européenne, N. 2495, March 4, 1927.
26. Berthold Molden, "Europa?" *DAZ*, October 5, 1926.
27. Ebed Vandervlugt, "Les Etats-Unis d'Europe," *Monde Nouveau*, January 15, 1926, 1061.
28. *Verhandlungen des Reichstags*, vol. 388, 4492 D, November 24, 1925.

29. Cohen, "Locarno und Kontinentalpolitik," *Sozialistische Monatshefte*, December 10, 1925: 731ff.

30. "Ein wirtschaftliches Locarno," *Gewerkschaftszeitung*, November 21, 1925.

31. Richard Kuenzer, "Der glückliche Ausgang," *Germania*, October 17, 1925.

32. Karl Anton Rohan, "System und Leben," *Abendland* 1, no. 3 (1926): 173.

33. "Erster Paneuropa-Kongreß," *Vossische Zeitung*, October 4, 1926.

34. Wilhelm Heile, "Von Versailles über Locarno nach—Europa," *Hilfe*, no. 21 (1925): 488.

35. "Simons über Pan-Europa," *Vossische Zeitung*, February 27, 1927.

36. *Verhandlungen des Reichstags*, vol. 388, 4610C, November 24, 1925.

37. Kuenzer, "Locarno."

38. Wilhelm Heile, "Locarno. Ein erster Schritt zu den 'Vereinigten Staaten von Europa,'" *Germania*, November 27, 1925.

39. Lancelle, "Die Vereinigten Staaten von Europa," *Deutsche Zeitung*, December 11, 1925.

40. Joseph Barthélémy, "Après Locarno: Vers les Etats-Unis d'Europe," *Revue Politique et Parlementaire*, November 10, 1925: 239, 244, 246.

41. Henri Hertz, "Locarno, Canossa de l'Europe," *Monde Nouveau*, November 15, 1925: 916–18.

42. Albert Mallet, "Le pacte rhénan est adopté," *Figaro*, October 16, 1925.

43. Auguste Gauvain, "Les traités de Locarno," *Journal des Débats*, October 21, 1925.

44. J.-M. Bourget, "La valeur stratégique des accords de Locarno," *Journal des Débats*, December 9, 1925.

45. Jean-L. Dauriac, "Pour une meilleure organisation de la paix," *Homme libre*, September 28, 1926; Nicola Politis, "La sécurité de l'Europe," *Monde Nouveau*, February 15, 1927: 1454.

46. Heinz-Otto Sieburg, *Geschichte Frankreichs* (Stuttgart: Kohlhammer, 1989), 399.

47. Ludwig Quessel, "Die neue weltpolitische Situation," *Sozialistische Monatshefte*, June 27, 1927: 30.

48. Grabowsky, "Problem Paneuropa," *Zeitschrift für Politik* 5 (May 17, 1928): 697.

49. Saint-Brice, "Où reparaît 'Paneuropa'?" *Revue universelle*, August 1, 1929, 360.

50. "Le discours de M. Briand," *Le Temps*, September 7, 1929.

51. Derek Heater, *Europäische Einheit—Biographie einer Idee* (Bochum: Winkler, 2005), 223.

52. Peter Krüger, "Die Ansätze zu einer europäischen Wirtschaftsgemeinschaft," in *Wirtschaftliche und politische Integration in Europa*, ed. Helmut Berding (Göttingen: Vandenhoeck und Rupprecht, 1984), 167.

53. Richard Kleineibst, "Europäisches Zwischenspiel," *Sozialistische Monatshefte*, June 10, 1930, 531.

54. Reinhold Georg Quaatz, *Vereinigte Staaten von Europa?* (Langensalza: Beyer, 1930), 24–29.

55. Bruno Rauecker, "Europäische Wirtschaftsgemeinschaft?" *Hilfe* 25 (February 1930): 196–97.

56. Hermann Ullmann, "Paneuropa? Europa!" *Kunstwart* 43 (July 10, 1930): 211.

57. Albert, "Illusion Paneuropa," *Akademische Blätter*, no. 12 (1929): 288.

58. Erich Obst, "Berichterstattung aus Europa und Afrika," *Zeitschrift für Geopolitik*, no. 10 (1929): 868.

59. Wilhelm von Kries, "Pan-Europa," *Deutsches Adelsblatt*, May 24, 1930: 295.

60. Hans Herdegen, "Paneuropa oder Mitteleuropa?" *Preußische Kreuzzeitung*, January 5, 1930.

61. "Gestern Balkanisierung Europas, heute Paneuropa," *Das freie Deutschland*, no. 1 (1931): 630.

62. Axel Schmidt, "Paneuropa und der Osten," *Hilfe*, no. 6 (1930): 632.

63. Richard Hennig, *Geopolitik* (Leipzig: Teubner, 1931), 322.

64. Carl von Ossietzky, "Coudenhove und Briand," *Weltbühne*, no. 26 (May 1930): 785.

65. *Verhandlungen des Reichstags*, vol. 444, 916A, February 11, 1931.

66. Emil Daniels, "Paneuropa," *Preußische Jahrbücher*, no. 6 (1930): 331–32.

67. "Briand in Genf," *Völkischer Beobachter*, September 7, 1929.

68. Gürge, "Paneuropa oder Mitteleuropa?" *Volk und Reich* 6 (May 1930): 490.

69. Quaatz, "Vereinigte Staaten von Europa?" 24–29.

70. Wolff, "Die Vereinigte Staaten von Europa," *Arbeitgeber* 19 (October 1929): 556ff.

71. "La France a invité hier les 25 Etats du vieux continent," *Volonté*, May 18, 1930.

72. "Un événement historique," *Quotidien*, May 18, 1930.

73. "Le discours de M. Briand," *Temps*, September 7, 1929.

74. "L'Union Fédérale Européenne nouvelle étape vers la guerre antisoviétique," *Humanité*, May 18, 1930.

75. "Le mirifique succès des Etats-Unis d'Europe," *Action francaise*, September 7, 1929.

CHAPTER 10

Attempts at a Franco-German Economic Rapprochement during the Second Half of the 1930s

Frédéric Clavert

Hitler's seizure of power in 1933 was not welcomed in France, but Paris believed that it had the means to contain Nazi Germany. The Third Republic was counting on the diplomatic policy developed since 1919. It was based on an "alliance de revers" with Poland and the Little Entente (Czechoslovakia, Yugoslavia, and Rumania). Two great conferences, the economic and financial conference in London and the disarmament conference in Geneva, collapsed in 1933, which was to Berlin's advantage. It led France to build the Gold Bloc, which soon proved a failure, and encouraged Germany to withdraw from the League of Nations. Furthermore, the French position in Eastern Europe worsened when Poland signed an agreement with Germany in January of 1934. The "alliance de revers" was dying. Paris and Berlin nonetheless tried to come to an agreement on disarmament, but Louis Barthou, the French foreign minister, explained in April 1934 that France would decide alone what was in its national interests. The disarmament talks were over.

On an economic level, France wanted Germany to refund the Dawes and Young loans. Hjalmar Schacht, president of the Reichsbank, halted all financial and commercial transfers in foreign currencies. As a result, France and Germany concluded a clearing agreement in July 1934. Paris accepted to buy more German goods, and Berlin would pay its debts in francs instead of blocked marks. However, this treaty malfunctioned in the weeks following its signing.[1]

On a diplomatic level, Paris, London, and Rome then tried to establish a front against Germany. The Stresa Conference in April of 1935 had no positive consequences for the French position toward Germany: Great Britain signed an agreement with the Third Reich that allowed the latter to rebuild its navy (June 18,

1935). Moreover, the deplorable Franco-British management of the Ethiopian crisis at the end of 1935 and the remilitarization of the Rhineland in March 1936 definitely ended the Third Republic's supremacy on the European continent. France's attempt to contain Nazi Germany had failed.

This altered the balance of power between the two countries in favor of Germany. It highlighted the need for better commercial and political relations if there was a chance of avoiding war. France and some Nazi dignitaries looked for an agreement that could link politics and economics. The failure of this attempt was followed by the last efforts toward rapprochement: Munich and the Franco-German declaration of December 1938.

1936: A Modification of the European Atmosphere

The democracies tried to learn from the diplomatic shift in favor of Germany after the remilitarization of the Rhineland. In France and Germany, evolution at the head of the two nations and the transformation of segments of French public opinion occurred parallel to each other.

Changes in Europe

The remilitarization of the Rhineland and the failure of the sanctions imposed by the League of Nations in 1935 created a new balance of power. Although the "Axis" had not yet been formed, Europe in the summer of 1936 seemed more and more divided between democracies on the one hand and fascist dictatorships on the other. This division raised two questions. What kind of economic relations could be established between democratic and fascist states? Could the United States play an economic role in Europe again? The involvement of the United States on the European continent was seen as an element favoring France and the United Kingdom.

The question of the relationships between democracies and fascist regimes became important with the decision to end economic sanctions against Italy, made during an extraordinary meeting of the Assembly of the League of Nations. On July 4, 1936, Belgian Prime Minister Paul van Zeeland ended his final speech as president of the assembly with these words: "In a great many countries the revival is evident; but it is almost entirely confined to the home markets. . . . Such being the case, does not wisdom demand that the next assembly should extend the scope of deliberations, and that, without neglecting in any way that which must be done in the political sphere, it should again make a comprehensive and strenuous effort to set in motion an economic revival."[2] This speech marked the beginning of a two-year period characterized by attempts at rapprochement between democracies and dictatorships in the economic field. The franc's devaluation in September of 1936 and a private initiative of reconciliation carried out by the French financial attaché in London, Emmanuel Monick, highlighted the fact that France and the United Kingdom needed help from the United States.

The French economic situation made American support all the more pressing. After two years of an ineffective deflation policy, the center-right majority was, in fact, waiting for the 1936 elections to devaluate the currency. In May of that year, the unexpected victory of the Popular Front, a left-wing coalition bringing together Communists, Socialists, and Radicals[3] led by Socialist Léon Blum, adopted a policy of "reflation," that is, neither deflation nor devaluation. Nevertheless, the social reforms of June 1936 threatened the price level and the government had to devaluate the franc on September 26, 1936. The currency lost 26 percent of its gold value.[4]

However, Blum was conscious of the need for France to avoid an isolated economic and monetary policy. In fact, he obtained international support for the devaluation of the franc with a tripartite agreement among France, the United Kingdom, and the United States, announced on September 25, 1936. This imprecise declaration contained the notion of "monetary alignment." Since the 1933 failed economic conference in London, the Third Republic had desired to convince the United Kingdom and the United States to carry out joint monetary action. France now seemed to have reached this goal, though the tripartite declaration ultimately had no practical effects. Yet, the prospect of a monetary agreement with the United States raised hopes in Western Europe. Within weeks of the signing of the tripartite agreement, Belgium, Switzerland, and the Netherlands had joined in. This success raised questions for the foreign policy of both France and the United Kingdom: What was to be done with Germany? Would the United States accept a larger commitment in Europe without any understanding with Germany?

Emmanuel Monick's initiative to U.S. president Franklin Roosevelt demonstrated that America was not ready to increase its engagement in Europe, unless relations between France and Germany improved. Monick submitted to the American ambassador in Paris, William Bullitt, an informal memorandum called "President Roosevelt and the War Debts," dated November 22, 1936. On December 20, Bullitt commented negatively on this memorandum to Roosevelt but insisted on the need for better relations between France and Germany. He also noted that Italy and Germany had no interest in collaborating with France and the United Kingdom.[5] Was he drawing conclusions from the recent political change in France and Germany?

National Political Changes

After the Rhineland remilitarization, two events marked the year 1936: the Popular Front's democratic seizure of power in France and the rise of Hermann Göring in the economic field with the launching of Hitler's Four-Year Plan, an economic program whose goal was to revitalize the German economy in anticipation of war.

On May 3, 1936, the Popular Front won the French legislative elections. Léon Blum, the new prime minister, made his first declaration about international relations at the end of June. He assigned three priorities to French foreign policy:

collective security, peace, and disarmament.[6] In Blum's eyes, collective security was an implement for peace and ought to be combined with general disarmament. Blum's experimentation with peaceful suggestions was less out of sheer idealism rather than a means to preserve the political status quo in Europe—of which France was a main defender—in light of ever-stronger revisionist, totalitarian regimes and to strengthen it through cooperation with its principal challengers, that is, Hitler's Germany and Mussolini's Italy. This appeared all the more urgent since French diplomacy faced a new political configuration in Europe owing to gradual Italian-German rapprochement. During the summer and autumn of 1936, the Belgian claim of "independence," the signing of the tripartite agreement, and the franc's devaluation forced the French government to consider talks with Germany. However, the most important changes that France had to consider were in the economic power structures of the Third Reich during 1936.

In fact, Hjalmar Schacht, the economics minister, and Göring, the head of the Luftwaffe, were struggling against one another to gain control over the economy. Schacht, who had been president of the Reichsbank from 1924 to 1930, met Göring and Hitler in December 1930 and January 1931. This tactical rapprochement served him well: He became president of the Reichsbank again in March of 1933. Schacht's management of Germany's external private debts in 1933 and 1934, which led to a "bilateralization" of the German financial and economic foreign relations, enabled him to replace Kurt Schmitt as economics minister, who opposed the financial consequences of German rearmament.[7] In 1935, serving also as "general plenipotentiary for the war economy," Schacht exerted a dominant influence on the German economy. In the autumn of 1934, he initiated the "New Plan," a mercantilist economic policy aimed at assuring the arms industry a sufficient supply of raw materials, which neglected the consumer products sector. Furthermore, the mismanagement of the farming sector provoked tensions between Schacht and Agriculture Minister Walter Darré. Hitler then asked Göring to arbitrate between the two ministers during the winter of 1935. From that point on, Schacht progressively lost power to Göring. During the summer of 1936, Hitler wrote a "memorandum for a Four-Year Plan," which implicitly opposed Schacht's policy. Under Göring's direction, it officially became the Four-Year Plan, whose aim was to speed up rearmament through autarchy.

Despite his loss of power, Schacht was still useful to the Third Reich. Indeed, as central banker, he had strong connections abroad, notably through the Bank of International Settlements in Basel. The Popular Front's rise to power caused a reshaping of the Banque de France. Emile Labeyrie, its new governor, met Schacht in Berlin at the beginning of August 1936. The two bankers agreed that the latter would go to Paris at the end of the month. When Schacht arrived in Paris, a segment of French public opinion was ready for better relations with the Third Republic's eastern neighbor.

Since 1933, Germany had tried to influence French public opinion.[8] The aim was to take advantage of pacifist feelings in the French population in order to undermine the Versailles Treaty system. Berlin had several means to achieve this goal. French newspapers were experiencing financial difficulties which could be solved by German funds.[9] In 1934, Otto Abetz founded a French office of the Dienststelle Ribbentrop,[10] a Nazi organization that functioned parallel to the German Foreign Ministry; this initiative allowed Germany to exploit different ideological streams in its favor: pacifism, right-wing authoritarianism, and Alsatian and Breton autonomism. One of the most important elements of German propaganda in France was the foundation of the Deutsch-Französische Gesellschaft or Comité France-Allemagne in October 1935. These actions generated a favorable atmosphere for a rapprochement with Berlin while reassuring French public opinion about Germany's intentions.

The Impossible Link between Politics and Economics (August 1936 to July 1937)

Though Paris wished to improve relations with Berlin, it would not do so at all costs. Schacht's visit to Paris was the occasion for Germany and France to measure the potential for a "détente." Blum clearly wanted a general and political agreement with Germany on peace in Europe before accepting any economic settlement. The conclusion of the tripartite agreement gave France the occasion to integrate bilateral talks into larger discussions that gave birth to the van Zeeland mission (April 1937). The fall of the Blum government in June 1937 and his replacement by the "radical" Camille Chautemps altered French diplomacy: With the conclusion of a new clearing agreement in July, politics was subordinated to economics. The political agreement that France was looking for was still not in sight.

Schacht, Blum, and van Zeeland

Emile Labeyrie, governor of the Banque de France, came to Berlin at the beginning of August 1936. This courtesy visit led to Schacht's trip to Paris between August 26 and 28 of 1936. The discussions that followed this visit between Blum and Schacht on one hand and France and the United Kingdom on the other led to the van Zeeland mission.

In August of 1936, Schacht met in Paris with Blum and other members of the Cabinet. André François-Poncet actively prepared those discussions and believed that Schacht's visit could help influence Hitler toward moderation.[11] On August 28, 1936, Blum told Schacht that he was ready to discuss a general system guaranteeing peace in Europe thanks to disarmament negotiations.[12] Schacht seemed receptive and promised a European system of nonaggression that would indirectly include the USSR. The most delicate part of the discussion was the question of the compensation France could offer Berlin. Schacht asked for concessions that he had supported since the 1920s: the return of Germany's colonies. Though Blum could not see how such a proposal would ease German economic conditions, he was ready to contact the British government on the subject. The two men considered the possibility of an international conference between Germany, Italy, France, the United Kingdom, and the United States.

Back in Berlin, Schacht informed Hitler about the discussions in Paris. Even though Hitler did not have any interest in colonies or believe in the future of the Blum government, he authorized Schacht to engage in those talks and insisted on the importance of a German colonial domain at the 1936 Party Rally.[13] The loss of the country's overseas possessions was actually one of the last terms of the Treaty of Versailles not yet abolished.[14] The ambiguity of Hitler's behavior was the most serious obstacle to a Franco-German rapprochement in the period from 1936 to 1938.

The following months showed to what extent the objectives of the August 1936 Blum-Schacht talks were blocked by the ambiguity of German and British actions. Blum contacted Anthony Eden of the British Foreign Office in September 1936. Eden welcomed Schacht's propositions but played a "wait-and-see" game and basically refused any colonial concessions. The Franco-British talks on Schacht's ideas had reached a deadlock. Neither Paris nor London could leave the German propositions unanswered or take any initiative to make the tripartite agreement more concrete. With the Spanish Civil War in the background, the French and British governments asked Belgian Prime Minister Paul van Zeeland in April 1937 to undertake a private diplomatic mission on the possibility of economic cooperation in Europe. Van Zeeland seemed the right man for the task since he had successfully combated economic problems in his country.

One of the most important actors in van Zeeland's mission was Schacht. From August 1936 to his dismissal from the Economics Ministry in November 1937, his main goal was to bring Germany back into a "normal" set of international economic arrangements. Part of this involved increasing Germany's raw material supplies. New colonies or privileged access to resources in the hands of colonial powers could in his view be a solution. His demand was nonetheless ambiguous because raw materials could be used for rearmament. Even so, the president of the Reichsbank tried to use the van Zeeland mission to accelerate a Franco-British answer to his August proposals. During the mission, Schacht was back in Paris from May 25 to 29, officially to inaugurate the German Hall at the World Exposition of 1937. He met Blum again and spoke to the members of the Comité France-Allemagne and of the German Chamber of Commerce. Schacht adroitly played off French expectations: *Le Temps* had a false presentiment that he would propose something extraordinary.[15] In fact, his actions reflected an internal conflict within the Nazi government on economic issues. Schacht faced major opponents such as Göring, Ribbentrop, Darré and Robert Ley (head of the German Labor Front), so the colonial and raw materials questions became a matter of his political survival. Within this context, the van Zeeland mission and negotiations with France to conclude a new clearing agreement were particularly important to him.

Schacht's trip to Paris was characterized by the all-pervasive raw materials question. A new discussion between Blum and Schacht revealed the gap between the two men: The prime minister wanted a political agreement whose goal was to favor general solutions to European problems, disarmament, and Germany's return to the League of Nations, whereas the banker wanted to accelerate the conclusion of the Franco-German clearing agreement. For Blum, politics was the highest priority, whereas Schacht's prime concern was economic in nature. A change at the head of the French government proved opportune for Schacht and his priorities.

From Blum to Chautemps

Politically weakened, the Blum government fell on June 22, 1937. The new French government, led by Camille Chautemps, gave Schacht the opportunity to accelerate the signing of a new clearing agreement between Germany and France. Chautemps's economic priority replaced Blum's political priority. Was this shift in France's diplomatic goal successful?

Camille Chautemps's arrival at the head of the French government started a second phase in the policy of the Popular Front. He was a "radical" and thus presided over a more center-left government. Soon after he came to power, France and Germany signed the 1937 clearing agreement, replacing the 1934 settlements that France had denounced in 1935. Between 1935 and 1937, Franco-German commerce had functioned on a kind of extralegal basis. Chautemps favored a clearing agreement, because he thought that an economic agreement would strengthen the position of the "moderate" German dignitaries, such as Schacht or even Göring who was usually considered a conservative rather than a Nazi extremist. This policy of economic appeasement aimed at stabilizing Germany and the European Continent through better economic relations.

The clearing agreement was a victory for Schacht. It could be considered a first step toward a Franco-German rapprochement and a colonial solution to Germany's economic problems.[16] At that time, van Zeeland was in Washington and the European powers were aware that a global solution capable of heading off a war was dependent on U.S. action in Europe. This implied a settlement of Franco-German disputes. Would the clearing agreement be the first step toward a more general treaty? That was France's wish and, perhaps, Schacht's hope.

However, the 1937 Franco-German economic settlement did not work as expected. The agreement concluded on July 10, 1937, was not compatible with the Four-Year Plan, and Chautemps's goal of obtaining a political agreement through better commercial relations was not achieved. As soon as the end of 1937, commercial relations between the two countries worsened. French financial and monetary problems had not been resolved.[17] As a result, France's economy was not strong enough and the French market could not offer a sufficient outlet for German goods so as to improve bilateral commercial relations. The Third Reich used the July agreement to further its rearmament. In fact, neither better commercial relations nor a political agreement was possible. Moreover, the most significant clause of the clearing agreement, the iron and coal settlement, proved unworkable as early as 1938.[18]

At the end of 1937, Germany seemed more and more dangerous to the other European states. French and British heads of government noted the weakening of Schacht's position in the Nazi polycratic power structures. For Chautemps, Schacht now had the "voice of a ghost."[19] France and Germany continued to discuss the possibility of a colonial solution to the German problem, but Schacht, no longer heading the Economics Ministry, was now out of the game.

Approaching the Nightmare

At the same time that Schacht was losing his influence in the Third Reich,[20] London and Paris were looking for a way to draw Germany away from the path to war through a return of colonies. The definitive failure of van Zeeland's mission and rising tensions over Czechoslovakia pushed the Franco-German rapprochement into the background. The signing of the Munich Agreement at the end of September 1938 nevertheless paved the way for an illusory Franco-German declaration. However, the entry of German troops into Prague destroyed any hope of a bilateral rapprochement considered as a first step to pacification of Europe.

The Failure of the Colonial Solution

Paris and London tried one last time to dissuade Germany from building an autarkic economy while discussing the possibility of returning its former colonies. In Germany, some ministers were using the colonial question to profit from Schacht's loss of power. Walter Darré, for instance, argued that colonies would enable Germany to achieve agricultural autonomy.[21] Following these declarations, Mussolini claimed on November 5, 1937 that Germany had a right to receive colonies. Then on November 27, Schacht's departure from the Economics Ministry became public.[22] On November 19,[23] Chautemps, Chamberlain, and their foreign ministers had considered the retrocession of colonies to Germany in exchange for German concessions in Central Europe. Such a general agreement with Berlin was not possible judging from German reactions after the publication of van Zeeland's memorandum (January 26, 1938).

The determination to improve Franco-German relations could not be separated from Franco-British cooperation in the form of van Zeeland's mission. His memorandum suggested a very progressive way to free commercial relations by lowering tariffs and improving the European political atmosphere. German officials reacted in two ways. Hitler indirectly refused any implementation of the ideas during his speech of February 28, 1938.[24] The Reichsbank suggested rejecting van Zeeland's proposals, because they would force Germany to change its trade system with Eastern and Central Europe and thus give up a large part of the Reich's influence in those regions.[25] The definitive failure of van Zeeland's mission was logical considering the changes in Germany. At the beginning of February 1938, the most influential conservative politicians in Germany were expelled from power and replaced by convinced Nazis. All hope then vanished for a Franco-German rapprochement so as to avoid another war stemming from political, military, and economic disputes in Central and Eastern Europe. The annexation of Austria to the Reich the following month confirmed this fact. Between

February of 1938 and March of 1939, French and British appeasement policy focused on Czechoslovakia.

Munich and the December 1938 Franco-German Declaration

After the annexation of Austria, Franco-German relations improved because Paris agreed during the summer of 1938 to integrate Austrian trade into the 1937 clearing agreement. Nevertheless, this did not bring about any improvement in the system: German exports to France fell. The 1938 Czechoslovakian crisis complicated these trade relations even further. Until the Franco-German declaration of December 6, political negotiations were prioritized over economics and were essentially led by the British Prime Minister Neville Chamberlain. With the signing of the Munich agreement at the end of September 1938, the two democracies capitulated: the Third Reich could occupy and annex the Sudetenland in accordance with Hitler's will.

In France, Edouard Daladier, successor to Chautemps as prime minister, and Georges Bonnet, foreign minister since March 1938, signed the Munich Agreement. Back in France, they asked for a joint declaration with Germany, which resembled the one concluded with Britain in Munich. After some insistence, they obtained it on December 6, 1938. This text had a strong political significance: Officially, France and Germany had no conflicts in Europe any longer.

Nonetheless, the most important fact concerning a practical rapprochement between the two powers was the economic negotiations following the declaration.[26] To develop the disappointing trade relations between the two countries, Germany offered to augment its purchases in France and its Empire. It also suggested initiatives to promote contacts between French and German companies and citizens as well as Franco-German cooperation in other countries.[27] These proposals aimed at a kind of "clearing" of the Franco-German trade dispute.[28] Both countries negotiated on this basis. If a monetary problem in the tourist field, one of France's most vital economic sectors, could not be solved, they could start negotiations on the iron and coal agreement again. On March 10, 1939, trade from the Sudetenland was inserted into the 1937 clearing agreement. German economic circles believed that these negotiations would improve political relations with France.[29] At the beginning of March 1939, they even reproached the French delegation in Berlin as being too timid.[30] On March 15, 1939, the last step toward Czechoslovakia's dismemberment put an end to all attempts at Franco-German rapprochement.

Conclusion

When Léon Blum became prime minister of France in June of 1936, European sentiment was in favor of a rapprochement with Germany. This possible "détente" could have been the basis for a general agreement on Europe, including the United Kingdom and the United States. Although Hjalmar Schacht seemed to agree with Blum's plans mainly because he wanted a success abroad to counter

Hermann Göring's competition, the Third Reich nevertheless favored an economic rather than a political understanding. The goal was to secure supplies for the German economy, which was straining from the extraordinary pace of rearmament.

Among the numerous initiatives aimed at improving economic relations, Blum's strategy of "politics first" could not succeed because it contradicted Göring's Four-Year Plan. Confronted with this failure, Blum's successor at the head of the French government, Camille Chautemps, tried to reverse this logic by concluding the 1937 Franco-German clearing agreement. This settlement was a first step in encouraging a larger treaty that the mission of Belgian Prime Minister Paul van Zeeland would bring about. The result was very disappointing: The clearing system did not work. Schacht, at that time advocating a Franco-German rapprochement, lost the Economics Ministry. The van Zeeland mission largely failed.

In 1938, the Sudetenland crisis transformed attempts at rapprochement into a policy of appeasement. French appeasers temporarily believed that the Munich agreement and the declaration of December 1938 allowed an economic rapprochement. From December 1938 to March 1939, talks between the two countries sketched out an ambitious scheme to revive trade relations. The dreams of the appeasers fell apart when Germany dismembered Czechoslovakia.

Interpreting these attempts at rapprochement is not easy. On Germany's side, Schacht's position in the Third Reich is a noteworthy feature of the conflicts between German offices. To slow Göring's rise in the economic field, the central banker tried to obtain a success abroad: An economic agreement with France could have improved the flow of supplies to the German economy. Schacht could not convince Blum to reverse his priorities, but it was not in the interest of France to conclude an economic agreement without a political one. Blum probably wanted to obtain U.S. and British support for his foreign policy objectives. Chautemps seemed more reliable: The new Franco-German clearing agreement was signed, but Schacht's hope of obtaining significant results and Chautemps's goal of concluding a political agreement collapsed because of the radicalization of the Third Reich that occurred between the fall of Schacht and the Sudetenland crisis. The meaning of rapprochement changed accordingly. Its aim was no longer a peaceful stabilization of the continent but the appeasement of the German dictatorship, then preeminent in Europe. Although the December 1938 Franco-German Declaration gave birth to illusory economic talks, this policy definitively failed in March 1939.

Notes

1. Sylvain Schirmann. *Les relations économiques et financières franco-allemandes, 1932–1939* (CHEFF, Ministère de l'économie et du budget: Paris, 1995), 98.
2. *Journal Officiel de la Société des Nations*, supplément no. 151 (1936): 70.
3. At that time, "radicalism" was a center-wing political movement, divided into different parties.

4. Schirmann, *Les relations économiques*, chap. 13; Frédéric Clavert, "Hjalmar Schacht, financier et diplomate" (unpublished PhD, Université Robert Schuman, Strasbourg 3, 2006), chap. 6.
5. Jean-Baptiste Duroselle, *La décadence* (Paris: Imprimerie Nationale, 1979), 312.
6. Ibid., 292.
7. The process of "bilateralization" began under the Brüning government (March 1930–May 1932), when the Reich faced the 1931 banking crisis. Cf. Clavert, "Schacht," 192ff and following.
8. Charles Bloch, "La place de la France dans les différents stades de la politique extérieure du Troisième Reich (1933–1940)," in *Les relations franco-allemandes. 1933–1939*, ed. F. G. Dreyfus (Strasbourg: CNRS, 1976), 14–31.
9. Cf. *Le Figaro*, very favorable to Germany. Bloch, "La place de la France dans les différents stades."
10. Otto Abetz, *Histoire d'une politique franco-allemande, 1930–1950, Mémoires d'un ambassadeur* (Paris: Stock, 1953).
11. Documents Diplomatiques Français (DDF), 1932–1939, 2e série, volume 3, no. 196, François-Poncet à Delbos, August 24, 1936.
12. DDF, ser. 2, vol. 3, no. 196, François-Poncet à Delbos, August 24, 1936.
13. Ibid.
14. Ibid.
15. DDF, 2e série, Tome V, no. 442, François-Poncet à Delbos, May 21, 1937.
16. Ibid.
17. Chautemps devaluated again the Franc at the end of June 1936.
18. Schirmann, *Les relations économiques*, 197. Those collaborations included cooperation in French colonies (199).
19. DDF, 2e série, Tome VII, no. 296, François-Poncet à Delbos, December 2, 1937.
20. Schacht was dismissed in November 1937 from the ministry of economics, but he abandoned de facto his ministerial functions as soon as the beginning of September 1937. Clavert, "Schacht," 396.
21. Ibid., 460.
22. Schacht remained president of the *Reichsbank* until January 1939.
23. DDF, 2e série, Tome VII, no. 287, Conversations franco-britanniques du 29 novembre.
24. DDF, 2e série, tome VIII, no. 255, François-Poncet à Delbos, February 23, 1938.
25. Ibid.
26. Raymond Poidevin, "Vers une relance des relations économiques franco-alle mandes en 1938–1939," in *La France et l'Allemagne entre les deux Guerres mond iales. Actes du colloque tenu en Sorbonne (Paris IV) 15–16–17 janvier 1987*, ed. Jacques Bariéty, Alfred Guth, and Jean-Marie Valentin (Nancy: Presses Universitaires de Nancy, 1987).
27. Poidevin, "Vers une relance des relations économiques," 264.
28. Ibid., 269.
29. Ibid., 271.
30. Ibid.

CHAPTER 11

France and the German Economy 1945–48

An Imperialist Policy?

Martial Libera

Was it France's intention at the end of the Second World War to become the Old Continent's leading economic power? In other words, did France take advantage of Germany's defeat by appropriating its economic assets and turning the European industrial balance in its favor? For over thirty years this question has featured in the historiography of Franco-German economic relations, as historians have long considered France's post-1945 policy toward Germany to be imperialist. According to the majority of these historians, the sole purpose of French plans for political and economic detachment of the Ruhr and Rhineland was to weaken Germany and at the same time strengthen its own economic potential. By detaching the Ruhr, France would gain control of the bulk of German coal and steel reserves—the very fundament of economic and military power at the time. But since the mid-1980s this theory has lost ground. Instead, argue modern historians, it was rather the imperatives of security and reparations that shaped French policy toward Germany, and detachment of the Ruhr was the only means whereby France could reconcile these two conflicting objectives.[1] If the detachment of the Rhineland is to be interpreted as an imperialist act, then it was driven out of political and militaristic need rather than economic greed, as can be explained by the creation of a buffer zone—a by-product of detachment—protecting France from Germany.[2]

Is this to say that in 1945 France renounced all imperialist economic policies toward Germany, more precisely, expansionist policies that would reduce the former Reich to be economically dependent on France?[3] A study of the plans put forward

This article was translated from French by Bianca Jacobsohn. I am deeply grateful for her work.

for these policies indicates not. This chapter analyzes the nature of French economic imperialism by introducing the proponents of these plans and expounding on their content and objectives. In doing so, the decision-making processes prevailing in German affairs during this period are also explored. Were these imperialist ambitions shared by French decision makers and industrialists alike? Did the French Government support these ambitions and, if so, were they truly representative of France's policy toward Germany? French economic imperialism between 1945 and 1948 is embodied in three plans. The first—the "iron and steel" dream—was conceived in 1945 by Pierre Mendès France, General de Gaulle's Finance Minister. The second was elaborated a year later by André Philip, Finance Minister of the Provisional Government of the French Republic (PGFR), and Gaston Cusin, General Secretary of National Economy. Third, from 1946 France's policy of acquisition of holdings in German business became the Trojan horse of its economic ambitions in Germany.

Pierre Mendès France's "Iron and Steel Dream"

During the spring of 1945 Pierre Mendès France proposed his iron and steel plan.[4] He advocated measures that were, in every respect, contrary to France's policy toward Germany, a policy that the government was still in the process of defining. Unlike the majority of the Provisional Government of the French Republic (PGFR), he believed that Germany would no longer present a military threat in the future and consequently opposed the detachment of the Ruhr—advocated by de Gaulle and the PGFR—which he considered unrealistic and dangerous. Instead, Mendès France feared that the Ruhr basin, if internationalized, would prosper and constitute for France "a very serious economic danger."[5] He warned that "if the French government allows the Rhine iron and steel industry to be superior to that of Lorraine, France will eventually lose its authority in Europe."[6] Mendès France asserted that Germany would continue to pose a threat on an economic level and that, for the sake of peace, France would need to impose on Germany "certain artificial economic measures that would allow France to overturn the natural ratio between the French and German economies in its favor."[7] By stamping out German economic competition, Mendès France believed that France would bloom into a top industrial country and recover its position as a major power in Europe. In fact, Mendès France considered that "Anglo-Saxon powers would in future need to rebuild the western part of the European continent around a great power." It was thus necessary to avoid the "weaknesses of the French economy," which would eventually "encourage them [the Anglo-Saxon powers] to turn to Germany in ten years."[8]

To achieve this, Mendès France counted on the reversing of the balance of power in the European iron and steel industry to the benefit of France and the Benelux countries. This meant the transfer of part of the German iron and steel industry potential to these countries so that the latter could produce enough steel to meet internal needs and those of Germany. Concretely, this plan effectively sought to ban Germany from producing more steel than its own iron ore reserves would enable her. Three measures inserted into the peace treaty would allow for the maintenance of this new balance of power in the European iron and steel industry. First, all iron ore exports to Germany would be banned. Second, Germany would be allowed to import iron and steel products only from France, Belgium and Luxembourg to meet its own needs, which were in any event strictly limited by the Allies. Finally, in return for these deliveries, Germany would be required to provide the fat coal or coke necessary for steel production corresponding to German iron and steel imports, on the one hand and, most importantly, to the needs of France, Belgium and Luxemburg, on the other hand.[9] Deeply imperialist, Mendès France's iron and steel plan nurtured vast economic ambitions for France.

Implementing this plan would be highly profitable indeed. First, it would give France control of the German economy, steel being one of the most essential raw materials to industrial development. By increasing its steel production, France would build up its economic and military power. The adoption of Mendès France's plan would force the French industry to increase its production capacity above French domestic needs in order to ensure the supply of steel to Germany.[10] The expansion of the national iron and steel industry also formed an integral part of Mendès France's plan to reconstruct the French economy and for France to renew and "update its equipments to become a modern state."[11]

In July 1945, the PGFR enacted its first directives concerning Germany.[12] The primacy of security was maintained as the Ruhr, the Rhineland, and the Saarland were to be detached along with the former Reich, which was also to be disarmed economically and militarily, thus preventing any resurgence of a German threat. These directives therefore sanctioned the rejection of Mendès France's proposal. Three reasons explain this dismissal. Mendès France had resigned in April and was therefore no longer in a position to defend his ideas. Moreover, his project opposed the views that most of the decision makers held and therefore had little chance of being accepted. Furthermore, the decision-making process prevailing over German affairs was not at all favorable to the Ministry of National Economy, its representatives having been stripped of their key positions. Indeed, in January 1945, a commission for German relations, created in December 1944 and comprised of representatives from most of the French ministries, set about the task of preparing the policy toward Germany of the PGFR. Until March 1945, the secretary of the subcommittee, responsible for the drafting of reports, was a representative of the Ministry of the National Economy. He was subsequently replaced by a government official from the Quai d'Orsay.[13] Third, and most important, the PGFR rejected Mendès France's plan as it opposed the detachment of the Ruhr—a measure that, in July 1945, the French Government was unwilling to forgo. Following the requested detachment of the coal-rich basins of East Germany by the Soviets, Paris believed that the detachment of the Rheno-Westphalian basin, west of the previous Reich, should occur for geopolitical reasons and to maintain a balance of power in Europe.[14] Furthermore, French public opinion—anti-German and largely in favor of a dismemberment of the

Reich[15]—would interpret the abandonment of detachment plans, which underpinned General de Gaulle's German policy since February 1945,[16] as an act of defeat by France. The PGFR was eventually hostile toward Mendès France's proposal also because it gave industrialists a key role within France's economic policy toward Germany at a time when de Gaulle had emphasized the role of the State. De Gaulle was also partial to the measures defended by the majority of decision makers who oversaw the strict control of private interest in an internationalized Ruhr. Mendès France's proposal, forged within the dynamic context of France's iron and steel industry and poised to overtake its neighbor, did not reflect the existing ideals of the steel manufacturers and therefore did not win their approval.[17] In July 1945, the Mendès Frances iron and steel dream crumbled and collapsed.

German Industrial Disarmament: A Lever for French Supremacy?

In February 1946 Finance Minister André Philip and General Secretary of National Economy André Cusin proposed a second imperialist plan to the French Government.[18] Their proposal opposed the policy that the PGFR upheld during negotiations with the Allies before the adoption of the Plan for Reparations and the Level of Post-War German Economy. Concretely, this plan entailed setting German peacetime production levels and the extent of its economic and industrial disarmament. They agreed on prohibiting its war industries and permanently reducing its industrial potential. They also concurred that the German economy should, as a matter of priority, be oriented toward its domestic market in order to meet its population's needs. In more detail, the differences between the Allies influenced the extent of the limitations to which each industrial sector was subjected.[19] Since the PGFR gave precedence to security, he consequently advocated a major cutback in industrial activities that could possibly jeopardize peace. The iron and steel and engineering industries in particular were targeted. The French Government ordered that German steel production be reduced to approximately six million tons and declared that consumption and production of German steel should be balanced, one not exceeding the other. To ensure security, German engineering output would also be the subject of a major cutback and would be restricted to the domestic market, ruling out all exports. To pay for food imports, Germany could, on the other hand, continue to export products from its light industrial and textile industry that posed less of a security threat. This management of the German economy presented two sets of advantages to the French Government. First depriving Germany of its most threatening industries would reinforce security. This reorientation of the German economy would also be economically rewarding. High-ranking officials at the Ministry of Industrial Production believed that limiting Germany's iron and steel and engineering industries would facilitate the development of these industries in France, which take advantage of the market gap created by the shut down of German exports. On the whole, the proposition would be highly advantageous to France.[20]

Precisely these effects were contested in February 1946 by Philip and Cusin. They believed that, far from ensuring France's security and economic influence, the French Government's position would weaken them. Their criticism was leveled at two key measures of the Government's plan. First they argued that it was dangerous to balance German steel production and consumption. If ever German needs proved to be higher than what was initially authorized, the adoption of the Government proposition would inevitably lead to an increase in steel production and therefore threaten security once more. They also argued that modifying the trade flows of the engineering, light industrial, and textile industries would constitute a second error. France would not benefit in the least from the liberation of the engineering industry as it possessed neither the labor force nor the commercial organization necessary to become a major producing country and exporter of engineering goods. Instead, these markets would go to warlike nations. At the same time, France would have to encounter German competition in sectors of the light and textile industries, sectors that could, however, immediately be developed. For the Ministry of National Economy, represented by Philip and Cusin, the Government measures were therefore doubly disadvantageous as they would eventually both jeopardize security and further weaken the country's economy. The absolute primacy of security would lead to an impasse, they argued, and should, therefore, be revised.[21]

The two decision makers recommended a turnaround in the priorities of France's policy toward Germany: economic considerations should, from that point onward, take precedence over security concerns. In February 1946 they presented to the government a plan aimed at transforming France into a large industrial power. Composed of two measures, the plan took the opposite view of the Government's proposal. First, they advocated that a distinction be drawn between German steel production, which should be set at a very low level, and German consumption of iron and semifinished steel products, which could evolve according to German requirements. Second, the export of engineering products—a great source of income that Germany would need in order to finance its imports—should be authorized. However, they also advocated a ban on exports from the light industry and textile industry. These measures, they believed, would be far more beneficial to France.[22]

Limiting Germany to the textile industry and light industry—optics, measuring instruments, watchmaking, surgical instruments, jewelry, and furriery—would effectively allow French counterparts to fill the market gaps within these activities. In addition, distinguishing between the production and consumption of German steel would be profitable for two reasons. First, it would encourage the development of the French metallurgical industry by giving it a permanent outlet for its semifinished steel products, one that did not exist within its domestic market. Indirectly, security would also be improved primarily as a result of increased iron and steel production, but also because German steel production would remain at a much lower level, making Germany dependent on foreign sources for a good part of its supply of iron and semifinished steel products. Finally, this distinction would indirectly allow Germany a high enough production to meet its needs while exporting its engineering products to finance its imports. The proposal of the Ministry of National Economy would therefore allow for an appropriate standard of living in Germany, thereby limiting the risk of political and social unrest.[23]

Within the French Government, however, the plan made little headway. For the majority of the decision makers, the measures put forward by the Ministry of Industrial Production seemed more suitable because of the massive reduction of German steel production it advocated. It was therefore unsurprising that the PGFR rejected Philip and Cusin's plan. Yet again, security took precedence over economic ambitions.

Toward Financial Imperialism?

From summer 1946, French imperialist plans took a radical turn. During the conference of foreign affairs ministers of the Allied occupying powers in Paris during June and July 1946, French policy makers became convinced that they would not obtain the detachment of the Ruhr and the Rhineland. Furthermore, at the end of the conference officials from Britain and the United States made public their intention to merge their zones of occupation. In a speech in Stuttgart in September 1946, United States Secretary of State James Byrnes announced the relaxation of the United States policy toward Germany to encourage the recovery of its economy. These developments, which eventually lead to the creation of the Bizone in December 1946, rendered null and void the PGFR's policy toward Germany. France was losing its grip on Germany. It was within this context that certain high-ranking officials advocated a new form of economic expansion to ensure the enduring domination of France over Germany. This policy, which deviated from the industrial-oriented plans of Mendès France and Philip, pre-scribed financial control of German businesses. It was at this point that industrial imperialism gave way to financial imperialism.

From autumn 1946, the French administration opted for a policy of acquisi-tion of holdings in German businesses as a way of securing for France a "long-lasting influence capable of surviving the occupation period."[24] The government initiated this policy and charged French industrialists with implementing it. Their investments in Germany remained, however, dependent on the agreement of a *commission des participations financières* (acquisition of holdings commis-sion), created in December 1946. This interministerial organ could authorize or reject applications from French industrialists.[25] The government therefore retained the control over acquisitions of holdings, even if it needed the support of private investors.

The advantages were both economic and political.[26] A report from French occupation authorities emphasized that "from an economic point of view, these investments would identify companies which manufacture goods, whose pro-duction is substandard or nonexistent in France, and would orient their production towards satisfying the demands of the French domestic market." This control would "also apply to establishments in competition with French business." Such establishments would be cut back or redirected toward "outlets where they would not be competing with French products of the same nature."[27] Politically, the existence of French interests in Germany would sustain France's influence there while ensuring that Germany—beyond the period of occupation—adhered to the conditions imposed by the Allies. The acquisition of holdings had to be, first of all, selected by suppliers or competitors in sectors of German production relevant to the French economy. They also had to be made in innovative industrial activities trademarks known outside of Germany, and in companies in foreign markets that France could then take over. The state, however, rejected requests to invest speculatively.[28]

By June 1948, which saw the radical transformation of foreign investment conditions in Germany resulting from the monetary reform and the signing of the London agreements,[29] French earnings were very disappointing. Indeed, French businesses had acquired holdings in fifty-three German companies, but the accumulated capital from companies remained limited (26.8 million Reichsmark), the French share being even lower (12 million Reichsmark).[30] Moreover, apart from just a few exceptions, these strategic acquisitions were not made in big businesses.[31] Compared to the results of the other powers, the outcome of the French policy appeared even more modest. By summer 1948 the total of French acquisition of holdings in Germany, carried out before and since the war, rose to approximately 200 million Reichsmark. Against a total figure of 3 billion Reichmarks by other Western allies, the French component was negligible.[32]

The French effort was thus a resounding failure for three reasons: The Allies did not allow French acquisition of holdings in their occupied zones. France was therefore left with no option but to limit its ambitions to the French Zone of Occupation (FZO).[33] Hopes of broad control of the German economy were consequently dashed. Financing acquisitions of holdings constituted another major stumbling block as mixing French legislation and interallied regulations posed insurmountable problems.[34] This failure unquestionably resulted from the caution of French industrialists who did not share the views of the French administration. The long-term control of the German economy was of little importance to the industrialists. They were instead more interested in the profitability of their investments in Germany, which remained speculative within the shifting context of an occupied Germany. Up until 1947 and into 1948 they feared that France's policy toward Germany, which remained undefined, would continue to prioritize the industrial dismantling of Germany—a measure unfavorable to their interests. The future of the economy and also of the German currency too remained uncertain and this did not encourage industrialists to invest.[35] Furthermore, French industrialists were also concerned that the future German government would contest the legality of their acquisition of holdings and would try exposing these as acts of pillage.[36] They also had more short-term concerns and were especially worried that the strict control of the new rulers in power would prevent them from transferring their profits back into France.[37] The situation was paradoxical: the industrialists could not rely on the assistance of French authorities for such transfers and yet, at the same time, the French authorities called upon the industrialists to acquire holdings in Germany. In short, the system envisaged by the State cast the French industrial establishments as the key actors in France's economic expansion in Germany. They were expected to accept all the risks entailed but without any certainty of the profits their investments would yield. Moreover, because they had to submit their plans to the acquisition of holdings commission their activities were constrained. Thus it becomes clear at this point that these industrialists were not entirely willing "to bring to the French Government the competition it hoped for to facilitate its policy of permanent industrial control of Germany."[38] Uninterested in cooperating with the Germans, after fours years of occupation and despoliation the French industrialists opted for a levying policy in the FZO as a more ready source of income.[39]

Conclusion

Between 1945 and 1948, economic imperialism undoubtedly formed a part of France's policy toward Germany. Certain French leaders dreamt of transforming their country into a great industrial power by taking over Germany's economic assets. Against this background, a certain permanence of conceptions runs from one postwar period to another.[40] In 1919 the French plans for economic expansion could be defined as a "poor man's imperialism"[41] in that they made "outside economic influence dependent not on France's own industrial power, but on the weakening of Germany and of the assets of a victorious country."[42] Also, as in 1919, "governmental initiative prevailed over private initiative."[43] For the industrialists, "the income and profitability of the investments represented an end, while for the policy-makers, economic interests only constituted a means" to enduring control and domination of Germany.[44] Despite this, both postwar periods differ from one another. In 1945, French industrial expansionism fast gave way to financial imperialism. During the second postwar period, the proponents of an imperialist policy were also a small minority. The indifference, indeed, the *opposition* of industrialists to expansionist plans was evident. However, the majority of the decision makers were also hostile toward them—an unprecedented reaction. In the end, the overweening ambitions of the French plans stand in stark contrast to the modesty of their achievements. And so, from 1947, French dreams of imperialism were no longer permitted.

Notes

1. See Raymond Poidevin, "Frankreich und die Ruhrfrage 1945–1951," *Historische Zeitschrift* 228, no. 2 (1979): 317–34; Idem, "La France et le charbon allemand au lendemain de la deuxième guerre mondiale," *Relations internationales*, no. 44 (1985): 365–77; Marie-Thérèse Bitsch, "Un rêve français: le désarmement économique de l'Allemagne (1944–1947)," *Relations Internationales*, no. 51 (1987): 313–29; John Gillingham, "Die französische Ruhrpolitik und die Ursprünge des Schuman-Plans. Eine Neubewertung," *Vierteljahrshefte für Zeitgeschichte* 35, no. 1 (1987): 1–24; Werner Bührer, "Frankreich und das Ruhrgebiet—Mythos und Realität," in *Die*

deutsch-französischen Wirtschaftsbeziehungen 1945–1960. Les relations économiques franco-allemandes 1945–1960, ed. Andreas Wilkens (Sigmaringen: Jan Thorbecke Verlag, 1997), 225–27.

2. See Georges-Henri Soutou, "La politique française à l'égard de la Rhénanie 1944–1947," in *Franzosen und Deutsche am Rhein: 1789–1918–1945*, ed. Peter Hüttenberger and Hansgeorg Molitor (Essen: Klartext, 1989), 47–66.

3. See Jean Bouvier, René Girault, and Jacques Thobie, *L'impérialisme à la française 1914–1960* (Paris: La Découverte, 1986), 64–65. In this short study, matters of a scientific nature discussed by Marie-France Ludmann-Obier will not be examined.

4. There were two successive versions of Pierre Mendès France and the Ministry of the National Economy's proposals: "politique économique de la France à l'égard de l'Allemagne," ministère de l'Economie nationale, 19 mars 1945, Archives du ministère de l'Economie et des Finances, Centre des archives économiques et financières (CAEF), 5 A 25; and "note sur le problème allemand," ministère de l'Economie nationale, 28 mai 1945, Archives du ministère français des Affaires étrangères, Archives diplomatiques du Quai d'Orsay (AMAE-Paris), direction économique, affaires allemandes et autrichiennes (DE-AAA), tome (t.) 7.

5. Mendès France, "note sur le problème allemand."

6. Mendès France, "politique économique de la France à l'égard de l'Allemagne."

7. Mendès France "note sur le problème allemand." See also "recommandations du Conseil de coopération économique en matière de sidérurgie," Commission tripartite de l'acier, annexe II à l'accord franco-belgo-néerlandais-luxembourgeois, sans date (20 mars 1945), Archives nationales (AN), F12 10110.

8. Mendès France, "note sur le problème allemand."

9. Mendès France, "politique économique de la France à l'égard de l'Allemagne."

10. Ibid.

11. Michel Margairaz, *L'Etat, les finances et l'économie. Histoire d'une conversion 1932–1952* (Paris: Comité pour l'histoire économique et financière de la France, 1991), 784.

12. The "directives pour notre action en Allemagne" of July 19, 1945 were published by Rainer Hudemann in *L'Allemagne occupée 1945–1949*, ed. Henri Ménudier (Bruxelles: Complexe, 1990), 169–82.

13. Refer to the letters from Hervé Alphand, director of economic affairs at the Ministry of Foreign Affairs, addressed to Jacques Rueff, 13 mars, AMAE-Paris, DE-AAA, t. 5, and the "procès-verbal de la réunion de la sous-commission économique pour les affaires allemandes et autrichiennes," 24 juillet 1945, AN, F12 10104. In summary, the National Economy had a very meager representation within the commission.

14. In February 1944, General de Gaulle used this line of argument upon learning that the Soviets wanted to dismantle the industrial areas of eastern Germany. Charles de Gaulle, "L'unité 1942–1944," in *Mémoires de guerre*, vol. 2 (Paris: Plon, 1956), 618.

15. Dietmar Hüser, "Frankreich, Deutschland und die französische Öffentlichkeit 1944–1950: innenpolitische Aspekte deutschlandpolitischer Maximalpositionen," in *Vom "Erbfeind" zum "Erneuerer." Aspekte und Motive der französischen Deutschlandpolitik nach dem Zweiten Weltkrieg*, ed. Stefan Martens (Sigmaringen: Jan Thorbecke Verlag, 1993), 19–64; and Jean-Pierre Azéma, "Rapports de préfets et sondages," *Le rétablissement de la légalité républicaine (1944)*, ed. Fondation Charles de Gaulle (Bruxelles: Complexe, 1996), 782–87.

16. Radio broadcast of General de Gaulle's speech, February 5, 1945, in Charles de Gaulle, *Discours et messages 1940–1946* (Paris: Berger-Levrault, 1946), 558–63.

17. Françoise Berger, "Les patrons de l'acier en France et en Allemagne face à l'Europe (1930–1960)," in *Milieux économiques et intégration européenne en Europe occidentale au XXe siècle*, ed. Eric Bussière and Michel Dumoulin (Arras: Artois Presses Université, 1998), 190.

18. The proposal of the Ministry of National Economy is set out in three documents: "note sur l'établissement de la balance commerciale," ministère de l'Economie nationale, 4 février 1946, CAEF, 5 A 25; correspondence from the Ministry of National Economy to the Ministry of Industrial Production "fixation du niveau de l'industrie allemande," 13 février 1946, CAEF, 5 A 25; and "communication de Monsieur le ministre de l'Economie nationale, ministre des Finances, sur le taux d'activité des industries allemandes" au CEI (document n° 226 du CEI), 15 février 1946, AN, F60 902.

19. Pierre Guillen, *La question allemande (1945–1995)* (Paris: Imprimerie nationale, 1996), 17.

20. The position of the French Government is recorded in a memorandum of the Ministry of Industrial Production. See "position française relative au désarmement économique de l'Allemagne," ministère de la Production industrielle, service des affaires allemandes et autrichiennes, 6 février 1946, AMAE-Paris, DE-AAA, t. 7. Refer also to Bitsch, "Un rêve français," 316–320.

21. See endnote 19 for the different elements of the National Economy's plan.

22. Ibid.

23. Ibid.

24. "Politique suivie en matière de participations financières," gouvernement militaire de la zone française d'occupation (GMZFO), direction des finances, service du contrôle des biens, juillet 1947, Archives du ministère français des Affaires étrangères, Archives de l'occupation française en Allemagne et en Autriche, AMAE-Colmar, affaires allemandes et autrichiennes (AAA) 1369/1.

25. "Les participations financières françaises en Allemagne. Recherche d'une politique de participations," GMZFO, division économie et finances, Lionel Favereau, 20 décembre 1948, AMAE-Colmar, AAA 1369/1. Refer to the acquisition of holdings commission transcripts in AMAE-Colmar, AAA 1369/1 and in AMAE-Paris, DE-AAA, t. 80.

26. "Note sur les participations financières," Jean Filippi, directeur général de l'économie et des finances du GMZFO, 26 octobre 1945, AMAE-Colmar, AAA 1369/2.

27. Correspondence from the General Commission for German and Austrian Affairs (CGAAA) to French ministers pertaining to the "participations financières françaises en Allemagne," 8 août 1946, AMAE-Colmar, AAA 1369/1.

28. "Politique suivie en matière de participations financières."

29. In reevaluating the Deutsche Mark against the French Frank, monetary reform reduced the interest borne on acquisition of holdings. The anticipated merge of the FZO with the Bizone also limited the flexibility of the French.

30. Sylvie Lefèvre, "La politique française de prises de participations financières dans sa zone d'occupation (1945-49)," in *Aspekte der deutsch-französischen Wirtschaftsbeziehungen (1945–1957)*, ed. Werner Scholz (Leipzig: Leipziger Universitäts-Verlag, 1993), 26.

31. "Note au sujet des possibilités d'une politique d'investissements français en Allemagne," CGAAA, service des affaires économiques et sociales, 28 avril 1948, AMAE-Colmar, AAA 1370/1; and Jean-François Eck, *Les entreprises françaises face à l'Allemagne de 1945 à la fin des années 1960* (Paris: CHEFF, 2003), 43–44.

32. "Note annexe. Développement et financement des participations françaises en Allemagne," Haut-Commissariat de la République française en Allemagne, René Plas, 17 janvier 1950, CAEF, B 61 216.

33. "Note au sujet des possibilités d'une politique d'investissements français en Allemagne," CGAAA, service des affaires économiques et sociales, 28 avril 1948, AMAE-Colmar, AAA 1370/1; Sylvie Lefèvre, *Les relations économiques franco-allemandes de 1945 à 1955. De l'occupation à la coopération* (Paris: CHEFF, 1998), 106–7.

34. "Les participations financières en Allemagne"; Eck, *Les entreprises françaises*, 58–59.

35. Eck, *Les entreprises françaises*, 43–44.

36. "Note au sujet des possibilités d'une politique d'investissements français en Allemagne," CGAAA, service des affaires économiques et sociales, 28 avril 1948, AMAE-Colmar, AAA 1370/1;

37. Sylvie Lefèvre, "La politique française," 24; and Eck, *Les entreprises françaises*, 44.

38. "Note au sujet des possibilités d'une politique d'investissements français en Allemagne," CGAAA, service des affaires économiques et sociales, 28 avril 1948, AMAE-Colmar, AAA 1370/1; Eck, *Les entreprises françaises*, 35, 38.

39. Eck, *Les entreprises françaises*, 48–49.

40. This quote, adapted for this article, was taken from Catherine Nicault in *La libération de la France, juin 1944–janvier 1946*, ed. André Kaspi et al. (Paris: Perrin, 1995), 243.

41. Georges Soutou, "L'impérialisme du pauvre: la politique économique du gouvernement français en Europe centrale et orientale de 1919 à 1929. Essai d'interprétation," *Relations internationales*, no. 7 (1976): 219–39.

42. Robert Frank, "Le dilemme français: la modernisation sous influence ou l'indépendance dans la décadence," in *La puissance française en question 1945–1949*, ed. René Girault and Robert Frank (Paris: Publications de la Sorbonne, 1988), 144.

43. René Girault and Robert Frank, *Histoire des relations internationales contemporaines*, tome 2: *Turbulente Europe et nouveaux mondes, 1914–1941* (Paris: Masson, 1988), 104. See also Eck, *Les entreprises françaises*, 60–61.

44. Girault and Frank, *Histoire des relations internationales*, 104. For further reading on the opposition between the government and steel manufacturers after 1918, see Jacques Bariéty, *Les relations franco-allemandes après la première guerre mondiale, 10 novembre 1918–10 janvier 1925, de l'Exécution à la Négociation* (Paris: Pédone, 1977), 143.

PART III

Postwar Franco-German Relations

CHAPTER 12

On the Path to a "Hereditary Friendship"?

Franco-German Relations since the End of the Second World War

Ulrich Lappenküper

From "Hereditary Enemies" to Bonne Entente Franco-Allemande

"What a strange, cruel, beautiful and intense adventure it has been for these two fraternal peoples who needed more than a millennium to recognize each other as they are, to acknowledge each other, and to unite."[1] Dramatic in tone and wholly fitting in content, French President François Mitterrand's remarks reminded the Germans of the vicissitudes of Franco-German "brotherhood" on the occasion of the fortieth anniversary of the end of the Second World War. Arising from the breakdown of the Carolingian Kingdom of the Franks, the historical twins Germany and France could look back on a convoluted thousand-year history. After hundreds of years in which repulsion and crossfertilization characterized their relationship, antagonism became the determining factor after the Franco-Prussian War of 1870–71. Instrumentalized by interested groups, the resort to arms seemed to be the consequence of a "hereditary enmity."

After the catastrophe of the Second World War, Franco-German relations had to be reshaped because of fundamental transformations in international relations.[2] The Old World was relegated to a subordinate role compared to the new superpowers and saw itself confronted by the bipolar universalism of the East–West conflict. France was not content with the status of a minor power. Although weakened internally by wartime occupation and collaboration, this "second-class victor" over Hitler's Germany strove for a dominant place in Europe and at the same time sought security against the Germans.

The answer to the "German question" provided jointly by France, Great Britain, and the United States in 1949 fell below expectations. With the coming of the cold war, France had given up its initial concept of dominance for one of integration, but resentments toward its neighbor across the Rhine were by no means overcome.[3]

Not the subject but quite simply the object of international politics, the newly founded Bonn republic felt itself bound by other goals. The recovery of sovereignty, equality among Western powers, security partnership with the United States, participation in the coming together of Europe were the goals of the first chancellor, Konrad Adenauer. Below this plateau, an understanding with France played a very important role for the Christian Democrat.[4] His conception would by no means enjoy unlimited support among the West German population. First, this was because in the course of a revolutionary reorientation of German foreign policy, Adenauer was demanding that the West Germans "sacrifice" by accepting an alliance with the West. Second, he was calling for an understanding with a nation that seemed only to want a piecemeal incorporation of the Federal Republic into the realm of democratic states.

Adenauer's willingness to take French security needs into account and to favor Germany's incorporation into the West over reunification gave him an advantage in the eyes of the French over the opposition leader in Bonn, Kurt Schumacher, for whom independence, self-determination, and equality of Germany were the clear priorities. The French leadership however did not think of turning this goodwill into a political *rapprochement*, even when in early 1950 the United States and Britain supported a gradual modification of the most important means of control available to the Allies, the Occupation Statute. When its policy of obstruction ran into a dead end, the government in Paris saw itself forced into a process of rethinking out of which would emerge the "Schuman Plan," the spectacular project for a unification of the European coal and steel industry.[5] Under the pressure of increasingly loud calls by the Federal Republic for sovereignty, France also finally approved a reworking of the Occupation Statute. In order to prevent West German remilitarization, France initiated the formation of a supranational European army under the umbrella of NATO and called for the founding of a European Political Community.[6]

The Franco-German relationship gained a new foundation with the implementation of the European Coal and Steel Community (ECSC) in 1951, the signing of two treaties on the abolition of the Occupation Statute, and the founding of a European Defense Community (EDC) in 1952. But what Adenauer and French Minister Robert Schuman celebrated as a historical development seemed an impertinence to many of their countrymen.

Contrary to their hopes, a majority in the Bundestag gave its support to Adenauer's policy and approved the Western treaties in 1953. The National Assembly however rejected the treaty on the EDC in 1954 and thereby also torpedoed the statute for a European Political Community, which had been worked up in the meantime. The benefits of the Franco-German understanding, which had been achieved only with great difficulty, now seemed obsolete; the reestablishment of sovereignty and the rearmament of West Germany and European unity were up in the air. Thanks to intensive diplomatic consultations, however, the Western powers were able to produce a credible substitute solution in a matter of weeks. With the Paris Treaties of October 23, 1954, they freed the Federal Republic of the yoke of the Occupation Statute, brought the country into the Atlantic Alliance, and opened the door for its entry into the newly created Western European Union. Parallel to this, Bonn and Paris agreed to promote cultural exchanges, to deepen economic relations, and seemingly to have settled the torturous Saar question.[7]

Twosome Political Union

When the Treaties of Paris came into effect on May 5, 1955, a new era seemed to begin, but the burden of mistrust between the two peoples was by no means eliminated.

Largely thanks to the "thaw" in the East–West conflict, however, political relations between the two nations led to a "good Franco-German entente."[8] Given that the two superpowers were sending signals of an exclusive understanding between them, the Federal Republic and France even intensified their mutual cooperation out of concern for influence and security. They also undertook a new attempt at European integration. Shaken by the "impotence"[9] of the old Continent in the double world crisis of 1956, namely the Suez and Hungary, the two neighbors reached an agreement on the return of the Saar region to Germany, overcame hurdles in negotiations on the founding of the European Economic and Atomic Community, and agreed under the strictest secrecy on the joint production of nuclear missiles.[10]

After the demise of the Fourth Republic and the 1958 rise of Charles de Gaulle to power, these achievements in Franco-German cooperation threatened to evaporate.[11] Among the German public, a widespread anti–de Gaulle feeling developed that arose primarily from objections to the Algerian War[12]. Chancellor Adenauer responded to the general with deep suspicion, associating him with the Franco-Soviet Alliance of 1944 and the quest for prestige, and independence. Almost as if he had undergone a conversion on the road to Damascus, however, Adenauer saw de Gaulle completely differently after their first meeting in September 1958. However, this euphoria lasted only a few days, for the new French president was soon calling for the restructuring of the Atlantic Alliance into a triumvirate without German participation. Bonn's indignation over this affront did not result in a lasting disagreement thanks primarily to the Second Berlin Crisis unleashed by the Soviet Union; whereas Britain and the United States practiced conciliation, France stood firmly by the Federal Republic.

De Gaulle's stance was not a matter of altruism but of calculation. With the background of his ultimately unsuccessful efforts toward a three-power restructuring of NATO and a failed East–West summit on the "German question," the French president began in 1960 to implement a highly ambitious defense and foreign policy program. He led the development of the "force de frappe" (a French nuclear force) and urged Adenauer to participate in an intensification of European cooperation on the basis of a "Franco-German entente."[13] Since he aimed to empty both NATO and the European Economic Community (EEC) of their substance, the Federal Republic initially refused to go along with the general the general. Only after John F. Kennedy took office as president of the United States in 1961 did Adenauer and de Gaulle resolve their differences. The more stubbornly the United States stressed its role as leading power of the Western Alliance in its defense policy turn from "massive retaliation" to "flexible response" while simultaneously seeking détente with the Soviets, the more closely the chancellor and the president came together.

In 1962, Adenauer even accepted an offer from the French president for a bilateral entente in the wake of renewed détente signals between the two superpowers. Freed of the burden of the Algerian War, de Gaulle made in July 1962 the sensational offer of a political Union "à deux" in place of the failed union of six states, which the rejected Fouchet plan, initiated by de Gaulle himself, would have created.[14] All the efforts of politicians in Bonn to dissuade Adenauer from going down this path and to get him to commit himself to the West German foreign policy of multilateralism that had prevailed since 1949 proved fruitless. On January 22, 1963, the chancellor and the general signed a treaty of friendship that was aimed at anchoring Franco-German relations in international law.[15] In their remarks after the signing, the two old men buried their nations' status as "hereditary enemies."

Whereas a majority of the German and French peoples supported the agreement, there was massive opposition in political circles, heightened by de Gaulle's earlier very strong criticisms of American nuclear policy and of British entry into the EEC. In mid-May, the Bundestag blunted the bilateral alliance by inserting a preamble to the Elysée Treaty emphasizing the Federal Republic's multilateral relations. With their "close Franco-German entente,"[16] the two men had introduced a fundamentally new element into the politics and psychology of their peoples. Nevertheless, they failed because they had placed too heavy demands on their political environment.

The Rejected Option for France

After Adenauer's resignation in October 1963, the work of building the Franco-German relationship came to an almost complete halt. Under the new chancellor, Adenauer's fellow party member, Ludwig Erhard, bilateral relations were mired in three years of constant conflicts, manifested above all in European policy but also in security and Eastern policy. The French president now envisioned a "European Europe" in which nation-states would be preserved and which, under French leadership, would act on the world stage with a status equal to that of the superpowers. For his part, Erhard countered with a supranational "Europe of the free and equal" as an equal alliance partner of the United States.[17]

The moment of truth came in July of 1964 when the general invited the Bonn government to participate in a project for a Europe independent of the United States, one based on a Franco-German union. Feeling that he was being forced into this option by France, the chancellor rejected the offer and ignored the bait of participation in the "Force de frappe."

Indignant over the West German leadership's support of the United States, de Gaulle now began applying the political thumbscrews. First, he attacked the Americans' and West Germans' plans for a Multilateral Force (MLF), which was to offer the Federal Republic a certain amount of participation in nuclear policy. He then refused his support for Erhard's plan for a new "European relaunch" and sought to force him to accept his thesis that resolution of the "German question" was essentially a European problem that concerned the United States only secondarily.

De Gaulle's jabs were all the more painful for the West German government because it was accompanied by vehement admonitions from well-known coalition politicians to finally bring the Franco-German Treaty to fruition. Although this conflict—which reached the level of self-destruction between the so-called "Atlanticists" and "Gaullists" in the Christian Democratic Union (CDU) and its Bavarian sister party the Christian Social Union (CSU)—afflicted Erhard very much, he held steady on his course. He knew that he was in agreement with his foreign minister, Gerhard Schröder, the majority of the Bundestag, and the public, who unequivocally viewed partnership with the United States as a priority over friendship with France and who expected a "policy of movement" to Eastern Europe.[18]

Angered over the defiance of the West German government, and indeed that of his European partners in general, France demonstrated its determination with its "policy of the empty chair" in the EEC even as it planned closer contacts with the Soviet Union and withdrew in 1966 from military integration in NATO. Three years after its signing, the Elysée Treaty had lost both its spirit and substance. Its only remaining effect lay in its requirement for consultation, which meant that the leaders in Bonn and Paris could not give up on dialog. Despite some points of contact, the more power-political orientation of de Gaulle and the more economic orientation of Erhard could not be brought together. They functioned like two pyramids abutting one another at their bases; despite a common foundation, they grew further and further apart as their height increased. When in the autumn of 1966 the Federal Republic was threatened with isolation because of a damaged relationship not only with France but also with the United States, the government forced the resignation of the luckless chancellor.

No "Preferential Cooperation"

The grand coalition of the CDU/CSU and the SPD, which assumed power on 1 December 1966, awakened hopes of a better bilateral relationship. The new leadership in Bonn transferred its foreign policy priorities from the West to the East.

But it also made assurances that despite seeking new shores, there was absolutely no desire to dissolve old bonds. With a pragmatic alliance policy, Christian Democratic Chancellor Kurt Georg Kiesinger differentiated himself from Erhard's deference to the United States and Adenauer's focus on France. In agreement with Social Democratic Foreign Minister Willy Brandt, he sought to avoid having to commit to either the Atlantic or the Gaullist option.[19]

De Gaulle approved of the Federal Republic's turn, which fit with his call for more European self-confidence and an easing of tensions across the Continent. He also found it refreshing and enjoyable that the West German chancellor let him play first violin in the European orchestra. Warmer relations between Bonn and Paris could not, however, hide that bilateral cooperation remained very narrow because contradictions in their respective conceptions of NATO or the second British application for entry into the EEC had not been resolved. De Gaulle's flirtation with Russia, his insistence on independence, and his pressure for recognition of the Oder-Neisse border meant further dissonance. In the eyes of the general, the Germans and French did not share a "common fate" regarding the Soviet threat, as Kiesinger believed, but rather shared "common interests" vis-à-vis an American challenge.[20]

The German chancellor was by no means immune to the general's admonitions. The arrogant manner in which the United States cajoled the Federal Republic to sign onto the Treaty on the Non-Proliferation of Nuclear Weapons in 1967 aggravated him just as did the "atomic complicity" of the two superpowers.[21] Nevertheless, there was in his view no question of dispensing with the transatlantic partnership. In stark contrast to de Gaulle, the West German government offered no criticism of the Vietnam War, and during the Six-Day War in the Near East, the Germans stood by the United States and Israel rather than the Arabs, as the French were doing.

Despite growing unrest in the coalition, Kiesinger held to his entente with France.[22] Yet, because he repeatedly rejected de Gaulle's offers of "preferential cooperation,"[23] he could not eliminate the tension—in fact, the opposite was the case. In late 1968 during the European currency crisis, "the miracle of the Franco-German reconciliation" was in danger of suffering severe damage.[24]

Economic cooperation between France and the Federal Republic had developed in a very positive manner since the 1950s, however, but a blemish remained in the balance of trade that had, since 1965, been fundamentally in West Germany's favor and assumed dramatic dimensions in 1968 in the wake of grave French monetary and economic problems. When the West Germans stubbornly rejected all demands by France and other Western industrial states to raise the value of the German mark and for the first time implicitly transformed economic power into political strength, fears of German hegemony emerged among the French public and the political class. De Gaulle was even worried that West Germany might seek both economic and military dominance in Europe. Disillusioned with the possibility of privileged cooperation with the Federal Republic, he revealed to Kiesinger in March 1969 with disarming clarity how difficult it had been for France since the Second World War to reach out its hand to its eastern neighbor. According to de Gaulle, it was owing to French "self-mastery" alone that "a completely different policy" had not been pursued and "revenge" taken.[25]

"Elementary Entente"

With the resignation of the general in the spring 1969 and the shattering of the grand coalition the following autumn, the cards of Franco-German relations were reshuffled.[26] For the first time in its history governed by a social-democrat-liberal coalition (SPD-FDP), the Federal Republic saw its international stature significantly increase thanks to its "new Eastern policy" and its replacement of France as the leader in détente. The difficult relationship between the leading personalities in Paris and Bonn, the Gaullist Georges Pompidou and the Social Democrat Willy Brandt, added a personality problem to the shift in the balance of power between the two countries.

To limit the severity of this shift in the bilateral balance of power, the French president accelerated France's industrial and social progress—and indeed with the close cooperation of the Federal Republic! He declared that political relations were no longer the priority but rather were now only one element, something wholly acceptable to the West Germans. After years of dashed hopes, a return to greater realism now seemed possible. Fixated on the two superpowers, Brandt's political calculus assigned France a subordinate role, yet, he never forgot that it was only through a constructive relationship with his Western neighbor that reconciliation with the East could be maintained and his "new Eastern policy" could be supported in the West.

Bonn's *élan* in the politics of reconciliation gave rise to significant discomfort in Paris. In order to defend against the danger of a "Germany adrift," Pompidou worked to maintain the "Four-Power Prerogatives" over the Federal Republic and strongly supported the continued presence of U.S. troops on the Continent. He toyed with the idea of a Soviet reinsurance alliance and, with the close cooperation of Brandt, sought a "European relaunch" that would bring Great Britain into the EEC, expand the Common Market, end the Community's status as a political lightweight, and take up the issue of a common economic and currency policy.

When in 1973 the United States embarked upon a rebalancing of the international state system, reducing its European partners to nothing more than a regional power, Brandt's so-called elementary entente[27] with France suffered severe turbulence. With the intention of protecting his country from Washington's hegemonial behavior, Pompidou's Foreign Minister Michel Jobert sought to raise Western Europe to the level of an autonomous force in world politics, one that could stand up to the United States. The oil crisis and intensification of world economic problems after the Yom Kippur War meant that his call for European solidarity went unheard. Relations between Bonn and Paris became very cold in early 1974.

Inclination toward Marriage of Convenience

The sudden death of Georges Pompidou on April 2, 1974 and the abrupt resignation of Willy Brandt on May 6 ushered in a new epoch in Franco-German relations marked by disillusionment in détente policy between the superpowers and a change in personnel at the highest levels in the Western world. In Paris, Valéry Giscard d'Estaing was now at the helm and his German counterpart was Helmut Schmidt. Less visionaries than shrewd analysts, the liberal president and the social democratic chancellor devised a "marriage of convenience out of inclination."[28] Due to the economic dislocations unleashed by the oil crisis, Giscard and Schmidt aimed primarily at securing Europe's ability to act and pragmatically advancing European integration. In order to work against the primacy of economics, they initiated in 1974 the formation of a "European Council" as the highest decision making body of the EEC heads of state and of government.

The Soviet deployment of modern medium range missiles and the election of Jimmy Carter as president of the United States gave the "duo" of Giscard and Schmidt new impetus in 1977. This remained the case even when elements of French society accused the Federal Republic of "torture methods" in its struggle against the leftwing terrorism of the "Red Army Faction." Convinced of the necessity of filling the leadership vacuum in the Western alliance created by Carter's weakness, Giscard and Schmidt initiated the European currency system to bolster the political autonomy of the EEC. They sought to prevent the deteriorating détente between East and West from breaking down completely. They succeeded in advancing Franco-German relations by publicly celebrating their friendship and the "Copernican revolution" it involved.[29]

Admittedly, the two statesmen were not always of one mind, and in their social relations, there were still reservations. In the first direct elections to the European Parliament in 1979, France's communists and Gaullists accused the president of seeking to erect a supranational Europe under German hegemony. Giscard protested against the return of anti-German resentments but also took care not to endanger the autonomy that French foreign policy had maintained since de Gaulle. France rejected West German encouragement to use the Four-Power venue in order to advise the United States and Soviet Union on SALT II arms reduction negotiations. Giscard also refrained from joining the NATO Double Resolution of December 1979 that Schmidt had, to a great extent, prepared. For his part, the chancellor refused to go along with the French demand for independence vis-à-vis the United States despite his own disordered relations with the American administration: "America is our most important ally; France is our closest ally," as he put it in the press.[30]

Worried by the growing friction within the Atlantic community and between the superpowers in the wake of the Soviet invasion of Afghanistan, Schmidt and Giscard attempted in 1981 to shape more closely their mutual cooperation along a broad front. They were not to have the opportunity to implement this ambitious program, however, because Giscard lost his office to his challenger François Mitterrand in the elections of May 1981.

"The Franco-German Couple"

The arrival of the first socialist in the Elysée Palace since 1954 caused much uneasiness in the Franco-German relationship.[31] By inviting four communists into the cabinet after the left's landslide victory, Mitterrand irritated even those German observers who had welcomed the socialist turn in France. "Cognitive dissonances"[32] and political differences of opinion soon multiplied to the level of a dangerous potential for conflict. Shaking their heads, Germans looked on as the new president embarked upon an economic experiment aimed at nationalizing key sectors, one that ended in disaster after two years. For their part, the French reacted with incomprehension to the Federal Republic's growing environmental movement, which denounced military and civil use of nuclear energy with unshakable dogmatism.

Despite his emphasis on continuity in foreign policy, Mitterrand added two new accents at the beginning of his presidency. He broke off Giscard's friendly policy toward the Soviets and refused to grant the Federal Republic a special role in France's foreign policy system, accepting a "good entente" but not any "Paris-Bonn axis."[33]

After a solid year of this, internal difficulties in both states made it necessary for him to reconsider his course. Paris was being afflicted by turbulence in its finance policy over which it only gained control thanks to measures of support from Bonn. In the Federal Republic, the debate over NATO's Double Resolution broke the consensus on Schmidt's policy of balance, a development that, in French eyes, raised the specter of German neutrality.

Shortly after the fall of Schmidt's government in early October of 1982, Mitterrand made use of the twentieth anniversary of the Elysée Treaty in order to strengthen the new Christian Democratic-Liberal coalition under Chancellor Helmut Kohl against its opposition. Transcending all social, political, and character differences, he and Kohl ushered in a new blossoming of Franco-German cooperation.

In clear contrast to the harmonious relationship at the governmental level, new clefts opened up between the societies on each side of the Rhine. France's belief in progress and the wide consensus on the civil and military use of nuclear power met with much incomprehension in the Federal Republic. For their part, many French worried about the German state of mind in light of the environmental and pacifist movements in the Bonn republic.

The political leadership in Bonn and Paris forged a "Franco-German couple" in stark contrast to the dissonance between the two societies.[34] With the background of a waning ice age in the East–West conflict, Mitterrand postulated for both peoples the historical duty to construct a European union. The Single European Act passed by the governments of the EEC in 1986 was, however, difficult to harmonize with such lofty ideals.

With the transformation of world politics in 1989 and 1990, the "fronts" in the governmental and societal viewpoints on Franco-German relations shifted significantly on both sides of the Rhine. Whereas a majority of the French welcomed the fall of the Berlin Wall, segments of the Parisian political class reacted with uncertainty, even rejection. Mitterrand himself did not contest in principle the legitimacy of a German nation-state but did wish to see its rebirth pushed off so far into the indefinite future that it never would happen. With disappointment and even bitterness, the Germans perceived the coolness with which the president defended French *raison d'état* in light of what he erroneously thought to be the threat of German reunification to the "power geography" of Europe.[35]

The reestablishment of German unity in 1990 poured Franco-German relations into a new foundation. Now the largest state in Europe, Germany had undeniably become the leading political-economic power on the Continent. Such actions by the German government as its haste in recognizing Croatia and Slovenia during the Yugoslavian conflict in 1990 or its conceptions for a new European security architecture after the fall of the Soviet Union in 1991 did not serve to reduce French mistrust as to the ambitions of their now fully sovereign neighbor. Only with difficulty did the "duo" of Kohl and Mitterrand once again find its footing, but it functioned so well thereafter that negotiations over the European Union could be successfully concluded in 1992.[36]

The "Miracle" of Reconciliation

With the end of Mitterrand's term in 1995 and Kohl's election loss in 1998, Franco-German relations once again entered a new period. The impression quickly set in that those now in power, two generations removed from the postwar visionaries, presided over the bilateral friendship without enthusiasm. Although the neo-Gaullist President Jacques Chirac sought a refounding of the relationship, it met with such difficulties given the eastward expansion of the EU and the debate on a European constitution that the press began speaking of a "requiem" for the Franco-German "axis."[37] It was only when the conflict between the United States and Iraq manifested itself that the two nations once again closed ranks. Challenged by severe accusations from the American government, Chirac and Social Democratic Chancellor Gerhard Schröder forged an antiwar alliance augmented by Russia, offering the vision of a multipolar world in place of the unilateralism of George W. Bush.

Without cultivating an exclusive private relationship as had Giscard and Schmidt or Kohl and Mitterrand, Chirac and Schröder proclaimed a rebirth of understanding on the fortieth anniversary of the Elysée Treaty in 2003. With their symbolic embrace at the commemoration of D-day in Normandy in 2004, they ostentatiously placed themselves in the ranks of their predecessors and resumed the grand gestures of Franco-German reconciliation.

In the CDU opposition, there was much doubt as to the traditional conviction that German-American and German-French friendship were compatible.[38] Whereas some Christian Democrats advocated the establishment of a firm Franco-German "axis" that would put the EU in a position to save the United States from the "hubris of power," the party leader stood unequivocally on the side of the United States. Even before her election as the first female chancellor of the Federal Republic, Angela Merkel did nevertheless demonstrate that she would avoid subservience to America along the lines of an Erhard: Against the wishes of Washington, she voiced her agreement with the French neo-Gaullists that Turkey should not become a full member of the EU but rather should only enjoy a "privileged partnership."

Charles de Gaulle had characterized Franco-German reconciliation after the Second World War as the "miracle of our time."[39] In light of the nationalistic excesses of the nineteenth and twentieth centuries, this reconciliation between Germany and France can indeed be regarded as a "miracle." Initiated by Adenauer and Schuman in 1950, the process gained international legal form thanks to Adenauer and de Gaulle in 1963. On the foundation of their Elysée Treaty, there arose a network of contacts that may well be unique among sovereign states. Meanwhile, then, there is no reason to undertake a transfiguration of the "hereditary friendship."[40]

Notes

1. Address by François Mitterrand, May 8, 1995, in François Mitterrand, *De l'Allemagne, de la France* (Paris: Odile Jacob 1996), 241.
2. Julius W. Friend, *The Linchpin. French-German Relations 1950–1990* (New York: Praeger, 1991); Gilbert Ziebura, *Die deutsch-französischen Beziehungen seit 1945. Mythen und Realitäten* (Stuttgart: Neske, 1997).
3. With dissenting theses Cyril Buffet, *Mourir pour Berlin. La France et l'Allemagne 1945–1949* (Paris: A. Colin, 1991); Dietmar Hüser, *Frankreichs "doppelte Deutschlandpolitik". Dynamik aus der Defensive—Planen, Entscheiden, Umsetzen in gesellschaftlichen und wirtschaftlichen, innen- und außenpolitischen Krisenzeiten 1944–1950* (Berlin: Duncker & Humblot, 1996); Geneviève Maelstaf, *Que faire de l'Allemagne? Les responsables français, le statut international de l'Allemagne et le problème de l'unité allemande (1945–1955)* (Paris: La Documentation Française, 1999).
4. Ulrich Lappenküper, *Die deutsch-französischen Beziehungen 1949–1963. Von der "Erbfeindschaft" zur "Entente élémentaire,"* 2 vols. (München: Oldenburg, 2001); Klaus Schwabe, ed., *Konrad Adenauer und Frankreich 1949–1963. Stand und Perspektiven der Forschung zu den deutsch-französischen Beziehungen in Politik, Wirtschaft und Kultur* (Bonn: Bouvier, 2005).
5. Ulrich Lappenküper, "Der Schuman-Plan, Mühsamer Durchbruch zur deutsch-französischen Verständigung," *Vierteljahrshefte für Zeitgeschichte* 42 (1994): 403–45; Klaus Schwabe, ed., *Die Anfänge des Schuman-Plans 1950/51, The Beginnings of the Schuman-Plan. Beiträge des Kolloquiums in Aachen, 28.-30. Mai 1986* (Baden-Baden: Nomos, 1988); Andreas Wilkens, ed., *Le Plan Schuman dans l'histoire. Intérêts nationaux et projet européen* (Brussels: Bruylant, 2004).
6. Seung-Ryeol Kim, *Der Fehlschlag des ersten Versuchs zu einer politischen Integration Westeuropas von 1951 bis 1954* (Frankfurt am Main: Peter Lang, 2000); Lutz Köllner, et al., *Die EVG-Phase* (München: Oldenburg, 1990); Dieter Krüger, *Sicherheit durch Integration? Die wirtschaftliche und politische Integration Westeuropas 1947 bis 1957/58* (München: Oldenburg, 2003).

7. Rainer Hudemann and Raymond Poidevin, eds., *Die Saar 1945–1955. Ein Problem der europäischen Geschichte. La Sarre 1945–1955. Un problème de l'histoire européenne* (München: Oldenburg, 1992); Sylvie Lefèvre, *Les relations économiques franco-allemands de 1945 à 1955. De l'occupation à la coopération* (Paris: CHEEF, 1998); Hélène Miard-Delacroix and Rainer Hudemann, eds., *Wandel und Integration. Deutsch-französische Annäherungen der fünfziger Jahre, Mutuations et intégration. Les rapprochements franco-allemands dans les années cinquante* (München: Oldenburg, 2005).

8. Circular telegram from Antoine Pinay to French embassies, May 4, 1955, Ministère des Affaires étrangères, *Documents Diplomatiques Français (DDF) 1955* (Paris: La Documentation Française, 1987), 571–73.

9. Meeting between Adenauer und Guy Mollet of September 29, 1956, quoted in Lappenküper, *Beziehungen*, 1027.

10. Georges-Henri Soutou, *L'alliance incertaine. Les rapports politico-stratégiques franco-allemands 1954–1996* (Paris: Fayard, 1996).

11. Frédéric Bozo, *Deux stratégies pour l'Europe. De Gaulle, les Etats-Unis et l'Alliance atlantique, 1958–1969* (Paris: Plon, 1996); Martin Koopmann, *Das schwierige Bündnis. Die deutsch-französischen Beziehungen und die Außenpolitik der Bundesrepublik Deutschland 1958–1965* (Baden-Baden: Nomos, 2000); Knut Linsel, *Charles de Gaulle und Deutschland 1914–1969* (Sigmaringen: Thorbecke, 1998); Maurice Vaïsse, *La grandeur. Politique étrangère du général de Gaulle 1958–1969* (Paris: Fayard, 1998).

12. Jean-Paul Cahn and Klaus-Jürgen Müller, *La République fédérale d'Allemagne et la Guerre d'Algérie (1954–1962). Perception, implication et retombées diplomatiques* (Paris: Editions du Félin, 2003); Ulrich Lappenküper, "Adenauer, de Gaulle und der Algerienkrieg 1958–1962," *Revue d'Allemagne* 31 (1999): 603–15.

13. Meeting between de Gaulle and Adenauer, September 30, 1960, in *DDF 1960* (Paris: La Documentation française, 1996), 176.

14. Meeting between Adenauer and de Gaulle of July 5, 1962, in *DDF 1962* (Paris: La Documentation Française, 1999), 40.

15. Corinne Defrance and Ulrich Pfeil, eds., *Der Elysée-Vertrag und die deutsch-französischen Beziehungen 1945–1963–2003* (München: Oldenburg, 2005).

16. Meeting between de Gaulle and Eisenhower, September 2, 1959, in *DDF 1959* (Paris: La Documentation Française, 1995), 284.

17. Ulrich Lappenküper, "'Ein Europa der Freien und der Gleichen.' La politique européenne de Ludwig Erhard (1963–1966)," in *Crises and Compromises: The European Project 1963–1969*, ed. Wilfried Loth (Baden-Baden and Brussels: Nomos and Bruylant, 2001), 65–91.

18. Franz Eibl, *Politik der Bewegung. Gerhard Schröder als Außenminister 1961–1966* (München: Oldenburg, 2001); Torsten Oppelland, *Gerhard Schröder (1901–1989). Politik zwischen Staat, Partei und Konfession* (Düsseldorf: Droste, 2002). On the domestic conflict over the course of Bonn's foreign policy, cf. Reiner Marcowitz, *Option für Paris? Unionsparteien, SPD und Charles de Gaulle 1958 bis 1969* (München: Oldenburg, 1996).

19. Philipp Gassert, *Kurt Georg Kiesinger 1904–1988. Kanzler zwischen den Zeiten* (München: DVA, 2006); Henning Türk, *Die Europapolitik der Großen Koalition 1966–1969* (München: Oldenburg, 2006).

20. Meeting between de Gaulle and Kiesinger, July 13, 1967, in *Akten zur Auswärtigen Politik der Bundesrepublik Deutschland (AAPD) 1967* (München: Oldenburg, 1998), 1053.

21. Address by Kiesinger to the Verein Union-Presse, February 27, 1967, excerpted in Reinhard Schmoeckel and Bruno Kaiser, *Die vergessene Regierung. Die große Koalition 1966–1969 und ihre langfristigen Wirkungen* (Bonn: Bouvier, 1991), 135.

22. Andrea H. Schneider, *Die Kunst des Kompromisses. Helmut Schmidt und die Große Koalition 1966–1969* (Paderborn: Schöningh, 1999); Daniela Taschler, *Vor neuen Herausforderungen. Die außen- und deutschlandpolitische Debatte in der CDU/CSU-Bundestagsfraktion während der Großen Koalition (1966–1969)* (Düsseldorf: Droste, 2001).

23. Meeting between Kiesinger and de Gaulle, September 28, 1968 in *AAPD 1968* (München: Oldenburg, 1999), 1258.

24. Meeting between Kiesinger and Sandys, October 23, 1968 in *AAPD 1968*, 1370.

25. Meeting between de Gaulle and Kiesinger, March 14, 1969 in *AAPD 1969* (München: Oldenburg, 2000), 405.

26. Franz Knipping and Matthias Schönwald, eds., *Aufbruch zum Europa der zweiten Generation. Die europäische Einigung 1969–1984* (Trier: Wissenschaftlicher Verlag Trier, 2004); Horst Möller and Maurice Vaïsse, eds., *Willy Brandt und Frankreich* (München: Oldenburg, 2005); Haig Simonian, *The Privileged Partnership. Franco-German Relations in the European Community, 1969–1984* (Oxford: Clarendon, 1985); Andreas Wilkens, *Der unstete Nachbar. Frankreich, die deutsche Ostpolitik und die Berliner Vier-Mächte-Verhandlungen 1969–1974* (München: Oldenburg, 1990).

27. Willy Brandt, *Begegnungen und Einsichten. Die Jahre 1960–1975* (Hamburg: Hoffmann und Campe, 1976), 341.

28. Kurt Becker, "Eine Vernunftehe aus Neigung," *Die Zeit*, January 14, 1983, 3; cf. the basic account in Hélène Miard-Delacroix, *Partenaires de choix? Le chancelier Helmut Schmidt et la France (1974–1982)* (Bern: Peter Lang, 1993); Michèle Weinachter, *Valéry Giscard d'Estaing et l'Allemagne. Le double rêve inachevé* (Paris: L'Harmattan, 2004).

29. Quoted in Ulrich Lappenküper, "Auswärtige Angelegenheiten: Auf dem Weg zu einer gleichgerichteten Haltung in Fragen gemeinsamen Interesses?" in *Elysée-Vertrag*, ed. Defrance and Pfeil, 120.

30. Quoted from Simonian, Partnership, 303.

31. Urs Leimbacher, *Die unverzichtbare Allianz. Deutsch-französische sicherheitspolitische Zusammenarbeit 1982–1989* (Baden-Baden: Nomos, 1992).

32. Ziebura, *Beziehungen*, 280.

33. François Mitterrand, *Politique, vol. 2, 1977–1981* (Paris: Fayard, 1981), 279.

34. Henri Ménudier, ed., *Le couple franco-allemand en Europe* (Asnières: PIA, 1993).

35. Tilo Schabert, *Wie Weltgeschichte gemacht wird. Frankreich und die deutsche Einheit* (Stuttgart: Klett-Cotha, 2002), 13; cf. Frédéric Bozo, *Mitterrand, la fin de la guerre froide et l'unification allemande. De Yalta à Maastricht* (Paris: PUF, 2005); Elke Bruck, *François Mitterrands Deutschlandbild. Perzeption und Politik im Spannungsfeld deutschland-, europa- und sicherheitspolitischer Entscheidungen 1989–1992* (Frankfurt am Main: Peter Lang, 2003).

36. Valérie Guérin-Sendelbach, *Frankreich und das vereinigte Deutschland. Interessen und Perzeptionen im Spannungsfeld* (Opladen: Leske und Budrich, 1999).

37. Joachim Fritz-Vannahme, "Requiem für eine Achse," *Die Zeit*, July 18, 2002: 4.

38. Ulrich Lappenküper, "'Die Partei der deutsch-französischen Freundschaft.' Die CDU und Frankreich 1945–2005," in *Brücke in eine neue Zeit. 60 Jahre CDU*, ed. Günter Buchstab (Freiburg: Herder, 2005), 265–87.

39. After-dinner speech by de Gaulle, July 3, 1962, in Charles de Gaulle, *Memoiren der Hoffnung. Die Wiedergeburt 1958–1962* (München: Molden, 1971), 450.

40. Hans-Peter Schwarz, *Erbfreundschaft. Adenauer und Frankreich* (Bonn: Bouvier, 1992).

CHAPTER 13

A New Framework for Franco-German Relations through European Institutions, 1950 to 1954

Victor Gavin Munte

At the end of the Second World War, the policy of the Allied Forces toward Germany was one of punishment. The defeated nation was made to feel the weight of its guilt, as was established in the instructions of the Allied governments for the occupation authorities. The country was divided into four occupation zones, each one under the military control of one of the four victors of the Second World War (the United States, the Soviet Union, the United Kingdom, and France). Germany was demilitarized, its productive capacity severely limited, part of its industrial infrastructure dismantled, and the country was ultimately transformed into an international pariah, without self-government and under Allied tutelage.

The immediate goal was to make the Germans feel the weight of their national guilt. The hard line taken in daily dealings with the German population and the country as a whole was reflected in a directive sent to the U.S. military governor for immediate application in the zone under his control (JCS 1067, October 17, 1945) in which it was established that "Germany will not be occupied for the purpose of liberation but as a defeated enemy nation. . . . You will strongly discourage fraternization with the German officials and population."[1]

In the case of France, a country that had suffered German occupation and for which the invasion of 1940 was the third attack made by its eastern neighbor in seventy years—following the Franco-Prussian War of 1870–71 and the First World war of 1914–18—similar principles and aims were established in the instructions sent to the French commander in Germany on July 7, 1945: "the essential target is the military, economic, and financial disarmament of the ancient Reich."[2]

This aggressive stance lasted only a short time. The beginning of the cold war brought with it a change of enemy. The Soviet Union, an ally during the war, then became the new enemy to fight and to contain, thereby making Germany's recovery necessary. This situation completely changed all of the principles previously mentioned, initially in the political sphere by transforming the three Western occupation zones into the Federal Republic of Germany in 1949, with its capital in Bonn and Konrad Adenauer as chancellor, as well as the substitution of civilian high commissioners for the Allied military governors. There was also a change in economic policy toward western Germany.

The new circumstances demanded the end of the politics of punishment toward Germany and instead called for its economic recovery and its integration into a Western Europe reconstructed along the lines dictated by the Marshall Plan. Through the Marshall Plan, the United States government had committed itself not only to the economic and material recovery of Western Europe but also to its reorganization by overturning the restrictive nature of nation-state frontiers in favor of an integrated continent able to offer Europeans a market of similar proportions and potential as the American model, which in turn could produce the type of stability and prosperity enjoyed on the other side of the Atlantic.[3]

France: The Recovery of Germany as a Problem

In France, Jean Monnet, at the head of the General Commissariat for the Modernization and Equipping of the French Economy, was working not only to regain prewar economic levels but also to establish a sufficiently solid base to ensure the economic future and prosperity of France as a first-rank power.[4] Monnet understood that to attain this objective, it would be necessary to change the manufacturing structure of the country by means of an ambitious program of investment in six basic sectors: coal, electricity, steel, cement, agricultural machinery, and railroads. This was the Monnet Plan,[5] and it was not created with only French territory in mind but rather in relation to neighboring countries, particularly Germany, the most powerful economy in continental Europe before the war. The main industries in France during this period, coal and steel, suffered historically from a serious structural problem: reliance on other nations for the supply of raw materials, fundamentally the coking coal used in the production of steel. The principal supplier of this resource was Germany, which raised the issue that most worried Monnet. Since Germany sold its coal on the foreign market at a higher price than on the domestic market, French industry suffered a serious problem of competitiveness, giving the Germans a clear advantage in terms of production costs. In light of the condition of Germany at the end of the war, it is no wonder that France saw an opportunity to overcome its historical disadvantage once and for all.[6]

With the politics of punishment and the dynamics of occupation, France saw its desires fulfilled. When Allied treatment of Germany changed, it was necessary to use other means to ensure that the trade practices of the past did not return. Indeed, Georges Bidault, French minister for foreign affairs, had already made clear to a cabinet led by Robert Schuman that "there is not the slightest possibility of combining the benefits of the Marshall aid with the rejection of a Germany that will be configured according to our views, halfway at least. There are moments when it is necessary to be able to conclude matters. If we wish to advance alone we will lose everything."[7] That scene took place in 1948. Two years later, Robert Schuman as the minister of foreign affairs was faced with the task of providing a practical and viable answer to U.S. plans for the future of Europe. These had been outlined in a letter to Schuman from U.S. Secretary of State Dean Acheson in which the Frenchman was asked to lead the integration of the Federal Republic of Germany (FRG) into a Europe reformed according to the criteria of the Marshall Plan.[8]

Europe as a Solution? The European Coal and Steel Community (ECSC)

It was at this point that the concept of Europe emerged, of the construction of a new Europe whose institutions would be a positive means of exercising control over the former enemy. A note written by François Seydoux, chairman of the European Desk of the French Ministry of Foreign Affairs, clears up any doubts on this matter:

> Germany will not recover its complete independence; the current system of tutelage will pass directly to another system under which other restrictions will limit its freedom, but these limitations will have to be assumed by all the members. . . . No time will exist during which Germany can be the master of its destiny; it will exit the present framework to enter into another one, easier to bear, firstly because it will be less rigid, secondly because it will not be confined to the borders of Germany. Germany will enjoy equality of rights, but this equality will only be applied to limited rights.[9]

The problem was that nobody could find a formula capable of translating such ideas into a practical proposal, particularly because France, which had to take the initiative, was unable to see the advantage of imposing restrictions upon itself simply in order to restrain Germany. It was Jean Monnet who discovered the advantage.

Monnet was trying to end French dependency on German coking coal and the commercial practices stemming from it. If Bonn could be prevented from managing its coal resources unilaterally and for its own benefit, the problem might be solved. At that time, this role was being fulfilled by the administration of the postwar occupation in Germany, but if this regime was nearing its end, why not pass on the role to a European authority dedicated to managing not only the German resources but those of all the states wanting to participate, an authority working for the benefit of all. This was Monnet's reasoning. As part of this new authority, France—although it would lose its capacity to manage its coal and steel resources unilaterally—would be liberated from the German commercial practices that were damaging to its industry. This reasoning gave birth to the Schuman Declaration of May 9, 1950, which would develop into the European Coal and Steel Community (ECSC), the first institution of the new European community. It had been given the task of managing the Franco-German production of coal and steel under a European High Authority. Four other states joined the initiative: Italy, Belgium, Luxembourg, and the Netherlands. [10]

Two paragraphs of the Schuman Declaration will go into the history books. The first declares that the above measures will remove all possibility of a new war between France and Germany; the second describes the initiative as the first step toward a European federation. In other words, what France was publicly offering was a comprehensive plan to federalize Western Europe, with the ECSC as just the beginning. In this way, a concrete solution to a concrete problem of France's coal and steel industry was introduced as an ambitious political plan able to resolve the never-ending problem of European wars and to include a new and free Germany without any risk to its neighbors. In truth, the principal motivation behind the Schuman Declaration was more practical, as Monnet himself had written in a memorandum six days earlier: "The continuation of the recovery of France will be halted if the question of German industrial production and competitiveness is not solved rapidly . . . the base of the superiority that the French industrialists recognize traditionally in Germany is its production of steel at a price against which France cannot compete. From this, they conclude that French production as a whole suffers a handicap."[11] The political value of the Schuman Declaration and the beginnings of European integration centered on France and Germany—coming only five years after the end of the Second World War—is undeniable. Yet, it seems obvious that the real motivation behind the decision was not to construct a federal Europe or to overcome the nation-state borders for their own sake, as the classical approach to this subject argues, but instead to resolve a concrete problem of French industry and to keep Germany under control after the occupation ended.[12] Besides, the international acceptance of the plan and especially that from Washington, DC promised to give France another interesting asset: the opportunity to entrust the whole question of German political evolution to a European project under French leadership. That way, Paris would hold the key to the future evolution of the Federal Republic of Germany.

This last point brings us to another of the key issues: Why did the FRG agree to become part of the Europe outlined by the Schuman Plan? We can surmise that this was essentially because the proposal was presented as the only means the West was prepared to offer the Federal Republic for its return to international normality with equality of rights and obligations. The aim of constructing a European federation outlined in the Schuman Declaration was directed both at the United States, eager to see a reconstruction of Europe in accordance with a model similar to its own, and at the FRG, pointing out that coal and steel marked the beginning of a path that would lead to a new Europe in which the new Germany could find a place without suffering any discrimination. The problem for the FRG in general and for Adenauer in particular was that Paris had no proposals to follow the Schuman Plan because France had no intention of federalizing Europe and thus being diluted within it. This was a problem because it was impossible for either the West German chancellor or his country to remain indefinitely in this initial stage.[13]

An Undesired Evolution: The European Defense Community (EDC)

When the Atlantic Council met in New York in September of 1950, only four months after the launching of the Schuman Plan, Washington demanded the rearmament of the FRG as an indispensable condition for the United States to commit itself to the defense of Western Europe against a possible Soviet invasion. Paris reacted negatively. The U.S. demand, if accepted, would mean granting the new German government a military capability that would clash with the French objective of keeping its eastern neighbor disarmed and under permanent control within a framework indisputably led by France—as the Schuman Plan promised and the North Atlantic Treaty Organization (NATO), within which West German rearmament would take place, did not. On the other hand, linking the United States with the defense of Western Europe in peacetime was a priority for the European states ever since the end of the Second World War. This meant that all of the NATO capitals, with the exception of Paris, accepted the U.S. demand, even though most of them shared France's feelings toward the Germans.

Assuming that without support it would be impossible to block indefinitely the U.S. commitment to the defense of Western Europe, the French government again accepted the help of Jean Monnet, for whom the U.S. demand represented above all the opening of an alternative route to the Schuman Plan through which Germany could return to international normality.[14] The solution then had to be found within the Schuman Plan framework and in accordance with its principles. Essentially, it consisted of replacing the national armies of the six states of this first European community (France, the FRG, Italy, Belgium, the Netherlands, and Luxembourg) with a European force integrated at the level of the smallest unit and under the authority of a European minister of defense. Under this plan, German soldiers would be used but no new German army would be raised. This would, however, come at an enormous cost to the five other states, that of relinquishing their own armies in favor of the new European force. This plan was accepted by the French government due to the lack of alternatives capable of breaking the impasse in the Atlantic Council and was launched by Prime Minister René Pleven on October 24, 1950. Hence it was called the Pleven Plan and later became known as the European Defense Community (EDC).[15]

The virtue of the Pleven Plan for Paris was that it placed the issue of German rearmament within the framework defined by the Schuman Plan, thus providing the continuity promised in the declaration of May 9, 1950 and obliging the United States to support it at the risk of being brought down by the incoherence of rejecting the very principles it had espoused just five months before. If we add to this the fact that France was indispensable for the defense of Europe and that the Pleven Plan was introduced as a sine qua non for France's acceptance of German rearmament, we will understand why the Pleven Plan was accepted, despite doubts about its practical application.

For What Purpose Do We Want Europe?

France was now faced with a considerable task—it had to lead the integration of Western Europe beyond the level of the coal and steel industry, creating a European army that in turn implied the creation of a political Europe, something that had never been considered by those behind the Schuman Plan. The situation was an interesting one: A policy that had been designed to control Germany seemed to be moving beyond the control of its designer. The situation in the following four years was marked by a dramatic contrast. On the one hand, the gradual construction of a federal, or confederal, Europe was in theory advancing. The treaty establishing the European Defense Community was signed in 1952,[16] and a project for a European constitution, the basic law of the future European Political Community (EPC), was drawn up in 1953.[17] Yet France continually used all means at its disposal to delay the practical application of the agreements, demanding guarantee after guarantee to assure itself a higher status than the other European Community states and to limit the FRG's freedom to maneuver. The circumstances became more complicated with the progressive alienation of the supporters of the European policy defined by the Schuman Declaration from the power centers in Paris due to election processes, especially the legislative election of June 17, 1951, and the decision of Jean Monnet to leave Paris for Luxembourg to chair the High Authority of the ECSC, the main organ of the new community. In short, the enemies of the European policy will gain the control of the situation. Most of them were in the French Ministry of Foreign Affairs, as a note of January 26, 1953, from its Central European Desk made absolutely clear: "If France has taken the initiative in projects aimed at the common management, in certain areas, of the resources and energy of the countries of continental Europe, this in no way means abandoning its position as a world power or neglecting any responsibilities with regard to the French Union." Moreover, the author of the note added that "the uniting of Europe is not for us a mystical phenomenon but politics. We are seeking to carry out transfers of sovereignty appropriate to settling those problems for which the solution exceeds the national framework."[18] The problem for the French government was how to state publicly that the aims it had set forth in the Schuman Declaration in 1950 for the creation of a European federation were mere rhetoric or, at most, were to be achieved in an undetermined but very distant future but certainly not in 1953 or 1954, that the EDC, as established by the Chief of the Juridical Service of the French Ministry of Foreign Affairs, was nothing other than "a political device resulting from the American precipitation in favor of German rearmament" or that the project of a political community was a way "of making the adversaries of the politics of the government since 1950 fall into their own trap."[19] All this at a time when U.S. Secretary of State John Foster Dulles was threatening an "agonizing reappraisal" of the European policy of the United States if the EDC were not made a reality.[20] Let us not forget Konrad Adenauer, the West German chancellor who had invested all his political capital in the success of a European policy that was to free his country from the discrimination caused by its recent past.

Pierre Mendès France or the End of the Federal Dream

The arrival in June 1954 of a French prime minister with no link to the European policy of the country, Pierre Mendès France, was necessary for finding a solution to the problem. He decided to reveal the reality of the situation in his first meeting with Dulles.[21] After the certain defeat of the EDC project in Paris, Mendès France immediately looked to the United Kingdom for help in finding a solution and in redefining the European project so that it was in line with French and British interests. Having earlier felt no affinity for the European project, the British government decided to help the French prime minister following a meeting between Mendès France and Winston Churchill at the latter's private residence, Chartwell. During the meeting, Mendès France assured his British colleague that the future alternative solution for including Germany in the defense of Western Europe would mean the FRG's entry into NATO, precisely what France had refused four years before.[22] For their part, the British decided that their assistance would be provided only after the nonratification of the EDC, which had to be entirely the responsibility of the French. Meanwhile, public pronouncements in favor of U.S. efforts supporting the ratification of the EDC would be continued.[23]

Previously, at a conference in Brussels from August 19 to 22 of 1954, the French prime minister proposed to his European colleagues that a revamping of the EDC—stripped of all its main supranational features and with an integrated army only for Germany while the other five states would keep their national armies—was the only way of obtaining its ratification in Paris. Adenauer, puzzled, initially even refused a bilateral meeting with Mendès France, but it finally took place at the end of the conference and was a complete success. Mendès France assured Adenauer that if the French National Assembly refused the EDC Treaty and the United States and United Kingdom proposed returning full sovereignty to Bonn, he would accept it and defend the measure before the French parliament and stand against any solution involving the neutralization of Germany and the end of the chancellor's pro-Western policies.[24] From this moment on, Mendès France was, in Adenauer's eyes, the French politician responsible for settling the German question, whether by means of ratifying the EDC in the National Assembly, for which the chancellor would abstain from any public pronouncement in favor of an alternate solution, or by accepting an alternative formula that safeguarded the vital interests of the FRG. No wonder, then, that after four years of delays, Adenauer declared before the Commission of Foreign Affairs of the Bundestag that he did not consider the Brussels Conference to be a defeat.[25] Moreover, as Hans Peter Schwarz explains, it soon became clear that it was Mendès France, so criticized for his policies, who achieved the ratification of the agreements that would permanently ensure Germany's inclusion in the Western system of security,[26] a task for which the political realism of Adenauer would prove invaluable. Joseph Luns, the Dutch foreign minister, confided to the French ambassador in The Hague, Jean-Paul Garnier, that Adenauer had claimed (without specifying to whom) that for his policies to succeed he did not want to see the creation of any group in which France was less powerful than the Federal Republic.[27]

Finally, the European Defense Community was derailed by the National Assembly in Paris on August 30, 1954. At the end of the same year, West Germany was accepted into NATO on the condition that all its troops be placed within the NATO structure and that it renounces the production of nuclear, chemical, and biological weapons. Its full sovereignty had been restored except for the Allied special rights, which would be retained pending a final peace treaty with Germany, signed some thirty-six years later.

Conclusion

The years from 1950 to 1954 were the period in which France realized that, in order to resolve its problems with Germany, it had to change the parameters of the relationship. The national framework of bilateral relationships had proven incapable of providing a stable and lasting solution, and so the time for supranational solutions had come. France did not arrive at this point through any conviction about the need to reorganize Europe according to a supranational or federal model, however, but through an analysis of a competitiveness problem in its main industry. Convinced that the solution to this problem demanded a new framework in its relationship with Germany, one that removed the German state's unilateral capacity to decide on the use of its coal resources, France used the idea of the federalization of Europe, supported by the United States government since the launching of the Marshall Plan, to articulate its plans and to introduce them to the international community in a positive light. The plan was introduced to the FRG as its only way back to international normality, though within a new Europe federalized under French leadership and in which the new German state could exist without discrimination. That is the very reason why this is the only time in the history of the European integration process that the words "federation" or "confederacy" were used, though only rhetorically. The need to rearm West Germany and the subsequent failure of the European Defense Community project uncovered the rhetorical use of these words and made plain that the acknowledged need to base the Franco-German relationship on new foundations in any case implied the political will to reorganize Europe along federal lines. The European construction continued after 1957 with the European Economic Community, focused on economic development through the creation of a common market and around a Franco-German axis established by Konrad Adenauer and Charles de Gaulle with the Elysée Treaty of 1963, a simple but effective agreement to harmonize the two countries' foreign policies. The terms "federation" or "confederacy" have not since appeared in official documents of the EEC and EU, but Europe has since experienced unprecedented economic development, peace, and stability—and all with the FRG as its main engine.

Notes

1. For documents related to the Occupation, see Beate Ruhm von Oppen, ed., *Documents on Germany under Occupation 1945–1954* (Oxford: Oxford University Press, 1955); Velma Hastings Cassidy, ed., *Germany 1947–1949. The Story in Documents* (Washington, DC: U.S. Government Printing Office, 1950). The JCS 1067 is in the latter 21–33. For further reading on the occupation from a U.S. viewpoint, see the biography of the U.S Military Governor Jean Edward Smith, *Lucius D. Clay. An American Life* (New York: Henry Holt and Co., 1990).

2. Sylvie Lefèvre, *Les Relations économiques franco-allemandes. De l'occupation à la coopération* (Paris: Comité pour l'Histoire économique et Financière de la France, 1998), 25

3. Two excellent works explaining the Marshall Plan period and the rebuilding of Europe according to the U.S. model are Michael Hogan, *The Marshall Plan. America, Britain and the Reconstruction of Western Europe* (Cambridge: Cambridge University Press, 1987); and David Ellwood, *Rebuilding Europe. Western Europe, America and Postwar Reconstruction* (Harlow: Longman, 1992).

4. On Jean Monnet, see Jean Monnet, *Memoirs* (New York: Doubleday, 1978); François Duchene, *Jean Monnet. The first statesman of interdependence* (New York: Norton, 1994).

5. On the Monnet Plan, see Frances M. B. Lynch, *France and the International Economy: from Vichy to the Treaty of Rome* (London: Routledge, 1997).

6. On the subject of the rebuilding of France after the war there are a lot of works, but two excellent ones in English are Irwin Wall, *The United States and the Making of Postwar France, 1945–1954* (Cambridge: Cambridge University Press, 1991); and William I. Hitchcock, *France Restored. Cold War Diplomacy and the Quest for Leadership in Europe, 1944–1954* (Chapel Hill: The University of North Carolina Press, 1998).

7. René Girault and Robert Frank, eds., *La puissance française en question 1945–1949* (Paris: Publications de la Sorbonne, 1988), 107; my translation.

8. Acheson's letter, October 30, 1949, in *Foreign Relations of the United States* (hereafter *FRUS*) 13 (1949), 621–25.

9. Note from the Direction d'Europe, Quai d'Orsay, a/s L'integration de l'Allemagne dans l'Europe occidentale, April 7, 1950, Ministère des affaires étrangères (herafter MAEF), Europe 1944–1960, Generalités, vol. 133; translation of the author.

10. The Schuman Declaration can be found in The European Navigator: http://www.ena.lu. Lots have been written on the ECSC, but the author strongly recommends the following: John Gillingham, *Coal, Steel, and the Rebirth of Europe, 1945–1955: The Germans and French from Ruhr Conflict to Economic Community* (Cambridge: Cambridge University Press, 1991). Another essential work, which argues that the ECSC and the rebuilding of Europe and European integration were a means to advance national interests of the states, was written by Alan S. Milward, *The Reconstruction of Western Europe, 1945–51* (London: Routledge, 1992). A more classical approach is offered by Pierre Gerbet, *La construction de l'Europe* (París: Imprimerie Nationale, 1999).

11. Monnet's Memorandum, May 3, 1950 in *Politique étrangère*, no. 1 (1993): 121–25; translation of the author.

12. This classical approach can be found, for example, in the main work of Pierre Gerbet or in Monnet's memoirs (refer to endnotes 4 and 10), and in the works of Raymond Poidevin, *Robert Schuman, homme d'Etat (1886–1963)* (Paris: Imprimerie nationale, 1986); and Robert Schuman, *Pour l'Europe* (Paris: Les éditions Nagel, 1963). The opposite viewpoint is defended by the British historian Alan Milward—whose position this article supports—with works such as *The Reconstruction of Western Europe* (see note 10) or *The European rescue of the Nation-State* (Berkeley: University of California Press, 1992).

13. On Adenauer, see the impressive biography of Hans Peter Schwarz, *Konrad Adenauer. A German politician and a statesman in a period of war, revolution and reconstruction. Vol. 1: From the German empire to the federal republic, 1876–1952, Vol. 2: The statesman, 1952–1967* (Oxford: Berghahn Books, 1997).

14. *Jean Monnet-Robert Schuman. Correspondance 1947–1953* (Fondation Jean Monnet pour l'Europe, Lausanne, 1986), 56–59.

15. The text of the Pleven Plan in The European Navigator: http://www.ena.lu. The list of works on the EDC is not as long as in the case of the ECSC, but two excellent works are: Edward Fursdon, *The European Defence Community: A History* (London: MacMillan, 1980); and Michael Creswell, *A question of Balance. How France and the United States Created Cold War Europe* (Cambridge: Harvard University Press, 2006). A contemporary work is Daniel Lerner, *France defeats EDC* (New York: Praeger, 1957).

16. The text of the EDC Treaty is accessible at the European Navigator: http://www.ena.lu.

17. The text of the Project for a European Constitution is accessible at: *American Foreign Policy 1950–1955. Basic Documents, vol. 1*, 1201–32.

18. Politique Européenne, Direction Générale des Affaires Politiques, Europe. Direction d'Europe Centrale, 26 January 1953, Archives Nationales (hereafter AN), Paris, Papiers Bidault, 457 AP 44; translation of the author.

19. Note pour le Secrétaire Général: Bilan des engagements du Gouvernement Français en matière de politique européenne, le jurisconsulte, January 17, 1953, AN, Paris, Papiers Bidault, 457 AP 38; translation of the author.

20. On John Foster Dulles see Richard H. Immerman, ed., *John Foster Dulles and the Diplomacy of the Cold War* (Princeton: Princeton University Press, 1990).

21. For the verbatim of the meeting between John Foster Dulles and Pierre Mendès France, see Declassified Documents Reference System (DDRS), Tuesday, July 13, 1954, 7:30–8:30 pm, Ambassador Dillon's Residence, Paris.

22. Conversations at Chartwell with M. Mendès France, August 23, 1954, Public Record Office [hereafter PRO], Kew Gardens, PREM 11/672.

23. CAB 128 / 27, CC (54) 57th, August 27, 1954, PRO, Kew Gardens. On the United Kingdom, the EDC and West German rearmament, see Kevin Ruane, *The Rise and Fall of the European Defence Community: Anglo-American Relations and the Crises of European Defence, 1950–55* (New York: St Martin's Press, 2000).

24. Pierre Mendès France, *Gouverner, c'est choisir (1954–1955)* (Paris: Gallimard, 1986), 241–44.

25. Telegram from François-Poncet to Mendès France, a/s déclarations de M. Von Eckardt, Chef du Service de Presse et d'information du Gouvernement Fédéral, sur la Conférence de Bruxelles, August 30, 1954, MAE, Europe 1944–60, Généralités,

vol. 155; Armand Berard, *Un Ambassadeur se souvient. Washington et Bonn, 1945–1955* (Paris: Plon, 1978), 566–69.

26. Hans-Peter Schwarz, *Adenauer*, 1176.

27. Telegram The Hague (Garnier) to the Quai d'Orsay, August 24, 1954, MAE, Europe 1944–60, Généralités, vol. 155; translation of the author.

CHAPTER 14

The *Relance Européenne* and the Nuclear Dimension of Franco-German Rapprochement

Mathieu L. L. Segers

Introduction

After the breakdown of negotiations in October of 1956, deadlock threatened European consultations on the Common Market and the European Atomic Energy Community, commonly known as EURATOM. At the same time, international tensions were increasing tremendously because of the Suez Crisis. This tense situation, notwithstanding, West German Chancellor Konrad Adenauer decided to go ahead with a previously scheduled visit to his French counterpart, Guy Mollet. On November 6, during Adenauer's stay in Paris, the outlines of a Franco-German compromise concerning the European Economic Community (EEC) and EURATOM were agreed upon. The Adenauer-Mollet agreement ushered in a series of Franco-German accords which finally cleared the way for the signing of the Treaties of Rome on March 25, 1957.

This chapter can be seen as a contribution to the detailed debate between the so-called traditionalists, who claim that the Rome Treaties were the result of decisions based on geopolitical reasoning,[1] and "revisionists," who stress the crucial importance of the socioeconomical and commercial interests of the member states of the European Coal and Steel Community (ECSC).[2] The discussion sparked by the simultaneity of the decisive European consultations on the EEC and the international crisis in the autumn of 1956 is illustrative of this debate. Traditionalists claim that "the successful outcome of the EEC negotiations was a historical accident, initiated by Nasser's Suez crisis,"[3] whereas revisionists judge the simultaneity as no more than a "striking coincidence of timing."[4]

Passages concerning the West-German position are based on: Mathieu Segers, "The FRG and the Common Market," in 1956, ed. Carole Fink, et al. (Leipzig: Leipziger Universitätsverlag, 2006), 169–90. The author owes thanks to the editors of this volume for the translations of many of the German and French quotations used in the present chapter.

Both traditionalists and revisionists cite historical research in support of their analyses. This chapter aims to provide a contribution to that research by focusing on some relatively underrated aspects. First of all, the historical evidence presented here demonstrates that it was Adenauer—and not his French counterpart[5]—who, under the pressure of international circumstances, decided to compromise in order to save "Europe" on November 6, 1956. Furthermore, the chapter challenges the widespread claim that from the mid-1950s, the United States no longer played an essential role in the European integration process.[6] This picture is far from correct: U.S. influence, especially on the position of the Federal Republic of Germany (FRG), was an indirect yet crucial element in the development of the Franco-German entente, which led to the Adenauer-Mollet agreement.

Finally, the chapter seeks to counter an "irony of historiography" by drawing attention to the importance of nuclear cooperation, which (instead of the now famous Common Market), was the primary issue at stake at the time.[7] After the short-lived hope of détente, which had become an illusion after the failure of the Geneva Conferences of 1955, the cold war reality of nuclear rivalry dominated international politics more than ever in 1956.[8] From this perspective, it is no surprise that available primary sources indicate that the rationale behind the *relance européenne* of 1956–57 appears to have been inspired especially by French and West German endeavors to obtain nuclear striking power and form a "European counterweight" to the superpowers.

A World Divided into Two Categories

On December 26, 1954, during a highly secret meeting of the French cabinet, a select group of ministers discussed the possibility of the military use of nuclear energy. On this occasion prime minister Pierre Mendès France concluded that the world was divided "between the nuclear powers and the others."[9] According to the prime minister, France had to join the first category as soon as possible. This was all the more important because of "the advantage which France had in these matters vis-à-vis the FRG since the West Germans renounced the production of nuclear weapons"—within the framework of the Paris Agreements, the FRG had indeed unilaterally and voluntarily renounced the production of nuclear, biological, and chemical weapons. Subsequently, Mendès France ordered a secret nuclear study program and preparations for the construction of a French atomic bomb and submarines with the capacity to carry nuclear weapons.

When the Mendès France government collapsed in February of 1955, the French cabinet had not yet taken a decisive stance on the issue. Nevertheless, the *Commissariat à l'énergie atomique* (CEA) had already begun the secret study program.[10] Moreover, the CEA shared the Gaullists' opposition to the idea of a European nuclear Community for the peaceful use of nuclear energy, which was the new project of Jean Monnet, the "father" of the ECSC.

Contrary to the CEA vision, Monnet's idea was well received by the Quai d'Orsay. The French Ministry of Foreign Affairs was increasingly anxious over the possibility of U.S.-FRG collaboration in the nuclear field. The new Monnet project seemed a possible and promising "double solution" to this problem.[11] Within a nuclear Community, France could on the one hand prevent the creation of an independent West German nuclear sector. On the other hand, a nuclear Community was the key for France to gain access to the FRG's financial and industrial resources, which would benefit the country's own nuclear ambitions.[12]

At this time, France depended on imports from the United States for some 90 percent of its enriched uranium (U235), which was essential for producing nuclear weapons. The United States systematically opposed French plans to develop a military nuclear capacity, however. During the early months of 1955, the CEA took the first steps toward building a plant for nuclear fission, but these attempts largely foundered due to the Anglo-American monopoly on enriched uranium. On February 4, the British government announced the immediate end of Franco-British consultations on the production of enriched uranium because the United States had exercised its veto over any form of nuclear cooperation with France. Moreover, the ambitions of the CEA were frustrated by American control over the quantity and quality of exported uranium and American unwillingness to share information. Under these circumstances, the CEA's skepticism about a European nuclear Community shrank rapidly.[13] On April 22, 1955, the French cabinet declared its support for the project.[14]

In the spring of 1955, Belgian minister of Foreign Affairs Paul-Henri Spaak together with his Dutch counterpart, Jan-Willem Beyen, drafted a memorandum combining the new initiatives for European integration (after the failure of the EDC). This so-called Benelux Memorandum, developed in close cooperation with Monnet and his aide Pierre Uri, was sent to the ECSC member states in mid-May of 1955. The document called for a *relance européenne* based on Dutch plans for a Common Market and further sector integration in the fields of energy, transportation, and especially nuclear cooperation—the latter through a separate European Community for the peaceful use of nuclear energy. A meeting of the Foreign Ministers of the Six was announced for June 1 and 2 in Messina to discuss the Benelux initiative.

At the Messina Conference, instructions from Paris compelled Antoine Pinay, the French minister of foreign affairs, to work for progress on the nuclear Community but at the same time to shelve the Common Market.[15] Finally, the ministers of the Benelux states managed to win Pinay over to a preliminary study, concerning the Common Market and the nuclear Community. A committee representing but not binding the governments would carry out this "study" and report its findings by November 1, 1955.[16] The results of the conference were laid down in the so-called Messina Resolution, which was to symbolize the *relance européenne* after the debacle of the EDC. Shortly after the Messina Conference, "the Six" appointed Spaak as the "political personality" who would lead the deliberations of the committee.[17]

Discussion in the Spaak Committee soon turned out to be an uphill battle. On September 6, 1955, at the interim conference of foreign ministers in the Dutch seaside resort of Noordwijk, Spaak requested that the report deadline be postponed.[18] The most important incident occurred at the margins of the Noordwijk Conference when Pinay confidentially warned Spaak that France was not prepared to renounce the military use of nuclear energy within a European nuclear Community. According to Spaak's memoirs, he fixed these cautious words carefully in his mind.[19]

La Bombe atomique and the Unity of the West

Chancellor Adenauer did not give priority to the deliberations of the Spaak Committee in Brussels. He considered other matters of foreign policy more important, especially resolution of the lingering Saar question, the two four-power Geneva Conferences (in the summer and winter of 1955) and, above all, the further *Gleichberechtigung* of the FRG—after the Paris Agreements had come into force—especially in the sense of (possible nuclear) rearmament. As a result, the formulation of the West German negotiating position in Brussels remained relatively unclear. At the end of 1955, deliberations on the Common Market and EURATOM—as the nuclear Community was now called—were put on hold as a result of the collapse of the Faure government. Moreover, progress was severely hindered by the opposition of Franz-Josef Strauss, the new, high-handed West German minister of nuclear affairs, who supported the German nuclear sector in its preference for bilateral cooperation with the United States over the uncertain adventure of a nuclear Community of "the Six."[20]

It was only at the end of 1955 that Adenauer decided to reactivate his European policy in a pro-European manner by actively supporting the Messina Program. The chancellor came to this conclusion in reaction to the surprising outcome of the Saar referendum on October 23, 1955,[21] the imminent failure of the (second) Geneva Conference, and two personal conversations with Pinay and Spaak at his home in Rhöndorf in mid-November. In the second of these meetings, Adenauer reassured the Belgian minister of foreign affairs, who was worried about the lack of West German support for the nuclear Community, that he "would give strong instructions 'along the right lines' to Strauss."[22] One day before the meeting with Spaak, Adenauer and Pinay had succeeded in relieving much of the tension in Franco-German relations caused by the Saar referendum. Pointing to the poor results in Geneva, they used the subsequent press conference to emphasize the importance of their joint wish to strengthen European integration in the very near future.[23] The appearance of détente, which the Geneva Conference had taken on when talks started in July, vanished completely during the second half of 1955.

After the failure of the Geneva Conferences, it became clear that the U.S. State Department was of the opinion that objections to the sharing of confidential nuclear information with the new European Community only caused useless discussions. After all, France's efforts to acquire nuclear striking power, one way or the other (i.e., unilaterally or multilaterally), would in any case result in its entry into the category of nuclear powers in the foreseeable future. Given this reality, the dominant vision in the State Department focused on possible damage control:

creating a supranational European nuclear Community to prevent the (potentially disastrous) disintegration of Western Europe as a result of French ambitions. A strong and functioning EURATOM was thus of the utmost importance for the American power position vis-à-vis the Soviet Union.

It was this geopolitical calculation that made Dulles conclude that the American government had to give an extra impulse to EURATOM rather than being reluctant with its support and the sharing of confidential information.[24] The international reality after the Geneva Conferences dictated that absolute priority be given to the unity of the West and of Western Europe in particular.

On January 31, 1956, a new French government under the leadership of the Socialist Guy Mollet came to power. A prominent member of Monnet's Action Committee for the United States of Europe, Mollet made European integration a top priority of his minority government. Despite the fact that the Action Committee was promoting EURATOM explicitly as integration in the field of the *peaceful* use of nuclear energy, the Mollet government consistently carried on France's quest for the military use of nuclear energy. On February 6, 1956, French President of the High Authority of the ECSC René Mayer traveled to Washington for high-level consultations on EURATOM. In a confidential discussion with Dulles, he stressed that he could not imagine "that France would ever give up for all time the right to have atomic weapons if others had them."[25]

Only a few days later, on February 11, 1956, an informal ECSC Conference of Foreign Ministers was scheduled in Brussels at the instigation of the French government. This meeting gave new French Minister of Foreign Affairs Christian Pineau the opportunity to break the official silence over France's intention of making military use of nuclear energy within EURATOM. As a compromise, Pineau suggested a five-year moratorium on the production of nuclear weapons. According to estimates in Paris, France needed that amount of time to make the necessary preparations for the testing and production of *la bombe atomique*.[26] Spaak, acknowledging that the Six had to find a formula to meet France's requirements in order to save the whole Messina project, agreed to lay the groundwork for such a five-year moratorium.[27]

Laying the Foundation of the Franco-German Entente and Relance européenne

The Spaak Committee presented its final and unanimous report on April 21, 1956. It took no position on the military use of nuclear energy. According to the document, the heads of delegation agreed that "the problem of the possibility of the military use of nuclear energy represented an issue of such a political nature that it went beyond the competences of the committee.[28] On April 26, Spaak sent a side letter on the issue to the foreign ministers of the Six in which he presented a proposal for a five-year moratorium on the production and testing of nuclear weapons.[29]

The Spaak Report was the main topic at the ECSC Venice Conference on June 1, 1956, where Pineau's announcement of the French position came unexpectedly.[30]

France had until then been the major opponent of the Common Market. Suddenly, it appeared to accept the Spaak Report as the basis for negotiations to establish both EURATOM *and* the Common Market. The gathering concluded with an announcement of an intergovernmental conference to draft two treaties.

The "EURATOM debate" in the Assemblée nationale, from July 5 to 11, 1956, meant a second success (after the Venice Conference) for the European forces in Paris. After Mollet had made the crucial pledge that EURATOM would not place any barriers to the French military nuclear program—provided that France not carry out any test explosions before 1961—the parliament voted in favor of EURATOM (332 to 181).[31] Moreover, the "1961 clause" mentioned by Mollet made a moratorium clause *de facto* superfluous in a future EURATOM treaty.

At the same time, the military use of nuclear energy gained a sense of urgency in the eyes of Konrad Adenauer. On July 13, Adenauer was unpleasantly surprised by a new American foreign policy concept presented in the *New York Times* as the Radford Plan. It was consistent with the so-called New Look, which represented a shift in American military priorities toward further development of its nuclear arsenal. In order to put together the necessary budget, the Radford Plan foresaw significant cutbacks in conventional American armed forces, especially those stationed overseas.[32] To the West German chancellor, unilateral troop reduction by the United States meant playing with fire because more than 250,000 men were under arms in the Soviet Zone. A U.S. troop withdrawal would encourage Moscow to provoke trouble at any time anywhere along the great length of the Iron Curtain. Adenauer feared that "the FRG . . . would be swept away" because of the simple fact that "if the Radford Plan were realized, the Americans would only be able to sit by and watch, because American intervention would mean starting a nuclear war."[33] To make things worse, it became clear during the summer that the American government was unwilling to give Britain and France military backing in the escalating Suez Crisis. According to Adenauer, this situation made "the impotence of Europe frightfully clear" and compelled the continent to establish "a strong joint European foreign policy" as soon as possible.[34]

In reaction to the Radford Plan, Adenauer concluded that the FRG had to reconsider the ban on the production of nuclear weapons as formulated in the Paris Agreements. In his new capacity as defense minister, Strauss decided to act on the revised West German position by agreeing to initiatives for far-reaching Franco-German cooperation in the field of security policy, which French diplomacy had confidentially been proposing to Bonn since April 28, 1956.[35] Under the Mollet government, the Quai d'Orsay tried to refloat this Franco-German ship. In addition, the Mollet government appeared to further pave the way for a Franco-German entente by taking a constructive stance on the Saar.[36]

On September 17, Adenauer held consultations on EURATOM with French State Secretary of Foreign Affairs Maurice Faure in Bonn. At the end of this meeting, Faure stated that the Paris Agreements prohibited the FRG from producing nuclear weapons but not from possessing them. Faure made it clear that

French government believed that "if political developments indicated . . . the FRG should be armed with nuclear weapons."[37]

Twelve days later, on September 29, Adenauer and Mollet met at Schloss Ernich, the residence of the French ambassador to West Germany, in order to discuss the last issues concerning the Saar question, which had heavily mortgaged postwar Franco-German reconciliation. On the margin of these concluding talks, the statesmen also discussed EURATOM. Adenauer took the opportunity to underscore once again that the FRG had renounced the production of nuclear weapons but not the possession of them. Again, the French delegation did not oppose him.[38] During the press conference, Adenauer emphasized that European integration was entering an era in which the aim should be that "Europe and the European nations would maintain their significance and position in the world." According to the chancellor in this time of Franco-German rapprochement, "European unity was stronger than ever before."[39]

During a special cabinet meeting on October 5, 1956, Adenauer stated that he "wanted to obtain, through EURATOM, the possibility of producing nuclear weapons as soon as possible."[40] However, after the failure of the ECSC Paris Conference (October 20 and 21),[41] the chancellor seemed to believe that his main priority, that is, obtaining nuclear weaponry within a framework of further European cooperation, required a Western European Union (WEU) track parallel to the EEC and EURATOM.[42]

Under the pressure of the Suez Crisis (and the brutal suppression of the Hungarian uprising by the Red Army), however, Adenauer eventually acted on the advice of the Ministry of Foreign Affairs to accede to French wishes so as to break the deadlock threatening the *relance européenne*.[43] The chancellor made the decision to outmaneuver Economics Minister Ludwig Erhard[44] by using an already scheduled visit to Paris on November 6, 1956, to save the Messina project. In addition, Adenauer seemed to anticipate acquiring nuclear weapons for the FRG in the foreseeable future through a further strengthening of the Franco-German entente. Although time was short, West German diplomacy managed to bring the FRG's position in line with that of the French. Additional concessions concerning social harmonization, especially with respect to the harmonization of wages, were made.[45]

The Real Rivalry of the Nuclear Age

In a November 5, 1956, broadcast on Radio Moscow, Soviet Prime Minister Nikolai Bulganin warned that the Suez Crisis would escalate into a world war if France and the United Kingdom did not end their colonial aggression against the Egyptian people. At the same time, the two European countries were forced to conclude that the United States, despite the Soviet nuclear threats,[46] was persisting in its rejection of the Franco-British military actions in Egypt and refusing to give its NATO partners nuclear support.

The following day, November 6, Mollet and Adenauer immediately focused their discussion on the tense international situation. The chancellor referred to a letter from Bulganin to Eisenhower: "The Soviet Union and U.S. . . . are two great powers possessing all the most modern forms of armaments, including atom and hydrogen weapons. . . . If Govts of USSR and USA firmly announce their will to guarantee peace and will condemn aggression, the aggression will be terminated and there will be no war. . . . Mr. President, in these threatening hours when the highest principles of morality . . . are being subjected to an ordeal, Soviet Govt turns to Govt of U.S. with a proposal for close cooperation to stop aggression and end further bloodshed."[47] According to Adenauer, this letter contained an "offer to divide and rule the world," one which the United States had not rejected. Pineau declared that the French government shared this analysis.[48]

Adenauer then proceeded to outline his vision of Europe and argued that the moment had come for the states of Western Europe to unite "against the United States." The chancellor stated that American interests in Western Europe were steadily decreasing, and he cited the Radford Plan to reinforce his arguments.[49] He also urged his French partner by saying: "And now we have to make Europe!"[50] Before the end of their meeting, Mollet and Adenauer had accepted the proposals concerning the Common Market and EURATOM worked out earlier that day by experts.[51] Adenauer had de facto given in to French demands concerning the EEC. Afterward, Pineau informed France's diplomatic representatives that Mollet and Adenauer "gave their complete agreement to the propositions of the experts, thanks to the constructive attitude of the West German delegation."[52]

The Federal Republic's concessions finally cleared the way for the establishment of the EEC and EURATOM.[53] On March 25, 1957, the heads of state of "the Six" signed the treaties in Rome. Moreover, on January 17, 1957, French Defense Minister Maurice Bourgès-Maunory and his West-German counterpart Franz-Josef Strauss signed an agreement at Colomb-Béchar concerning further Franco-German cooperation in the field of (nuclear) defense.[54] The Colomb-Béchar agreement laid the groundwork for cooperation among France, Italy, and West Germany, which started in November of 1957 and resulted in the short-lived trilateral treaty of April 8, 1958, on the building of a nuclear fission plant in Pierrelatte in southeastern France.

Conclusion

The Adenauer-Mollet agreement of November 6, 1956, ushered in a series of Franco-German accords which finally cleared the way for the signing of the Treaties of Rome and can be seen as the birth of the famous Franco-German axis in European integration. From the second half of 1955, both Paris and Bonn acknowledged that international realities compelled "Europe" to join forces and treat the military use of nuclear energy as "an end in itself" (independent of the United States).[55] The definite establishment of a bipolar world after the Geneva Conferences prompted the Western bloc to seek stronger unity but first and foremost speeded up the Franco-German entente, as did the solution of the Saar question in the second half of 1956. Moreover, the tense international situation resulting from the Suez Crisis contributed to the development of a joint Franco-German quest to safeguard the geopolitical position of European nations in the "new world" of the superpowers and to counter a nuclear power play with European cooperation.

Notes

1. For instance, Hanns-Jürgen Küsters, "West Germany's foreign policy in Western Europe, 1949–58," in *Western Europe and Germany. The beginnings of European integration 1945–1960*, ed. Clemens A. Wurm (Oxford: Berg, 1995).
2. The two most prominent revisionist works are: Andrew Moravcsik, *The choice for Europe* (London: UCL Press, 1998); and Alan S. Milward, *The European rescue of the nation-state* (London: Routledge, 1992). In 2003, Craig Parsons widened the debate by arguing against Moravcsik's "liberal intergovernmental explanation" from a constructivist perspective in *A Certain Idea of Europe* (Ithaca: Cornell University Press). For an introductory overview of the theoretical dimension of the debate, see Michelle Cini, ed., *European Union Politics* (Oxford: Oxford University Press, 2006).
3. Küsters, "West Germany's foreign policy," 69.
4. Moravcsik, *The choice*, 87, 107; cf. Milward, *The European rescue*, 208.
5. As is often supposed in traditional analyses, see f.i.: Hanns-Jürgen Küsters, "The origins of the EEC treaty," in *Il rilancio dell'Europa*, ed. Enrico Serra (Brussels: Bruylant, 1989), 233.
6. For a critical review of this assumption see: Geir Lundestad, *'Empire' by integration* (Oxford: Oxford University Press, 1998), 129.
7. On the mentioned "irony," see Jonathan E. Helmreich, "The United States and the formation of EURATOM," *Diplomatic History* 15, no. 3 (1991): 388–89.
8. Fink, et al., eds., *1956*, 10.
9. Bertrand Goldschmidt, *Les rivalités atomiques 1939–1966* (Paris: Fayard, 1967), 206–7.
10. See Lawrence Scheinman, *Atomic energy policy in France under the Fourth Republic* (Princeton, NJ: Princeton University Press, 1965), 112–15.
11. See Georges-Henri Soutou, *L'alliance incertaine* (Paris: Fayard, 1996), 38.
12. See Historical Archives of the European Union (HAEU), Florence: MAEF/OW/304, Note, April 14, 1955.
13. See Helmreich, "The United States," 390.
14. See Christian Pineau and Christiane Rimbaud, *Le grand pari* (Paris: Fayard, 1991), 162.
15. See Jean-Marie Palayret, "Les décideurs français et allemands, 1955–1957," in *Le couple France-Allemagne et les institutions européennes*, ed. Marie-Thérèse Bitsch (Brussels: Bruylants, 2001), 111.
16. Michel Dumoulin, *Spaak* (Brussels: Racine, 1999), 508.
17. See HAEU: CM3/1, MAE/SEC 13/4: III. Le Comité Intergouvernemental.
18. Ibid., V. La Conférence de Noordwijk.
19. See Paul-Henri Spaak, *Combats inachevés*, vol. 2 (Paris: Fayard, 1969), 89.
20. See Mathieu Segers, "Zwischen Pax Americana und Pakt Atomica," *Vierteljahrshefte für Zeitgeschichte* 55, no. 3 (2006): 439–40.

21. That is, against the pro-French so-called Saar Statute, in favor of which Adenauer had lobbied in spite of fierce opposition within the FRG (also within his own CDU/CSU). In this respect, Adenauer seemed of the opinion that the fragile Franco-German reconciliation and West-German *Gleichberechtigung* should not be put on the line, all the more taking stock of the West-German interests in the (then-approaching) Geneva Conference(s).

22. *Foreign Relations of the United States, 1955–57, Vol. IV (FRUS IV)*, doc. 140, 371.

23. See *Archiv der Gegenwart* (AdG), Deutschland 1949 bis 1999, vol. 2 (Sankt Augustin: 2000), 1603.

24. See *FRUS IV*, doc. 147, 388–89. The issue of the property right of EURATOM in relation to the military use of atomic energy would develop as the trickiest question in this respect. See *FRUS IV*, doc. 220, 520–21.

25. *FRUS IV*, doc. 155, 406.

26. See HAEU: MAEF/SG I. Conversation franco-allemande, Bruxelles, 11 Fevrier 1956; Gérard Bossuat, *L'Europe des Français 1943–1959: La IVe République aux sources de l'Europe communautaire* (Paris: Publications de la Sorbonne, 1997), 300, 305.

27. See Politisches Archiv des Auswärtigen Amts (PAAA), Berlin: Abteilung 2, vol. 904/nr.A9020–21, Brüssel, February 28, 1956; Entwurf des Protokolls.

28. Comité Intergouvernemental, secrétariat, MAE 120 f/56 (corrigé), 122.

29. See Bundesarchiv Koblenz (BArch): N1337/642, Regierungsausschuß, Brüssel, April 26, 1956.

30. With agreement on the possibility of military use of atomic energy close at hand, Mollet, sensing the need to clarify France's position, gave his foreign minister carte blanche for the impending conference in Venice (cf. Pineau and Rimbaud, *Le grand pari*, 207–8).

31. See Pascaline Winand, *Eisenhower, Kennedy and the United States of Europe* (New York: St. Martin's Press, 1993), 98.

32. See Catherine Kelleher, *Germany and the Politics of Nuclear Weapons* (New York: Columbia University Press, 1975), 43.

33. Konrad Adenauer, *Erinnerungen 1955–1959* (Stuttgart: DVA, 1989), 200.

34. Ibid., 200, 215–19, and 223.

35. See Ulrich Lappenküper, *Die deutsch-französischen Beziehungen, 1949–1963*, vol. 1 (Munich: Oldenbourg, 2001), 1163.

36. See Nassima Bougherara, "La coopération militaire atomique franco-allemande," in *Les relations internationales au temps de la guerre froide*, ed. Paul Vaiss and Klaus Morgenroth (Bern: Peter Lang, 2006), 45–46.

37. PAAA: B1/155. Aufzeichnung, Bonn, September 19, 1956.

38. PAAA: B1/155. Aufzeichnung, Besprechung, September 29, 1956.

39. AdG, vol. 2, 1799–1800.

40. BArch: N1254/84 and N1337/643, geheim, Auszug aus dem Kurzprotokoll der 155. Kabinettssitzung.

41. See Segers, "The FRG," 182–83.

42. See HAEU: JMAS/33; BArch: N1337/537, London, October 25, 1956.

43. BArch: N1337/643, geheim—Abteilung 2, Bonn, October 29, 1956.

44. Since the start of his second period in office, Erhard had pleaded for an Anglo-European free-trade area instead of an extension of the "French and *dirigiste*" Europe of the Six.

45. See BArch: N1337/643, Aufzeichnung, Bonn, November 3, 1956.

46. In a letter to Prime Minister Anthony Eden, Bulganin asked the question "in what situation would Britain find herself if she were attacked by stronger states, possessing all types of modern destructive weapons?" *FRUS, 1955–57, Volume XVI*, doc. 511, 1003, fn. 2.

47. *FRUS, 1955–57, Volume XV*, doc. 505, 993.

48. HAEU: MAEF/SG. Proces-Verbal de l'entretien Mollet- Adenauer du 6 novembre 1956.

49. Ibid.

50. Pineau and Rimbaud, *Le grand pari*, 222–23.

51. See PAAA: B1/156, Aufzeichnung, Bonn, November 9, 1956.

52. MAE (1989), *Documents Diplomatiques Français (DDF), Tome III, 1956*, doc. 146, 249.

53. See Segers, "The FRG," 188–89.

54. The ban on production of ABC-weapons on German soil was maintained in the Franco-German agreement.

55. Soutou, *L'Alliance*, 56.

CHAPTER 15

More than a Geriatric Romance

Adenauer, de Gaulle, and the Atlantic Alliance

Ronald J. Granieri

The relationship between Konrad Adenauer and Charles de Gaulle was crucial for postwar Europe. Although Franco-German reconciliation enjoyed its first successes before de Gaulle's return to power in 1958 and endured periods of relative coolness over succeeding decades, the regular consultations Adenauer and de Gaulle codified in the Elysée Treaty of 1963, built on five years of regular tête-à-têtes, and provided a framework for intergovernmental cooperation irrespective of the political makeup of subsequent French and German governments.

Two photographs of Adenauer and de Gaulle offer enduring images of Franco-German reconciliation. One shows them at Mass in Reims Cathedral in the summer of 1962, standing near the altar, surrounded by the Gothic glories of the coronation site of French kings. The other shows them embracing after signing the Elysée Treaty, symbolically overcoming centuries of enmity between their peoples. Those images have encouraged a great deal of mythmaking about both their relationship and about Franco-German reconciliation in general. Some of that mythmaking was intentional, as Adenauer and de Gaulle each used symbolism and rhetoric to cultivate public support for their policies. Symbolism came with a price, however, encouraging sour reactions from critics who accused the two statesmen of pursuing impractical policies based on sentimentality. A sarcastic American Undersecretary of State George Ball, angry over Adenauer and de Gaulle's refusal to accept the American "Grand Design" for an Atlantic community, was contemptuous of their "geriatric romance." British historian A. J. P. Taylor, reflecting his own lack of enthusiasm for European integration, acidly dismissed them as two "old gentlemen . . . lost in the dreams of their youth," calling their "Franco-German community built on Roman Catholic conservatism . . . the fantasy of a world which has passed away."[1] Former Secretary of State Dean Acheson offered withering criticism of Adenauer's "serious" mistake in signing the Elysée treaty and endorsing de Gaulle's "dangerous and anachronistic" vision, deeming it an act of "singular misperception" by someone who "has never understood General de Gaulle's design, nor the undignified role designed for him or for Germany."[2] Just as Adenauer and de Gaulle claimed to be pursuing historical opportunities, their opponents claimed they were lost in the past.

Neither critics nor supporters can be blamed for emphasizing the personal nature of the Adenauer-de Gaulle relationship. Their very appearance contributed to the impression that they embodied "old Europe." Both wanted Europe to be an independent actor in world affairs and saw themselves as defenders of European traditions against both Soviet aggression and American imperial hubris. This attitude encouraged a particular sort of cultural arrogance that inspired negative reactions. As Adenauer told a receptive de Gaulle in 1963, "it would be better if the Americans listened more to [de Gaulle's] advice, not just in issues relating to France and America, but in world affairs in general. After all, the Americans are pretty much all alone. In 1900 they didn't even have a foreign policy."[3]

Both the "two old gentlemen" and their critics, however, knew there was more to Franco-German reconciliation than symbolism and sentiment, and that a great deal of calculation went into the relationship on both sides. Although both men were certainly capable of symbolic gestures, both were also practical statesmen who used the relationship to serve particular purposes. The personal relationship was undoubtedly important, and helped them return to discussions even when policy differences could have led to deeper estrangement. The historical significance of their collaboration, however, lies in how their cooperation reflected the complexity and possibilities of the Atlantic alliance, both during the cold war and after.

To contemporary observers, they had much in common. Both were products of the nineteenth century—Adenauer born in 1876, de Gaulle in 1890—and began their careers before the First World War. Both sprang from Catholic milieus with a strong sense of the fallen nature of human beings that shaped their philosophies and political views. Both were often distant and imperious, with few close friends. Those qualities made them appear to be soul mates, especially to American interlocutors such as John Kennedy, who came from another generation and another, more optimistic world.

At the same time, however, the two men were quite different. De Gaulle was a soldier, while Adenauer proudly declared he had never served in uniform. Adenauer was a child of the upwardly mobile urban middle class, who rose within the political machine of his native Cologne, while the well-bred officer de Gaulle never hid his distaste, even contempt, for the compromises of party politics. De Gaulle also conceived of foreign policy in national terms, and considered his primary mission to be the restoration of French *grandeur*. Adenauer reflected the ambivalence of most Rhineland Catholics toward the Prussian-German Reich and German national traditions. That ambivalence, combined with the realities of Germany's situation after 1945, meant that Adenauer's government could not pursue a purely national foreign policy and would rely much more on plans for European and Atlantic integration.

What brought and held them together, despite external pressures and their own disagreements, was not some mystical bond, but rather the way they related their principles to the political situations at hand. Both practiced their own versions of Realpolitik, though their contrasting traditions encouraged different priorities. Adenauer, for example, told a gathering of party allies: "In foreign policy . . . individual interests are decisive, and we should not assume that anybody is going to help us Germans based on our good looks and charm."[4] De Gaulle was no less convinced of the need for nations to pursue their own interests, though at the same time he believed firmly that France, the embodiment of Enlightenment values, was "loved" around the world, an attitude that led him to believe he could run greater risks in pursuit of its policies. Critics often claimed the General overdrew on this bank of good will, but that does not mean it was not there.[5] That attitude was foreign to Adenauer, but their differences as much as their similarities shaped their relationship as they responded to the changed situation in postwar Europe.

Adenauer's geographical roots helped shape his political conception, which combined a firm attachment to the idea of a unified Christian West built on Franco-German reconciliation with a pragmatic evaluation of the European situation. As early as October 1945, he considered the division of Europe a "fact" that Western Europe and West Germany should accept and that Europe should unite to protect against further encroachments from the East. His commitment to European integration is not surprising. Much more intriguing, however, was his attitude toward the United States. Despite holding reservations about American society common among European conservatives, Adenauer recognized the United States was the indispensable defender of a rebuilding Europe, and had to be part of the new West. He would develop famously close relationships with American leaders such as John Foster Dulles, and would work to bind the Federal Republic closely to the United States.

Adenauer's belief that the Germans needed both to secure the protection of the United States and to pursue European integration based on Franco-German reconciliation led him to pursue a policy that moved between these two poles. Even as he demanded that the Germans abandon their traditional *Schaukelpolitik* between East and West, he did seesaw between European and Atlantic priorities, which in practical terms meant between the United States and France as preferred partners, based on his sense of the Federal Republic's insecure position in the postwar world. If other states acted in their own interests, he was determined his policy would be equally fixed on German interests as he defined them, maneuvering between the allies to secure the sovereignty and stability that came with *Westbindung*.[6]

Drawing on his unique interpretation of French history and traditions, de Gaulle pursued his own vision of French revival and reconstruction. Even more than the rather ascetic Adenauer, de Gaulle used grand rhetorical and historical analogies to build support for his policies. As far back as 1950, for example, de Gaulle speculated on Franco-German cooperation in Western Europe by claiming that Franks, Gauls, Romans, and Germans had united once to defeat the Huns at Chalons. By the summer of 1962, during his triumphal state visit to the Federal Republic, he praised—in German—the "great German people" for their successful reconstruction and to proclaim the great things Germans and French would do together for Europe. At the same time, however, de Gaulle focused his attention on regaining France's international position as a great power, and resented American imperial pretensions. He was also ambivalent about Germany's role in his plans. In the immediate postwar years, starting with his decision to sign a treaty with Stalin in 1944, de Gaulle envisioned a Europe led by France—with Britain if possible, without Britain if necessary—in which Germany would be partitioned and weak. As the cold war developed, de Gaulle was willing to imagine a European role for West Germany, and spoke well of Adenauer. Nevertheless, he and his followers rejected plans for Europe that placed France and the Federal Republic on the same footing or which would have placed France too much at the mercy of the United States. Those sentiments found clear expression in the Gaullist vote against the European Defense Community (EDC) in August 1954. Even as he later recognized the value of Franco-German partnership, de Gaulle did not want to see a strong German state, but believed the long-term basis of any European cooperation had to be "a direct accord, without intermediaries, between the people of France and the German people."[7]

Two events in 1958, the French political crisis that returned de Gaulle to power and the Berlin crisis, brought them together, as each saw the other as a potential ally in a dangerous time. At their first official meeting in Colombey, despite Adenauer's initial misgivings, the two gentlemen quickly agreed on the need for greater European cooperation built on their "permanent consultation." Correctly gauging his guest's mood as Adenauer criticized American policy, de Gaulle highlighted the need for European independence from the United States. Although he asserted the importance of relations with Washington, Adenauer agreed that it would be a "catastrophe" if the Europeans allowed themselves to become merely "instruments of the United States."[8] Adenauer's desire for closer cooperation with France intensified during the Berlin crisis, which dovetailed with de Gaulle's plans to restore France's position as the leader of continental Europe. As the Americans and British suggested compromises on Berlin, de Gaulle rejected negotiations with the Soviets, earning Adenauer's trust and gratitude. Even as he hoped de Gaulle would be a reliable ally, however, Adenauer's motivation was as rooted in concern as it was in confidence. From the start, he recognized that de Gaulle had great power ambitions, and was always on the lookout for signs France intended to go over Germany's head, either by seeking a rapprochement with the Anglo-Saxons or with the Soviets.[9]

Adenauer was right to be uncertain. Within a month of their meeting in Colombey, de Gaulle upset Adenauer with his first formal proposal of a joint Anglo-American-French "directory" within NATO. Far from seeking European solidarity, de Gaulle appeared more interested in guaranteeing France a place among the great powers. Adenauer even criticized French plans to British Prime Minister Harold Macmillan—a rare gesture of trust in the British.[10] In order to avoid a "disagreeable" public debate and preserve the "memory of the atmosphere of Colombey," however, Adenauer also wrote to de Gaulle expressing his own desire for NATO reform.[11] Ultimately, the Anglo-Saxons (de Gaulle's favorite if inaccurate collective term for the British and Americans) rebuffed the directory proposal, though he repeated it in 1960. Although one wonders whether de Gaulle's grand vision for Europe could have withstood the temptation of admission to the Anglo-Saxon Special Relationship, itself a combination of convenience and sentimentality, de Gaulle's frustration with the Anglo-Saxons encouraged further solidarity with Adenauer, at least as long as no better offer came along.

Areas of dissonance nonetheless remained within their ever-closer relationship. Security policy was one such area. The last government of the Fourth Republic under Guy Mollet, seeking financial support for the French nuclear weapons program, had negotiated an agreement on tripartite cooperation between France, the Federal Republic, and Italy on joint research and production of nuclear weapons in April 1958. Upon arriving in office in May, however, de Gaulle canceled the agreement, preferring nuclear development within a national framework, much to the disappointment of Adenauer and Defense minister Franz Josef Strauß.[12] Although de Gaulle would occasionally hint at German participation in the *force de frappe* to undermine American-led NATO nuclear plans, this symbol of national self-assertion remained firmly in French control. His attitude toward nuclear cooperation reflected de Gaulle's overall feelings about NATO. Although he endorsed the alliance in general, he rejected integration limiting French sovereignty. As he told the cadets at St. Cyr in 1959, "the defense of France must be French."[13] No German leader could make such a statement, nor could the Germans, on the front line in a divided Europe, be so dismissive of an alliance that guaranteed their security.

The most complex aspect of the Adenauer-de Gaulle relationship, however, was the area in which they also tried to express the most agreement, European cooperation. Adenauer, like many German Christian Democrats, strongly advocated European political integration, and was willing to sacrifice national sovereignty to the cause—which was of course much less of a sacrifice for the semisovereign Germans than for their proud French allies. As the chances for supranational integration faded after the collapse of the EDC, however, Adenauer was willing to be more flexible, arguing in a 1956 speech in Brussels that Europeans should pursue greater cooperation as soon as possible rather than waiting for ideal structures, through international and federal channels, to reduce dependence on the "patronage" of the United States.[14] This was a sort of Gaullism avant la lettre, even if Adenauer left no doubt that the ultimate goal should be a federal Europe.

De Gaulle skillfully appealed to Adenauer's European enthusiasm. At their meeting at Bad Kreuznach in late 1958, he reassured Adenauer that, despite rumors to the contrary, he did not want to withdraw France from the EEC, but instead asserted the need for a politically more autonomous Europe based on

Franco-German cooperation. The Americans needed to be "allies, not masters," de Gaulle claimed. "We [Europeans] are closer in spirit . . . America is another world. We must never let them govern us."[15] Nevertheless, de Gaulle never advocated a federal Europe. He did not hide this feeling from Adenauer but also was not above using the Chancellor's frustration with the Americans to try to pull him to the French position. At their July 1960 meeting in Rambouillet, after the failed Paris summit exposed differences on Berlin, he wooed Adenauer with a plan for European cooperation based on government consultations rather than supranational institutions and hinted at a looser Atlantic alliance.[16] Adenauer was receptive, and only after his return to Bonn, where advisers reminded him that the Germans were in no position to abandon NATO or the EEC, did he distance himself from the plans.[17]

De Gaulle was disappointed but also persistent, advocating intergovernmental cooperation instead of political integration in the Fouchet Plans of 1961 and 1962. Other EEC partners, especially Belgium and the Netherlands, concerned that the plans institutionalized French dominance and unwilling to create structures that would keep the British out of Europe, rejected them.[18] Decrying British meddling, however, de Gaulle won over Adenauer, himself increasingly skeptical about British membership in the EEC. Adenauer called the defeat of the second Fouchet Plan on April 17, 1962 a "black day for Europe." The failure of these plans for political union *à six* led Adenauer and de Gaulle to pursue cooperation *à deux* with the exchange of state visits in 1962 and the Elysée Treaty. De Gaulle's patient cultivation of Adenauer thus appeared to bear fruit.

Adenauer considered the Elysée Treaty the culmination of his pursuit of Franco-German cooperation. He also defended it as a first step toward deeper European integration by offering a forum for political consultation, despite criticism of the anti-Anglo-Saxon tones struck by de Gaulle, who had vetoed British membership in the EEC only a week before.[19] Adenauer even expressed shock at the negative American reaction, claiming, "John Foster Dulles would have embraced me joyously" at the news of such close cooperation between former archenemies.[20] De Gaulle also considered the treaty a major success, though for different reasons. De Gaulle did not much care whether John Foster Dulles, let alone John Kennedy, approved his plans nor did he see intergovernmental cooperation as a step toward deeper integration. Though he was open to the possibility that the rest of the Six would join in consultations, his goal was to use consultation with the Germans to secure French influence within Europe, even if the resulting controversy produced tension within the Atlantic alliance.

Despite the differences in their longer-term visions, there was logic to their cooperation. Though his critics accused him of being disingenuous, Adenauer consistently claimed his goal remained European integration within an Atlantic alliance. From his perspective, only an assertive Europe could balance the Anglo-Saxons, and Adenauer knew that the Federal Republic could not assume the leading role in such a Europe. Thus, in preparation for his visit to France in July 1962, Adenauer sent foreign policy assistant Horst Osterheld to de Gaulle with a letter expressing his hope that France would assume the position in Europe "to which it is entitled."[21] This choice was not based primarily on sentiment. Adenauer wanted to "bind France tightly to Germany, so it could not ally with the Russians against us." Adenauer presented himself as a pragmatic but consistent supporter of Franco-German reconciliation and European integration. There were three types of politicians he told one visitor, "Hyper-Europeans, Europeans, and Anti-Europeans. He was a European."[22] De Gaulle could not have said it better. Though differences remained on the horizon, in the early 1960s their visions aligned.

Adenauer and de Gaulle's partnership marked a significant phase in the process of postwar Franco-German reconciliation. It coincided with general economic and political stability, leading to a degree of harmony impossible in the early 1950s. The Federal Republic had become a reliable partner in both the Atlantic and European communities, and the Fifth Republic was strong enough to cooperate with the Germans in ways the more fragile and fractious Fourth Republic could not. Both sides had practical motives and made use of the sentimental elements of reconciliation, but the converse was also true. Greater harmony of interests made the rhetoric of reconciliation that much more appealing, as the enthusiastic public response to their respective state visits in 1962 and the signing of the Elysée Treaty demonstrated. The combination of practical interests and desire for reconciliation reinforced its own momentum. The result was, in both political and moral terms, a golden age of Franco-German reconciliation.

Golden ages, though, like gold itself, maintain their value precisely because they are rare. To return to George Ball's "romantic" metaphor, it is necessary to see how the relationship continued after the heady days of the honeymoon. Even as Adenauer and de Gaulle sealed their commitment to reconciliation, their immediate plans were doomed to decline. Under pressure from party colleagues, Adenauer prepared to retire in October 1963. Meanwhile, the Kennedy Administration, in alliance with Atlantic-minded members of the German political elite, conspired to undermine the Paris-Bonn Axis, first by adding a preamble to the Elysée Treaty emphasizing the German commitment to the Atlantic alliance, and then by their own symbolic offensive, capped by President Kennedy's June 1963 visit to Berlin. De Gaulle responded with pragmatic realism. At a meeting with French parliamentarians on July 2, 1963, on the eve of the first governmental meeting foreseen by the Elysée Treaty, the last with Adenauer as Chancellor, a week after Kennedy's triumphal performance in Berlin, de Gaulle commented that treaties were "like roses and young maidens; they bloom and quickly fade." Adenauer was not so quick to resign himself to failure. At the welcome banquet in Bonn on July 4, Adenauer, whose home in Rhöndorf was surrounded by the most famous rose garden in Germany, reminded his guests that "the rose, which I know something about, is the hardiest plant there is . . . it survives every winter."[23] He preferred to see the future of Franco-German relations as less an act of fate than a matter of will, dependent on the ingenuity of the "gardeners" in both capitals to secure the blooms through seasons of frost.

Changing circumstances, however, provided stony ground for the gardeners. Adenauer tried in his last years, as Chair of the Christian Democratic party

(CDU) and national scold, to convince his colleagues and the German public to pursue a closer relationship with France. He even engaged in a bit of revisionist history, claiming Franco-German reconciliation in general and the Elysée Treaty in particular were the most important accomplishments of his years in office, downplaying other accomplishments such as West German membership in NATO or the EEC. For his part, de Gaulle advocated Franco-German coopera-tion but remained focused on his vision of French interests in Europe. He proph-esied that the day would come when even the Germans would find American dominance of NATO "difficult to bear," and a reorganized West would allow Europe to reassert its historic place in the world.[24] As it became clear that the new team of Chancellor Ludwig Erhard and Foreign Minister Gerhard Schröder had little interest in choosing Paris over Washington, however, his response was unsentimental. At the July 1964 Franco-German meeting in Bonn, de Gaulle made an impassioned case for more intense cooperation, but Erhard and Schröder were unreceptive. A bitter Horst Osterheld wrote in his diary: "many participants . . . had the feeling of being witnesses to the destruction of a historic friendship." De Gaulle, with a preference for gendered references that deserves an essay all its own, told Adenauer that the Franco-German marriage remained unconsummated; he "returned to Paris a virgin."[25]

To his advisers de Gaulle was harsher, dismissing the German leadership as "poor types" and the Federal Republic in general as "a broken-backed State" unable to resist American hegemony.[26] Erhard and Schröder were "the Americans' men, they don't like France." On major issues, "as soon as there is a concrete problem, they always choose the American solution."[27] Although he made a renewed effort to cultivate the Germans during the Grand Coalition that succeeded the Erhard government and some so-called German Gaullists such as Franz Josef Strauß developed plans for a more autonomous Europe based on Franco-German coop-eration, de Gaulle's spectacular coups against NATO and the EEC from 1965 to 1966 showed that then as earlier he was not willing to compromise his vision of French interests to make things easier for the Germans.[28]

Although the grander visions for a Gaullist Europe did not come to pass, Adenauer and de Gaulle's efforts to shape Europe and the Alliance have lasting historical significance. Their model of regular consultations, for example, pro-vided a forum for Gerhard Schröder and Jacques Chirac in January 2003 to assert their opposition to Anglo-American policy in Iraq. Recent historical assessments, profiting from greater distance from the controversies of the 1960s, portray de Gaulle less as the destroyer of the Alliance than as a creative spirit who encour-aged important reforms.[29] Similarly, even as he criticized American decisions, Adenauer did not give up on the possibility that the United States and Europe would someday achieve a partnership of equals. This is not to say that either Adenauer or de Gaulle was always correct, or always sensible in advancing their arguments. Nevertheless, in light of the problems that have plagued the post–cold war Atlantic alliance, many of which spring from Europe's failure to speak clearly as an equal and critical partner for the United States, historians should recognize the value of what Adenauer and de Gaulle wanted Europe to be.

That Europe was not simply the product of romanticism, geriatric or otherwise. It was based on recognition of the necessity of European cooperation in an increasingly complex world. During the spring 1966 crisis over French withdrawal from NATO command, when France and Germany appeared destined for renewed estrangement, for example, Adenauer looked not to the past, but to the future. In a letter to his former chief of staff, Hans Globke, he declared that France "will always remain our neighbor, even when the present period, in which America must help us, is over," and concluded that "the gentleman in Paris is as convinced as I am that as neighbors we will share the same fate."[30] That sense of common destiny, beyond personalities, was the foundation of Adenauer and de Gaulle's historic contribution to the Franco-German relationship.

Notes

1. Frank Costigliola, France and the United States: The Cold War Alliance since World War II (New York: Twayne Publishers, 1988), 143; Stiftung-Bundeskanzler-Adenauer-Haus, Konrad Adenauer im Spiegel von Zeitgenossen: 30 Jahre danach (Bad Honnef, 1993), 21–22.

2. Dean Acheson to Kurt Birrenbach, February 19, 1963, Archiv für christlich-demokratische Politik (ACDP) Nachlass (NL) Birrenbach 01–433–186/2.

3. Adenauer-de Gaulle conversation, January 22, 1963. Horst Möller and Klaus Hildebrand, ed., Die Bundesrepublik Deutschland und Frankreich: Dokumente 1949–1963 (BDFD) 4 vols. (Munich: Oldenbourg, 1997–99), vol. 1, doc. 311, 941–50.

4. Adenauer, remarks to the CSU, October 5, 1963, Stiftung Bundeskanzler Adenauer Haus, Rhöndorf (StBKAH), 02/31.

5. Lord Gladwyn, De Gaulle's Europe, or Why the General Says No (London: Secker and Warburg, 1969), 142–43.

6. Ronald J. Granieri, The Ambivalent Alliance: Konrad Adenauer, the CDU/CSU, and the West, 1949–1966 (Oxford and New York: Berghahn, 2003).

7. De Gaulle Press Conference, November 14, 1949, BDFD, vol. 3, doc. 4, 69–71. See also de Gaulle, Discours et Messages, vol. II (Paris: Plon, 1970), 327–29.

8. Meeting between Adenauer and de Gaulle at Colombey, September 14, 1958, Documents Diplomatiques Français 1958 (DDF) (Brussels: P.I.E. Peter Lang, 1993), vol. II, doc. 155, 341–45.

9. Brentano to Washington, June 16, 1958; Jansen to Auswärtiges Amt, June 19, 1958, Leduc to Couve de Murville, July 17, 1958, and Blankenhorn Diary, July 18, 1958, BDFD, vol. 1, docs. 222–26, 698–708.

10. See Seydoux to Couve de Murville, October 11, 1958 and October 14, 1958, DDF 1958, vol. II, docs. 237 and 246, 498–99, 514–15.

11. Adenauer to de Gaulle, October 13, 1958, included in Couve de Murville to embassies Washington, London, Bonn, and NATO, October 13, 1958, ibid., doc. 240, 503–4.

12. Memorandum of conversation, Strauß, Pierre Wormser, and others in Paris, November 19, 1958, BDFD, vol. I, doc. 260, 790–94.

13. De Gaulle, Speech at St. Cyr, November 3, 1959, ibid. doc. 266, 807–8.

14. Adenauer address, "Europa muss sich einigen," September 25, 1956. Konrad Adenauer Reden: Eine Auswahl, 1917–1967, ed. Hans-Peter Schwarz (Stuttgart: DVA, 1975), 327–33. See also his interview with Charles Thayer, October 18,

1956. *Adenauer Rhöndorfer Ausgabe: Teegespräche, 1955–1958*, ed. Hans Peter Mensing (Berlin: Siedler, 1986), 134–43, especially 135.

15. Transcript of the meeting at Bad Kreuznach, see *DDF 1958*, vol. II, doc. 370,754–63. De Gaulle's quotes are on 762. On Adenauer's concerns, see Carstens to all embassies, November 29, 1958, *BDFD*, vol. 1, doc. 229, 712–13.

16. Adenauer-de Gaulle meeting at Rambouillet, July 30, 1960, *BDFD*, vol. 1, doc. 272, 819–23.

17. Adenauer to de Gaulle, August 15, 1960, ibid., doc. 273, 824–26.

18. On the Fouchet plans, see Jeffrey Glenn Giauque, *Grand Designs and Visions of Unity: The Atlantic Powers and the Reorganization of Europe, 1955–1963* (Chapel Hill: University of North Carolina Press, 2003).

19. De Gaulle Press Conference, January 14, 1963, *Discours*, vol. 4, 66–70, 75–78.

20. Hans-Peter Schwarz, *Adenauer: Der Staatsmann 1952–1967* (Stuttgart: DVA, 1991), 823.

21. Here and below see Horst Osterheld, *"Ich gehe nicht leichten Herzens": Konrad Adenauers letzte Kanzlerjahre, Ein dokumentarischer Bericht* (Mainz: Matthias-Grünewald-Verlag, 1986) [Osterheld I], 122–25 (June 9, 1962). This direct quotation from the handwritten letter is on page 125.

22. Osterheld I, 125–27 (June 14, 1962).

23. Ibid., 236–37.

24. De Gaulle comments to Adenauer, July 4, 1963, *Akten zur Auswärtigen Politik der Bundesrepublik Deutschland* [AAPD] 1963 (Munich: Oldenbourg, 1994), vol. 2, 701. See also de Gaulle press conference from October 28, 1966, summarized in Horst Osterheld, *Außenpolitik unter Bundeskanzler Ludwig Erhard* (Düsseldorf: Droste, 1993) [Osterheld II], 368–69.

25. Osterheld II, 98–99 (July 4, 1964); Anneliese Poppinga, *Meine Erinnerungen an Konrad Adenauer* (Stuttgart: DVA, 1970), 111–12.

26. Jean Raymond Tournoux, *La Tragédie du Général* (Paris: Plon, 1967), 463; Gladwyn, *De Gaulle's Europe*, 79.

27. De Gaulle from August 1964. Alain Peyrefitte, *C'était de Gaulle*, vol. 2 (Paris: Ed. de Fallois, 1997), 264. Quoted in N. Piers Ludlow, *The European Community and the Crises of the 1960s: Negotiating the Gaullist Challenge* (London: Routledge, 2006), 111.

28. In general, see Ludlow, *The European Community*.

29. See Frédéric Bozo, *Two Strategies for Europe: De Gaulle, the United States, and the Atlantic Alliance*, trans. Susan Emanuel (Lanham, MD: Rowman & Littlefield 2001), especially 245–58.

30. Adenauer to Globke, April 20, 1966, ACDP NL Globke 01–070–052/2.

CHAPTER 16

The Soviet Factor in Franco-German Relations, 1958–69

Garret Martin

Introduction

The Paris-Bonn-Moscow triangle had already a long history by the time French president Charles de Gaulle and West German chancellor Konrad Adenauer signed the Elysée Treaty on January 22, 1963. Since the end of the nineteenth century, there was a tradition of bilateral alliances being formed against the third player. This included, on the one hand, the Franco-Russian alliance of 1893 and the Franco-Soviet pact of 1935 and, on the other hand, the Rapallo Treaty of 1922 and of course the Nazi-Soviet pact of 1939.[1]

The cold war proved no different, and this chapter will highlight the role played by the Soviet factor in the Franco-German couple between 1958 and 1969. Whereas the rivalry between Paris and Washington for Bonn's favours often appeared more strident, the role played by Moscow in the Franco-German relationship was in many ways more complex, at times helping to unite the two states, and at other times pushing them apart. Considering the role played by the Soviet Union is thus vital to get a full picture of Franco-German relations in the crucial period of de Gaulle's presidency. After all, this dynamic triangle between Paris, Bonn and Moscow helped shape not only the Western world, but also East-West détente in Europe.[2]

1958–63: The Soviet Threat and the Franco-German Rapprochement

De Gaulle came back to power in 1958 determined to recapture France's prestige and Great Power status. He realized that he could only fulfil this ambition by creating a Western European entity that would be led by France and independent of the two superpowers. For this, he needed a partnership with West Germany in which his country would play the dominant role. Thus, as early as September 1958, de Gaulle began to court Adenauer, a task that, in the following four years, was facilitated by the Soviet threat.

Indeed, Soviet leader Nikita Khrushchev proposed, during a speech on November 27, 1958, the signature of a German peace treaty that would recognize the existence of two Germanies and "the free city of West Berlin." For four years, the second Berlin crisis, which culminated in the erection of the Berlin Wall, kept Europe, the Soviet Union, and the United States in a state of extreme tension.[3]

Throughout the Berlin crisis, de Gaulle's intransigent attitude toward the Soviet Union comforted Adenauer and created common ground between both leaders. On the one hand, the French president strongly opposed any negotiations with Moscow as long as it maintained its threatening attitude.[4] Consequently, the Franco-German Treaty of January 1963 aimed in part an attempt at strengthening Western Europe's ability to stand up to the Soviet Union. As de Gaulle indicated, "we did not sign the Franco-German treaty to please the Soviet Union."[5] On the other hand, since Adenauer was firmly opposed to any form of *Ostpolitik* and often lamented that "we are the victims of America's détente policy," de Gaulle realized that he could maintain leverage over the West German chancellor by taking a tough line toward negotiations with Moscow.[6]

This tactic was evident during the limited détente following the Cuban Missile Crisis. The superpowers realized that they needed to make their relations more predictable and guarantee a minimum of cooperation. This culminated in the Partial Test Ban Treaty (PTBT) of August 1963 and Khrushchev's proposal for a nonaggression pact between the Warsaw Pact and the North Atlantic Treaty Organization (NATO). The French leaders opposed the PTBT because it threatened to undermine their emerging independent nuclear arsenal, and because they viewed the superpower talks as a false détente. They worried that Washington and Moscow might acquire the habit of deciding the fate of the world without consulting other states.[7]

Paris also believed it could capitalize on Bonn's uneasiness about the PTBT. The West German government eventually signed the treaty, but it was very upset by the "upgrading" of East Germany as a signatory; additionally, it criticized the nonaggression pact proposal, because it risked giving a certain degree of recognition to Pankow and permanently codifying the status quo in Central Europe.[8] De Gaulle seized on the opportunity to warn Adenauer that both France and West Germany were threatened by the relations between the Anglo-Saxon powers and the Soviet Union.[9] The French decision makers also claimed that the talks between the Anglo-Saxon powers and the Soviet Union might lead to the neutralization of West Germany and hence be catastrophic for Western Europe.[10]

On the surface, it seemed as if France and West Germany were firmly united in their opposition to the Soviet Union. In reality, though, the ties were less rigid than they appeared on first glance. For Adenauer, signing the Franco-German

Treaty allowed him to prevent the recurrence of a Franco-Russian alliance as had happened in the past—a clear sign that the old chancellor did not fully trust his French counterpart.[11] Similarly, Moscow's reaction to the Franco-German Treaty was not as straightforward as expected. Undoubtedly, the Kremlin leaders felt that the Paris-Bonn axis was unequivocally hostile to the Soviet Union.[12] Yet, certain voices within the Soviet foreign policy community promoted a more nuanced assessment. They claimed that while the Franco-German rapprochement presented a danger for world peace, it also contributed to the decline of the American presence in Europe; in other words, Soviet policy toward Western Europe needed to be more flexible and play on existing divisions within the Atlantic Alliance.[13]

This applied specifically to France. Aware of the ever-worsening Franco-American relations, many Soviet scholars pointed out that Moscow could gain from de Gaulle's centrifugal pull away from NATO and Washington.[14] These arguments had some influence on the Soviet leaders, who began to moderate their criticisms of France and sought instead to benefit from any tensions between France and its Western partners. Thus, on May 17, 1963, a day after the Bundestag ratified the Franco-German Treaty, the Soviet government sent a note to its French counterpart. Beside the usual attacks against the Franco-German Treaty, the note not so subtly referred to past Franco-Soviet cooperation against Germany during World War II, and expressed hope that both countries might cooperate once again for the sake of European peace.[15] In July, Khrushchev repeated similar arguments and invited de Gaulle to visit the Soviet Union.[16]

Finally, de Gaulle returned to power in 1958 with a long-term blueprint for relations with the Soviet Union and for European security. He was convinced that Russia would eventually discard Communism and accept to play a traditional balancing role in a modernised version of the Concert of Europe. This would be a continental system centred on two main pillars, the Soviet Union and a Western European grouping led by France. Together, they would contain Germany, while the United States would revert to its role of arbiter from afar. While Khrushchev's threatening behaviour during the 1958–62 Berlin crisis prevented de Gaulle from effectively dealing with Moscow, the French president nonetheless still sent a certain number of signals to the Soviet Union during this period. Thus, in 1959, he recognized the Oder-Neisse line and referred to a "Europe from the Atlantic to the Urals." In 1962, he publicly claimed that close Franco-German cooperation would make possible the establishment of a new European equilibrium between East and West.[17]

1964–65: France's Shift to the East

Even in the period between 1958 and 1963, the Paris-Bonn-Moscow triangle did not remain static, and this trend continued in the following years. Indeed, 1963–64 witnessed a sharp deterioration in relations between France and West Germany, marked by numerous disagreements in various key issues. First, under pressure from Washington and from within his own party, Adenauer had to accept the inclusion of a preamble to the Franco-German Treaty, which stated that the latter did not affect Bonn's loyalty to NATO, the Atlantic Alliance, and the European Economic Community (EEC). This effectively neutralised de Gaulle's ambition of creating a privileged partnership between France and West Germany. Secondly, in October 1963, Ludwig Erhard, minister of the economy, replaced Adenauer as chancellor. Unlike his predecessor, he was less keen on a close partnership with France. Finally, and more importantly, both states became estranged because of their differing attitudes toward the United States. Whereas Bonn wanted to avoid jeopardising its ties with Washington at all costs, Paris did not hesitate to challenge American leadership within the Atlantic Alliance. By the summer 1964, a crossroad had been reached. De Gaulle in particular had accepted that his objective of creating a Paris-Bonn axis was unfeasible in the immediate future because of West Germany's subordination to the United States.[18]

Some scholars have argued that the general chose to initiate a rapprochement with the Soviet Union precisely at the moment when relations with West Germany were deteriorating.[19] On closer inspection, the switch did not prove so straight-forward. Undoubtedly, obsessed by the future of West Germany and its possible nuclear ambition, De Gaulle was constantly tempted to look for "fall-back" allies.[20] Both privately and publicly, the French leaders warned that they were ready if need be to revert to the traditional alliance with Russia in order to contain Germany.[21] Yet, in the summer of 1964, a rapprochement with Moscow was out of the question because of Khrushchev's lack of interest. Focused on his dialogue with the United States, he remained ambivalent toward the French President.[22] Only in the fall of 1964, following the Multilateral Force (hereafter MLF) affair, did Paris and Moscow draw closer.

Initially proposed in December 1960 by U.S. secretary of state, Christian Herter, the MLF project sought to establish an integrated nuclear force for NATO. In January 1963, de Gaulle declared France would not participate in the MLF but added that he had no objection to it going ahead, in part because he believed it would never come to be. This assumption changed after Erhard publicly mentioned the possibility of a German–U.S. bilateral agreement over the MLF in October 1964.[23] The French government immediately launched a virulent crusade against the project, claiming for instance that the MLF was not compatible with the Franco-German Treaty.[24] Paris opted for this particularly strong reaction for two reasons. Not only did it perceive the MLF as an American weapon aiming to divide Europe, but it also feared that the MLF would allow West Germany to indirectly possess nuclear weapons.[25] Since French plans for cooperation with West Germany had always centred on Bonn' subordination, it would be harder for France to exert future leverage on its neighbour if it could have access to nuclear technology. By adopting such a tough stance during the MLF crisis, France found itself defending positions that were very close to the Soviet ones.[26]

The MLF crisis created an important common ground between Paris and Moscow and led France and the Soviet Union, albeit for different reasons, to consider future cooperation as potentially beneficial. Moscow became more sensitive to the opportunities offered by de Gaulle's policies to undermine American influence in Europe and isolate West Germany.[27] Soviet officials systematically began to push their French counterparts for more regular consultation on issues where they adopted similar views, including Southeast Asia, the MLF, or Germany's borders.[28] In France's case, the tension over the MLF contributed to a further deterioration of relations with West Germany. De Gaulle, in particular, felt very bitter against the Germans, with his mood toward them reminiscent of that toward the British in January 1963.[29] It pushed him to seek diplomatic alternatives: "we [France] are getting closer to the Russians to the extent that the Germans are moving away from us."[30]

At the same time, common opposition to Bonn's nuclear ambitions was not the sole factor bringing Moscow and Paris together. Despite Khrushchev's downfall on October 14 and his replacement by the troika of Leonid Brezhnev, Alexei Kosygin, and Anastas Mikoyan, the French president remained wary of Soviet intentions and did not know what value to give to their openings.[31] While he believed both countries had a lot in common and that Russia was taking into account France's growing prestige in the World, he also feared that the Soviets' courtship could be just another way to gain an edge over the United States. However, his conviction that Europe was witnessing dramatic changes, especially the crumbling away of both blocs slowly making the cold war obsolete, helped the general overcome his doubts.[32] In particular, he seemed to believe that the growing emancipation of the satellite states behind the Iron Curtain would continue, which could enable one day the reunification of Germany.[33]

In this context, the general gave his all-important press conference of February 4, 1965, or twenty years exactly after the start of the Yalta conference. He used the speech as an opportunity to reflect on the recent developments in East–West relations and to clearly outline his vision of how the division of Germany could be overcome in a European framework.[34] He argued that the German problem could not "be solved by the confrontation of the ideologies and the forces of the two camps opposed to each other" but by "the entente and conjugated action of the peoples that are and will remain most interested in the fate of Germany, the European nations."[35] Yet, he carefully pointed out that such a solution could only occur in the long-term and depended on many conditions. A solution to the German question was only conceivable once a general "détente, entente and cooperation" had developed between all the European states.[36]

1965–66: Priority to East-West Détente

Not only was this press conference significant for East–West relations in Europe, but it also marked a definite turning point for French foreign policy.[37] It marked a signal of a change in French strategic priorities. Since de Gaulle had temporarily given up on his hopes of seeing a more independent Western Europe centred on the Franco-German axis, he now pinned his hopes for a radical transformation of the European system on his emerging *Ostpolitik*. In the following two years, the rapprochement with the Soviet Union—and its satellite states—gathered momentum and was symbolised by the growing number of high-profile visits. Thus, Soviet foreign minister, Andrei Gromyko, came to Paris in April 1965, and his French counterpart, Maurice Couve de Murville, returned the favor in the fall. More importantly, de Gaulle announced in January 1966 his intention to visit the Soviet Union later that year.

Common opposition to the American intervention in Vietnam helped the improvement of relations between Paris and Moscow but not as much as the relative convergence of interests on the German question. A certain overlap in the position of both countries now allowed a dialogue on Germany.[38]

While relations between France and the Soviet Union warmed considerably in this period, relations between France and West Germany went in the opposite direction. De Gaulle and his close collaborators felt increasingly frustrated by Bonn's enduring desire to have a say in the Atlantic Alliance's nuclear defense matters and by its close ties with the United States. Countering the apparent resurgence of German nationalism was yet another reason to revert to the historic policy of an alliance with Russia.[39] As for West Germany, the government was undoubtedly annoyed by the growing ties between France and the Soviet Union and by de Gaulle's idea of solving the German problem within a European framework.[40] If the Soviet threat had previously brought France and West Germany together, it was now keeping them apart.[41] Yet, Bonn worried even more about the fact that France's shift to the East was happening in parallel to its policy of seemingly challenging the foundations of the Western Alliance. Following its attack against the dollar's role in the international monetary system and its boycott of the EEC institutions in 1965, France shocked its partners by announcing on March 7, 1966, its withdrawal from NATO's integrated military structure.

Despite the general giving priority to relations with the Soviet Union and his tendency to frighten his Western partners, he had no intentions of switching sides. Rather, he sought to find the right balance between showing independence from the Atlantic Alliance and reaching out to the Eastern Bloc. French leaders actually went to great lengths to reassure their Allies and public opinion about the aims of de Gaulle's visit.[42] They downplayed the possible impact of his trip. During a meeting with Adenauer, de Gaulle made it clear that he was not naïve and that he did not plan any early far-reaching agreement with Moscow.[43]

De Gaulle wanted to convey the impression that his trip to Moscow could actually help the cause of German reunification: "it is not at the moment when the two blocs are cracking up that I am going to think of leaving one bloc for the other . . . I will speak for Western Europe."[44] At the same time, the general believed that his trip could be vital for his long-term goal of transforming the European order, since the Soviet Union, rather than West Germany, had become France's main partner.[45] Moreover, as Couve de Murville said in an interview for Soviet radio on June 4, 1966, Franco-Soviet cooperation on European matters could act as a role model for their respective allies and encourage them to follow the path leading to peace on the continent.[46]

The meetings between the French president and the Kremlin leaders highlighted many areas of agreement, ranging from Vietnam to a shared opposition to any speedy German reunification. The general also took a step in the Soviet direction when he showed a certain support for the project of a European security conference, even if he suggested that this was not an immediate prospect. At the same time, during the first talk with Brezhnev, Kosygin, and Podgorny, de Gaulle clearly underlined existing differences and made it clear he would not recognize East Germany. His key aim, though, was to probe Soviet intentions. In effect, he wanted to know whether the Soviet Union would accept to go along with his vision of a new European system.

1967–69: High Hopes and Rapid Disillusion

At the end of 1966, Gaullists felt euphoric as Europe seemed to be evolving toward the path outlined by the French president. After the fall of Erhard's government in September 1966, the new grand coalition government in West Germany, headed by the Christian Democrat chancellor Kurt Georg Kiesinger and the socialist foreign minister Willy Brandt, was intent on improving relations both with France and the Eastern bloc.

The first meeting in January 1967 between the grand coalition and the French government proved to be a great success.[47] Kiesinger announced that West Germany had given up on the Hallstein doctrine and the MLF and also accepted de Gaulle's analysis that German reunification could only happen through a rapprochement with the Eastern Bloc. Bonn was now ready to establish diplomatic relations with all satellite states, except East Germany.[48] Moreover, Brandt and Kiesinger repeatedly asked France to champion their *Ostpolitik*, in particular by vouching for them during talks with Eastern Bloc leaders[49]. The January meetings had largely convinced de Gaulle that "they [the Germans] are going through key changes. They realise that détente is the most promising path for them. They are getting closer to us."[50] He further hoped that if France supported Bonn's *Ostpolitik*, this could help to guarantee German solidarity in other Western matters, including monetary questions and the imminent British application to the EEC. Thus, the friendlier attitude of the new German government presented both a great opportunity and challenge for the General: "It is essential to push Germany towards a rapprochement with Russia. We have to disarm their reciprocated aggression. It is our game, it is the only one."[51]

De Gaulle's high hopes for a German-Soviet rapprochement, though, quickly gave way to disillusion. A more permanent improvement in Franco-German relations could only have occurred if the Soviet Union had decided to treat West Germany less harshly.[52] By 1968, however, Moscow was just not ready to do business with Bonn.[53] Under pressure from the more conservative elements of the Warsaw Pact, the Kremlin leaders felt deep-rooted anxiety about the controllability of a sweeping European détente, and this only worsened when unrest developed in Czechoslovakia in 1968.[54] Moreover, the core of Bonn's new *Ostpolitik* implied that it would now take greater control over its own fate rather than rely on others to speak on its behalf.[55] Even if it followed France's détente policy with great interest, West Germany only expected limited gains from its cooperation with Paris, and the possibilities of common actions toward Eastern Europe could not be overstated. Germany could take "decisive steps" toward the Eastern Bloc at the bilateral level.[56]

Paris's ability to play the mediator between Bonn and Moscow quickly deteriorated in this period. After the initial bout of optimism, relations between France and West Germany soured quickly, in large parts because of de Gaulle's stance during the Six Day War and his second veto of the British application to join the EEC. Similarly, the Soviet doubts about détente meant that they were not at all receptive to the General's plea for a more open attitude toward Germany's *Ostpolitik*.[57] To make matters worse, de Gaulle's ambition to create a new European order was dealt two further major blows in 1968. The May events in France largely damaged the General's prestige and reminded him that he could no longer ignore domestic problems, while the Soviet decision to crush in August the reform movement in Czechoslovakia highlighted the fact that the leaders in the Kremlin were not ready to accept a loosening of their control over the states of Eastern Europe. In a final twist, the Czech affair caused another crisis in Franco-German relations. Already disappointed by Moscow's behaviour, Paris also criticized Bonn for its adventurist policy toward Eastern Europe, especially multiplying contacts with Prague during the unrest and in effect causing more anxiety in Moscow.[58]

Conclusion

The year 1968 was thus a turning point for de Gaulle's policy of *grandeur* and his ambition to create a new European order, as Hervé Alphand, the Quai d'Orsay's general secretary, stated in his diary: "It is maybe indeed the end of a grand effort to reunite two worlds beyond ideology. . . . So the General's disappointment must be very profound, after the unrest of May and June, and the blows to the country's economy and finance, as well as to his morale."[59] The French president survived the events of May and June, but they left him in a very fragile position. His resignation in April 1969, following a referendum that was rejected by popular vote, was essentially a delayed reaction to May 1968. In September of that year, Brandt became chancellor and initiated a more ambitious *Ostpolitik*. West Germany took over France as the leading force in the European process of East–West détente.

De Gaulle's presidency marked a crucial period for Franco-German relations, one that witnessed rapprochement, drama, and numerous disputes. The general never considered the Franco-German reconciliation as an end in itself but rather as the basis for the reshaping of Europe and enabling the continent to overcome the divisions inherited from the cold war. In that respect, the Soviet Union was to play a vital role in that grand design. On one level, ever wary of Soviet and German military power, de Gaulle's strategic aims depended on a double containment of Moscow and Bonn.[60] At the same time, however, his vision went beyond simply playing one power against the other. Ultimately, the French president realized that his country's long-term security objectives would be better served by tying both competitors, the Soviet Union and West Germany, to a European structure of cooperation.[61]

Notes

1. Jean-Paul Bled, "Le général de Gaulle et le triangle Paris-Bonn-Moscou," in *De Gaulle et la Russie*, ed. Maurice Vaïsse (Paris: CNRS éditions, 2006), 199.

2. For more on Franco-Soviet and Franco-German relations in this period see Thomas Gomart, *Double Détente: Les relations franco-soviétiques de 1958 à 1964* (Paris: Publications de la Sorbonne, 2003); Marie-Pierre Rey, *La tentation du rapprochement: France et URSS à l'heure de la détente (1964–1974)* (Paris: Publications de la Sorbonne, 1991); Thierry Wolton, *La France sous influence: Paris-Moscou, 30 ans de relations secrètes* (Paris: Grasset, 1997); Georges-Henri Soutou, *L'Alliance incertaine: Les rapports politico-stratégiques franco-allemands 1954–1996* (Paris: Fayard, 1996); and Pierre Maillard, *De Gaulle et le problème allemand: Les leçons d'un grand dessein* (Paris: Guibert, 2001).

3. Vladislav Zubok, Constantine Pleshakov, *Inside the Kremlin's Cold War: From Stalin to Khrushchev* (Cambridge, MA: Harvard University Press, 1996), 194–95.

4. Marie-Pierre Rey, "De Gaulle, l'URSS et la sécurité européenne, 1958–1969," in *De Gaulle et la Russie*, ed Vaïsse, 220–21.

5. Alain Preyrefitte, *C'était de Gaulle, vol. 2* (Paris: Edition de Fallois: Fayard, 1997), 63, 226.

6. Erin Mahan, *Kennedy, De Gaulle, and Western Europe* (New York: Palgrave Macmillan, 2002), 145.

7. De Gaulle-Chang-Huan meeting, February 9, 1963, Ministère des Affaires étrangères Français (hereafter MAEF): Cabinet du Ministre (hereafter CM), Couve de Murville (hereafter CD), vol. 376.

8. William Glenn Gray, *Germany's Cold War: The Global Campaign to Isolate East Germany, 1949–1969* (Chapel Hill: University of North Carolina Press, 2003), 143; Anna Locher and Christian Nuenlist, "What Role for NATO? Conflicting Western Perceptions of Détente, 1963–65," *Journal of Transatlantic Studies* 2, no. 2 (2004): 189.

9. Charles de Gaulle, *Lettres, Notes, et Carnets: Tome IX* (hereafter *LNC: IX*) (Paris: Plon, 1986), 364.

10. De Gaulle-Dixon meeting, September 17, 1963, MAEF: CM, CD, vol. 376; Paris to FO, Telegram (hereafter TG) 217, September 10, 1963, The National Archives (hereafter TNA): Foreign Office (hereafter FO) 371/172077.

11. George McGhee, *At the Creation of a New Germany: From Adenauer to Brandt, An Ambassador's Account* (New Haven, CT: Yale University Press, 1989), 30.

12. Vojtech Mastny, "Détente, the Superpowers and their Allies, 1962–64," in *Europe, Cold War and Coexistence, 1963–1965*, ed. Wilfried Loth (London: Frank Cass, 2003), 217.

13. Michael Sodaro, *Moscow, Germany and the West from Khrushchev to Gorbachev* (London: I. B. Tauris, 1991), 49.

14. Julie Newton, *Russia, France and the Idea of Europe* (New York: Palgrave Macmillan, 2003), 20.

15. Laboulaye to Couve, TG 2613–2636, May 17, 1963, MAEF: Europe, URSS 1961–1965, vol. 1931.

16. Dejean to Couve, TG 3810–3834 and 3835–3836, July 17, 1963, Documents Diplomatiques Français: 1963, Tome II, 119–23.

17. Georges-Henri Soutou, "De Gaulle's France and the Soviet Union from Conflict to Détente," in *Europe, Cold War*, ed. Loth, 173–75.

18. Garret Martin, "Untying the Gaullian Knot: France and the Struggle to Overcome the Cold War Order, 1963–1968," (unpublished PhD diss., London School of Economics and Political Science, 2006), chap. 1.

19. Bled, "Triangle Paris-Bonn-Moscou," in *De Gaulle et la Russie*, ed. Vaïsse, 201.

20. Maurice Vaïsse, *La grandeur: politique étrangère du Général de Gaulle 1958–1969* (Paris: Fayard, 1998), 566.

21. Peyrefitte, *C'était de Gaulle: vol. 2*, July 7, 1964, 261; MAEF: Secrétariat Général (hereafter SG), Entretiens et Messages (hereafter EM), vol. 22: Couve-Schroeder meeting, July 4, 1964.

22. Zubok and Pleshakov, *Inside the Kremlin's Cold War*, 181; and Sodaro, *Moscow, Germany*, 51.

23. Helga Haftendorn, *NATO and the Nuclear Revolution: A Crisis of Credibility, 1966–1967* (Oxford: Clarendon, 1996), 132.

24. Vaïsse, *La grandeur*, 575.

25. Couve-Hasluck meeting, November 4, 1964, and De Gaulle-Adenauer meeting, November 9, 1964, MAEF: SG, EM, vol. 23.

26. Laboulaye to Couve, TG 5513, November 7, 1964, MAEF: Europe, URSS 1961–1965, vol. 1931.

27. Thomas Wolfe, *Soviet Power and Europe: 1945–1970* (Baltimore: Johns Hopkins University Press, 1970), 288.

28. Note of the *Directeur Politique* to Couve, November 19, 1964, MAEF: Europe, URSS 1961–1965, vol. 1931.

29. Note of the *Directeur Politique* to Couve, November 19, 1964, TNA: FO 371/177867.

30. Peyrefitte, *C'était de Gaulle: vol. 2*, November 18, 1964, 62.

31. Hervé Alphand, *L'étonnement d'être: journal, 1939–1973* (Paris: Fayard, 1977), January 3, 1965, 445.

32. Peyrefitte, *C'était de Gaulle: vol. 2*, January 4, 6, 12, 1965, 313–17.

33. De Gaulle-Mende meeting, December 2, 1964, MAEF: CM, CD, vol. 378; see Martin, "Untying the Gaullian Knot," chap. 2.

34. Soutou, "De Gaulle's France," in *Europe, Cold War*, ed. Loth, 180.

35. Charles de Gaulle, *Discours et Messages: Tome IV* (hereafter DM: IV) (Paris: Plon, 1970), 341.

36. Ibid.

37. Bohlen to Rusk, TG 4451, February 5, 1965, National Archives Record Administration (hereafter NARA): Record Group 59 (hereafter RG59), Central Foreign Policy Files (hereafter CFPF), 1964–1966, Box 2178.

38. Soutou, "De Gaulle's France," in *Europe, Cold War*, ed. Loth, 181; Maurice Couve de Murville, *Une politique étrangère, 1958–1969* (Paris: Plon, 1971), 205.

39. CIA Intelligence Info Cable, August 25, 1965, Lyndon Baines Johnson Library (hereafter LBJL): Presidential Papers (hereafter PP), National Security Files, Country Files, Box 172; Kissinger-Grandville meeting, January 23, 1966, LBJL: PP, Confidential Files, Box 8.

40. Vaïsse, *La grandeur*, 578; François Seydoux, *Dans l'intimité franco-allemande: Une mission diplomatique* (Paris: Albatros, 1977), 50.

41. Soutou, *L'Alliance incertaine*, 283.
42. Vaïsse, *La grandeur*, 425.
43. De Gaulle-Adenauer meeting, March 10, 1966, MAEF: CM, CD, vol. 382; Charles de Gaulle, *LNC: X* (Paris: Plon, 1987), 306.
44. Bernard Lefort, *Souvenirs et secrets des années gaulliennes, 1958–1969* (Paris: A. Michel, 1999), 149.
45. De Gaulle, *LNC: X*, Exposé during the Council of Foreign Affairs on West Germany, 246–49.
46. Bohlen to Rusk, Airgram number 2425, June 24, 1966, NARA: RG59, CFPF, 1964–1966, Box 2180.
47. See MAEF: SG, EM, vol. 29.
48. De Gaulle-Kiesinger meeting 1, January 13, 1967, MAEF: SG, EM, vol. 29.
49. See Couve-Brandt meeting, January 13, 1967, MAEF: SG, EM, vol. 29.
50. Alain Preyrefitte, *C'était de Gaulle: vol. 3* (Paris: Edition de Fallois Fayard, 2000), January 18, 1967, 194.
51. Peyrefitte, *C'était de Gaulle: vol. 3*, December 5, 1966, 206; see De Gaulle-Kosygin meeting 1, 8 December 1966, MAEF: CM, CD, vol. 385.
52. Seydoux, *Dans L'intimité franco-allemande*, 85.
53. Timothy Garton Ash, *In Europe's Name: Germany and the Divided Continent* (New York: Random House, 1993), 56.
54. Newton, *Russia, France*, 79–80
55. Willy Brandt, *People and Politics: The Years 1960–1975* (London: Collins, 1978), 168–69.
56. Andreas Wilkens, "L'Europe en suspens. Willy Brandt et l'orientation de la politique européenne de l'Allemagne fédérale 1966–1969," in *Crises and Compromises: The European Project 1963–1969*, ed. Wilfried Loth (Bruxelles: Bruylant, 2001), 331.
57. See De Gaulle-Zorin meeting, February 20, 1968, MAEF: SG, EM, vol. 32; De Gaulle-Zorin meeting, October 4, 1967; MAEF: CM, CD, vol. 391.
58. Vaïsse, *La grandeur*, 588; Couve de Murville, *Une politique étrangère*, 282.
59. Alphand, *L'étonnement*, August 25, 1968, 513.
60. Mahan, *Kennedy, De Gaulle*, 22.
61. Edward Kolodziej, *French International Policy under de Gaulle and Pompidou: the Politics of Grandeur* (Ithaca, NY: Cornell University Press, 1974), 324.

CHAPTER 17

What Role for Europe in the International Arena of the Early 1970s?

How France and Germany Were Able to Matter

Katrin Rücker

The 1970s were a period of change in international relations influenced in part by Europe and European states, such as France and West Germany. The privileged partnership between the two countries mattered not only in Europe but also in the wider cold war world. An analysis of the Franco-German pair thus helps explain why integrated Europe managed to speak with one voice on some issues and failed on others.

During their years in office from 1969 to 1974, French president Georges Pompidou and West German Chancellor Willy Brandt witnessed four major elements of change that highlighted the perceptible shift of power in Franco-German relations.

When Willy Brandt became West German chancellor in October 1969, he immediately started to refashion an old cold war issue, the German question, into a new form of détente between East and West. His *Ostpolitik* led to the Moscow and Warsaw Treaties ratified by the Bundestag on May 5, 1972. Later that same year, the Federal Republic of Germany (FRG) and the German Democratic Republic (GDR) also signed a treaty. In 1973, both German states became members of the United Nations (UN), and the GDR acquired international status, one of the consequences of Brandt's détente policy. Despite constant official support, Brandt's *Ostpolitik* provoked mixed reactions in Paris and burdened bilateral relations.

Georges Pompidou's overture to the United Kingdom and his launching of The Hague Summit in 1969 led to accession negotiations among the European Communities and the four applicants, Great Britain, Ireland, Denmark, and Norway. On January 1, 1973, the Common Market integrated all applicants except Norway. This new Europe of Nine posed an economic challenge to the two superpowers: The European Economic Community (EEC) encompassed a larger population than that of the United States or the Soviet Union, represented one third of global commerce, and constituted the second largest industrial power in the world. Pompidou's agreement to enlarge the EEC removed a major point of contention that had poisoned Franco-German relations since the early 1960s and helped relaunch European integration after nearly a decade of stagnation.

Thanks to the West German chancellor, monetary cooperation was also initiated at The Hague Summit, but any attempts to establish a common European policy failed, largely due to U.S. President Richard Nixon's decision to suspend the dollar's convertibility into gold and impose a 10 percent surtax on imports in order to cut rampant inflation. Economic and trade relations between the EEC and the United States suffered from the collapse of the Bretton Woods system. European policy concentrated on restoring the international monetary system and supporting regional currency stability.

Finally, the first oil and energy crisis following the Yom Kippur War of 1973 intensified international monetary and economic problems and posed a threat to European integrity. In 1973–74, the European Communities (EC) were prone to speak with a single voice in the international arena, but the decision by Organization of Arab Petroleum Exporting Countries (OAPEC) to politicize a resource revealed the vulnerability of EC member states to pressure, particularly from the U.S. superpower. This sparked a transatlantic squabble and an intra-European, notably a Franco-German, crisis that threatened the emergence of political cooperation in Europe.

Détente policy in Germany and Europe, British membership in the EEC, the international monetary crisis, and the first oil shock were undoubtedly four important events of the early 1970s, which tested Franco-German effectiveness in dealing with global challenges. This essay will therefore focus on and analyze the Franco-German dimension of this series of events. Doing so will shed light on why some European initiatives succeeded and some failed and demonstrate how the "elementary entente" between West Germany and France had become an essential prerequisite for the integration of Europe.[1]

France, West German Ostpolitik, and European Integration

The Federal Republic's policy of openness toward the East was not a solely German product but was instead deeply embedded in the context of U.S.–Soviet détente after the Cuban Missile Crisis and the Eastern policy of French President Charles de Gaulle in the 1960s. Without the approval or at least acquiescence of Washington, London, Paris, and Moscow, this West German overture vis-à-vis the East would not have been possible. In June 1963, the "red telephone" between Washington and Moscow was established, and arms control discussions began thereafter. In the period from 1969 to 1972, Americans and Soviets met in Helsinki to talk about a first round of Strategic Arms Limitation. Starting in 1966, Willy Brandt, West German foreign minister under the grand coalition headed by Chancellor Kurt Georg Kiesinger, initiated an early version of what subsequently would become the New *Ostpolitik* once he had been elected chancellor in October 1969. Even if Brandt's *Ostpolitik* represented continuity with previous American and French détente policies, Brandt and his senior diplomatic adviser, Egon Bahr, are considered the real architects of West Germany's new policy toward the Eastern Bloc. The German-Soviet treaty, signed in Moscow in August 1970, confirmed the peacetime territorial status quo and hence laid the groundwork for a series of other agreements and treaties, notably with Warsaw in December 1970. Brandt's *Ostpolitik* pursued a dual objective. Its primary and immediate objective was to improve German-German relations so to alleviate the consequences of Germany's division. But it also intended to promote political détente, a means by which the Federal Republic would gain maneuver room for its diplomacy and to increase trade. Indeed, as the FRG was the largest western importer of Soviet goods, a number of trade agreements did follow. In September 1971, a quadripartite Allied Agreement between the United States, France, the USSR, and the United Kingdom laid down conditions for travel by West Berliners and the Allies on the transit routes. Three months later, an agreement between the two Germanies and a convention concluded between the Berlin Senate and the GDR eased transit conditions for civilian goods and for West Berliners visiting relatives in the FRG. A basic Inter-German Treaty was signed in December 1972.

France was said to be very reluctant and skeptical toward German *Ostpolitik*, fearing a sort of new German power, but that assumption needs to be profoundly revised. Georges Pompidou's reaction was actually more complex and nuanced than has previously been presented.[2] Since their first bilateral meeting in January 1970, Pompidou had assured Brandt of his support for *Ostpolitik*, and the French president would not abandon this attitude at least officially or publicly. However, it is also true that especially toward the end of his presidency, he showed increasing signs of discomfort and dropped warning hints to Brandt. Nevertheless, French doubts were not related to what seemed to be an excess of West German power but instead to West German engagement with others in the EC.

On December 3, 1971, Georges Pompidou explained to Willy Brandt his vision of détente in Europe: "For me, the policy of rapprochement with Eastern Europe, ours and yours, presupposes a strong Western Europe. If Western Europe is splitting up, this policy will quickly become dangerous."[3] According to the French president, such a rapprochement with Eastern Europe would indeed necessitate a forceful, united Western Europe. In November 1973, during a meeting with British prime minister Edward Heath, Pompidou expressed surprise that German *Ostpolitik* had been successful so rapidly.[4] The French president did not fear Willy Brandt, but Pompidou worried in general about Germany's long-term future, notably about German reunification as an enduring cold war problem. Indeed, a few months earlier, the French president had asked Brandt how he imagined Germany's future, especially with regard to reunification. The chancellor had to reassure him that the priority of his country still was and would continue to be European integration. Along the same lines, Pompidou had also reiterated in a press conference in September 1973 the fundamental importance of Franco-German relations for European integration and stability, thus signaling to Brandt that he should not neglect these relations.

Anticipating Allied and French long-term skepticism, the West Germans adopted a reassuring stance on what they preferred to call "Entspannungspolitik," détente policy, of which *Ostpolitik* was only one component. "*Ostpolitik* starts in the West" was indeed a well-known formula.[5] As foreign minister (1966–69), Brandt had already suggested that a successful West German policy of peace and security needed a strong "Westpolitik."[6]

In September 1969, one week before the federal elections, Egon Bahr drafted the European policy of a future government under left-wing leadership:[7] The FRG needed the "good will" of its allies and partners, above all in Western Europe, in order to pursue *Ostpolitik*. Concerning the FRG's policy toward its Western partners, Bahr underscored four important points. First, Westpolitik means politics with France; second, he thought that there was a division among EEC member states, namely between France and the five others; third, Bahr called for EEC enlargement and British accession independently of the United Kingdom's ability to adopt Common Market rules; last, enlargement of the EC implied that "substantial regulations must be changed"[8] to facilitate the entry of new member states. According to Brandt's special advisor, the FRG's Westpolitik determined its détente policy. A Western European policy aimed at good relations with France and British membership in the Common Market would secure a strong Western base for its *Ostpolitik*.

The success of détente policy under Chancellor Willy Brandt may well have been due not only to the fact that it was embedded in the cold war context and followed the détente policy of American and French predecessors but also to its crucial link to European integration and cooperation with France. As a matter of fact, Allied and French doubts about *Ostpolitik* did not have concrete consequences. They did not derail the treaties and agreements the FRG was planning to sign, and for European integration, *Ostpolitik* was perhaps even beneficial because West German and French leaders wanted it deeply rooted in the West.

A Franco-German Entente on British Accession to the EEC

The Franco-German elementary entente during the enlargement negotiations between the EEC and the four candidates seems important for explaining the success of British accession in 1973.

Almost since the creation of the Common Market in 1958, the issue of enlargement, namely the question of Great Britain's membership, had been on the European agenda. Two French vetoes, one in January 1963 and another one in 1967, prompted the collapse of accession negotiations with Great Britain and other members of the European Free Trade Association (EFTA).

When de Gaulle left office and Georges Pompidou was elected president in June 1969, he pursued the same European objectives, albeit with a different style.[9] Lifting de Gaulle's veto against British entry into the Common Market, Pompidou was said to be different than his predecessor, because he apparently privileged the London-Paris axis rather than the Franco-German pair.

Changes in French attitudes under Pompidou were more a question of style than of substance, however. De Gaulle's harshness and Pompidou's overture were not only a matter of character but a matter of timing as well. Both men had the same objectives—rescue the relatively young Common Market and assure its continued and successful existence—but timing resulted in a different, less conflict-laden diplomatic strategy in the 1970s than it had in the 1960s. Whereas a Common Market of six member states under French leadership corresponded to French interests in the early years of the European Community, enlargement was in the French interest ten years later due to fears that the EEC would otherwise break up.

In June 1969, Pompidou's officials confirmed that, during the last two years, there had been no French objection to the principle of EEC enlargement. In October 1969, preparing for The Hague Summit, Pompidou declared that "the refusal to talk with the British, which has happened twice, has now become unsustainable, unless we are to accept the end of the Common Market."[10] He insisted on the essential character of the EEC, its current crisis, and its remedy via enlargement. However, he referred to the financing of the common agricultural market, which remained France's first EC priority, as the "greatest obstacle to British accession." According to French European Commissioner Jean-François Deniau, the French government perceived "the British accession and the enlargement of the European Community as a good opportunity to transform the treaties in a reasonable way and in accordance with French interests."[11] He affirmed that the ideal would be to remain at six but that enlargement of the EEC certainly had become a necessity.

During The Hague Summit of EEC European leaders in December 1969, France accepted enlargement under two formal conditions: the "acceleration" and "deepening" of the Common Market. Pompidou thus conceded ground on the question of enlargement in order to be in a stronger position on the completion of the common agricultural policy and institutional reform—he rightly assumed that Britain would not accept any drift toward supranationalism. All in all, however, France attached more political importance to enlargement and acceleration—both considered a test of British commitment to the Community—than it did to deepening, for which French officials lacked well-thought-out proposals.

The subsequent enlargement negotiations in the early 1970s did not, however, deprive Franco-German cooperation in Europe of its relevance. Willy Brandt valued a direct understanding between the French president and the British prime minister during the EEC negotiations with London and, conversely, in a letter to

Brandt in May 1971, British Prime Minister Edward Heath underscored the role of the West German chancellor in initiating his important summit that same month with Pompidou: "You had made it clear to me that you thought that a meeting between us could be constructive, both for the negotiations for the enlargement of the European Communities and for the future of Europe more generally. So indeed I found it to be, and I hope you will feel that our meeting has fulfilled the hopes which you had for it."[12] Thinking in terms of European powers, the British government considered West Germany and France to be the member states holding the key to the United Kingdom's entry into the EC and sometimes tried to play one off against another according to its own interests.[13]

Even if there were many differences on practical issues between France and West Germany during the EC–UK negotiations, Paris and Bonn had a common objective—to save the "acquis communautaire." This was not solely a Franco-German goal but was also shared by the other EC partners and the European Commission. The Dutch and the European Commission, by no means support-ers of French Gaullists and hardliners, both appreciated the French role in defending the Common Market rules or acquis communautaire, especially con-cerning agriculture and its budget.

Although it implied confronting interests within General Agreement on Tariffs and Trade (GATT), the U.S. reaction to EEC enlargement was positive. In a conversation with U.S. president Richard Nixon in February 1969, chancel-lor Kurt Georg Kiesinger, Brandt's predecessor, compared the West German sit-uation to that of a "funambulist" trying to balance French and British interests in Europe.[14] Bonn would be neither pro-French nor pro-British, but the postwar Franco-German friendship, the chancellor affirmed, was essential nevertheless. Nixon's sympathetic reaction to Kiesinger's attitude that was tacitly more pro-French than pro-British epitomized Washington's general approach to European integration and the Franco-German pair in the 1960s.

The Breakup of the Bretton Woods System and the Failure of European Monetary Integration

In contrast to the issue of EEC enlargement, France and West Germany had less success with the timing of European monetary cooperation models. Willy Brandt's ambitious proposal at The Hague Summit of 1969 had almost been derailed by the first oil crisis. If timing was fatal to the plan for a European Monetary Union (EMU), Franco-German differences of opinion also accounted for the failure of the EMU project.

The world economic crisis of the 1970s was primarily the result of long underlying trends. The OAPEC decision triggered the crisis but cannot fully explain the long-lasting economic slowdown that followed. Serious problems had begun to develop in the mid-1960s with U.S. budgets designed to produce deficits in order to finance Vietnam-related expenditure and inflation rose sharply.[15] The Bretton Woods system based on the dollar came increasingly under pressure and criticism, notably from French president Charles de Gaulle who sharply attacked the dollar hegemony and finally collapsed in August 1971 when Nixon officially suspended the dollar's convertibility to gold. Nixon's decision implied that all Community countries would be obliged to abandon fixed parity.

There was no lack of willingness to reform the international monetary system, at least in Europe. The first tangible attempt was made in February 1969, when Raymond Barre, French vice president of the European Commission, presented a memorandum on the coordination of economic policy and monetary cooperation in the EC. The French franc was devalued by 12.5 percent in August 1969; the West German mark was revalued by 9.3 percent in October. Monetary stabilization was fundamental because if exchange rates fluctuated too widely, it would be difficult for the EEC to assure uniform intervention prices as set up by the Common Agricultural Policy (CAP) and assure free trade.

With European monetary cooperation "in the air" at the end of the 1960s, the European leaders agreed at The Hague Summit in December 1969 on a proposal from Willy Brandt to draw up a step-by-step plan with a view to creating a European economic and monetary union by 1980. The project was entrusted to a committee chaired by Luxembourg's Prime Minister Pierre Werner. The Werner Plan envisioned three main stages on the road to EMU. In February 1971, the Six decided to implement the first stage but they were forced to acknowledge in 1973 that the transition to the second stage appeared impossible due to increasing monetary instability. In March 1972, they had created the European currency snake as an attempt to guarantee a certain amount of stability among European currencies by narrowing the fluctuation limits of their exchange rates. The European snake was only a partial success because many currencies, such as the French franc and the British sterling were forced to abandon it, though they were able to rejoin later. Although the EEC did not achieve EMU and the European currency snake largely proved ineffective during Brandt's chancellorship and Pompidou's presidency, the Community did succeed in creating the European Monetary System in 1979, a prerequisite for the future Euro.

Explanations for the failure of the Werner Plan for EMU usually focus on the debate between French "monetarists" and German "economists" over the strategy to be adopted to achieve a monetary union.[16] The former believed that monetary integration had to start first and that economic and political integration would follow; by contrast, the latter argued that economic convergence between the national economies must occur before monetary integration can set off. Others emphasize that the time was not yet ripe for a single European currency bloc.[17] However, a closer look at the Franco-German partners with their differences and similarities sheds light on why the ambitious plan for a European Economic and Monetary Union ultimately failed.

Indeed, the supranationalism involved in EMU was certainly far more than President Pompidou would ever have been willing to accept.[18] On the other hand, even the West German government expressed doubts about the feasibility of European monetary projects. Already during the preparations for The Hague Summit in December 1969, the West German government showed signs of discomfort with Brandt's planned proposal; it was especially the Ministry of Economic Affairs that disagreed with the chancellor's ideas. Concerning the "acceleration, deepening, enlargement" formula, even Brandt regarded deepening as less important than enlargement.[19] Paris was of the same view. Both countries lacked viable deepening proposals and eventually considered enlargement as the priority. Moreover, there certainly were French monetarists and German economists, but as Pompidou's advisor Jean-René Bernard demonstrated, the gap between them was not so wide that it could not have been bridged.[20]

Concerning the so-called inconsistency between the goal of establishing a European currency bloc and its relationship with the Bretton Woods system of fixed exchange rates against the dollar,[21] France and the FRG differed on some points. Except for a small group of high civil servants Pompidou's France did not envision a system of fluctuating monetary parity or a nonsystem that actually followed the breakup of the Bretton Woods system. Conversely, discussions among French, West German, and European officials within the Monetary Committee of the EEC also revealed that Bonn found it easier to think in terms of fluctuating money than did Paris. Nevertheless, the French attitude changed in 1973, and France consented to the principle of joint Franco-German floating against the dollar.[22] Finally, Paris and Bonn also agreed that the Werner Plan for EMU was too ambitious.

Furthermore, the economic slowdown and the shift of the terms of trade against industrial producers of the 1970s had different impacts on West Germany and France. On the one hand, the Federal Republic's competitive advantage was based on strong industry able to export goods. Indeed, the country led many technological sectors. As a consequence, the strong West German mark was compatible with a low unemployment rate and low inflation. On the other hand, France lacked such competitive advantages. To maintain the exchange rate between the French franc and the mark, Paris had to curb inflation at the expense of employment, first with its stabilization program in 1977 and then with its "disinflation" policy in 1983.

Europe's Emerging Political Cooperation and the Energy Crisis of 1973

The first oil crisis of 1973 severely hit the Western oil-importing economies by both raising inflation and increasing budget deficits. However, this was only the trigger for the crash in economic growth. The roots of the slowdown were structural monetary and economic factors.

Between 1950 and 1972, oil consumption had almost doubled to account for over 60 percent of total energy consumption in Western Europe. The Common Market was particularly vulnerable with its 99 percent oil import ratio and its dependency on oil to meet 60 percent of total energy needs. The first oil crisis therefore reinforced the economic crisis already affecting Western Europe, and a recession put an end to the long period of economic growth after World War II.

On the political side, the energy crisis of 1973 was a challenge for European political cooperation and meant a failure rather than a success for Franco-German relations. After The Hague Summit, a committee chaired by the Belgian Etienne Davignon had been set up in March 1970 to draft proposals for deepening political cooperation within the Community with a view toward future enlargement. A forum for European Political Cooperation (EPC) was inaugurated in Munich in November 1970.

The Davignon proposals were very cautious, however. They did not include a joint institutional framework or consultations on external security and defense issues. Consequently, in 1972, Brandt and Pompidou jointly proposed the creation of a secretariat for political cooperation. Both leaders agreed on the principle of an independent body that should provide impetus for political cooperation, but they disagree on its location. Georges Pompidou refused to have the permanent political secretariat established in Brussels, as suggested by Willy Brandt.

Political cooperation in the 1970s was, in fact, more driven by the essential need to achieve and enlarge a Common Market rather than by a willingness to see a truly supranational political Europe emerge. Only through a long incremental process would political cooperation shape the international relationships of the European member states.

During the Pompidou-Brandt era, EPC was confirmed in October 1972 during the Paris Summit and seen in action during the subsequent Middle East crisis. The nine EEC member states demonstrated their solidarity in their joint appeal for a ceasefire on October 13, 1973. The first time EPC truly became successful was after the Pompidou-Brandt years, however, when the Final Act of the Helsinki Conference on Security and Cooperation in Europe was signed in July 1975.

A French "neo-Gaullist reflex" in reaction to Kissinger's Year of Europe, a speech that proposed a new charter redefining Euro-American relations, and the oil crisis did indeed overshadow the last part of the Brandt-Pompidou era. Without illusions, German officials noted a mentality in Europe in which everyone "saves his own—national—bacon." European unity at the Washington Energy Conference in February 1974 was a mere façade. The Nine had failed to agree on a comprehensive mandate for their acting president, the West German foreign minister. Everyone except the French foreign minister rallied in favor of the U.S. draft communiqué calling for the establishment of a group of officials to coordinate measures in the energy field. At the ministerial meeting of EPC in Bonn in March 1974, the nine member states approved the French-inspired scheme for a Euro–Arab dialogue. The West Germans upset the French, however, when they attempted to devise a coordination scheme that would be agreeable to the United States.[23] As the French saw no difference between Euro-American consultations and direct U.S. intervention in the decision making of the EC in foreign policy matters, discussions among the member states had made little progress when Pompidou died in office on April 2, 1974. One month later, Willy Brandt was forced to step down as chancellor following an FRG-GDR spy affair.

Conclusion

To conclude, Paris and Bonn certainly played a major role in the international arena of the early 1970s, both as a pair and singly, but above all thanks to their membership in the common EEC structures. West German *Ostpolitik* mattered because it followed American and French examples and was conditioned by European integration policy. EEC enlargement was a success because West Germany and France used different tactics but shared common goals, not only together but also with the other member states, the candidates, and even the American State Department. In contrast, European monetary plans and EPC failed or had very limited success during the Pompidou-Brandt era. Responsible were not only Franco-German divergences but also the international economic, monetary, and political context that did not facilitate cooperation in these fields.

Therefore, we can say that France and West Germany had more impact in the world when they acted together as partners than when they acted on their own as competitors. They were even more successful when their partnership benefited European integration.

Notes

1. See the articles by Georges-Henri Soutou, "Willy Brandt, Georges Pompidou et l'Ostpolitik," Andreas Wilkens, "Willy Brandt, die deutsch-französischen Beziehungen und die Europapolitik 1969–1974," and Katrin Rücker, "Willy Brandt, Georges Pompidou et le sommet de La Haye en 1969," in *Willy Brandt und Frankreich*, eds. Horst Möller and Maurice Vaïsse (München: Oldenbourg, 2005), 121–55, 181–215. See also Claudia Hiepel, "Willy Brandt, Georges Pompidou und Europa. Das deutsch-französische Tandem in den Jahren 1969–1974," in *Aufbruch zum Europa der zweiten Generation. Die Europäische Einigung 1969–1984*, eds. Franz Knipping and Matthias Schönwald (Trier: Wissenschaftlicher Verlag Trier, 2004), 28–47.
2. Georges-Henri Soutou, "L'attitude de Georges Pompidou face à l'Allemagne," in *Georges Pompidou et l'Europe*, ed. L'Association Georges Pompidou (Bruxelles: Editions Complexe, 1995), 267.
3. French National Archives (AN), 5 AG 2, 1011: Brandt-Pompidou in Paris, December 3, 1971.
4. AN, 5 AG 2, 1014: Entretiens franco-britanniques à Chequers, 16 et 17 novembre 1973, très secret, 3e entretien samedi 17 novembre 1973 de 10h30 à 13h15.
5. AN, 5 AG 2, 104: Entretien Pompidou-Brandt, 30 January 1970, see also: Wilkens, "Willy Brandt," 199.
6. Willy Brandt, *Friedenspolitik in Europa* (Frankfurt am Main: Fischer Verlag, 1968), 137. See also Henning Türk, *Die Europapolitik der Großen Koalition 1966–1969* (München: Oldenbourg, 2006).
7. Akten zur Auswärtigen Politik der Bundesrepublik Deutschland (AAPD) 1969, vol. 2, doc. 296, note by Egon Bahr, September 21, 1969, 1047–57.
8. Ibid.

9. See Maurice Vaïsse, "Changement et continuité dans la politique européenne de la France," in *Georges Pompidou et l'Europe*, ed. Association Geoges Pompidou (Bruxelles: Editions Complexe, 1995), 29–45.

10. AN, 5 AG 2, 1042: 22 October 1969, note de JR Bernard à M Jobert, projet de compte-rendu du Conseil sur les Affaires Européennes du 21.10.

11. AN, 5 AG 2, 1042: Conseil restreint du 21 octobre 1969 sur la préparation de la conférence de la Haye, note de JF Deniau sur l'évolution du marché commun, non signé, non daté, 10p.

12. Archiv der sozialen Demokratie der Friedrich-Ebert-Stiftung, Willy-Brandt-Archiv, Bestand Bundeskanzler, vol. 52: Heath to Brandt, May 22, 1971.

13. NA, PREM 15–370, Rippon to Heath, April 1, 1971.

14. AAPD 1969, vol. I, doc. 79, Discussion Kiesinger-Nixon, February 26, 1969, p. 275.

15. John Gillingham, *European Integration 1950–2003. Superstate or New Market Economy?* (Cambridge: Cambridge University Press, 2003), 100.

16. Richard T. Griffiths, "A dismal decade? European Integration in the 1970s," in *Origins and Evolution of the European Union*, ed. Desmond Dinan (Oxford: Oxford University Press, 2006), 181.

17. Olaf Hillenbrand, "Die Wirtschafts- und Währungsunion," in *Europa-Handbuch*, ed. Werner Weidenfeld (Bonn: Bundeszentrale für politische Bildung, 2002), 465.

18. See the two articles: Gérard Bossuat, "Le president Georges Pompidou et les tentatives d'Union économique et monétaire," and Robert Frank, "Pompidou, le franc et l'Europe," in *Pompidou*, ed. Association Georges Pompidou, 339–71, 405–49.

19. Politisches Archiv des Auswärtigen Amtes, B20, vol. 1439, note by Staden, November 18, 1969.

20. AN, 5 AG 2–58, Bernard to Pompidou, June 28, 1970.

21. Griffiths, "A dismal decade?" 182.

22. Wilkens, "Willy Brandt," 211.

23. Aurélie Gfeller, "A Contested Identity. Kissinger, France and the Year of Europe, 1973–1974," paper for the second international RICHIE conference, The Road to a United Europe, December 7–10, 2006, Copenhagen University, 16.

CHAPTER 18

Franco-German Relations in the Giscard-Schmidt Era, 1974–81

Michèle Weinachter

Beginning in the 1960s, both Valéry Giscard d'Estaing and Helmut Schmidt had important ministerial responsibilities in their respective countries. Both were in charge of economic and monetary affairs at the beginning of the 1970s and thus took a leading role in shaping Franco-German relations when it came to addressing international monetary turbulence and launching the Economic and Monetary Union (EMU) decided in 1969 at the Hague summit. Between 1969 and 1972, the relations between Giscard and his German counterpart, Karl Schiller, were strained. Both the working atmosphere and actual cooperation improved when Helmut Schmidt took over Schiller's position. Giscard and Schmidt got along very well right from the beginning, and this personal relationship would play an important role in the years to come. In the spring of 1974, the two men came to occupy the highest positions of power in France and Germany, and the pair would remain in office until 1981. A number of factors contributed to the ensuing reinvigoration of the Franco-German alliance, which had suffered from the restrictions added by the German Bundestag with a preamble to the Elysée Treaty.

The two men's vision and the circumstances of the moment favored rapprochement. This translated into not only a reinforcement of Franco-German cooperation in the European Community (EC) but also a rapprochement in views on East–West relations.

Context and Conception

In 1974, Europe was in crisis. While the Brandt-Pompidou period had begun under good auspices thanks to an improvement in the cooperative climate,

The author wishes to thank Marion Picker, assistant professor in German at Dickinson College, Pennsylvania, who translated this article from French into English, and Daniel Erkenbrack who proof-read the translation.

enlargement of the EC and projects concerning European integration, notably the EMU, the period ended with an overall worsening of the situation. The EMU project was moribund; the oil crisis divided the Nine; the Franco-German relationship was worsening; and Pompidou's distrust of *Ostpolitik* (Eastern Policy) was increasing toward the end of his term. During the election campaign of 1974, Valéry Giscard d'Estaing announced that if elected, he would take swift initiatives toward the Federal Republic of Germany (FRG), thus profiting from the French presidency of the Community in the second half of 1974. After his meeting with Helmut Schmidt on June 1, 1974, he affirmed his objective to see the Community maintain "its personality, its cohesion," notably "in taking and defending common positions on the big monetary, economic, and political problems of the world."[1] In 1980, at the time of an official visit to West Germany, he again affirmed: "it is the task of our two countries, our two peoples, to take steps together in order to put an end to the fading of Europe in the world and to give it back its strength and influence in the affairs of the world." For the new French president, this involved moving beyond "Reconciliation," which he believed had been achieved by General de Gaulle, toward a Franco-German "Entente" in the service of Europe. Germany was France's indispensable partner, whose "natural vocation" was to lead Europe on its way toward unification. This could only be accomplished on the basis of a well-balanced partnership, however. Preventing German domination of Europe was an enduring concern for Giscard, who wanted France to live up to its European role.[2] Above all, he intended to use the Franco-German dynamic in such a way that Europe might recover its global influence. For his part, Schmidt was interested in closer cooperation with France, notably to increase the leeway of the Federal Republic in the international domain.

The improvement in bilateral relations that took place under Giscard and Schmidt was largely due to the friendly and trustful relations both leaders had developed early on. They possessed a proven record of effective cooperation as finance ministers. They shared similar ideas on monetary issues and viewed themselves as finance experts. The fact that they came from different parts of the political spectrum did not hinder close cooperation. In reality, Giscard belonged to the moderate, European-oriented right while Schmidt belonged to the right wing of the Social Democratic Party (SPD). Moreover, Giscard and Schmidt represented a new generation of politicians and consequently adopted a new style in the conduct of bilateral relations. For instance, they met at each other's private homes, and they mostly spoke English together. All this helped strengthen the intimacy between the two leaders.

Circumstances also favored the rapprochement: Giscard was all the more successful in interesting Schmidt in his projects because the United States, the other privileged partner of West Germany, had disappointed and irritated the chancellor. In light of the worsening situation in Europe on the one hand and the deterioration of East–West relations on the other, the two leaders increased their cooperation, and tried to make their other partners follow in their wake.

The way the Giscard-Schmidt "couple" functioned was satisfying for the French president because Schmidt, conscious of Germany's historical handicap, formally gave Giscard the leading role in joint procedures. This configuration permitted them to form a closely allied duo thanks to a shared outlook and a joint handling of international relations both at the summit level and among "experts."

Institutionally, Franco-German relations under Giscard and Schmidt functioned on the basis of the Elysée Treaty. In contrast to their successors, Giscard and Schmidt did not create new tools for bilateral governmental cooperation. In practice, though, relations at the summit level would go well beyond the rules established by the treaty. Without counting numerous telephone conversations and written notes, Giscard and Schmidt met dozens of times during the French president's seven-year term. Thanks to the good personal understanding between the two, the Franco-German dialogue intensified considerably, often bypassing the official channels and agendas—the most significant example being that of devising the European Monetary System (EMS) in Schmidt's private apartment in Hamburg in 1978. This rapprochement made possible a certain number of advances toward greater European solidarity.

Giscard, Schmidt, and the Unification of Europe

While monetary questions had been at the center of both the Franco-German discussions and the two leaders' cooperation between 1972 and 1974, the difficult circumstances of 1974 did not permit an immediate choice of this particular terrain for a revival. This task was therefore delegated to the institutions. If the preceding periods had been strongly characterized by "ideological" quarrels, the pragmatism of Giscard and Schmidt permitted certain breakthroughs.

Institutional Progress

Concerning the institutional form of the organization of Europe, Giscard officially maintained his profession of the "confederal" faith of his predecessors up until the end of his seven-year term, in part not to alienate the strong Gaullist faction within his majority. Giscard explained in 1979: "the European Confederation will have a unique structure of three branches: an executive branch constituted by the European Council; an administrative branch for common issues, constituted by the Commission; and a deliberative and legislative branch for common questions, constituted by the Assembly."[3] Only after 1981 did Giscard affirm that he was a federalist or, at least, was in favor of a "federative Europe." The term "confederation" was flexible enough to permit substantial advances.

Helmut Schmidt shared Giscard's pragmatic approach. While in previous eras, the Germans had insisted on progressing toward a political Europe in the face of a reluctant France, the Giscard-Schmidt era revealed a new configuration, if not an exchange of roles. Schmidt, although willing to advance, did not have supranational objectives—at any rate not to any greater extent than did Giscard, as he acknowledged.[4] The two men could thus find a "middle" position between the traditional federal project dear to Germany and that of an intergovernmental Europe ignoring, if not sabotaging, communal institutions—a traditional Gaullist attitude. Both Giscard and Schmidt were determined to achieve progress, especially in light of the difficult international situation, which emphasized the need to reinforce the solidarity among Europeans and also vis-à-vis the wider world. In 1974, France officially took the initiative on the institutional terrain by proposing the creation of the European Council and the election of European parliamentary members by universal suffrage at the summit of Paris in December of 1974.

The creation of the European Council was in reality only the realization of existing plans that were very far advanced. On Jean Monnet's initiative, these plans had already been perfected under Pompidou without having been put into practice. Even if the final project was limited, Monnet pronounced himself satisfied after the December summit in 1974.[5] The idea of holding such meetings to push the construction of Europe was not totally new. Four "summits" had already taken place since the 1960s. In systematizing the procedure, however, Giscard and Schmidt—true to their image of a working duo—had institutionalized a method and a practice. The role of the European Council would be decisive in the later evolution of European integration. In the 1970s, it became the privileged institution for Franco-German cooperation, the means by which Giscard and Schmidt tried to get their European partners to move along and to obtain their commitment to joint projects—for example the EMS.

European parliamentary elections by universal suffrage—already anticipated in the treaty of Rome—were also decided upon at the end of 1974 and then put into practice in 1979. Even before his election, Giscard had come out in favor of this measure, which shows that there was no major "concession" to the Germans on this point. However, his position constituted no less than a break with the attitude of his predecessors, who feared a strengthening of the European Parliament's powers and a step toward a supranational Europe. The first elections of the European Parliament by universal suffrage took place in June of 1979. In France, they became a success for the president. But the violence of the attacks that came from the Gaullist camp (notably from Jacques Chirac) and from the communists showed how little leeway Giscard had in this area.

Giscard and Schmidt were committed to the confederal line between 1974 and 1981. Moreover, the accession of Great Britain to the Community in 1973 hardly eased the way toward integration. Margaret Thatcher took pains to impede all progress toward European integration, particularly after 1979. With the conception of the EMS, Giscard and Schmidt had succeeded in initiating the creation of a zone of monetary stability in Europe before the arrival of the "Iron Lady." They also hoped—Schmidt most of all—to obtain a better coordination of economic policies.

Economic and Monetary Cooperation in the 1970s

The development of Franco-German economic and monetary cooperation in the 1970s was closely tied to the evolution of the international situation. The Europeans had to react to the consequences of two oil shocks and the disintegration of the Bretton Woods monetary system. Facing increasing economic interdependence, Europe's interest—according to Giscard and Schmidt—was to maintain a united front so as to stabilize Europe and the national economies together. However, the increase in oil prices created a deficit of balances and payments. The economic crisis led directly to inflation and unemployment. The international monetary system, greatly undermined by the end of fixed exchange rates anchored to gold and by dollar instability, was in shambles. These difficulties threatened to break up the European Community, and so France and Germany took the initiative.

The priority was not to succumb to the protectionist temptation in a situation featuring common problems and increasing interdependence. Each of the two countries had become the principal economic partner of the other. From 1975 onward, France and Germany tried to show the way with different strategies to coordinate their economic policies.

Yet, in reality, the convergence never actually occurred except during a brief period after the appointment of Raymond Barre as French prime minister (in office from 1976 to 1981).[6] At first sight, this failure could be attributed simply to the differences of economic cycles having to adjust to the oil shocks. Yet, it also revealed fundamental structural differences between the French and the German economies that in themselves implied diverging modes of functioning.[7] In all these respects, France and Germany were very different. Between 1974 and 1979, Germany had an average annual inflation rate of 5 percent, while in France it exceeded 10 percent. The harmonization of the French and German economies desired by Giscard and Schmidt called for a difference of less than two or three points.[8] Raymond Barre's economic agenda would have led to a clear convergence of the two systems, if it had achieved the expected results.[9]

The recognition of the Western economies' interdependence drove Giscard and Schmidt to initiate the creation of the "G 7." In effect, they wanted a coordination of economic and financial policies at the international level as well. France, West Germany, Great Britain, Italy, the United States, and Japan were soon joined by Canada. The first meeting took place at Rambouillet in November of 1975. The results did not always live up to hopes. The meetings have nevertheless continued to the present day. As far as attempts at coordination of economic policies are concerned, the results appeared limited. Yet, Giscard and Schmidt's declared intentions attested to a new attitude: the rejection of "every man for himself" in a period of difficulty, the desire to join together in the struggle against the consequences of the crisis, and the affirmation of a "community of destiny" between France and Germany.[10] The will to reinforce the "primary circle of solidarity"—the European Community—was translated, with more success this time, into the monetary domain.

Giscard and Schmidt initiated a decisive revival of the move toward the Monetary Union with the creation of the EMS in 1979, conceived from the beginning as a step toward a common currency. Since the 1960s, Giscard had been persuaded that Europe would be made through its currency. The introduction of a common currency also seemed to be the means for France to shake off the Federal Republic's monetary domination in Europe.

The creation of a monetary Europe was fixed as a goal since the 1969 summit in The Hague. After many difficulties, the persistent worsening of the international context pushed the Europeans to move forward in this domain. The European Council was the decision-making body that allowed Giscard and Schmidt to win over their partners at the summits in Copenhagen, Bremen, and Brussels in 1978. The concretization of the monetary projects became possible thanks to favourable factors both in terms of circumstances and personalities. The paternity of the EMS goes back to Jean Monnet. At the end of the 1960s, he had asked experts to work on these questions, the result of which was the Triffin report on "the monetary and economic solidarity of the countries in the Community." Raymond Barre had also been involved in reflections on the issue since 1968.[11] After the summit in The Hague in 1969, attempts at a monetary rapprochement took off. Giscard and Schmidt took part in these as principal players. From 1972 to 1973, after the abandonment of a fixed exchange rate and in light of the American agenda, they thought that without a monetary union, Europe would find itself at the mercy of the United States. The two men's later initiatives, supported by Barre, were thus based on acquired experience. Concerning the actors, the combination of Giscard, Schmidt, and Barre thus constituted, according to the latter,[12] the "best possible trio" to reach a shared outlook and good personal understanding given their knowledge of the matter. The economic policy adopted by France in 1976 further contributed by reassuring the West German chancellor as to the extent that Barre was steering his country toward monetary stability, a paramount objective for the Germans. In fact, Barre imposed strict policies to curb inflation and public spending; the French economy recovered significantly starting in 1978 and above all in 1979—before the second oil shock.

The French political calendar also played a role in the choice of the moment when ideas were to be implemented: Giscard could not attach himself to the EMS project until after the parliamentary elections of 1978 in France, which confirmed the existing majority. According to the president of the Commission at the time, Roy Jenkins[13]—who had played an important role since 1977 in the promotion of the project[14]—the West German chancellor was ready to take action: Jenkins also noted that Schmidt had a rather sudden change of heart in favor of the immediate creation of the EMS. In practice, this signified Schmidt's abandonment of the "crowning theory," traditionally defended by the Germans and notably Karl Schiller. This theory assumed that the Monetary Union would not come until the end, as a "crowning" of the process, that is, the creation of a Monetary Union would only occur after the effective convergence of economic policies. The explanation comes from the deterioration of German-American relations after the election of U.S. president Jimmy Carter in November of 1976. This had multiple consequences. Giscard confirmed in his memoirs that it "now created in Helmut Schmidt an availability" for European projects, and, notably, for advancing the monetary project.[15] The annoyance of Giscard and Schmidt at American monetary policy was reinforced by the Jamaica Accords of 1976. In effect, these agreements opened the way for free flotation of currencies, resulting in very strong fluctuations of the dollar and the instability of European currencies,[16] with severe consequences for the Mark and the West German economy. All this led the chancellor to favor a solution that would foster monetary stability at least among Europeans rather than having to continue suffering the consequences of dollar instability. The combination of these political and economic, national and international circumstances, as well as the human factor thus permitted action to be taken in 1978.

The realization of the project was itself characteristic of the methods by which Giscard and Schmidt worked: at the summit, in exclusive company, and outside institutional circuits. The new system—one of exchange rates that were fixed but adjustable—foresaw the creation of the European reserve, the use of a common currency (the ECU, the European Currency Unit), and the setting of new fluctuation limits in relation to a basket of currencies. The West German chancellor and the French president elaborated the system together[17] in informal work sessions, each aided by one close advisor.[18] They worked together not only on the grand principles but also on all the important details[19] before submitting the project directly and personally to their European colleagues.[20] The political will would get the better of technical and bureaucratic constraints. The two men kept their project quasi secret for as long as possible, avoiding giving out details that would have ruined their plan. Something close to that actually did happen after its announcement: the French president was accused of sacrificing French interests by allying himself with Germany in such a fashion, while Schmidt, on the contrary, was accused by Helmut Kohl and the Bundesbank of sacrificing West German political stability by allying himself with countries having as high an inflation rate as France. It was at the European Council of Bremen on July 6 and 7, 1978, that the pair presented the new mechanism to their partners, who accepted it. The EMS could finally become effective on March 13, 1979.

In creating the EMS in 1978, Giscard and Schmidt had probably seized the only window of opportunity during which it was possible to accomplish the project due to a combination of the objective circumstances, the international and national conditions, and subjective circumstances, the political will of both leaders, previously described. From the end of 1978, economic conditions deteriorated once again after the outbreak of the revolution in Iran and thus the second oil crisis.

With this new system, Giscard and Schmidt pursued various objectives both economic and political. At the European level, the priority was to ameliorate the situation within the internal European market and to ensure better profits for businesses. Vis-à-vis the outside, the EMS would shelter Europe from the fluctuations of the dollar, thus making it the instrument of greater autonomy from the

United States. Lastly, it would lead to a reinforcement of the EC by the eventual creation of a common European currency capable of measuring up to the American dollar and the Japanese yen. The two men thus simultaneously had short-term, medium-term, and long-term objectives in mind.

Between 1974 and 1981, relations between Paris and Bonn were also marked by the intensity of exchanges about the evolution of East–West relations. Facing the unraveling of détente, "Europe"—this time in the reduced form of the Franco-German partnership—would try to develop its own stance.

Giscard and Schmidt between East and West

The end of the 1970s was marked by a profound modification of the international political climate. Détente culminated in 1975 with the Helsinki conference, but as of 1977, the Soviets began to deploy SS-20 missiles directed against Western Europe, thus triggering a return to the arms race. On December 12, 1979, the Western world responded with the "Double-Track Decision" adopted by NATO and elaborated at a summit meeting of France, Germany, Great Britain, and the United States in Guadeloupe in January of 1979. The double-track decision combined an offer by NATO to the Soviet Union for mutual limitation of medium and intermediate range ballistic missiles with a threat to deploy American cruise missiles throughout Western Europe in the event the Soviets rejected the Western demand concerning the SS-20 missiles. Tensions culminated first with the invasion of Afghanistan by Soviet troops at the end of December 1979, and then with the Polish crisis that led to the declaration of martial law by General Wojciech Jaruzelski in December of 1981. The world had entered a "new cold war." This period also saw widespread antinuclear protests in a number of Western countries, particularly in West Germany. The protests originated in a reaction to the 1977 decision of President Carter to arm U.S. forces in Europe with the famous "neutron bomb." In April of 1978, Carter unexpectedly revoked his decision—an episode that definitively altered relations between Helmut Schmidt and the American president and preoccupied Europe. Facing the wave of pacifism sweeping over the Federal Republic, France worried about the possibility of "German drift."[21] But Giscard, having hardly any doubts that Schmidt was solidly anchored in the West, did not share these reservations insofar as the European status quo resulting from Yalta had been reconfirmed at Helsinki. More than ever, Europe seemed stuck in its divided state. For the French president, the "German question" was, if not completely settled, then at least indefinitely put off.

The end of the 1970s saw a simultaneous weakening of the two pillars on which had rested the security of all Europeans for decades: détente and deterrence. Europeans became conscious of their vulnerability. Aside from European questions, East–West relations constituted another main discussion topic between Giscard and Schmidt.[22] On the basis of a common analysis of the situation and a large share of mutual trust, the two leaders looked to defend European interests in a difficult period. Indeed, President Carter's erratic conduct of international relations confirmed a gradual disenchantment with American leadership in foreign policy, while at the same time, the Soviet Union's attempts to widen its sphere of influence in the Middle East and Africa disquieted France and the Federal Republic, both of which favored rapprochement.

Regarding military and strategic questions, Giscard did not remain unaffected by Schmidt's reasoning concerning the danger of the Soviet SS-20 missiles. At the time of the Guadeloupe summit in January of 1979, he lent the chancellor support that made it possible to decide on NATO's "double track decision," which was to prove its importance in the years to come.

The Franco-German partnership both defined and displayed a common position vis-à-vis the events in Afghanistan and Poland. The two leaders' attitude during this period featured a number of common points, which made it more and more distinct from the ever hardening American line. Politically, they worked in favor of maintaining a dialogue with the Soviet Union. Economically, they refused to apply the sanctions against the USSR then being demanded by the Americans. Despite the suspicions of complacence regarding the Soviet Union that weighed them down, they expressed on several occasions their identical view of the political attitude to be taken toward the USSR. The Franco-German convergence found its boldest expression in the joint Franco-German declaration of February 5, 1980 on the situation in Afghanistan, released at the thirty-fifth Franco-German summit. A year later, Giscard and Schmidt released a new joint declaration concerning the situation in Poland.[23]

The Franco-German rapprochement, devised to safeguard European interests vis-à-vis Washington and Moscow, was real. It was intended to favor the emergence of a European identity in the international arena. Giscard certainly had reasons to pursue closer ties with Schmidt in that difficult period. In backing the chancellor at Guadeloupe, for example, he indirectly opened the path to restoring French security in regard to the USSR. But the French partner was also valuable to the chancellor during this difficult period. Leaning on his partner to the west, he could better validate his own views.

The rapprochement also had its limits, however. The desire of the French president to restore Europe's role on the international scene did not translate into decisive measures on cooperation in security and defense issues. Giscard appeared to be hovering between the will to aid progress toward a unified Europe on the one hand and the perseverance of a Gaullist military doctrine of "independence" on the other, a doctrine that assured France a special position and certain superiority in respect to its partners, including the FRG. Concrete progress in cooperation on matters of defense thus remained limited. As for joint Franco-German declarations on the international situation, they were the fruit of a bilateral and hence intergovernmental consultation, while more obvious progress in matters of European political cooperation would have required new joint institutions, and thus a transfer of sovereignty, something which Giscard would not and could not consider at that time. The Giscard-Schmidt understanding at least led to the emergence of a Franco-German partnership in the international arena. While the leeway granted to the Europeans had traditionally been reduced in periods when détente was in crisis, a European identity had begun to assert itself this time.

Conclusion

Between 1974 and 1981, Giscard and Schmidt showed new cohesion by their partnership's very steadfastness and consistency, both at the center of the European institutions and in the international arena. Without a doubt, they formed the first Franco-German "couple," if one presumes that this term implies a minimum of common strategic vision. Certainly the objective of creating a "European Union," declared in 1972 by the heads of state at the summit of Paris and taken in hand by Giscard in 1974, was not implemented in 1980 as planned. Little progress on policies or communal institutions was achieved during this period. Yet, the two leaders did make the Franco-German alliance the "engine" of the creation and implementation of European projects, the importance of which would become obvious in the future.

Notes

1. Address in Bonn, July 7, 1980.
2. Michèle Weinachter, *Valéry Giscard d'Estaing et l'Allemagne: Le double rêve inachevé* (Paris: L'Harmattan, 2004), 77ff. The present chapter is based on this book, which develops many points mentioned here in more detail.
3. Interview with Valéry Giscard d'Estaing, *Der Spiegel*, January 1, 1979.
4. Author's discussion with Helmut Schmidt.
5. Marie-Thérèse Bitsch, "Jean Monnet et la création du Conseil européen," in *Jean Monnet, l'Europe et les chemins de la paix*, eds. Gérard Bossuat and Andreas Wilkens (Paris: Publications de la Sorbonne, 1999), 99–410.
6. Hélène Miard-Delacroix, *Partenaires de choix? Le Chancelier Helmut Schmidt et la France 1974–1982* (Bern: Peter Lang, 1993), 139. Raymond Barre replaced Jacques Chirac at the head of the French government in August 1976, until 1981.
7. For a comprehensive study comparing these differences in the era see R. Lasserre, W. Neumann, R. Picht, eds., *Deutschland-Frankreich, Bausteine zum Systemvergleich* (Stuttgart: Robert-Bosch Stiftung, 1981).
8. David Lawday, "The odd couple," *The Atlantic Community Quarterly* (Fall 1979): 309.
9. Henrik Uterwedde, "Soziale Marktwirtschaft à la française: Die Wirtschaftspolitik Raymond Barres," *Dokumente* 1 (1979): 69–71.
10. The notion was introduced by Valéry Giscard-d'Estaing on his official visit to Germany in 1980.
11. In 1969, he presented, on behalf of the European Commission, the "Barre plan of political, economic, and mutual monetary support." Barre was at the time vice president of the European Commission and presented the plan in his capacity of Commissioner for Economics and Finance.
12. Discussion with the author.
13. Author's discussion with Roy Jenkins.

14. Françoise de la Serre, "L'Europe communautaire entre le mondialisme et l'entente franco-allemande," in *La politique extérieure de Valéry Giscard d'Estaing*, eds. Samy Cohen and Marie-Claude Smouts (Paris: Presses de la FNSP, 1985), 97.

15. Valéry Giscard d'Estaing, *Le Pouvoir et la Vie* (Paris: Compagnie 12, 1988), 136.

16. Marie-Thérèse Bitsch, *Histoire de la construction européenne de 1945 à nos jours* (Brussels: Editions Complexe, 1996), 98.

17. Valéry Giscard d'Estaing and Helmut Schmidt were alone at the beginning of taking on this project. They wanted James Callaghan, their British counterpart, to be on board, but the English experts interfered and Callaghan was dissuaded. See Helmut Schmidt, *Die Deutschen und ihre Nachbarn* (Berlin: Siedler, 1990), 222.

18. One of the decisive meetings took place in Helmut Schmidt's private apartment in Hamburg on June 23, 1978.

19. Helmut Schmidt was pleased to emphasize that such a smooth functioning would have been completely impossible between Helmut Kohl and François Mitterrand, who were not experts on economic and monetary questions, and, in fact, were dependent on their entourage (author's discussion with Helmut Schmidt).

20. Schmidt, *Die Deutschen*, 219–32, and Giscard d'Estaing. *Le Pouvoir*, 142 ff. For a detailed analysis of this entire phase see also Peter Ludlow, *The Making of the European Monetary System* (London: Butterworths, 1982).

21. On several occasions, the following suspicion was to be heard in France: Germany would cede to some Soviet siren, who would entice it with the promise of reunification in exchange for a drifting to the East, neutralization and thus Germany's betrayal of the European and Western cause.

22. According to Valéry Giscard d'Estaing, half of his discussion time with the German chancellor was dedicated to the United States. See Giscard, *Le Pouvoir*, 139.

23. February 6, 1981 at the conclusion of the thirty-seventh Franco-German summit.

CHAPTER 19

A Special Relationship

Franco-German Relations at the Time of François Mitterrand and Helmut Kohl

Georges Saunier

Mere hours after his nomination on October 4, 1982, Helmut Kohl made his first visit abroad to Paris, where he met François Mitterrand. He was accompanied by Hans Dietrich Genscher, who had been foreign minister in the preceding coalition. Continuity was, in fact, the message that the chancellor had come to deliver: Franco-German relations were to remain a priority.[1] A lot has already been written on the differences of character between the two statesmen: they did not belong to the same generation or share the same political allegiances, culture, and so forth.[2]. However, the two men were able to find common ground, both driven by the same European will, supported by history.[3]

Mitterrand discovered Germany as a war prisoner in Thuringia. Like many men of his generation, however, far from nourishing resentment against German people, World War II created in him a kind of spirit of generation, of community of—tragic—destiny, which is mirrored in his writings. For him, the "German question" was linked very early on to the development of Europe and he supported the majority of European texts with exception of the European Defense Community. Regarding Franco-German relations, he preferred the expression "friendship" rather than "axis." He may well have considered Germany his most important partner, but he had no intention to be his only one. However, when he became president in May 1981, he lost no time to use the Franco-German lever, even though his relations with Helmut Schmidt in the '70s had not been particularly good.

Helmut Kohl was slightly younger than Mitterrand and did not experience World War II in the same way. The former was influenced perhaps more deeply by the postwar period than by the conflict itself. Kohl was born, studied, and built his political career in Rhineland-Palatinate, a region deeply marked by its proximity to France, particularly after 1945, when the French were both an occupying power and neighbors with whom the Germans should make peace. A patriot and a well-reasoned Francophile who had campaigned for closer relations between the two countries since his teenage years, Kohl pursued Adenauer's pro-European policy, with Franco-German reconciliation at its core.

Franco-German Agreement from the "Battle of Euromissiles" to the Revival of Europe, 1981–84

The Euromissiles crisis was the true starting point, "a founding act,"[4] for relations between Mitterrand and Kohl. The installation of Soviet SS-20 missiles led to the December 1979 NATO Council "double-track" strategy that planned for the deployment of American Pershing missiles starting in late 1983 in the event that disarmament talks with Moscow failed.

In West Germany, the deployment of these missiles was very much criticized, with part of the population opposing it. Germany's position was delicate. It needed both to force Washington to try diplomacy to satisfy public opinion without endangering Western cohesion—on which Germany's safety relied—on the one hand, and keep discussions with Moscow open within the framework of *Ostpolitik*, all while preparing to install American missiles. Like his predecessor, Chancellor Kohl favored the "double-track decision" and looked to Paris for support.

For the French, the "Battle of the Euromissiles" raised many questions. They feared a neutralization of Germany and wanted to help Kohl. But doing so could have brought France into the negotiations, a dangerous move since the independence of the country's power to deter left no room for discussion.

This contradiction did not prevent Mitterrand from openly supporting the "double-track decision" as early as May 1981 and calling for the deployment of new Pershings should the imbalance created by the SS-20s persist. On January 20, 1983, he openly supported this position before the *Bundestag*, on the twentieth anniversary of the signature of the Franco-German Treaty.[5] The speech had considerable political ramifications in Germany. It consolidated the position of the supporters of the "double decision," namely Helmut Kohl. On this basis, Franco-German relations could fully develop.

In the first half of 1983, Germany was to preside over the European Economic Community (EEC). But the EEC's institutions were paralyzed by the never-ending disputes between member states over the agriculture budget. No compromise seemed possible, and other important decisions were blocked.

In spite of a reaffirmed European commitment and obvious interests for the common market, Chancellor Kohl's team refused to increase European finances with nothing in exchange. Germany, the main contributor to the European community budget, feared overspending in the European budget. The French rejected the concept of a "just reward" defended by the British—a threat not only for the future of Europe but also the finances of the Common Agricultural Policy

(CAP) that benefited French farmers. Furthermore, even though Mitterrand had been calling for a revival of European integration since June 1981, it was not until March 1983 that he set aside certain French protectionist tendencies, a sign Germans saw as favorable.

By 1983, the advantages of a revival of European integration gained ground in both France and West Germany: the Common Market offered prospects for economic development and the European Monetary System (EMS) promised stability favorable to trade. Politically, the cohesion of the EEC guaranteed a foothold for Germany in the West while also providing interesting diplomatic leverage through European political cooperation. A Franco-German agreement took shape gradually from June 1983 to June 1984 and lead to the successful European Council in Fontainebleau. Thanks to the understanding between Mitterrand and Kohl, most of Europe's disputes were resolved. EC members agreed on a financing for the European community in the future, on a compensation for the British deficit to the EEC budget and on a limitation to agricultural expenditures. These decisions paved the way for the adhesion of Spain and Portugal to the EEC and the convocation of two committees assigned to study the future of Europe. Also at Fontainebleau, Mitterrand and Kohl agreed to appoint Jacques Delors as the European Commission's chairman.

Around the same time, François Mitterrand and Helmut Kohl announced the opening of Franco-German borders (July 1984). The decision served as the forerunner to European freedom of movement introduced a year later with the Schengen agreement. The two statesmen then met in Verdun for the famous handshake, a symbol of Franco-German reconciliation.

Most importantly, France and Germany overcame the opposition of the United Kingdom, Denmark and Greece and the principles of an intergovernmental conference (IGC) along with Delors' Single Market project were adopted in Rome in June 1985. These two decisions were important.[6] Indeed, the IGC resulted in the adoption of the Single European Act (SEA) in February 1986. Largely based on Franco-German documents, it was the first significant modification to the 1957 Rome Treaty. It opened the door to a new stage in European economic integration: goods, workers and services would be able to circulate without excessive constraints by 1993.

Friendship, Controversies, Europe: The "Cycle," 1984–89

The strategic agreement on Euromissiles, the success of Fontainebleau, the joint resolution of European issues, and so on, all indicated that as of the mid 1980s, the French-German couple was working. However, many disagreements between the two countries still existed. As Mitterrand pointed out in 1985, "our relations are founded on good, solid mutual realism, along with the hope and the common desire to build Europe. But our interests are not automatically identical."[7] Therefore, not only the close ties and the success of the French-German couple should be emphasized—which neither the *cohabitation* in France, nor the chancellor's difficulties at home were able to disrupt—but also the persistence of contradictions from 1984 to 1989. They did not prevent both governments from making every effort to achieve progress. What surprised observers was the involvement of Europe in every discussion: directly or indirectly; it was always about making Franco-German relations a model for the future. The Franco-German couple was designed as a sort of European laboratory.

The combination of French and German defense policies, started in 1982, reached a decisive stage with the creation of the Defense and Security Council in November 1987 to closely coordinate their policies. At the same time, a shift in French military doctrine was noticeable. By announcing the creation of a Rapid Action Force in April 1983, organizing joint military maneuvers and formations and, finally, based on a proposal by Kohl and accepted by Mitterrand, setting up a Franco-German brigade starting in June 1987, France accepted the idea of committing its troops in the context of the forefront battle. The brigade also had the support of an antitank helicopter (Eurocopter) that the two countries had decided to produce together, a symbol of their military cooperation. In February 1986, it was even agreed that the president and the chancellor would have a consultation in the event that France was considering the use of tactical nuclear missiles, a considerable progress given the strict autonomy of French deterrence policies. All this was obviously developed—as Mitterrand and Kohl insisted—with a European perspective and complemented Franco-German plans for a revival of the Western European Union (WEU) in 1984 and 1987.

Although real progress was being made, it had its limits. Eurocopter was a success, but other projects (tanks, fighter planes, observation satellites, etc.) never saw the light of day. Beyond the cost issue, these failures demonstrated a difference in strategy that remained a barrier between France and Germany. Germany wanted to bring France closer to the Atlantic Alliance and European defense was a means of bringing pressure to bear on Washington. The French approach was exactly the opposite. Close ties with Germany and the ensuing emergence of European defenses were designed to increase Europe's military independence and thereby more freedom of decision for France. Thus, Paris refused to get involved in any NATO organizations, even under the cover of Franco-German actions. This led to different attitudes in France and Germany to American proposals. Whereas France was strongly opposed to President Ronald Reagan's Strategic Defense Initiative (SDI) project, Germany accepted its basis, despite serious reservations and the risk it posed to the French-initiated project for European scientific cooperation (Eureka, 1985), developed as a European response to the SDI. Relations with Washington therefore remained a subject of tension between France and West Germany.[8]

Nevertheless, Franco-German cooperation remained a priority. Mitterrand and Kohl launched many projects in far-ranging fields such as culture (e.g., the Franco-German High Council for Cultural Affairs, French-German television channels), science and research, industry (Airbus A320, Ariane 5, the European Space Agency), education and youth (bilingual schools, creation of the

French-German middle school), and so on. Each of these initiatives preceded or accompanied the adoption of appropriate policies at the European level.

There were some notable exceptions however. Several projects, in particular in industry, never came to fruition (high definition television, high-speed train, space program). In many cases, they failed because of the different economic models of the two countries. In fact, the liberalism supported by Kohl and the interventionist socialism of Mitterrand caused serious disputes between the two countries. For example, the "European social space" that the French president wanted never received real support from the Germans. The same occurred when the Germans supported a new round of trade talks the United States wanted between 1986 and 1993, while the French dreaded them. Another dispute occurred when the Germans opposed the French proposal to strengthen the protectionist provisions of the EEC. The French finally won out but only thanks to a majority vote by the European Council. And so there was an ongoing succession of agreements and controversies between 1984 and 1989.

Controversies existed, but the teams at the Chancellery and at the Elysée were accustomed to them and the Franco-German relationship was working as Paris and Bonn intended. A kind of "trust" was established, each one knowing that the mechanics of Franco-German dialogue would make it possible to identify problems and find a compromise that might eventually lead to a new political initiative. New difficulties appeared at the beginning of 1989.

On the strategic level, the initiatives taken in 1987 by Mikhail Gorbatchev had pushed the Westerners to denuclearize Europe. However, Germany was the only country to still have short-range nuclear forces (SRNF), essentially the U.S. Pershings stationed in the Federal Republic of Germany (FRG). However, Kohl caught the French unawares by insisting that they be dismantled—the triple zero option—in April 1989. For Paris, it would logically involve the dismantling of the French SRNF and posed the question of the French autonomy of dissuasion.

The biggest disagreements concerned European issues. In the face of the resurgence of problems over the agricultural budget and the development of the European Community (single market and structural policies), Kohl seemed torn between his European focus and his electoral, agricultural and financial interests. With difficulty, an agreement—"Delors I"—was finally reached in June of 1988, again thanks to good Franco-German relations. But new problems were cropping up in connection with the Economic and Monetary Union (EMU).

Tied to the Deutschmark through the EMS, the Franc mirrored the changes in German monetary policy. While the situation offered real financial advantages, it gave French economic policy less leeway. French authorities looked for a way to make German monetary policy less unilateral, in particular by implementing the EMU.

Among those close to the chancellor, opinions on the EMU were divided. Genscher believed that it would provide the EMS with greater stability and thus be advantageous to the German economy. In addition, he stressed that the liberalization of capital flows within the common market made the step necessary. But other ministers in the federal government along with the Bundesbank believed that the EMU was premature, that the convergence of the European economies was by no means certain, and that giving up the *Deutschmark* would risk suffering the bad management of European countries with weak currencies.

France, however, had gone down the path of the EMU. The SEA brought up monetary issues; and at Nyborg, in September 1987, the Twelve had agreed to strengthen the EMS. Finally, in January 1988, in parallel with the creation of the Franco-German Defense Council, Paris had obtained the same for a bilateral Economic and Financial Council where the two countries were to harmonize their economic policies. Furthermore, three months later, Germany took the initiative by sending its partners a memorandum on the EMU. During the following European Council of Hanover, the concept of the EMU was adopted, to the great satisfaction of the French. Delors was assigned to write a report on the subject.

This report was presented in April 1989. It not only prescribed a three-stage implementation process for an ambitious EMU but also made major concessions to Germany. In particular, the future European central bank would be independent, a point hardly acceptable for the French, who eventually resigned themselves to it, expecting that the EMU project would be confirmed during the European Council of Madrid (June 1989). However, Kohl agreed at Madrid to set a date to move into the first stage of the EMU but refused to set a date to convene the IGC, which was necessary for the following stages. The Twelve, thus, left the council without any guarantee that the EMU would ever come to fruition, that is, move to a single currency.

As of summer 1989, Paris had every reason to worry about this subject, which it considered a priority. This was especially true since, in April, the German authorities had twice acted unilaterally to make important economic decisions.

Commenting on the conclusions reached by the Council of Madrid, Mitterrand spoke of the existence of a certain "fog,"[9] which was to be lifted during the second half of 1989. Over the following months, the French expected a new Franco-German agreement, certain that Kohl's commitment to Europe would win the day. Mitterrand had good reasons to hope. Germany had made the necessary gestures; relations between both leaders and foreign ministers were good, contacts were constant. Events in Eastern Europe shook this expectation to its core.

The Stakes of German Unification, 1989–90

Since 1949, although the reunification of Germany had been a constant concern for the German authorities, it was unlikely. Nevertheless, from 1985–89 and adapting to the events occurring in the East, Helmut Kohl refocused West German diplomacy on this objective. But he didn't rush things: discussions on the subject with the French remained very vague. Only in the wake of the noticeable changes happening in Poland, Hungary, and Czechoslovakia in the summer 1989 did he declare that the German question was "once again on the agenda."[10]

In France, particularly in the Ministry of Foreign Affairs, the possibility of reunifying Germany was discussed as of 1987–88, but it seemed impossible to achieve quickly. It was not until the summer of 1989 that a change in the wind was felt. Paris felt that the end of the cold war should be accompanied by expanding liberal Europe to include the democratized countries of Eastern Europe. This was both Mitterrand's analysis and the reason why he met with several Eastern European leaders, including Gorbatchev and Erich Honecker, at the time, a gesture that would lead to many controversial interpretations.[11] This way, the German question would find a solution. But, the European community had to be strong enough to handle the changes in Europe.

Mitterrand himself spoke on the topic on several occasions, notably to the German chancellor on 3 November 1989. Stating that he "wasn't afraid of reunification,"[12] he specified that the process was to be peaceful, democratic, respectful of existing borders—in particular the German-Polish border—and, most importantly, European: "as Eastern Europe evolves, Western Europe must be reinforced, and must strengthen its structures and define its policies."[13] In his eyes, reunification had to be carried out at the same pace as European integration. Nobody dared however to propose a schedule, either at the Chancellery, the Elysée, or in the other major Western capitals.

However, overnight, between November 9 and 10, the Berlin Wall fell. The country was nonetheless far from reunification. During this crucial period, France and Germany did not achieve any joint initiatives. Their priorities were different, as the discussions at the special European summit on November 18, 1989, demonstrated, along with the following events.[14]

For Kohl, who feared missing a historical occasion, reunification was now the priority. He worked with several collaborators in complete secrecy to draft a ten-point plan opening the way for a progressive reunification of West and East Germany. This far-reaching plan was presented to the Bundestag on November 28 and seemed to redefine the priorities of the German government for years to come.

In France, discovery of the plan sowed confusion. Did the Treaty of Elysée forecast not call for each partner to consult the other before taking any important initiative? Why had the Germans not done so? And although the chancellor's proposals seemed to be prudent and to demonstrate his desire to achieve reunification through a democratic process, he did not directly mention the question of East German borders; and, while he emphasized the importance of the European Community, he also called for a new organization of Europe. For the French, who certainly considered German reunification to be legitimate and inevitable, the priority was to respect the European agenda and in particular to ensure the implementation of the EMU. Reunification was likely to hinder these projects.

From the end of November 1989 and at least until the meeting between Mitterrand and Kohl in January 1990 at Latché, the private residence of the French president, Franco-German discussions were a series of questions. While insisting that Europe was still a priority, Kohl tried to gain time to manage the reunification as best as possible. Mitterrand, for his part, tried to impose his own views. As he reminded Kohl, France had interests and prerogatives. He pressured the chancellor to recognize the Oder-Neisse border as soon as possible, not to rush Mikhail Gorbatchev—a position France would continue advocating during the "2+4" negotiations[15]—and, above all, to set a date for the intergovernmental conference on the EMU.

Conflicting political objectives could have caused German reunification to lead to a major schism between France and Germany. This was not the case, however, mainly because the existing institutional structures, working habits, and so forth, made it possible to maintain dialogue throughout this period. In addition, reunification happened more quickly than expected. The democratization of East Germany accelerated its disintegration; and Mikhail Gorbatchev quickly made concessions during the "2+4" negotiations. Lastly, despite different agendas and objectives, Europe remained the priority in both countries. The chancellor understood that intensive European integration would facilitate German reunification.

When German reunification was achieved on October 3, 1990, it had occurred peacefully and democratically and the Polish question had been resolved according to French requests. Better yet, in agreeing, at the European Summit of Strasbourg on December 8–9,1989, to set a date for the opening of the IGC on the EMU and later confirming this decision, Helmut Kohl sent a clear signal to his partners in Europe. German reunification served as an extraordinary driving force for Europe. And indeed, over the following months, France and Germany were to experience one of the most prosperous periods of their cooperation: the move toward the European Union. Kohl and Mitterrand committed themselves together to it in a spectacular way.

Toward the European Union:
The Treaty of Maastricht, 1990–93

From 1990 to 1993, the Franco-German couple focused almost exclusively on European questions. Major initiatives by both countries marked the period. In light of the democratic and economic movements taking place in Eastern Europe, most of the Western European capitals accepted the idea of framing it within a strong European Community, the structures of which should therefore be reinforced.[16] The European agenda itself ordered some reforms, too. The extension of the European domestic market to most spheres of economic activity (industry, services, transportation, capital); the consolidation of freedom of movement for money and for people; the ongoing increase in the European budget and structural policies; and the prospect of a true EMU, made it necessary for member states to be more fully integrated. In other words, the new size of Europe called for a new step forward. Finally, from 1990 to 1992, the European Community began new negotiations on the agricultural budget. They ended in a new agreement—"Delors II"—which was adopted at the European Council of Edinburgh in December 1992. As with the previous dispute between 1980 and 1984, the final agreement owed much to the understanding between France and Germany, which was itself made possible by the prospect of a stronger European Community. Expanding the jurisdiction of the European Community involved constant collaboration.

Germany also wanted to confirm that the new Germany was committed to Europe in order to lie to rest the concerns of its partners during the country's reunification. As such, the increasing political power of Europe would offer support for the changes that a unified Germany would inevitably experience on the international scene. Therefore, after declaring that the "German house [would be] under a European roof,"[17] the chancellor announced in late 1989 his desire for European political integration to move into a new phase.

In France, this idea of a new phase was initially viewed with skepticism. Was this not an attempt by the Germans to delay the EMU negotiations, which remained a priority? But, this issue was solved at the European Council of Strasbourg with the decision to launch an IGC on the subject in late 1990. Consequently, the birth of a European Union with broader political jurisdiction, in particular in the fields of diplomacy and defense, should become a new objective. The Union thus needed a new perspective.

Very quickly, the teams at the Chancellery and the Elysée managed to agree on the basics. The jurisdiction of the future Union would be extended to new fields; institutional adjustments were needed; and for these two reasons a new treaty was required. On April 19, 1990, Mitterrand and Kohl sent an important letter to their partners, in which they invited the member states "to reinforce the Union's democratic legitimacy and coherence of action in the economic, monetary and political fields, and to define and implement a common foreign and security policy" (CFSP). Coming on the heels of a Belgian memorandum that had been sent out a few weeks earlier, the Franco-German initiative was the final push that launched negotiations on the treaty of Maastricht.[18]

During the Irish presidency in the first half of 1990, government leaders agreed to open an IGC devoted to political questions in parallel with the IGC on EMU. It was still necessary to set its mandate. This was the main objective of the Italian presidency in the second half of 1990. In the face of serious differences between the parties, the initiative came once more from France and Germany. On 6 December 1990, Mitterrand and Kohl sent another letter to their counterparts. Just days before the European Council of Rome, they explained their vision of the future political Union in three fields. They suggested broadening the European Community's jurisdiction in the fields of environment, health, social policy, energy, research and technology, and consumer protection; giving the Union new jurisdiction in the fields of immigration, visas, right to asylum, and the fight against international crime. They also mentioned the concept of European citizenship. In the institutional field, while planning to strengthen the powers of the European Parliament and to extend the majority vote in the Council of Minister, they wanted the European Council to become a high political authority within the future Union. The European Council—and Council of Ministers—would have exclusive jurisdiction over the CFSP and the justice-related tasks. In short, Kohl and Mitterrand drew up what was to be the future institutional structure of the Union, in pillars.

Despite opposition from Great Britain, the mandate given to the IGC by the European Council of Rome matched these points almost exactly. Over the chancellor's objections, Mitterrand also succeeded in setting a date to move to the second phase of the Euro. It was a small concession, however, since the Germans had won out on most of their demands related to the future single currency (independence of the central Bank, coordination of national economic policies rather than a joint economic policy, strict criteria for the change to the Euro).

On October 14, 1991, noticing the differences between member states and the hostility of the European Commission toward the institutional architecture of the future Union, Kohl and Mitterrand put forward one last initiative. Just before the conclusion of the two IGCs, they sent their partners a draft treaty. This draft was the basis for the final discussions at the European Council of Maastricht, on December 9 and 10, 1991. Franco-German agreement was complete—the chancellor even accepted a French proposal setting a date to move into the EMU's third stage. As in Fontainebleau, the close ties between France and Germany made it possible to isolate Great Britain and to achieve an ambitious treaty, which was largely of Franco-German inspiration.

Time for Farewells, 1993–95

With the end of the negotiations on the Treaty of Maastricht, a cycle of Franco-German relations reached an end. A new period and stage were inaugurated with a reunified Germany that was trying to find its bearings on the international stage.

The French-German couple tried to organize post–Yalta Europe with some difficulty. Problems—from opening up to Eastern Europe, the role of NATO to the Yugoslavian tragedy—were numerous. On the first point, Mitterrand had launched the idea of a European Confederation in December 1989. He considered it premature to expand the EEC. But the Germans rejected his proposal, preferring to act within the existing frameworks: European Union, Conference on Security and Cooperation in Europe, NATO. With regard to NATO, the development of East–West relations had made its reform necessary. But, while some believed that its mandate should be expanded, others thought that it should be replaced by an independent European defense system. At a meeting in La Rochelle in May 1992, Mitterrand and Kohl announced the creation of a European army corps within the WEU, soon joined by Spain, Belgium, and Luxembourg. In January 1993, another major agreement was reached between France, Germany, and the Supreme Allied Commander in Europe. Eurocorps could act within the framework of Atlantic Alliance missions. This meant that, for the first time since 1966, France agreed to work within the integrated command, first as part of the Franco-German brigade and then the European forces. Admittedly, in Paris, there were many reservations, but this decision opened the way to the European pillar of defense.

In spite of these achievements and another Franco-German letter in October 1993, it remained difficult to implement the CFSP. During the Gulf War, for example, Europe did not play any real part. Worse still, the tragedy in Yugoslavia demonstrated a divided Europe with France and Germany—the latter recognizing Croatia unilaterally—unable to come together on this issue.

Again, in terms of European and bilateral issues, results were mixed. Disagreements over negotiations within the framework of the General Agreement on Tariffs and Trade (GATT), the new reform of the CAP, and the rise in structural expenditures were overcome. During the monetary problems of 1992–93, the French-German couple showed real solidarity that made it possible to adapt the margins of the EMS while maintaining the objective of the EMU. But Franco-German initiatives were fewer, due in part to Germany's delay in ratifying the Treaty of Maastricht and also to some changes within the teams—Genscher's departure in 1992 and another *cohabitation* in France from March 1993. The Mitterrand-Kohl relationship was coming to its end, an impression undoubtedly accentuated by French president's ever more visible illness.

Nevertheless, many French-German "gestures" were made, starting with Kohl's direct and unprecedented intervention in the French political debate during the campaign over the referendum on Maastricht in 1992. Exemplary understanding between the two capitals was also shown on the thirtieth anniversary of the Treaty of Elysée, in January 1993, followed, on July 14, 1994, French national day, by the parade of German troops down the Champs-Elysées as part of Eurocorps, something that had not happened since the German occupation in the 1940s. These symbolic signs were Mitterrand's testament. In the last months of his term, he unquestionably wanted to complete the reconciliation of the two countries. In Berlin, on May 8, 1995, for the fiftieth anniversary of the end of the war in Europe, he declared that the victory of 1945 was not only a "victory of freedom over oppression" but also "a victory of Europe over itself." These words gave the real perspective of the Franco-German relationship.

Notes

1. Private documents, see also Jacques Attali, *Verbatim I. 1981–1983: chronique des années 1981–1986* (Paris: Librairie générale française, 1995), 491.
2. Helmut Kohl's and Mitterrand's personalities and encounter have been often described. In this respect two useful biographies and two studies on their years in power can be quoted: Jean Lacouture, *Mitterrand. Une histoire de Français*, 2 vol. (Paris: Seuil, 1998); Jean-Paul Picaper, Karl Hugo Pruys, *Helmut Kohl* (Paris: Fayard, 1996); Clay Clemens, William E. Paterson, eds., *The Kohl chancellorship* (F. Cass: London, 1998); and Pierre Favier, Michel Martin-Roland, *La décennie Mitterrand* (Paris: Ed. du Seuil, 1995).
3. Numerous studies have been devoted to Franco-German relations at the time of Mitterrand and Kohl. For the French side, we recommend in particular the following recent scholarly works based on archival research: Frédéric Bozo, *Mitterrand, la fin de la guerre froide et l'unification allemande. De Yalta à Maastricht* (Paris: Odile Jacob, 2005); Marion Gaillard, *La politique allemande de François Mitterrand, 1981–1995* (Thèse de doctorat de l'Institut d'Etude politique de Paris, dir. Pierre Milza, 2007); and Tilo Schabert, *Wie Weltgeshichte gemacht wird. Frankreich und die deutsche Einheit* (Stuttgart: Klett-Cotta, 2002). Bozo's work on Mitterrand and German unity

will be published in English in 2009 by Berghahn books. For the German side, we principally refer to the following published sources and academic studies: Dokumente zur Deutschlandpolitik, *Deutsche Einheit. Sonderedition aus den Akten des Bundeskanzleramtes 1989–90* (Munich: R. Oldenburg, 1998); Werner Rouget, *Schwierige Nachbarschaft am Rhein. Frankreich-Deutschland* (Munich: Piper Verlag, 2002); Hans Stark, *Kohl, l'Allemagne et l'Europe. La politique d'intégration européenne de la République fédérale 1982–1998* (Paris: L'Harmattan, 2004). See also the numerous memoirs published by the main actors, such as Jacques Attali, Verbatim, vol. 1, 2, 3 (Paris: Fayard, 1993–95); Joachim Bitterlich, "In memoriam Werner Rouget," in *Schwierige Nachbarschaft am Rhein. Frankreich-Deutschland,* Werner Rouget, ed. by Joachim Bitterlich, Ernst Weisenfeld (Bonn: Bouvier, 1998); Roland Dumas, *Le fil et la pelote. Mémoires* (Paris: Plon, 1996); Hans-Dietrich Genscher, *Erinnerungen* (Berlin: Siedler Verlag, 1995); Helmut Kohl, *Reden und Erklärungen zur Deutschlandpolitik* (Bonn: Presse- und Informationsamt der Bundesregierung, 1990); Helmut Kohl, *Ich wollte Deutschlands Einheit* (Berlin: Ullstein, 1996); François Mitterrand, *Réflexion sur la politique extérieure de la France. Introduction à 25 discours 1981–1985* (Paris: Fayard, 1986); François Mitterrand, *De l'Allemagne, de la France* (Paris: Odile Jacob, 1996); Horst Teltschick, *329 Tage. Innenansichten der Einigung* (Berlin: Siedler, 1991); and Hubert Védrine, *Les mondes de François Mitterrand: à l'Elysée, 1981–1995* (Paris: Fayard 1996).

4. Védrine, *Les Mondes de François Mitterrand*, 93.

5. Mitterrand's speech in front of the Bundestag, in *Les relations franco-allemandes depuis 1963*, eds. Pierre Jardin and Adolf Kimmel (Paris: La Documentation française, 2001), 261–63.

6. On the negotiations for the conclusion of the SEA, see John Gillingham, *European Integration 1950–2003: Superstate or New Market Economy* (Cambridge: Cambridge University Press, 2003), 152–294; Kenneth Dyson, Kevin Featherstone, *The Road to Maastricht. Negotiating Economic and Monetary Union* (Oxford: Oxford University Press, 1999); and Jean De Ruyt, *L'Acte unique européen* (Bruxelles: Ed. de l'Université de Bruxelles, 1987).

7. Press conference of François Mitterrand, president of the French Republic, at the end of the summit of industrialized countries, Bonn, May 4, 1985, in *Documents d'actualité internationale* (hereafter *DAI*), Paris, La Documentation française.

8. For a good study of the Franco-German strategic dialogue, refer to Stephen A. Kocs, *Autonomy or Power? The Franco-German Relationship and Europe's Strategic Choice, 1955–1995* (Westport: Praeger, 1995).

9. Press conference of François Mitterrand at the end of the European Council in Madrid, Congres Palace, June 27, 1989, *DAI*.

10. Declaration of Helmut Kohl on August 22, 1989, *DAI*.

11. For the most critical study on France's position on reunification, see Samy Cohen, ed., *Mitterrand et la sortie de la guerre froide* (Paris: PUF, 1998). One should also consult two articles by Daniel Vernert, a journalist at *Le Monde,* and notice his interesting evolution on this question: Daniel Vernet, "Mitterrand et la réunification dans les archives allemandes" (Politique étrangère, no. 2/1999, p. 395–403); and Daniel Vernet, "Mitterrand, l'Europe et la réunification allemande" (Politique étrangère, no. 1/2003, p. 165–79).

12. Joint press conference of François Mitterrand and Helmut Kohl at the end of the fifty-fourth Franco-German consultations in Bonn, November 2–3, 1989, in *Les relations franco-allemandes depuis 1963*, 338–39.

13. Ibid.

14. See, for instance, Bozo, *Mitterrand*.

15. See Bertrand Dufourq, "2+4 ou la négociation atypique" (Politique étrangère, no. 2/2000, p. 467 and following).

16. See N. Piers Ludlow, Frédéric Bozo, Marie-Pierre Rey, Leopoldo Nutti, eds, *Europe and the End of the Cold War* (London: Routledge, 2007).

17. Speech of Helmut Kohl in front of the Brandenburger Gate, December 19, 1989, *DAI*.

18. For a detailed analysis of bilateral bargaining before and after Maastricht, see Colette Mazzucelli, *France and Germany at Maastricht: Politics and Negotiations to Create the European Union* (New York: Garland Publishing, 1997).

CHAPTER 20

The "Other" Franco-German Relations

The GDR and France from 1949 to 1990

Ulrich Pfeil

With the demise of the "other" Germany, memories of the "other" Franco-German relationship vanished too. If we are to believe the writer Lutz Rathenow, France was the "most congenial form" of Western societal organization in the eyes of the adherents of the Socialist Unity Party (*Sozialistische Einheitspartei Deutschlands*-SED). As an advertisement might say, France was "the sweetest temptation since there have been class enemies."[1] As Rathenow asks himself, how was it that France and Paris in particular became the most desired travel destination in the imaginations of the Germans behind the Wall? He believes that the clichés were confirmed by reality. Thanks to pop singer France Gall and actress Brigitte Bardot, France presented itself not only as the "erogenous zone of Western civilization," but with its literature and philosophy, it also won over the subcultural milieu of intellectuals in the German Democratic Republic (GDR).

In the era of German division, the Federal Republic's claim to be the sole representative of the German side in relations with France took hold of historians and political scientists with the corollary that the GDR was no longer thought of in terms of links between Germany and France. Almost twenty years after the fall of the Wall, however, we must make a more detailed inquiry than has yet been the case as to place the GDR in these relations.[2] By incorporating the second German state, one ends up with a Franco-German-German triangular relationship. Questions arise as to the contact points among the three states and their societies, what role the French side played in the conflict between the two Germanies, what meaning the East German side had for the Franco–West German relationship, and in what form the West German side influenced Franco–East German contacts.[3]

The Unofficial Triangular Relationship:
A Political Perspective, 1949–73

The emergence of the two German states was a consequence of the East-West conflict, which became the most important determinant of Germany's double postwar history both in terms of international relations and domestic affairs. The policy of the GDR toward France between 1949 and 1973 was dominated by two factors: first, the Soviet Union and, second, the Federal Republic. From the beginning of its existence, the GDR was subject to the goals and interests of the hegemonic power to the east, for which it functioned as a "transmission belt" providing indispensable services on German policy. This allowed the Soviets to secure enduring and maximal political influence in Europe and Germany. Sharing an ideological foundation, the Communist Party of the Soviet Union (CPSU) and the SED determined the lines of socialist foreign policy as parties of the "ruling working class" and saw their main task in securing the "most favorable international conditions for the building of socialism and communism."[4] Even with the agreement on principles shared by these "brother parties," the SED depended on the political tutelage of Moscow. As an expression of this hegemonic relational hierarchy, the Soviets regularly assigned tasks to the GDR in the "agreed upon" French policy and expected their timely completion. Even if the GDR never overcame its function as cat's paw, it could make itself indispensable in the attempt to undermine the West's integration efforts and also gain its first freedom of action. In the process, there emerged as early as the 1950s divergent interests in that Walter Ulbricht had already opted to build a separate state whereas the Soviet Union left the final German settlement open in its 1952 notes to the West and regarded the GDR as a bargaining chip. It was in France especially that Moscow placed its hopes in a successful "Stalingrad Effect" and distrust of Western integration from the nationalist-oriented milieu. However, the concept of an unallied and unified Germany in the heart of Europe enjoyed majority support neither among the French population nor among its political decision makers. The shaky foundation of Soviet policy on Germany and the insecure position of the SED as ruling party, with its complete failure revealed to Western public opinion on June 17, 1953, were not lost on observers in Paris. A further reason that the self-confident appeals for peace made by the GDR to the French people were unable to reach their intended audience was that the SED could not use propaganda to eliminate the contradictions that characterized it; in international relations, it offered pacifistic discourse, while at home it continued to pursue the militarization of society using images of the West as the enemy.

With the GDR's permanent fixation on the second factor, the Federal Republic, there arose between the two German states a relationship that was soon being characterized as "asymmetrical linkage in differentiation."[5] Each had formulated its own claim to be the sole representative of the German people and its own theory of magnetic attraction, making use of every available means to "demagnetize" the other. Whereas the Federal Republic decided on integration into the West, the GDR aimed for the short-term reunification of Germany in accordance with the principles of the nation-state and applying an "anti-fascist-democratic" model. This meant the revolutionary extension of its own socialistic order into the Federal Republic. Since the GDR's foreign policy in this period was synonymous with German policy, the SED was never concerned with reciprocity in its promotion of a bilateral network of relations with France. Its French policy was part and parcel of efforts to legitimize the GDR as a sovereign and alternative German state.

After both German states had been integrated into their respective alliances, the GDR gained some freedom of action for the shaping of its foreign relations within the framework of its "Two-State Theory." Even as it had to hold onto the goal of German unity for domestic political considerations, the SED now began a policy of recognition—in dissociation from and competition with the Federal Republic—aimed at gaining influence over foreign states and portions of West German society and gaining economic advantages.[6] In France as elsewhere, this policy ran headlong into the Federal Republic's imperative for reunification, which held fast to the concept of German citizenship, the continued existence of the German nation, and the isolation of the GDR in international law. By seeking to expand its communication network in France, the East German government was attempting to undermine the Hallstein Doctrine proclaimed by the Federal Republic in 1955 and bring its own international recognition closer and to make its development as a separate state irreversible. In order to accomplish these goals, there could be a simultaneous willingness to cooperate and desire to dissociate from the end of the 1960s onward. This was characterized by the continued insistence on political dogmas and simultaneous pressure to conform to Western forms of communication.

The SED sought to gloss over this growing contradiction by trying to bring the GDR into Franco-German relations as an independent factor and present itself as the guarantor of a peaceful Germany that had learned the lessons of the past. At the same time, the SED painted a picture of a Federal Republic in which the old forces were still at work, those that had led to three wars against France within a seventy-year period. This policy successfully gained attention for the GDR in France and also benefited from a certain "underdog reflex" that accrued to the GDR almost automatically given the increasing economic might of the Federal Republic. Whereas the GDR was able to use the continued desire in all French political milieus to remain aloof from the powerful neighbor east of the Rhine, the Federal Republic remained a permanent magnet for the East Germans, one whose attractiveness had to be limited by SED foreign policy successes so as to cover up the GDR's domestic instability and compensate for it to a certain extent.[7]

The ever increasing output of and demands upon the Western and French apparatus within the SED ruling system were therefore an expression of that asymmetry with the Federal Republic. This became ever more difficult for the

GDR given the constant sociopolitical challenge from West Germany by 1973. A decisive role was played in all this by the fact that the GDR never succeeded in overcoming the constant ends-means conflict of the doctrine of peaceful coexistence: While hoping for political recognition and bilateral respect from France, the GDR persisted in ideological confrontation and, among other things, supported the Algerian opponents of French "imperialism."

Although the division of Germany was perceived with more or less open sympathy in all French political milieus, the German policy pursued by Paris into the 1960s concentrated unswervingly on the Federal Republic. Emblematic of this policy was the conclusion of the Franco-German Treaty in 1963, which demonstrated to the leaders of the SED the failure of their French policy up to that time but also further intensified the inequality between the two German states. Even when misunderstandings between the West Germans and the French over the Elysée Treaty manifested themselves publicly from 1964 onward, de Gaulle did not give Ulbricht an opportunity to overtake the FRG in Franco-German relations without allowing the West Germans to catch up. He made use of the GDR in his "policy of pinpricks" in order to demonstrate his anger to Bonn and once again bring it more closely into his orbit.[8] Additionally, it was difficult for the SED that although de Gaulle visited a number of communist states in the 1960s and sought increased cooperation with them, he excluded East Germany from his traveling diplomacy and thereby refused to concede it equal status.

During the presidency of Georges Pompidou, when the pressure for recognition in Bonn and Paris was constantly increasing, the GDR never transcended its status as a "lead weight" repeatedly placed by the French government on the foreign policy, including the new *Ostpolitik* of the Federal Republic's social-liberal coalition led by Chancellor Willy Brandt. Despite all its reservations as to the *Ostpolitik*, France proved itself a loyal ally with which relational networks were continually expanded. The practice of consultation mandated by the Elysée Treaty proved useful and developed into a stabilizing element in the Paris-Bonn axis during this delicate phase. Even with all its obligingness, France never took its eyes off its most important goal: the guarantee of its rights in Germany as a whole and in Berlin as one of the four victorious Allied Powers of the Second World War.[9]

Although the politicians in Bonn and the West German public were never completely sure that France would not one day succumb to the enticements of East Berlin and recognize the GDR prematurely, it was in fact the case that Franco–West German relations between 1949 and 1973 proved to be a stabilizing factor for the Federal Republic. Whereas the SED increasingly found itself on the defensive and the relationship between the party leadership and the East German populace reached a new low during the Berlin crisis, France assisted the Federal Republic on its way into the West as an equal. It was symptomatic that the West German public's trust in its own state neared a new high point at the signing of the Elysée Treaty.[10] Integration into the West and economic progress helped lessen the attraction of the national issue for West Germans and put the GDR in an increasingly negative position. The Paris-Berlin axis and the expansion of contacts were signs of the opening of West German society to the West and the increasing disinterest on the part of the West Germans in their "German brothers in the East."

The Unofficial Triangular Relationship:
A Perspective Full of Images, 1949–73

One of the characteristics of the cold war in Europe was that the conflict between the systems was not carried out by military means but rather by propaganda campaigns directed both inward and outward in connection with economic and political measures of various kinds. With enormous organization and material effort, the GDR pursued its informational work vis-à-vis France, which since 1957–58 had completely ruled out a policy of recognition. This effort was motivated by ideological competition but could not achieve its main goal. Although pressures mounted on the Hallstein Doctrine in the 1960s, no component of GDR foreign policy—political or economic or cultural—was able to topple it. Even when the French government found itself having to take the movement for recognition increasingly into its domestic and German policy considerations, the GDR's weight was insufficient to drive a wedge between Paris and Bonn. Because the social–liberal coalition was able to maintain the prospect of reunification in the Moscow Treaty by means of its policy of Change through Rapprochement (*Wandel durch Annäherung*),[11] the movement for recognition "from below" lost a portion of its political brisance.

Even though the SED's recognition policy did not succeed in establishing the GDR as an equal, sovereign state in international relations before the signing of the Basic Treaty (*Grundlagenvertrag*) and the country's reception into the UN, an examination of the French case demonstrates that as early as the 1960s, the GDR was perceived as having a distinct identity thanks to its targeted image policy. With its cultural achievements and economic development within the Eastern camp, East Germany had drawn attention even from outside the communist milieu. The cultural presence of the GDR in France and its self-understanding as the literary executor of authors such as Bertolt Brecht strengthened the image of an alternative German state and supplemented its geopolitical reality of 1949 with an identifiable existence in 1969.[12]

Beyond the boundaries of its worldview, the SED was able to expand its range of action into the French cultural and political milieu such that there developed a low level normality in relations even in this early phase.[13] A special bridge function was provided by the concept of antifascism, which the SED had initially used as a means of neutralizing domestic opponents and creating a founding myth for the GDR.[14] After antifascism had been built up into a cultural construct, it was massively employed in transnational communication with France in order to present the GDR as the morally "superior" Germany. Antifascism was used instrumentally in the attempt to link old French images of the German enemy to the Federal Republic. Without wanting to overemphasize its effectiveness, it was the case that antifascism provided the GDR an unprecedented domestic legitimization in the early 1970s that also exercised a stabilizing effect on the East German state on the international stage. The cautious developing tendencies in the perception of the GDR were promoted by the French image of the neighbor beyond the Rhine, in which there was room enough for several "Germanies" and in which the focus was always on the whole German-speaking sphere.

Even though the political and cultural landscape of France opened up possibilities for developing the GDR image and for its spread, it also demonstrated the limits of those possibilities. In contrast to other Western European industrial countries, the strength of the French Communist Party (Parti Communiste Français—PCF) and its bridgehead function were favorable factors only at first glance. It was the case that after a difficult initial period, the French comrades did facilitate the GDR's efforts to build a wide communication network from the end of the 1950s onward. Party, union, and friendship societies were always the first partners addressed. Yet, a lack of coordination of international and working class demands and national interests made the relations between the SED and PCF into a high-wire act, leading to repeated falls as in the months of the Prague Spring, for example. Because the GDR showed little flexibility as an exemplar of the communist camp, similarities in worldview were overshadowed by power-political differences and made relations with the PCF into a tense aspect of its Western policy.

The noncommunist leftist milieu in France also offered the GDR possibilities. Many saw the existence of the GDR as a guarantor of European security and freedom and also embraced East German cultural products with an astounding openness. Additional impetus was provided by the French Socialists' distrust of the West German Social Democrats. Yet even while crumbs falling from the table were snatched up by the GDR as confirmation of its policies, the repressive domestic policy of the SED prevented further successes.

In the phase of "zero relations" on the diplomatic level, the SED focused on relations between the largely state-dominated society it had created and the whole breadth of French civil society. It sought to politicize these relations in order to make use of their potential in the movement for recognition and increase the "pressure for recognition" on the French government. After it had shut down to the greatest extent possible all domestic civil society initiatives with their interactive or communicative character so as to achieve its monopoly on power, the GDR had to present itself as a communicating society in order to bring dynamism to its recognition policy and its image campaigns. It sought to achieve this goal via a façade of a civil society and therefore did not fully refuse societal encounters beyond the Iron Curtain. For better or worse, the East German leaders felt compelled to open up gaps for communication in the "antifascist protection wall," ones that did not eliminate the SED's monopoly on information but that did create a limited and modest public space. The network of relations that had meanwhile come into existence between the GDR and France meant that the contacts reaching beyond the systems became a balancing act between closure and openness after diplomatic recognition. The outcome of this balancing act was at that time still open.

The Official Triangular Relationship, 1973–90

With Europe as the main concern of French foreign policy and Franco–West German relations as a stabilizing and driving axis, there was little room left for the GDR. The leaders in East Berlin hoped for positive effects on their own position in the international structure stemming from de Gaulle's ambitious formulation of a Europe "from the Atlantic to the Urals" and also from the often pragmatic Eastern policy of his successors. Yet, throughout its entire existence, the GDR repeatedly had to recognize that the visionary goals for overcoming the bipolar world order remained mostly rhetoric unsupported by action that was not of value for weakening the West or for achieving breakthroughs in the competition between the two Germans states. Although it was constantly part of the repertoire of GDR French policy to sow discord between Paris and Bonn and to conjure up old demons and threatening scenarios, the relationship between France and West Germany was dominated by common interests in securing peace over potential national rivalries. This left the GDR with hardly any opportunity to put itself between the two partners. Moreover, despite all their conflicting interests and temporary disturbances in their relations, the economic power of the Federal Republic and the political leadership of France bound the two states together as complements of one another. The acceptance of this division of labor from the 1970s onward allowed the French to play the leadership role in the European Community, while the West Germans were to a great extent willing to forget, with the help of their neighbors to the west, the fact that theirs was a state of limited sovereignty within a divided nation.[15]

On this basis, France could develop its relations with the GDR on an official level after 1973–74 and to a greater extent after 1980–81. With a broader Franco–West German consensus than had existed in the 1960s, it was now possible to develop more expansive political contacts between France and the other Germany. Given the intensification of the "other" Franco-German relationship, the Federal Republic came to see itself in a German-German competition on French soil and so took measures to ensure that the GDR did not appear as an equally ranked German state. The relatively relaxed response of the Bonn leadership in this situation and the lack of an uproar in public opinion pointed to an increased self-confidence and a transformation of mentality in the Federal Republic. For the overwhelming majority of its citizens, the GDR was a negative factor whose existence had an affirmative and stabilizing effect on the "Bonn Republic."[16] Just as the governments in Paris and Bonn had become convinced that economic productivity and social consensus could only be achieved on the basis of the Common Market with the decisive leadership of the Franco–West German motor, so too had the certainty increased among the populace of the FRG that its political and cultural present and future could only lie in the West. Conversely, in relations between the two German states, contacts dwindled. At the same time, the East German populace fixed its gaze ever more strongly on the West due to frustrations over the unsatisfactory supply of consumer goods.

Both France and the Federal Republic had accustomed themselves in neighborly fashion to this balance by the time demonstrators began marching in East Berlin, Leipzig, and Dresden. The people in the streets sounded the death knell of SED dominance with their slogan "We Are the People" and the national variant "We Are One People," raising the German question once again, a question that seemed to have already been answered. In light of this unexpected development, the heretofore solid Franco–West German relationship became unfixed in the short term and confronted Paris with the challenge of directing relations between the two states into a new and sustainable system based on eventual equality of international legal status for the two states. François Mitterrand's answer was shaped by history and served to lengthen the thread of French policy on Germany even beyond the epochal boundary of 1989–90, as the network of connections of the Franco-German partners further intensified in terms of both Western and European integration policies. Thus, over the forty years of its existence, the GDR remained a stimulating element in the relationship between France and the Federal Republic because each of them pursued contrary interests vis-à-vis the East German state and having overriding motivations, sought to bring them into harmony: Because East Berlin attempted to exploit every sign of diverging interests and the Franco-German partners needed to work together in many fields, the reality of the East German state compelled them both to reach a close, permanent agreement that gave rise to a catalyzing effect. This needed to be redefined by France and the unified Germany after 1989–90.[17]

After official recognition in 1973, the SED had wrongly believed it had reached its goal and regarded the status quo in the German question as having been irrevocably secured. Its constructive participation in various international organizations[18] and the routine that came to characterize Franco–East German relations meant for an increasing stature and gave the GDR the appearance of normality on the international stage. In order to preserve this and further expand its range of action in foreign policy, the SED attempted—while maintaining a fundamental tendency toward reducing political tensions—to profit from the political and economic advantages of its Western contacts in order to shift the international balance of power in favor of the socialist states over the long term.[19] The successful implementation of this goal depended primarily on two factors: First, the GDR had to preserve its political and economic weight and, better yet, increase it so as to demonstrate in the West that it was an indispensable negotiating partner. Second, it had to resolve conclusively the dialectic of allowing as little openness as necessary and as much closure as possible vis-à-vis both the outside world and the East German populace if this policy was not to be turned against the regime on both levels.

While erosion had already set in behind a seemingly stable façade, Erich Honecker interpreted the willingness of politicians such as Mitterrand to engage in bilateral conversations at the highest level and the diplomatic conventions of the resulting press communiqués (disappointing the French communists) as the expression of the GDR's increasing weight. At the end of the Honecker era, the diplomatic successes of the GDR, manifesting themselves as Pyrrhic victories, numbed the sense of reality among the leadership of party and state, who had lost their ability to sense societal processes and international developments due to their monopolization of decision-making authority. Since every attempt to change the system called into question the unity of the party and society, the various warning signs were no longer in the leadership's field of vision. Nor was there any longer any impetus for correction coming from the centralized state organs or the mass organizations, because regulating mechanisms and the ability to diagnose errors had deteriorated under the SED regime.

In what amounted to a new cult of personality, reports of meetings with Western politicians made most members of the Politburo believe that the state leadership's prestigious trips to the West with their rituals of politeness and esteem stemming from diplomatic protocol served to increase the internal acceptance of the regime or would distract the populace from economic and societal deficiencies then coming to a crisis. The targeted use of symbols paired with domestic repression and the SED's belief in the future, to which it clung until the very end, all served to deceive Western observers as to the actual condition of the SED state. The fiction of its stability was wiped away in the autumn of 1989 by demonstrators.

The courageous stand taken by those demonstrators against a leadership unwilling to embrace reform was the final piece of evidence that the SED's high-wire act between openness and closure had failed. How was the SED to explain to its citizens on an ongoing basis that while its leading politicians were regular guests in Western capitals, those same citizens were hindered from making similar journeys by an insurmountable wall? How were they to maintain the image of the West as the enemy when Honecker and Mitterrand greeted one another amicably? How could they legitimize their policy of dissociation when they reprinted in their own press quotations from well-known French politicians who concurred with East German government policies? The SED saw an answer to all this in the expansion of the state security apparatus in the wake of international recognition so as to counter "political-ideological diversion by opponents."[20] However, given the freer flow of information and the increasing number of contacts with the West, the Ministry for State Security could in most cases only react or simply record its observations in innumerable reports.

The field of societal relations between the GDR and France demonstrates how foreign policy successes—such as diplomatic recognition in 1973, the Final Act of the Conference on Security and Cooperation in Europe in 1975, the cultural agreement with France in 1980—became a new burden for the SED in the medium term and further intensified its legitimation deficit. Whereas the state party understood the signing of international agreements as obvious for solidifying its external and internal position, it underestimated the new obligations and expectations that this "growing up" brought with it. As an equal member of the international community, it now had to accept reciprocal cultural and societal exchanges along with mutual transnational relations. In its Potemkin villages, the

SED regime had robbed itself of a societal "early-warning system" and of the ability for self-observation such that the party and the Western public perceived apparent foreign policy successes as a sign of further ability to function—a view that went unchallenged—and they did not register how, among other things, relations with France allowed the internal hollowing out to proceed uninterrupted and finally seal the internal dissolution.

On November 10, 1989, the head of the French Communist Party, Georges Marchais, promised his "comrade" Egon Krenz the full support of his party on the "voie du renouveau" (path of renewal) and saw in the expected new beginning the only feasible way forward for socialism.[21] This hope proved illusory as the attractiveness of the oppositional model offered by the Federal Republic permanently raised the pressure for unification, and the SED leadership was forced to recognize that even dictatorships could not maintain themselves with the "loyal unwillingness" of their citizens but needed a minimum level of belief in their legitimacy, loyal assent, and active participation.

Notes

1. Lutz Rathenow, "Die süßeste Versuchung, seit es Klassenfeinde gibt. Gedanken zum 40. Jahrestag des deutsch-französischen Freundschaftsvertrages," *Berliner Morgenpost*, January 22, 2003.

2. Edgar Wolfrum, "Wo ist der Ort der DDR in den deutsch-französischen Beziehungen? —Plädoyer für neue Forschungsaktivitäten," *Dokumente* 56, no. 1 (2000): 19.

3. Cf. Ulrich Pfeil, *Die "anderen" deutsch-französischen Beziehungen. Die DDR und Frankreich 1949–1990* (Köln: Böhlau, 2004).

4. Waltraud Böhme et al., eds., *Kleines politisches Wörterbuch*, 5th ed. (Berlin, Ost: Dietz, 1985), 104.

5. Cf. Arnd Bauerkämper et al., eds., *Doppelte Zeitgeschichte. Deutsch-deutsche Beziehungen 1945–1990* (Bonn: Dietz, 1998), 9ff.

6. Cf. Michael Lemke, *Einheit oder Sozialismus? Die Deutschlandpolitik der SED 1949–1961* (Köln: Böhlau, 2001), 514.

7. Cf. Ernst Richert, "Zwischen Eigenständigkeit und Dependenz. Zur Wechselwirkung von Gesellschafts- und Außenpolitik in der DDR," *Deutschland Archiv* 7, no. 9 (1974): 955–82.

8. Cf. Alain Peyrefitte, *C'était de Gaulle. La France reprend sa place dans le monde* (Paris: Editions de Fallois, 1997), 276.

9. Cf. Andreas Wilkens, *Der unstete Nachbar. Frankreich, die deutsche Ostpolitik und die Berliner Vier-Mächte-Verhandlungen 1969–1974* (München: Oldenbourg 1990); idem., "Accords et désaccords. La France, l'*Ostpolitik* et la question allemande 1969–1974," in *La RDA et l'Occident (1949–1990)*, ed. Ulrich Pfeil (Asnières: PIA, 2000), 357–78.

10. Cf. Corine Defrance and Ulrich Pfeil, eds., *Der Elysée-Vertrag und die deutsch-französischen Beziehungen 1945 – 1963 – 2003* (München: Oldenbourg, 2005).

11. Cf. Werner Link: "Die Entstehung des Moskauer Vertrages im Lichte neuer Archivalien," *Vierteljahrshefte für Zeitgeschichte 49*, no. 2 (2001): 295–316.

12. Cf. Ulrich Pfeil, "Die deutsche Zweistaatlichkeit in westlicher Perzeption—das Beispiel Frankreich," in *Deutsche Zeitgeschichte von 1945 bis 2000. Gesellschaft*

– *Politik – Geschichte. Ein Handbuch*, eds. Clemens Burrichter et al. (Berlin: Dietz, 2006), 216–51.

13. Cf. "Bericht über die Beziehungen der DDR zu den westeuropäischen Ländern im IV. Quartal 1956," Politisches Archiv des Auswärtigen Amts, Bestand Ministerium für Auswärtige Angelegenheiten, A 630, Bl. 74–76.

14. Cf. Ulrich Pfeil, "Antifascisme et dénazification en zone d'occupation soviétique (SBZ) 1945–1948," *Revue d'Allemagne et des pays de langue allemande* 32, no. 1 (2000):101–15; Henry Leide, *NS-Verbrecher und Staatssicherheit. Die geheime Vergangenheitspolitik der DDR*, 2nd. ed. (Göttingen: Vandenhoeck & Ruprecht, 2006).

15. Cf. Valérie-Barbara Rosoux, *Les usages de la mémoire dans les relations internationales. Le recours au passé dans la politique étrangère de la France à l'égard de l'Allemagne et de l'Algérie, de 1962 à nos jours* (Brussels: Bruylant, 2001), 64.

16. Cf. Christoph Kleßmann, *Die doppelte Staatsgründung. Deutsche Geschichte 1945–1955*, 5th ed. (Göttingen: Vandenhoeck & Ruprecht, 1991), 256ff.

17. Cf. Wichard Woyke, *Deutsch-französische Beziehungen seit der Wiedervereinigung. Das Tandem faßt wieder Tritt* (Opladen: Leske und Budrich, 2000).

18. Cf. Benno-Eide Siebs, *Die Außenpolitik der DDR 1976–1989* (Paderborn: Schöningh, 1999), 392.

19. Ibid., 417.

20. Cf. Clemens Vollnhals, "Denunziation und Strafverfolgung im Auftrag der 'Partei'. Das Ministerium für Staatssicherheit," in *Der Schein der Normalität. Alltag und Herrschaft in der SED-Diktatur*, eds. Clemens Vollnhals and Jürgen Weber (München: Olzog, 2002), 113–56.

21. Georges Marchais à Egon Krenz, 10 novembre 1989; Stiftung Archiv der Parteien und Massenorganisationen der DDR im Bundesarchiv, DY 30/IV 2/2.039/327, Bl. 11.

CHAPTER 21

The Franco-German-Polish Weimar Triangle

A Strategic Instrument of Franco-German Relations

Wolfram Vogel

Introduction

The notion of a triangle to describe the structure of cooperation between France, Germany, and Poland has never been adequate. It implies, at least theoretically, the equal importance of the three partners involved and some kind of interdependence; any bilateral action would have an impact on the third member. None of these assumptions hold true for the Weimar Triangle, and yet the concept figures whenever Poland is associated with the Franco-German couple.

This chapter will argue that the Weimar Triangle can be conceptualized as a strategic instrument of Franco-German relations. Created in 1991, and henceforth vaguely referred to as a "forum of dialogue" or "forum of consultation," the basic idea was to help Poland on its way back into the European family. The notion of a "triangle" was strategically helpful in making Poland feel an equal partner of France and Germany, although this has in fact never been the case. In order to better understand the motives of the Triangle's foundation, it is necessary to look at the historical determinants of each of the three bilateral relationships. They have each developed a path dependency of their own that continues to influence the power relationship within the Triangle today. At the same time, the profound change in the European environment challenges the Weimar Triangle in that it highlights both its potential and limits.

Historical Determinants

Franco-German Bilateralism

For every political scientist working on European integration, the fact that France and Germany have played a key role in the process of European integration has become virtually self-evident. Whether or not they will continue to do so is quite another question to which I will return later on.[1]

The Schuman Plan, announcing the foundation of the European Coal and Steel Community on May 9, 1950, can be seen as the mobilizing factor in the process of Franco-German reconciliation and laid the groundwork for genuine partnership. Of course, France's hidden agenda was not only to control Germany politically and to profit from its economic resources but also to set the agenda on European construction. For Germany, the close ties to France were intended to pave the way back into the European family as an equal partner. Henceforth, Franco-German cooperation and progress in European integration would be intrinsically linked.

The period of reconciliation between France and Germany culminated symbolically in the Elysée Treaty, signed in 1963. The treaty thus marked an important milestone at the end of a process of rapprochement. It solemnly sealed Franco-German partnership and inaugurated another process that now, after half a century, has become a kind of "hereditary amity."

The period that began after the ratification of the treaty can be described as the period of institutionalized cooperation. When saying that the Franco-German relationship became institutionalized, it is important to consider that there is no single form of bilateral relationship today but rather a series of multi-layered relationships[2]—on a bilateral basis and within multilateral structures such as the European Council, the G8 and the International Monetary Fund; also party contacts, albeit informal, within the European Party system. In effect, the relationship benefits from closely knit ties that are unknown in any other bilateral relationship within the European Union (EU).

Considering political institutional visibility, it can be said that the summit mechanism has produced remarkable effects. On both sides, the mere existence of the treaty created expectations of cooperation, which have regularly been fulfilled by the political actors. The sequential organization of the summits—replaced by joint Councils of ministers in 2003—established a mechanism of consultation that required regular cooperation between German and French civil servants.[3] The French term *concertation* is actually more precise in denoting what takes place on both sides before a summit. The pressure to find an agreement on the important issues at stake has become a guarantee of success. This, in turn, has created confidence. For both countries the burden of common history turned out to be a decisive factor in the development of consciousness of their special responsibility for Europe. Wherever possible, political actors looked for common ground to build upon. Of course, this rationale hinged upon other factors, too, such as the personal chemistry between the heads of government, and also upon the policy area concerned. Thus, cooperation was strong in the preparation for European Monetary Union that laid the basis for the Maastricht Treaty or, during the European Convention between 2002 and 2003, when both countries presented common propositions on the Constitutional Treaty, or in 2007 when they showed particular commitment in adopting the simplified treaty on the EU level.

The productive handling of divergence testified to a willingness in both countries to compromise, which turned out to be efficient for the process of European integration. It showed that the Franco-German couple was capable of political leadership. However, the two governments' ability to handle controversies and to bring about compromise has been put to the test over and over again. It is precisely because French and German starting positions have been frequently far removed from one another that the cooperation of both states has played a key role in the progress of European integration. Whenever France and Germany developed a common line, it was easier for the other European member states to follow suit. The mere fact that current issues in European integration are to a large extent an object of Franco-German divergence does not mean that both countries have lost their ability to find compromises. France and Germany both see their relationship as an instrument to bind each other, but are also conscious of its importance as a "motor" of European integration—a firm and enduring conviction and some kind of functional myth in the European integration process.

German-Polish Bilateralism

Similarly to Franco-German relations, German-Polish relations also have a long tradition. Poland's situation was, however, entirely different: Its collective memory was forged by three partitions (in 1772, 1793, and 1795), the Hitler-Stalin Pact of 1939 and the fact that it lost its existence as an independent state at the end of the Second World War. The situation in 1945 was marked first by the fact that Poland and parts of former Germany became part of the interest zone of the Soviet Union and thus part of the Eastern bloc. Second, the situation was characterized by the emergence of two German states and the birth of the German question as an essential element of the cold war, branding the relations between the two Germanys and Poland. Following important initiatives in the 1960s by the Polish Catholic Church to further the process of rapprochement with the Federal Republic of Germany, Chancellor Willy Brandt's *Ostpolitik* opened up a new chapter of German foreign policy. He invested in negotiations with the Soviet Union as the dominant power of the Eastern bloc and finally achieved improved relations not only with the Soviet Union but also with Poland. The signing of the German-Polish Treaty—known as the Treaty of Warsaw—in December 1970, acknowledging the Oder-Neisse line as the Western border of Poland, was the most important element of the improved relations. The treaty's greatest shortcoming was that it was meant to uphold the status quo of that time and did not contain any provisions for German reunification. The whole border question had therefore to be addressed again in the course of German reunification between 1989 and 1990.

Real reconciliation work began in the following years. Copying the Franco-German model, a German-Polish Youth Office was founded to shore up political rapprochement from the civil society side. However, a few issues remained unresolved: the dispossession of ethnic Germans after their expulsion in 1945, the Polish restitution of cultural goods and the new discussion among the expellees in Germany, about how (and where) their fate in 1945 should be commemorated, in Polish eyes, a discussion that aimed to rewrite history in order to depict Germany, too, as a victim of World War II. In no other bilateral relationship is history such powerful a part of daily politics as in the German-Polish case, and it continues to be so.

When German unification became increasingly realistic, the Polish Government wanted to be assured of its Western borders. On November 11, 1990, both governments signed a border treaty in Warsaw recognizing the Oder-Neisse line forever as the permanent German eastern border, putting a legal and political end to any territorial "claims" that were lurking beneath the surface of the German-Polish relationship. Having managed this, the relationship had to be formalized on an official basis. The answer was the "treaty between Germany and Poland for good neighborhood and friendly cooperation," signed on June 17, 1991.

Since rapprochement at the beginning of the 1990s, Poland has had an ambivalent relationship with Germany. German economic strength, in terms of exportation and crossborder commerce, is seen as useful for Poland's own economic development, while at the same time being perceived as a threat. Germany's political influence in Europe is considered helpful in supporting Polish integration into the West; on the other hand, Poland fears any kind of German dominance.

Franco-Polish Bilateralism

The relationship between France and Poland is in so far exceptional as the two countries have never gone to war with one another. France embarked upon its special relationship with Poland in the sixteenth century, when Henry de Valois saw cooperation with Poland as an effective way of encircling the Holy Roman Empire of the German Nation. The Franco-Polish alliance was finally sealed in the eighteenth century when Louis XV wedded Marie Leszczynska, daughter of the Polish King Stanislas Leszczynski. The image of Napoleon—cited in the Polish national anthem—is part of the romantic mythology of long-standing relations. Another important aspect in Franco-Polish relations was the continuous waves of migrations from Poland to France in the nineteenth and early twentieth centuries: intellectuals, artists, musicians, and researchers, as well as miners and other workers. These multilayered exchanges over centuries formed the backdrop for the image of a common cultural base that underlies the Franco-Polish relationship—and they laid the basis for the legend that there was in fact a common cultural ground.[4]

However, the decades after 1945 were years characterized by benign neglect, which had begun already in 1939, when France did not meet its security guarantee toward Poland. Another disappointment followed when France, as the first Western country, acknowledged the Lublin committee in 1944 and deepened the special interest it was developing for the Soviet Union. Striving for nuclear power status and as part of the winning coalition in 1945, France defined itself as equal to the other Great powers of that time, the United States and the Soviet Union. Generally speaking, after 1945, French policy toward Eastern Europe was predominantly oriented toward the Soviet Union.

Since the sixteenth century, one of the main fundaments of Franco-Polish relations had been mutual support in resisting the "German danger." After 1945, however, Germany was geographically diminished. Furthermore, West Germany and France succeeded in achieving reconciliation, an entirely new phenomenon. These factors explain why Poland has become less important for France's security needs.

However, it was in the basic interest of the French government to ensure that Germany accepted the losses of prewar German lands as a given and unchangeable fact. From a psychological point of view, this was essential for France, as border issues along the Rhine had caused a lot of bloodshed between the two neighbors. From this, one can determine another main feature of Franco-Polish relations: from the outset, mutual support against the possibility of German hegemonic policy in the East and in the West played a key role.

Slight but interesting changes in the Franco-Polish relationship took place after 1989. After German unification, France and Poland rediscovered their "traditionally close" relationship—if imagined or real is of minor significance—when the former supported the latter in its wish to participate in the so-called "2+4" talks concerning the border question and Germany's sovereignty. Even if Poland did not actively participate in these talks, it revealed once again the Franco-Polish reflex of mutual assistance when Germany was involved. The rediscovery of the relationship was formalized in April 1991, when a "Treaty of Friendship and Solidarity" was signed, intended as a "framework of political, economic, financial, cultural and educational cooperation." However, neither this treaty nor its German-Polish equivalent signed two months later contained the same kind of mutual obligation to consult each other on a regular basis and to cooperate when necessary, as did the requirements of the Elysée Treaty.

Aims and Motives of the Weimar Triangle

It is against this background that the trilateral relationship will have to be judged in the future. The Weimar Triangle was founded on August 28, 1991 on the initiative of the three ministers for foreign affairs Hans-Dietrich Genscher (Germany), Roland Dumas (France) and Krzysztof Skubiszewski (Poland). The order of appearance of the names is by no means coincidental, as the role of the driving force is attributed to Hans-Dietrich Genscher. Weimar was chosen—on Goethe's birthday—as it is associated not only with German literature but also with the nearby concentration camp Buchenwald. Weimar was seen as "an expression of historical responsibility emanating from recent European—and that means Franco-German and German-Polish—history."[5]

In the Common Declaration, which mirrored the principal outlines of the bilateral treaties that had been passed earlier, the three ministers emphasized the "binding responsibility" of Poland, Germany and France to succeed in establishing structures that would further European neighborhood. They upheld the role of the European Community (EC) for peace, democracy, and stability on the European continent; at the same time they acknowledged the "transatlantic dimension" and the explicit role of NATO and the WEU with regard to European security.[6]

Several motives can be isolated when taking a closer look at the inception of the Triangle. First, the prevailing idea was to transfer the successful model of Franco-German reconciliation to the German-Polish relationship. The experience France and Germany had gained in settling their conflicts, regaining confidence in each other and building up closely knit consultation structures was to be used in the German-Polish dialogue. This idea was more alive at the beginning than it is today, above all in the minds of the pro-European Polish elites, who frequently referred to the notion of a "model," and it was in the interest of the French and German governments to support this idea without insisting on it themselves.[7]

A second motive can be seen in the idea that by linking Poland to the Franco-German tandem, the division of the European continent, a throwback to the cold war, would be overcome symbolically: "France and Germany support all efforts to approach Poland and the new democracies to the European Community," the declaration says. By assigning this particular role to Poland, because of its geographic and demographic size and its painful history, the three "cultural archetypes" of the European continent—the Latin, the Germanic, and the Slavic element—were to be represented.[8]

Finally, the entire issue of security and stability on the European continent after the breakup of the Warsaw Pact was a driving force in establishing close ties to the biggest of all the Central and Eastern European countries. "Stability exportation or instability importation" was an expression used at the time.

The Strategic Interests of the Partners

Germany in particular was aware of the security aspect, as German reunification had a considerable geopolitical impact on the European continent. The German-Polish frontier became the new external border of the EC, which on the one hand automatically meant a new role for Germany with regard to the Central and Eastern European countries. On the other hand, it foreshadowed a changing power relationship between France and Germany. For Germany, the Weimar Triangle served as an instrument for reassuring France that Germany would not "drift to the East" and evoked the *incertitudes allemandes* that could be read about in the French press at that time. By considering France before going to Poland, Germany provided itself with the legitimacy it needed to reestablish the ties to Poland it had already had before in the economic sector and to intensify them on the bases of democracy and free-market economy. For Germany, the Weimar Triangle was the ideal framework to actively foster the discussions on enlargement of the EC that had already begun, for it was also in 1991 that the EC made the first cooperation agreements with Central and East European countries, after Mitterrand's Confederation plans (which did not aim at accession) failed in the face of strong resistance from Germany and the United States. Intrinsically linked to the question of the future status of the Central and East European countries was the hope that within the Weimar Triangle, France would more easily be convinced to show commitment and support for the reform processes in Eastern Europe and finally agree upon the necessity of enlargement.

For two reasons, France did not initially really consider the Weimar Triangle to be a platform for French support of political transformation in Eastern Europe. First, France's stance toward EC expansion was to a large extent a reaction to the German stance on EC expansion. Hubert Védrine, chief diplomatic advisor to François Mitterrand (and minister of foreign affairs 1997–2002) notes that the relations between the EC and the Central and East European countries aspiring to accession were marked by "demagogic support and precipitation of Germany vis-à-vis that region."[9] Second, France did not have a proper concept of a policy toward Eastern Europe encompassing the space between Germany and the Soviet Union. The Weimar Triangle provided France with the opportunity to control Germany's eastern European policy, to counterbalance the firm positions of the latter and "to prevent a German-Polish drift toward Central Europe."[10] Regular consultations with Poland became essential from the security policy angle, while economic reasons were less dominant. On security issues, French and Polish interests converged. In essence, France could use the Triangle to be present in the region without showing too much commitment.

Poland had the strongest interests in the Weimar Triangle. To be associated to the two biggest nations of the EC, to the couple which set the agenda for European integration, was more than an act of reverence, and hence was bound to create satisfaction and suspicion at the same time. Fears of an overtly dominant (and just unified) Germany were still present, and the fact that France was part of the game was a reassuring sign. The Weimar Triangle was thus a good means of managing the asymmetric power relationship between each of the three bilateral relationships. In the long run, Poland aspired to attain the same level of intense relations to Germany as France had achieved, in order to rebalance the existing disequilibrium.

A crucial aspect for Poland was France's hesitation in terms of EU enlargement. It was hoped that the Triangle would help to elicit French support for Poland's accession to the European Union (EU), German support having been given from the beginning. Almost by tradition, the road to EU membership passes through

Table 1 Interest dimensions within the Weimar Triangle

Interest dimension	France	Germany	Poland
Security	Control of Germany's Eastern policy	Politics of stabilization at its Eastern borders	Integration into the West
Economic	New commodity markets and capital investment in Eastern Europe	New commodity markets and capital investment in Eastern Europe; cross-border cooperation	New commodity markets and capital investment in Western Europe; cross-border cooperation
Historical	Prevention of German hegemony in Eastern Europe	Meeting security concerns of France and Poland	Prevention of German hegemony in Eastern Europe

NATO, as was the case with Germany, Spain or Rumania. Poland finally became member of NATO in 1999, an almost logical consequence of the breakup of the Warsaw Pact and a Russian neighbor that had never hidden "national" interests in the Eastern European courtyard. Finally, from the Polish perspective the Triangle could enable the reestablishment of contacts between Polish and French society. The French intellectuals' sympathy for *Solidarność* during the 1980s was helpful in this respect.

To sum up schematically, the strategic interests of the three countries had a security dimension, an economic dimension and a historical dimension (see Table 1).

A New Engine for the Enlarged European Union?

On balance, the annual meetings of the ministers of foreign affairs and the irregular meetings of the heads of state and government[11] that have taken place since 1991 have produced little output. If this output is to be measured by visible progress in deepening European integration or in solving European conflicts, then this often heard reproach is justified. However, as the Weimar constellation considers itself to be a forum of dialogue, exchange, and consultation, the claim is somewhat harsh. The Triangle's lack of institutionalization in a narrow sense is not seen as a problem but as an asset. Part of the analytical problem of what the Triangle can do today is the underlying idea of what it should be, yet it has never defined exactly what it is itself. Until the accession of Poland to NATO, the issues at stake concerned to a large extent Poland itself or the status of the preparations for negotiating accession of the Central and East European States, although Poland's accession to both NATO and the EU would have taken place without the Triangle, too.

Thus one may wonder why some analysts argue that the Weimar Triangle will become the engine of the enlarged EU.[12] The line of reasoning frequently goes as follows: the Franco-German couple alone is no longer capable of playing this role and making propositions that will convince the rest of the EU. In merely arithmetical terms, a bilateral relationship in the EU of nine, twelve or fifteen states was bound to have more influence than in an EU of twenty-five and more member states. As the EU is expanding to the East and Poland is geographically and demographically the biggest of the new member states, it is quite naturally the country to be attached to the Franco-German engine.

It is at this point that the historical determinants have to be recalled. On the fortieth anniversary of the Elysée Treaty, in January 2003, the French and German governments passed a Common Declaration that said (amongst other things) that France and Germany offered Eastern European countries a common vision of tomorrow's Europe and a privileged partnership for those countries striving for accession.[13] From a discursive point of view, it is a first sign of their consciousness that the EU would soon have twenty-five members, a fact that would certainly lead to the modification of their own vision of Europe. At the same time, France and Germany established their common position on the war in Iraq without consultation of their European partners, looking instead for an alliance with Russia. In so doing, the "axis Paris-Berlin-Moscow" was resuscitated, a dreadful notion for all Poles, who were reminded of the 1930s.[14] When at the end of 2003, France and Germany put pressure on Poland (and Spain) to ratify the European Constitutional Treaty, warning of a "two-speed Europe," the insinuation of good Europeans and bad Europeans stung. In 2006, as the EU experienced a major crisis with public support waning and the constitutional question remaining unsolved, Germany and France decided to put forward propositions for solving Europe's constitutional problem by virtue of their respective EU presidencies in 2007 and 2008—irrespective of the negative outcome of the referendum on the Constitutional Treaty in France.

These examples illustrate two things. First, the Weimar Triangle could not prevent any of the crises cited. During those crises none of the partners thought of using the triangular platform at any point nor could the triangle put forward any solutions.[15] Second, the Franco-German relationship is still the dominant axis. More precisely, Franco-German behavior on the European level ultimately reflects the attempt to justify the further existence of a special Franco-German relationship in the EU-27. This special relationship has frequently been counter-productive and has produced accusations of Franco-German hegemony in Europe.

However, it seems that France and Germany have learnt from this experience. At the Weimar Triangle summit in December 2006, it was decided to deal with specific subjects, such as organized crime, demographic, change or migration, at each of the meetings. The hard issues at stake for Europe's future—Constitutional Treaty, energy policy, European Neighborhood policy—were not on the official agenda. Instead, it was decided to create a "Weimar Battle Group" by 2012 and to expand the Franco-German exchange of ministerial civil servants to include the Polish counterparts.[16] This shows that it is possible to obtain fruitful results when the idea of the "motor of an enlarged EU" is jettisoned.

In 1991, the Franco-German couple had a hidden agenda. Fundamentally, the creation of the Weimar Triangle helped to underpin the central role of Franco-German bilateralism in its claim to shape the process of European integration and set the agenda for decisions to be taken in the future, even if the actual agenda-setting capacity would turn out to be much weaker than they had hoped. To this extent, the Weimar Triangle served as strategic instrument of Franco-German relations. The continuing existence of the Triangle in the EU-27 ultimately reflects the continuing importance of the Franco-German couple.

Notes

1. Cf. Wolfram Vogel, "Die deutsch-französischen Beziehungen," in *Länderbericht Frankreich. Geschichte, Politik, Wirtschaft, Gesellschaft*, ed. Adolf Kimmel and Henrik Uterwedde, 2d ed. (Wiesbaden: VS Verlag, 2005), 418–35.

2. Alistair Cole, *Franco-German Relations* (London: Longman, 2001), 47.

3. Cf. the stringent analysis by Louis Savadogo, "Quelques observations sur le Conseil des ministres franco-allemand," *Revue française de droit constitutionnel* 67 (2006), 571–83.

4. Cf. Artur Borzeda, "Les relations franco-polonaises. Poids de l'histoire et réalités économiques," *Documents* (Winter 2001–2), 48–53; Michaélstrike; Warchala, *Les Polonais et les Français. Leur image réciproque après l'adhésion à l'UE* (Warsaw: Fundacja Instytut Spraw Publicznych, 2006), 9–11.

5. Hans-Dietrich Genscher, "Europa in einer neuen Weltordnung: Fragen an Paris und Bonn," in *Der Elysée-Vertrag und die deutsch-französischen Beziehungen: 1945–1963–2003*, ed. Corine Defrance and Ulrich Pfeil (München: Oldenburg, 2005), 269.

6. Cf. *Bulletin des Presse- und Informationsamtes der Bundesregierung*, no. 92 (1991): 735–37.

7. Cf. Krzysztof Skubiszewski, "La coopération franco-allemande: Un modèle pour la Pologne et l'Europe centrale?" *Documents*, no. 1 (1993): 8–12; Adam Krzeminski, "Der polnische Blick auf Deutschland und Frankreich," in *Erbfreunde. Deutschland und Frankreich im 21. Jahrhundert*, ed. Wolfgang Bergsdorf, Manuela Spindler, and Wolfram Vogel (Weimar: Verlag der Bauhaus-Universität Weimar, 2007), 25. For theoretical discussion cf. Wolfram Vogel, "Le couple franco-allemand: un modèle pour les autres? Une esquisse de recherche," *Allemagne Aujourd'hui* (mai 2006), 82–91.

8. Cf. Ludger Kühnhardt, Henri Ménudier, and Janusz Reiter, *Das Weimarer Dreieck–Die französisch-deutsch-polnischen Beziehungen als Motor der Europäischen Integration*, ZEI Discussion Paper C72, Bonn 2000, 33.

9. Quoted in Jean-François Daguzan, "Les intérêts français et européens en Méditerranée comparés à ceux d'Europe centrale et orientale," in *A Balanced European Architecture*, ed. Hartmut Elsenhans (Paris: Publisud, 1999), 63.

10. Ingo Kolboom, "Polen: eine deutsch-französische Annäherung in Mitteleuropa," *Politische Studien* 52, no. 376 (March–April 2001): 57.

11. The first meeting took place on September 21, 1993 in Gdansk (PL), the second took place almost five years later, on February 21, 1998 in Poznan (PL); others followed on July 7, 1999 in Nancy (F); February 27, 2001 in Neustadt an der Weinstraße (D); May 9, 2003 in Wroclaw (PL); May 19, 2005 in Nancy (F) and on December 5, 2006 in Mettlach/Sarre (D).

12. Kühnhardt, Ménudier, and Reiter, *Das Weimarer Dreieck*.

13. See declaration commune franco-allemande à l'occasion du 40ème anniversaire du traité de l'Elysée, http://www.diplomatie.gov.fr/fr/article-imprim.php3?id _article=28890.

14. In the aftermath, Poland and other East European countries witnessed their allegiance to the United States as principle guarantor of security. It was returned by President Chirac's insult that they had missed a good opportunity to hold their tongue. See Henri Froment-Meurice, "Contre l'idée d'un 'axe' Paris-Berlin-Moscou," *Commentaire*, no. 111 (Automne 2005): 679–82.

15. However, the format is used by the planning staff of the ministries of foreign affairs and the governmental departments of the three countries, albeit on an irregular and informal basis and as a closed shop. And still, any trilateral meeting is preceded by bilateral consultations.

16. The corresponding Declaration as well as others can be found on the Web site http://www.weimarer-dreieck.com.

Abbreviations

ABC-weapons	Atomic, bacteriological and chemical weapons
ARBED	Aciéries Réunies de Burbach-Eich-Dudelange
CAP	Common Agricultural Policy
CDU	Christlich Demokratische Union
CEA	Commissariat à l'Energie Atomique
CFSP	Common Foreign and Security Policy
CPSU	Communist Party of the Soviet Union
CSCE	Conference on Security and Cooperation in Europe
CSU	Christlich Soziale Union
DAZ	Deutsche Allgemeine Zeitung
DDP	Deutsche Demokratische Partei
DFG	Deutsch-französische Gesellschaft
DFR	Deutsch-französische Rundschau
EC	European Community
ECSC	European Coal and Steel Community
ECU	European Currency Unit
EDC	European Defense Community
EEC	European Economic Community
EFTA	European Free Trade Association
EMS	European Monetary System
EMU	Economic and Monetary Union
EPC	European Political Community
EU	European Union
EURATOM	European Atomic Energy Community (also EAEC)
FRG	Federal Republic of Germany
FZO	French Zone of Occupation
GATT	General Agreement on Tariffs and Trade
GDR	German Democratic Republic
IGC	Intergovernmental Conference
IMF	International Monetary Fund
JCS	Joint Chiefs of Staff
MLF	Multilateral Force

MRP	Mouvement Républicain Populaire
NATO	North Atlantic Treaty Organization
OAPEC	Organization of Arab Petroleum Exporting Countries
OEEC	Organization for European Economic Cooperation
PCF	Parti Communiste Français
PGFR	Provisional Government of the French Republic
PTBT	Partial Test Ban Treaty
RPF	Rassemblement du Peuple Français
SEA	Single European Act
SED	Sozialistische Einheitspartei Deutschlands
SFIO	Section Française de l'Internationale Ouvrière
SRNF	Short-Range Nuclear Forces
SPD	Sozialdemokratische Partei Deutschlands
UK	United Kingdom
UN	United Nations
U.S.	United States
USSR	Union of Socialist Soviet Republics
WEU	Western European Union

Selected Bibliography

Aaslestad, Katherine B. "Paying for War: Experiences of Napoleonic Rule in the Hanseatic Cities." *Central European History* 39 (2006): 641–75.

Adamthwaite, Anthony P. *France and the Coming of the Second World War, 1936–1939.* London: Cass, 1977.

———. *Grandeur and Misery: France's Bid for Power in Europe, 1914–1940.* London: St. Martin's Press, 1995.

Alistair, Cole. *Franco-German Relations.* Harlow: Pearson, 2001.

Blanning, Timothy C. W. *The French Revolution in Germany. Occupation and Resistance in the Rhineland, 1792–1802.* Oxford: Oxford University Press, 1983.

———. *The Pursuit of Glory: Europe 1648–1815.* New York: Viking, 2007.

Boissieu, Christian, and Hans Eckart Scharrer. "Accord and Conflict in French -German Monetary Cooperation." In *Motor für Europa? Deutsch-französischer Bilateralimus und europäische Integration,* edited by Robert Picht and Wolfgang Wessels, 187–209. Bonn: Europa Union Verlag, 1990.

Boquet, Dominique, and Quentin Peel. *The Future of the Franco-German Relationship. Three Views.* London: Royal Institute of International Affairs, 1997.

Burrin, Philippe. *France under the Germans: Collaboration and Compromise.* 2nd ed. New York: New Press, 1996.

———. *Living with Defeat: France under the German Occupation, 1940–1944.* London: Arnold, 1996.

Calleo, David. "France and Germany in the New Europe." In *SAIS Review* 13, no. 2 (Summer–Fall 1993): 25–39.

Calleo, David, and Eric Staal, eds. *Europe's Franco-German Engine,* Washington, DC: Brookings Inst. Press, 1998.

Campbell, Edwina S. "The Ideals and Origins of the Franco-German Sister cities Movement, 1945–1970." *History of the European Ideas* 8, no. 1 (1987): 77–95.

Cole, Alistair. *Franco-German Relations.* Harlow: Longman, 2001.

Craddock, Walter R. *The Saar Problem in Franco-German relations, 1945–1957.* Chapel Hill: University of North Carolina, 1961.

Deutsch, Karl et al. *France, Germany and the Western Alliance. A Study of Elite Attitudes on European Integration and World Politics.* New York: Scribner, 1967.

Farquharson, John E. *Europe from Below. An Assessment of Franco-German Popular Conducts.* London: Allan and Unwin, 1975.

Fischer, Conan. *The Ruhr Crisis, 1923–1924.* Oxford: Oxford University Press, 2003.

Freymond, Jacques. *The Saar Conflict 1945–1955.* New York: Praeger, 1960.

Friend, Julius W. *The Linchpin. French-German Relations 1950–1990.* New York: Praeger, 1991.

———. *Unequal Partners—French-German Relations 1989–2000.* New York: Praeger, 2001.

Fritsch-Bournazel, Renata. "German Unification: A Durability Test for the Franco -German Tandem." *German Studies Review* 14, no. 3 (October 1991): 575–85.

Fryer, W. R. "The Republic and the Iron Chancellor: The Pattern of Franco-German Relations, 1871–1890." *Transactions of the Royal Historical Society* 29, no. 5 (1979): 169–85.

———. "The War of 1870 in the Pattern of Franco-German Relations." *Renaissance and Modern Studies* 28 (1974): 77–125.

Fuller, Joseph V. "The War Scare of 1875." *The American Historical Review* 24, no. 2 (1919): 196–226.

Germond, Carine. "'A Cordial Potentiality?' Charles de Gaulle and the Franco-German Partnership, 1963–1969." In *International Perspectives on de Gaulle's Foreign Policies*, edited by Christian Nuenslist, Anna Lochner, and Garret Martin. Oxford: Rowman & Littlefield, 2009.

Giauque, Jeffrey Glenn. *Grand Designs and Visions of Unity: The Atlantic Powers and the Reorganization of Europe, 1955–1963.* Chapel Hill: University of North Carolina Press, 2002.

Gillingham, John. *Coal, Steel, and the Rebirth of Europe, 1945–1955: The Germans and French from Ruhr Conflict to Economic Community.* Cambridge: Cambridge University Press, 1991.

Gordon, Philip H. *France, Germany and the Western Alliance.* Boulder: Westview, 1995.

Granieri, Ronald J. *The Ambivalent Alliance: Konrad Adenauer, the CDU/CSU, and the West, 1949–1966.* Oxford and New York: Berghahn, 2003.

Greisman, Harvey Clark. "The Enemy Concept in Franco-German Relations, 1870–1914." *History of European Ideas* 19 (1994): 41–46.

Haftendorn, Helga et al., eds. *The Strategic Triangle: France, Germany, and the United States in the Shaping of the New Europe.* Washington and Baltimore: Woodrow Wilson Center Press and The Johns Hopkins University Press, 2006.

Hagemann, Karen. "Occupation, Mobilization, and Politics: The Anti-Napoleonic Wars in Prussian Experience, Memory, and Historiography." *Central European History* 39 (2006): 580–610.

Haglung, David G. *Alliance within the Alliance? Franco-German Military Cooperation and the European Pillar of Defence.* Boulder, CO: Westview, 1991.

Hendricks, Gisela, and Annette Morgan, eds. *The Franco-German Axis in European Integration.* Cheltenham, UK: Edward Elgar Publishing, 2001.

Hensel, Paul, R. "The Evolution of Franco-German Rivalry." In *Great Power Rivalry*, edited by William R. Thompson, 86–121. Columbia: University of South Carolina Press, 1999.

Hitchcock, William I. *France Restored. Cold War Diplomacy and the Quest for Leadership in Europe, 1944–1954.* Chapel Hill: The University of North Carolina Press, 1998.

Howard, Michael. *Franco-Prussian War: The German Invasion of France, 1870–71.* 2nd ed. London: Routledge, 2001.

Kaiser, David E. *Economic Diplomacy and the Origins of the Second World War. Germany, Britain, France and Eastern Europe, 1930–1939.* Princeton, NJ: Princeton University Press, 1980.

Keeton, Edward D. *Briand's Locarno Policy: French Economics, Politics and Diplomacy, 1925–1929.* New York: Garland, 1987.

——— "Economics and Politics in Briand's German Policy, 1925–1931." In *German Nationalism and the European Response, 1890–1945*, edited by Carol Fink et al., 157–80. Norman and London: University of Oklahoma Press, 1985.

Kent, Bruce. *The Spoils of War. The Politics, Economics, and Diplomacy of Reparations 1918–1932.* Oxford: Clarendon, 1989.

Kocs, Stephen A. *Autonomy or Power? The Franco-German Relationship and Europe's Strategic Choices, 1955–1995.* New York: Praeger, 1995.

Krotz, Ulrich. "Social Content of the International Sphere: Symbols and Meaning in Franco-German Relations." Minda de Gunzburg Center for European Studies, Harvard University. http://www.ces.fas.harvard.edu/publications/docs/pdfs/Krotz2.pdf, accessed June 18, 2007.

———. "Structure as a Process: The Regularized Intergovernmentalism of Franco-German Bilateralism." Minda de Gunzburg Center for European Studies, Harvard University. http://www.ces.fas.harvard.edu/publications/docs/pdfs/Krotz3.pdf, accessed June 18, 2007.

———. "Ties that Bind? The Parapublic Underpinnings of Franco-German Relations as Construction of International Value." Minda de Gunzburg Center for European Studies, Harvard University. http://www.ces.fas.harvard.edu/publications/docs/pdfs/Krotz4.pdf, accessed June 18, 2007.

Laird, Robin. *Strangers and Friends: The Franco-German Security Relationship.* New York: St Martin's Press, 1989.

Langer, William L. *European Alliances and Alignments 1871–1890.* 2nd ed. New York: Alfred A. Knopf, 1950.

Leggiere, Michael V. *Napoleon and Berlin: the Franco-Prussian War in North Germany 1813.* Norman: University of Oklahoma Press, 2002.

Ludlow, N. Piers. *The European Community and the Crises of the 1960s: Negotiating the Gaullist Challenge.* London: Routledge, 2006.

Maes, Ivo. "On the Origins of the Franco-German EMU Controversies." University of Pittsburgh Library. http://aei.pitt.edu/622/, accessed August 15, 2007.

May, Ernest R. *Strange Victory: Hitler's Conquest of France.* New York: Hill and Wang, 2000.

Mazzucelli, Colette. *France and Germany at Maastricht: Politics and Negotiations to Create the European Union.* New York: Palgrave, 1997.

McCarthy, Patrick. *France-Germany, 1983–1993: The Struggle to Cooperate.* New York: St Martin's Press, 1993.

———. *France-Germany in the 21st Century.* New York: Palgrave, 2001.

McDougall, Walter A. *France's Rhineland Diplomacy 1914–1924.* Princeton, NJ: Princeton University Press, 1978.

Milward, Alan S. *The Reconstruction of Western Europe, 1945–51.* London: Routledge, 1992.

Mitchel, Pearl. *The Bismarckian Policy of Conciliation with France.* Philadelphia: University of Pennsylvania Press, 1935.

Mitchell, Allan. *Bismarck and the French Nation 1848–1890.* New York: Pegasus, 1971.

———. "German History in France after 1870." *Journal of Contemporary History* 2, no. 3 (1967): 81–100.

———. *The German Influence in France after 1870: The Formation of the French Republic.* Chapel Hill: University of North Carolina Press, 1979.

————. *A Stranger in Paris: Germany's Role in Republican France*. New York: Berghahn Books, 2006.

Moravcsik, Andrew. *The Choice for Europe. Social Purpose and State Power from Messina to Maastricht*. Ithaca, NY: Cornell University Press, 1998.

————. "De Gaulle between Grain and Grandeur: The Political Economy of French EC Policy, 1958–1970." *Journal of Cold War Studies* 2, no. 2 (Spring 2000): 3–43.

————. "De Gaulle between Grain and Grandeur: The Political Economy of French EC Policy, 1958–1970." *Journal of Cold War Studies* 2, no. 3 (Fall 2000): 4–68.

Morgan, Roger, and Caroline Bray, eds. *Partners and Rivals in Western Europe: Britain, France and Germany*. Hants: Gower, 1986.

Nolan, Michael E. *The Inverted Mirror: Mythologizing the Enemy in France and Germany, 1898–1914*. Oxford: Berghahn Books, 2005.

Pedersen, Thomas. *Germany, France and the Integration of Europe—A Realist Interpretation*. London: Pinter, 2001.

————. "Recent Trends in the Franco-German Relationship." *Journal of Common Market Studies* 41, no. 1 (September 2003): 13–25.

Pitts, Vincent J. *France and the German Problem: Politics and Economics in the Locarno Period, 1924–1929*, New York: Garland, 1987.

Planert, Ute. "From Collaboration to Resistance: Politics, Experience, and Memory of the Revolutionary and Napoleonic Wars in Southern Germany." *Central European History* 39 (2006): 676–705.

Puchala, Donald J. "Integration and Disintegration in Franco-German Relations, 1954–1965." *International Organization* 24, no. 2 (Spring 1970): 183–208.

Rowe, Michael. "Between Empire and Home Town: Napoleonic Rule on the Rhine, 1799–1814." *The Historical Journal* 42, no. 3 (1999): 643–74.

————, ed. *Collaboration and Resistance in Napoleonic Europe. State-formation in an Age of Upheaval, c. 1800–1815*. London and New York: Palgrave, 2003.

————. *From Reich to State. The Rhineland in the Revolutionary Age, 1780–1830*. Cambridge: Cambridge University Press 2003.

————. "Resistance, Collaboration or Third Way? Responses to Napoleonic Rule in Germany." In *Popular Resistance in the French Wars: Patriots, Partisans and Land Pirates*, edited by Charles J. Esdaile, 67–90. New York: Palgrave, 2005.

Schivelbusch, Wolfgang. *The Culture of Defeat: On National Trauma, Mourning and Recovery*. New York: Picador 2004.

Schmidt, Peter. "The Special Franco-German Security Relationship in the 1990s." Chaillot Paper, European Institute for Security Studies (Paris), no. 8 (June 1993). http://aei.pitt.edu/452/, accessed August 15, 2007.

————. "West Germany and France: Convergent or Divergent Perspectives on European Security Cooperation?" In *The Evolution of an International Actor. Western Europe's New Assertion*, edited by Reinhardt Rummel and Colette Mazzucelli, 161–97. Boulder, CO: Westview, 1990.

Schöttler, Peter. "The Rhine as an Object of Historical Controversy in the Inter-War Years." *History Workshop Journal* 39 (1995): 1–22.

Schuker, Stephen A. *The End of French Predominance in Europe. The Financial Crisis of 1924 and the Adoption of the Dawes Plan*. Chapel Hill: University of North Carolina Press, 1976.

Simonian, Haig. "France, Germany and Europe." *Journal of Common Market Studies* 19, no. 3 (March 1981): 203–19.

————. *The Privileged Partnership. Franco-German Relations in the European Community.* Oxford: Clarendon, 1985.

Steefel, Lawrence D. *Bismarck, the Hohenzollern Candidacy, and the Origins of the Franco-German War of 1870.* Cambridge, MA: Harvard University Press, 1962.

Steiner, Zara. *The Lights That Failed: European International History 1919–1933.* Oxford: Oxford University Press, 2005.

Stevenson, David. *French War Aims against Germany 1914–1919.* Oxford: Clarendon, 1982.

Stone, James. "Bismarck and the Containment of France, 1873–1877." *Canadian Journal of History* 29 (August 1994): 281–304.

————. "The War Scare of 1875 Revisited." *Militärgeschichtliche Mitteilungen* 53 (1994): 309–26.

Story, Jonathan. "Convergence at the Core? The Franco-German Relationship and its Implication for the Community." In *Economic Divergence in the European Community*, edited by Michael Hodge and William Wallace, 167–91. London: Allen & Unwin, 1981.

Taylor, Arnold J. P. *Germany's First Bid for Colonies 1884–1885: A Move in Bismarck's European Policy.* New York: Norton, 1970.

Trachtenberg, Marc. *Reparation in World Politics: France and European Economic Diplomacy, 1916–1923.* New York: Columbia University Press, 1980.

Trouille, Jean-Marc, and Mairi McLean, eds. *France, Germany and Britain—Partners in a Changing World.* New York: Palgrave, 2001.

Vanke, Jeffrey. "The European Collaboration of France and Germany, 1963–1966." In *Crises and Compromises: The European Project 1963–1969*, edited by Wilfried Loth, 93–108. Baden-Baden: Nomos, 2001.

Wawro, Geoffrey. *The Franco-German War: The German Conquest of France in 1870–1871.* Cambridge: Cambridge University Press, 2003.

Webber, Douglas, ed. *The Franco-German relationship in the European Union.* London: Routledge, 1999.

Wetzel, David. *A Duel of Giants: Bismarck, Napoleon III, and the Origins of the Franco-Prussian War.* Madison: University of Wisconsin Press, 2001.

Wienefeld, Robert H. *Franco-German Relations, 1878–1885.* Baltimore, MD: John Hopkins Press, 1929.

Willis F. Roy. *France, Germany and the New Europe, 1945–1967.* Stanford: Stanford University Press, 1968.

————. "Germany, France and Europe." In *West German Foreign Policy: 1949–1979*, edited by Wolfram F. Hanrieder, 93–109. Boulder, CO: Westview, 1980.

Woolf, Stuart. *Napoleon's integration of Europe.* London: Routledge 1991.

Wurm, Clemens A., ed. *Western Europe and Germany. The Beginnings of European Integration 1945–1960.* Oxford and Washington, DC: Berg, 1995.

Contributors

Frédéric Clavert, PhD, wrote his PhD thesis about "Hjalmar Schacht, Financier and Diplomat" at the University Robert Schuman in Strasbourg (France).

Laura Fasanaro, PhD, is a post–doctoral research fellow at the University of Roma Tre (Italy).

Hugo Frey, PhD, is head of the Department of History at the University of Chichester (UK).

Victor Gavin Munte, PhD, is associate professor of Contemporary History at the University of Barcelona (Spain).

Carine Germond held the Clifford Hackett Lectureship in the History of European Integration at Yale University (U.S.) and is currently finishing her PhD thesis at the University Robert Schuman.

Ronald J. Granieri, PhD, is assistant professor of Modern European History at the University of Pennsylvania (U.S.).

Stefan Jordan, PhD, is a research fellow at the Historische Kommission bei der Bayerischen Akademie der Wissenschaften and teaches at the Ludwig-Maximilians-Universität München (Germany).

Ulrich Lappenküper, PhD, is an associate researcher at the Otto-von-Bismarck Foundation in Friedrichsruh (Germany) and visiting professor in Contemporary History at the University of Bonn (Germany).

Martial Libera, PhD, is an instructor at the University Robert Schuman and the Institut d'Etudes Politiques, Strasbourg (France).

Reiner Marcowitz, PhD, is professor in German Studies at the Paul Verlaine University in Metz (France).

Garret Martin, PhD, is currently teaching at the George Washington University, Washington DC.

Nathan N. Orgill is a PhD candidate in Modern European History at Duke University (U.S.).

Elana Passmann is a PhD candidate in History at the University of North Carolina at Chapel Hill (U.S.).

Ulrich Pfeil, PhD, is professor in German Studies at the Jean Monnet University in Saint Etienne (France).

Katrin Rücker is a PhD candidate affiliated with both the University of Marburg (Germany) and the Political Sciences Institute in Paris (IEP de Paris, France).

Georges Saunier is project manager at the Institut François Mitterrand and associate lecturer at the University of Cergy-Pontoise (France).

Sylvain Schirmann, PhD, is the head of the Institut d'Etudes Politiques in Strasbourg (France).

Verena Schöberl has just completed her PhD in Modern History at the Humboldt-University of Berlin (Germany).

Mathieu L. L. Segers, PhD, is an assistant professor of International Relations and European Integration History at the University of Utrecht (Netherlands).

Bernhard Struck, PhD, is a lecturer of Modern History at the University of St Andrews (Scotland).

Henning Türk, PhD, is a lecturer in Modern History at the University Duisburg-Essen (Germany).

Jörg Ulbert, PhD, is an associate professor at the University of Bretagne Sud in Lorient (France).

Wolfram Vogel, PhD, is a researcher at the Deutsch-Französisches Institut (dfi) in Ludwigsburg (Germany), currently head of the dfi office in Paris.

Michèle Weinachter, PhD, is an associate professor in German Studies and chair of the German Studies Department at the University of Cergy-Pontoise (France).

Index